SPIES AGAINST

ARMAGEDDON

SPIES AGAINST ARMAGEDDON

INSIDE ISRAEL'S SECRET WARS

by Dan Raviv and Yossi Melman

LEVANT BOOKS
Sea Cliff, New York

LEVANT BOOKS
Sea Cliff, NY 11579
http://LevantBooks.info
LevantBooks@ymail.com

ISBN: 978-0-9854378-3-1

Cover photo credits:
 Suspects in 2010 slaying of Mahmoud al-Mabhouh (Dubai Police)
 Israeli F-15 jets (IDF Spokesperson)
 author photos by Emma Raviv and Haim Taragan
Cover design:
 Tanya Nuchols (TanyaNucholsDesign.com)
Layout and technical editor:
 Paul Skolnick

CONTENTS

To the Memory of Benjamin Raviv

To the Memory of Yitzhak and Anna Melman

To cherished Dori, Jonathan and Emma

To beloved Billie, Yotam and Daria

KEY FIGURES IN
ISRAELI INTELLIGENCE

The Directors of the Mossad

1951-1952	Reuven Shiloah
1952-1963	Isser Harel
1963-1968	Meir Amit
1968-1974	Zvi Zamir
1974-1982	Yitzhak Hofi
1982-1989	Nahum Admoni
1989-1996	Shabtai Shavit
1996-1998	Danny Yatom
1998-2002	Efraim Halevy
2002-2010	Meir Dagan
2011-	Tamir Pardo

The Directors of Military Intelligence (Aman)

1948-1948	Isser Beeri
1949-1950	Chaim Herzog
1950-1955	Binyamin Gibli
1955-1959	Yehoshafat Harkabi
1959-1962	Chaim Herzog
1962-1963	Meir Amit
1964-1972	Aharon Yariv
1972-1974	Eli Zeira
1974-1978	Shlomo Gazit
1979-1983	Yehoshua Saguy
1983-1985	Ehud Barak
1986-1991	Amnon Lipkin Shahak
1991-1995	Uri Saguy
1995-1998	Moshe Yaalon
1998-2001	Amos Malka
2001-2006	Aharon Zeevi Farkash
2006-2010	Amos Yadlin
2010-	Aviv Kohavi

The Directors of Shin Bet

1948-1952	Isser Harel
1952-1952	Izzy Dorot
1952-1963	Amos Manor
1964-1974	Yosef Harmelin
1974-1981	Avraham Ahituv
1981-1986	Avraham Shalom
1986-1988	Yosef Harmelin
1988-1995	Yaakov Perry
1995-1996	Carmi Gillon
1996-2000	Ami Ayalon
2000-2005	Avi Dichter
2005-2011	Yuval Diskin
2011-	Yoram Cohen

Directors of Science Liaison Bureau (Lakam)

1957-1981	Binyamin Blumberg
1981-1986*	Rafi Eitan

*Agency disbanded

Heads of Malmab
(Director of Security of the Defense Establishment)

1958-1986	Chaim Carmon
1986-2007	Yehiel Horev
2007-	Amir Kain

Directors of Nativ (for Jewish immigration)

1952-1970	Shaul Avigur
1970-1981	Nehemiah Levanon
1981-1985	Yehuda Lapidot
1986-1992	David Bartov
1992-1999	Yaakov Kedmi
2000-2006	Zvi Magen
2006-	Naomi Ben Ami

PROLOGUE

Prepare, in the chapters ahead, to learn what Israel's intelligence agencies—led by the Mossad—are doing, day and night, to protect their own country and, by extension, Western nations. From an Israeli point of view, it is an unceasing, secret war. And the Israelis feel they have no choice but to win every time.

Crisis Day is coming. Iran may try to rush toward construction of nuclear bombs; Muslim terrorists could again attack America—or both calamities might occur. The president of the United States would surely ask: What do the Israelis say? What do they know? What are they up to that they may *not* be telling us? And what can the Mossad do?

Just as the Statue of Liberty and McDonald's became snappy synonyms for America, "Mossad" has become an internationally recognized Israeli brand name. More importantly, with the Middle East almost constantly on the edge of upheaval, the Jewish state's foreign espionage agency is a player in some of the biggest, though hidden, dramas of our time.

Is the Mossad really so good at what it does? Yes, as we document in this book—especially considering Israel's lilliputian size—it is stunningly effective. Yet, the pages to come will show that in more than 60 years, Israeli intelligence has made its share of mistakes. It succeeds or fails due mostly to the quality of its people: They are excellent. They are motivated. But they are human and, thus, fallible.

The agency's full name is *HaMossad l'Modi'in u'l'Tafkidim Meyuchadim,* Hebrew for The Institute for Intelligence and Special Tasks. It has a few thousand employees, and in the past decade it has gone slightly public with a website.

Mossad.gov.il discloses that its staff has an official motto: "Where there is no counsel, the people fall; but in the multitude of counselors there is safety."

The noun "counsel" is in the translation chosen by the Mossad for its English-language internet page, but that fails to capture the flavor of the Hebrew word *takhbulot* in the Book of Proverbs, chapter 11, verse 14. It can also be translated as "deception," "trickery," "stratagem," or even "wise direction," but always is aimed at confounding the intentions of one's opponents.

The motto that the Mossad finds inspiring thus adds up to this: Without tricky plans, Israel would fall; but when there is plenty of information, Israel finds salvation.

A former Mossad director, Efraim Halevy, told us that an even more apt motto might be: "Everything is do-able." That attitude encapsulates the spirit of the Mossad.

The agency's reputation for decisive action and hyperactivity has inevitably led to a mystique: that it is all-powerful, all-knowing, ruthless, and capable of penetrating every corner of the world.

Israel may not have intentionally created the image, but surely takes advantage of it. When feats, some of them seemingly unbelievable, are ascribed to the Mossad by the international press and politicians, Israel's spymasters say nothing.

This policy of ambiguity magnifies the mystique, which in turn helps sow fear among Israel's enemies. The nation does not admit to having nuclear weapons, although a nearly complete history of how it achieved that status— and how the atomic ambiguity is preserved—will be found in these pages.

There is a misconception, however. The Mossad is just one part of the Israeli intelligence community, which includes other agencies that are no less important: the domestic Shin Bet and the military Aman.

These are the big three, and in fact Aman—military intelligence—has the greatest financial and human resources and contributes the most to Israel's national security.

This book will also reveal two smaller, specialized parts of Israel's clandestine defense. One, which can be termed "Jewish intelligence," helps Jews exercise Israel's legislated Right of Return to their people's ancient homeland— where they are granted instant citizenship—and also protects them when they get into trouble outside Israel.

The other small unit, which was launched officially for "science liaison" and was nominally disbanded after Jonathan Pollard was caught spying in the United States in 1985, has been responsible for building and protecting Israel's most important deterrent capability: secret, nuclear, and officially unconfirmed.

Like the country's nuclear ambiguity, the Mossad has chosen to remain mostly masked—leaving others to distort and misattribute many mysterious events. The distortions may be traced to glorification of the spy agency, hostility toward Israel, or mere speculation. As imaginations run amok, charlatans publish what they will: that when British publishing tycoon Robert Maxwell fell off his yacht, the Mossad drowned him; that Israeli intelligence caused the car crash that killed Princess Diana; that Mossad operatives are primarily artists of assassination; that every Israeli arrested for drug dealing is serving the Mossad; and, most absurdly, that the Mossad orchestrated 9/11.

This book intends to shed light on the true nature of the Israeli intelligence community, viewing its development—from the beginning until today— through the prism of the country's unique history.

The Jewish state has been at war from the moment David Ben-Gurion declared statehood in 1948. And Israeli leaders still consider themselves to be at war every day.

Yet, being "at war" differs entirely from the 1948 War of Independence. It is also not the lightning-quick six-day victory of 1967. And the intelligence community wants to ensure that there is no repeat of Yom Kippur in 1973, when a surprise attack by Arab militaries could have been thwarted had Israel listened to astoundingly well-placed agents in Egypt.

This is an even more hazardous era, in which war brings the lethal crash of incoming missiles that may have nuclear or chemical warheads, fired by enemies who also make their own technological advances.

One of the major roles of intelligence, therefore, is to avoid all-out war.

The goal now is to win—or, thinking of Iran, to distract and delay the enemy's most dangerous plans—without committing large numbers of troops and planes, and without putting a major part of the Israeli population at risk from attacks by hostile neighbors' forces.

This book will reveal more than Israel has ever been willing to declare publicly about assassinations as a tool, about its flattening in 2007 of a nuclear reactor in Syria, and about the sabotage and murders aimed at choking Iran's nuclear ambitions.

The original mission of intelligence in the Middle East's eternal, complex chess game focused on preparing for the next war. Now, Israel's spymasters continually wage war by stealth, sabotage, disinformation, and killing.

The soldiers, pilots, and sailors of the Israel Defense Forces, meantime, work closely in league with the country's intelligence agencies. The chapters to come will show how the modern, highly adaptive IDF does not limit itself to deploying soldiers with guns. Special-operations fighters, not necessarily uniformed, go on daring missions inside enemy countries. These military men and women are also spies, no less than are Mossad operatives.

Israel increasingly takes full advantage of its cutting-edge drone aircraft, eavesdropping systems, and spy-in-the-sky satellites that have become a vital part of the tiny nation's ever-widening defense network.

The entire intelligence community—not only the Mossad—reflects the Israeli condition: a small country, vastly at variance from its neighbors in religion, culture, and values; with neighbors who do not accept its right to exist, or at best are willing to coexist reluctantly.

Israeli intelligence thus developed a style that is bold, willing to take risks, and aspires to be innovative at all times. It has to get along with less, and it compensates for quantity deficiencies by developing qualitative excellence.

"The human factor is the biggest and most crucial for our society and our security services," said the late Meir Amit, who directed both the Mossad and Aman in the 1960s.

His observation remains valid today. The Mossad's "success and fulfillment of its complex tasks depend on the quality of the people who serve it, form its core, and are its driving force," the agency's current director, Tamir Pardo, writes on its website. He hopes that his employees are "only the finest and most suitable people," who see their work as a "contribution to the fortification of the State of Israel's security." To that they "dedicate their skills and talents, determination and persistence and values."

Several Israelis now serving as Mossad operatives have said that their main motivation is protecting their country and their families. They also tend to be the type of competitive people who want to excel at absolutely everything they do.

The Mossad website invites job applications from "people who are creative and fans of challenges, who look for interesting things and different and special work—a role that is interesting, unconventional, and dynamic," starting with a year of training.

Candidates should have "good teamwork ability, curiosity and openness to learning, high learning capabilities, creativity and thinking outside the box, foreign language capabilities at a high level, and a willingness to work irregular hours and to take frequent trips abroad."

A troubling fact for Israel, with the wartime mentality it has never shaken off, is the inherent contradiction between democracy and clandestine defense.

Israel—long before other Western societies faced the issue in the post-9/11 era—struggled to find a balance. Is it absurd to have a secret subculture protecting a nation's freedom? The cohabitation has been far from smooth.

For many years, Shin Bet security operatives lied in court and were willing to sacrifice democratic values on the altar of fighting terrorism. Most Israelis did not raise objections. They preferred to sleep at night, vaguely knowing that they were being protected.

Abuses were, to Israel's credit, exposed and dealt with by the courts, an active news media, and the desire by some in the public for transparency.

An additional dissonance exists. Even if intelligence personnel adhere to Israeli laws and values, their work routinely involves violating the sovereignty and legal systems of other nations—to the point of killing individual enemies in foreign capitals.

The heart of the issue, now familiar to the United States and other countries, is how to honor and strengthen our freedoms while combating hostile forces seeking to crush our values.

The intelligence communities in democratic societies have to cope with a no-win situation. The "good guys" have to respect the law, at least at home, while terrorists take advantage of a system they totally abhor: suing their interrogators, tying up courts in lengthy trials, and even demanding that judges release them from prison on human-rights grounds. These are liberties that they, in their countries of origin, would not think of granting to anyone.

Since the start in 1948, Israeli leaders have adopted as a guiding principle the sense that they have their backs against the wall. Their country is so small—and, especially in its pre-1967 borders, so narrow—that some analysts speak of calamities that could lead to the nation's destruction. A few nuclear bombs going off in the center of Israel would kill most of its population.

Armageddon, in Christian lore, is said to be the site of a final battle between good and evil. While the location is reputed to be a hill near Megiddo, in the Valley of Jezreel in northern Israel, Jews do not expect or seek an apocalyptic event. Yet, Israel's intelligence community—time and again—has had the task of waging secret war aimed at pulling its country back from the brink of an awful situation. Making mistakes in the current campaign against Iran's nuclear program could be highly destructive.

Twenty-two years ago, we wrote *Every Spy a Prince*, a history of Israeli intelligence that considered some of these issues. Since then, much has happened and many key figures and governments have been removed from the scene—some peacefully, and many violently. Egypt, since signing a peace treaty with Israel in 1979, had become a mainstay for stability in the region, but the fall of President Hosni Mubarak in 2011 shook all Middle East foundations to the core. Many Arab countries continue to quaver.

With the passage of time, as Israel's challenges changed, we obtained more access than before. Documents, once locked away, have become available; more people involved in these dramas became willing to talk; and agencies and officials, so clandestine that they could not legally be named, have stepped into the light. We have managed to interview most of the chiefs of the agencies and many top operatives.

Our mission is to shed new light on historical events. We intend to put into perspective the challenges that continue to emerge from a troubled and strategic region, once again on the verge of a major crisis that could affect us all.

Dan Raviv   Yossi Melman

Washington   Tel Aviv

June 2012

Chapter One

STOPPING IRAN

Authorized visitors and employees arriving on the third floor of Mossad headquarters—inside a highly secure campus at a major highway intersection north of Tel Aviv—see four Hebrew letters on the wall that spell *Ramsad*. In the intelligence world, full of abbreviations and acronyms, this one means *Rosh ha-Mossad*—Head of the Mossad.

The office of Meir Dagan, who held that powerful job from 2002 through 2010, revealed several clues about his thinking and how his personality was shaped. Mementoes of his military service, to be sure, dotted the walls, but unique was a photograph dating from the dark days of World War II.

On one wall was a black-and-white photo of a miserable scene: a Jewish man on his knees, wrapped in a striped *tallit* (prayer shawl), arms raised in surrender or prayer, surrounded by jeering Nazi soldiers.

Dagan would tell visitors that the Jew was his maternal grandfather, Ber Ehrlich Sloshny. He would say that his grandpa was shot a few minutes after the photo was taken, as the Germans wiped out all the thousands of Jews in the shtetl of Lokov in Ukraine.

Though not ordinarily thought of as a sentimental fellow, Dagan took along this photograph throughout his career. It hung on the walls wherever he served as a military officer. He also displayed it in his office as Ramsad.

There, it carried extra meaning: a reminder of the existential threats facing Israel throughout its history, inside a government agency tasked with countering such threats. Dagan felt that he had the special burden of ensuring the continued existence of the Jewish state.

There could be no heavier load on his shoulders than the primary one he had during eight years leading the Mossad: how to prevent Israel's virulent enemies in the Islamic Republic of Iran from developing nuclear weapons.

Dagan, when asked, seemed eager to tell how he obtained the photo of his grandfather. He explained that his father returned to Lokov from Russia after the war to look for surviving relatives. He learned that no one had made it through the Holocaust, yet he was approached by a Gentile neighbor. The man told of the Germans forcing him to bury the bodies of murdered Jews, and because he had a camera with him they boastfully ordered him to take pictures. Now, after the war, he gave the photo to Dagan's father, who ultimately brought it with him to Israel.

For Dagan, the photo carried more than the simplistic meaning Israeli political leaders often intend when they declare that Jews must "never again" be wiped out and need the power to defend themselves.

For him, the photo also conveyed a moral lesson. When Dagan looked at it, he was amazed how people could easily turn into persecutors and beasts. He realized that it could happen to almost anyone.

Certainly, as the Mossad chief with a wide variety of means at his control, that transformation could have happened to him. The Ramsad could have misled himself into thinking he was almost like God. He held vast power in his hands. He could seal the fate of practically anyone.

When Dagan weighed which powers to use, how and when, confronting Iran presented huge challenges and occasional dilemmas. Around two years into his term, in 2004, when Dagan concluded definitively that the ayatollahs' regime would be his number-one priority, there was a need to strategize how best to prevent them from developing nuclear weapons.

Iran's nuclear ambitions preceded the rise of the Shi'ite clerics and Ayatollah Ruhollah Khomeini's establishment of the Islamic Republic in 1979. Those ambitions began in the mid-1950s, during Shah Mohammad Reza Pahlavi's reign and his tacit appointment by the United States as the "policeman" of the region.

As Iran's monarch, the Shah was certainly the darling of the U.S. nuclear power industry. He was a fantastic customer, busily buying American-made power plants. They were meant to produce electricity, but the monarch did not hide his hope that one day he would use the technology for military purposes: to build bombs and extend his hegemonic influence.

In those pre-1979 days, Israel also wanted a piece of the lucrative Iranian pie. The Shah and his regime were close allies of the Jewish state since the 1950s. Israel was fighting the Arabs; and Iran, though majority Muslim, did not see itself as part of the Arab peoples and had friction with them. The Shah's aspirations clashed with those of Egypt's Gamal Abdel Nasser and Saudi Arabia's royal rulers. Getting together with Israel was a marriage of convenience.

Israeli intelligence trained Savak, the Shah's brutal secret police and espionage service. As part of the compensation, the Shah allowed the Mossad to operate on his soil as a base for recruiting agents in Iraq and other countries. Iran even provided documentation to enhance the Israelis' cover stories.

Israeli arms manufacturers did a thriving business with Iran. The Shah sold oil to Israel and financed joint weapons ventures, including an improved version of the Jericho ground-to-ground missile, made by Israel based on a design that France apparently shared willingly in the early 1960s.

The joint missile project, codenamed Flower, was supposed to provide a means of delivery for Israel's nuclear weapons. And the Shah, with his nuclear aspirations, was thinking just the same thing for *his* future arsenal.

Then came Shimon Peres, the defense official—and future prime minister and president of Israel—who was one of the creators of his own nation's secret nuclear program. Peres offered the Shah nuclear technology and the use of Israel Atomic Energy Commission experts.

Israel, decades later, would have felt deep embarrassment and regret had the Shah said yes. The Israelis would have been helping their future arch-enemy go nuclear. The Shah said no. He did not need the Israelis' help. He already had American, French, German, and Canadian companies queuing up for big contracts with him.

After overthrowing the Shah in 1979, the new Shi'ite rulers did not have time or resources to devote to a nuclear program. They were tied down by a decade-long war with Saddam Hussein's Iraq. That terrible conflict, which left over a million dead on both sides, prompted them to think again. The Iraqis were using chemical weapons and poison gas against Iranians along the front, while striking Iran's cities with long-range Scud missiles.

Ayatollah Khomeini noticed that the world was silent in the face of these war crimes, and the intense and brooding cleric was livid to discover that the United States was supporting Iraq. Iran's supreme spiritual leader had been opposed to non-conventional weapons, on the religious grounds that innocents are typically the victims of mass destruction. But after the war, Khomeini changed his mind, concluding that Iran needed to match its enemies—if only as a deterrent.

In the early 1990s, after Khomeini's death, Iran renewed its atomic bomb-building program. It had some help from Russia and China, but above all from Pakistan's notorious nuclear traveling salesman, Abdul Qader Khan.

The Iranians confined themselves to buying drawings and instruction sheets for the construction of "cascades" of centrifuges, to be used for enriching uranium. Enrichment centers would have to be built, but Iran felt quite able to do it—unlike the Libyans, who around 1992 bought a ready-to-use project entirely from A.Q. Khan.

Amazingly, at that point, Israeli intelligence and the defense ministry did not perceive Iran as a threat. They even allowed Israeli companies and middlemen to sell security and military gear to the ayatollahs.

The deals were secret, however, in part to hide them from the United States. The Americans would have vigorously opposed such deals, because of the humiliation of their 52 diplomats being held as hostages in Tehran from late 1979 to early 1981.

The most worrisome, far-reaching set of transactions involved Nahum Manbar. The Israeli businessman traveled to Poland in the late 1980s and started selling Polish weapons to Iran, which was desperate to replenish its arms supply after the punishing war with Iraq. Establishing solid contacts in the Iranian defense ministry, Manbar supplied raw materials from China and Hungary that Iran used to make chemical weapons.

Britain's MI6 spy agency noticed his activities, some conducted on British soil, but could not believe that an Israeli would be working so closely with the

Iranians. British intelligence analysts naturally concluded that Manbar was a Mossad operative who was out to penetrate Iran's chemical and defense secrets. He was not.

In fact, the Mossad and the Shin Bet domestic intelligence service—Israel's equivalent of the FBI—were just realizing that Iran should not be helped with its military ambitions. Tolerating arms transactions made no sense. In part because of concerns expressed by the United States, Manbar was put under surveillance. Israeli spies watched for any physical or telephonic contacts with Iranian government agents.

During one surveillance mission in 1993 in Vienna, Austria, two Mossad men who were riding a motorcycle late one cold night took a wrong turn. Their motorcycle crashed into a car, and both spies were killed. Public reports simply said that two Israeli tourists died. The Mossad conducted an investigation to make sure that the car driver had not been an enemy agent.

Though there was no reason to blame Manbar for the deaths, the incident strengthened the Mossad's determination to punish the Israeli chemical arms merchant.

He was arrested in 1997 and put on trial in Israel, with a gag order and military censorship preventing any mention of the case by the country's usually hyperactive press. The muzzling was a fairly routine way of handling a case involving espionage agencies and sensitive foreign affairs. Manbar was sentenced to 16 years in prison for doing business with an enemy nation.

Dagan's placement of Iran at the top of his priority list was fully in the spirit of what Prime Minister Ariel Sharon sought when he appointed his old friend and fellow former army general in 2002. Dagan was tasked with turning the Mossad into a lean, muscular, and focused organization with a clear sense of its primary missions.

Dagan believed that his agency had become unimaginative and sometimes even lazy. His goal, metaphorically speaking, was to restore a Mossad "with a dagger between its teeth." At various, well-chosen times, the dagger would be expertly hurled at Iran.

Both the Mossad and the military intelligence agency, Aman, had concluded that Iran's nuclear program was advancing on two tracks. One was civilian, to generate electricity and for research to help medical and agricultural needs. At the same time, Iranian scientists were clandestinely advancing along a military track, often using the civilian work as cover to develop an ability to make nuclear bombs. Just as some equipment was clearly "dual use," many of the experts were, too. University lecturers and researchers were also part of the bomb program.

Sharon instructed Dagan to be the top-level "project manager"—a term of art in organizing intelligence work. The Mossad chief would personally coordinate a wide range of Israeli efforts to challenge Iran: politically, economically, psychologically, and almost entirely covertly.

The most benign steps entailed diplomatic pressure on Iran. The ayatollahs and their government would receive messages through third countries that told them to stop the military side of their nuclear program, coupled with threats of stern action if they did not stop.

The next stage centered on persuading Iran's main trading partners to impose sanctions aimed at damaging the Iranian economy. These were mostly European countries, which had to be persuaded that Iran's weapons and missile programs could even threaten them. The hope was that Iranian leaders would decide that it was not worth it to pursue nuclear weapons, because sanctions on certain goods, financial transactions, and travel would make their people suffer. Israeli intelligence's assessment was that while Iran might look like a strict religious dictatorship, the government was actually quite aware of a need for public support.

The Mossad—and Dagan himself—devoted a lot of energy to learning everything possible about Iran's domestic public opinion and pressures within Iranian society. While half of Iran's population was Persian, the country was a multiethnic tapestry with Azeris, Kurds, Arabs, Baluchis, and Turkmen. The minorities were all oppressed, to one degree or another, and could be seen as weak links in the Iranian chain.

Such tensions could be exploited by psychological warfare, to stir up discontent inside Iran. Identifying deeply unhappy citizens also provided a pool of potential paid informants for the Mossad.

Covert action could take many forms: recruiting high-quality agents in Iran's leadership and inside the nuclear program, sabotaging nuclear facilities, and assassinating key figures in the program. The overall philosophy of this comprehensive action plan—in Dagan's analysis, voiced by him and others in the Mossad—was "to define and use tools to change the mind of a country."

Top-level Iranians would have to be persuaded, by actions and not just words, that pursuing nuclear weapons would backfire. They would have to be convinced that it would make their regime less likely to survive, not more. In the mentality of the Mossad, pressure and persuasion—by no means always gentle—would be a far better strategy than a massive air raid on nuclear facilities.

Israel had no direct communication with Iran's leaders, but several European and Asian governments could pass messages back and forth. And, from time to time, the United States and its allies had talks with Iran about its nuclear program.

Positive results, if any, were practically invisible. Disgusted by a lack of progress and a surfeit of deception, the Western nations in 2011 and 2012 significantly tightened economic sanctions aimed at key individuals and organizations inside Iran.

Israel's political leaders, while encouraging the Mossad to pursue methods well short of all-out war, often made bellicose statements for public consumption. They found that by hinting that they might have to send their air force to strike at Iranian facilities, the rest of the world sat up and took urgent notice of Iran's nuclear work. As early as 2002, when he installed Dagan at the Mossad, Sharon's hope was that other countries would take the lead in applying pressure on Iran. They had a lot more economic clout, and the Americans, in particular, had more powerful military capabilities.

Sharon—later followed as prime minister by Ehud Olmert and more robustly by Benjamin Netanyahu—repeatedly declared that Iran was not only Israel's problem, but an international one. Dagan absorbed that credo and, in the very private battle he was waging, tried to muster as much support as possible from other nations' security services.

The Mossad director did have a problem, however, persuading the intelligence agencies of other nations that Iran was racing to create nuclear weapons. That was a tough mission. Military analysts at Aman had cried wolf, several times, in their annual National Intelligence Estimate. In the mid-1990s, the Estimate predicted that Iran would have nuclear weapons by the dawn of the new millennium. That date was postponed to 2003, and later modified to 2005.

The Israeli case—that Iran's nuclear program was a huge and urgent matter—was severely dented by another Estimate, the NIE that America's intelligence community delivered to President George W. Bush in 2007. It said, with high confidence, that Iran stopped its nuclear weapons program in 2003, perhaps in a somewhat frightened reaction to the U.S. invasion of Iraq that year.

So why should the world believe that the Israeli analysis was more accurate? Governments everywhere were skeptical of everything that touched on Middle East secrets. American and British espionage agencies were burned by declaring with certainty in 2002 that Saddam Hussein had weapons of mass destruction—and thus faulty intelligence was one of the building blocks of the costly, unpopular war in Iraq.

Dagan laboriously deepened the Mossad's liaison relationships with numerous intelligence agencies in Europe, Asia, Africa, and America. He wanted first to persuade them that the Iranian danger was real, and he laid out the latest evidence with detailed data. Unlike in the past, with Israel's reputation for being very stingy with information—wanting to get a lot, without giving much at all—Dagan was showing a broad array of facts that added up to an Iranian nuclear program far bigger than anything Tehran could claim was required for peaceful purposes.

The Mossad chief frequently flew to meet counterparts in countries that had intelligence relationships with Israel, urging them to accept that causing problems for Iran's nuclear program was something that they all should want to do and could do. Dagan hit it off especially well with the four directors of the Central Intelligence Agency who were his American partners during his eight years: George Tenet, Porter Goss, Michael Hayden, and Leon Panetta.

To strengthen the approach of compiling—and then acting upon—the most current intelligence available, the Mossad teamed up with Aman's technology unit and the Israel Atomic Energy Commission. They compiled a list of all the components that Iran would need to build a nuclear bomb.

The IAEC was able to utilize experience gained by acquiring everything that Israel's nuclear program—a secret project that officials refused ever to speak about—had required. They came up with 25,000 items, from tiny screws to missile engine parts: an amazingly wide range including specialized metals, carbon fiber, valves, wiring, fast computers, control panels, and so much more.

Iranian purchasing networks, operating on five continents in a systematic effort guided by the masters of the nuclear program, were trying to get their hands on everything the program needed. As a first action move, Dagan urged his counterpart agencies to find legal ways in all their respective countries to stop the shipments to Iran. He had an easy time with the CIA, MI6, the German BND, the French DGSE, and a few others who understood the danger and had been monitoring Iran's nuclear project.

Soon, even the relatively small secret services of countries such as Poland joined this informal coalition of intelligence agencies. Joint steps included halting and seizing cargos. Based on tips from the Mossad, the CIA, and MI6, dozens of Iranian purchasing networks were exposed. Iran-bound shipments from such nations as Tanzania, Italy, Belgium, Spain, Ukraine, Azerbaijan, Turkmenistan were confiscated by European and other state authorities.

The Mossad strengthened its liaison relationships with intelligence agencies in former Communist countries in Eastern Europe, as they had contacts in Middle Eastern countries that were different—and often more useful—than Western agencies had. When a businessman or other traveler from the ex-Soviet bloc was in Iran, the authorities seemed to be less suspicious than they were when Westerners arrived. Israel was able to share in some of the intelligence gleaned by the visitors, who included undercover spies.

Friendly liaisons were illustrated when Dagan received awards from several countries, including an honorary citizenship bestowed upon him by formerly Communist Poland. The gesture was poignant, in light of his family's tragic history on Polish soil, and also saluted joint operations with the Mossad in the present.

Iran started feeling the pinch, because of disruptions to its supply chain, but the nuclear program was not deterred.

The international effort had to be stepped up. Hoping to benefit from having the United Nations as a central base for the pressure, Israel and cooperative foreign agencies needed more evidence to prove Iran's true intentions. That was achieved by the coordinated intelligence efforts of the Mossad, CIA, MI6, and BND. They continually provided sensitive information to the U.N.'s International Atomic Energy Agency.

It was the mandate of the IAEA, based in Vienna, to monitor Iran's program. The agency bought satellite imagery from private companies, and it sent inspectors to several Iranian facilities where U.N. cameras were then installed.

Though the field work of the inspectors was quite good, they were stopped from telling the full truth. International bureaucrats led by the IAEA Director-General, former Egyptian diplomat Mohamed ElBaradei, drafted the reports and watered them down so that the conclusions were soggy rather than strong. Israeli officials felt that he was far too eager to broker a deal that would allow the Iranians to keep enriching uranium.

When quarterly reports were issued at IAEA meetings, Vienna was turned into a scene from the Orson Welles 1948 movie, *The Third Man*. The "U.N. City" neighborhood on the Danube River was teeming with Mossad, CIA, and spies of other nations—typically traveling with signals intelligence (sigint) technicians. They tried to recruit members of the Iranian delegation and listened in on their conversations. This was a somewhat rare opportunity to approach Iranian government employees outside their country's very restrictive borders. Some of them were senior scientists and managers in Iran's Atomic Energy Organization.

ElBaradei, who genuinely feared that his agency was being manipulated by Western interests, was stubborn. He refused to succumb to their pressure or to rush to point an accusing finger at Iran. Among his international staff were around 20 Iranians, and the Israeli assumption was that the U.N. agency was penetrated by Iran's spies and those of other countries. The IAEA was a body full of holes.

The Mossad put together a thick dossier on ElBaradei, alleging a cozy relationship with Iran, and gave it to Omar Suleiman, who was President Hosni Mubarak's intelligence chief. Mubarak was no fan of Iran's, and Suleiman was very cooperative with Israel on various projects. Still, there was no sign of ElBaradei being reigned in by his home government.

Mossad operatives considered several ideas for embarrassing the IAEA director, in the hope that he would have to resign. One such plan was to penetrate his bank account and deposit money there that he would not be able to explain. The psychological warfare department then would spread rumors to journalists that ElBaradei was receiving bribes from Iranian agents. In the end, that did not occur. In fact, his prestige only rose when he and the IAEA together were awarded the Nobel Peace Prize in 2005.

ElBaradei did become tougher on Iran, just around that time, when solid information provided by Western intelligence agencies left very little to the imagination. Now it was clear that Iran was deceiving inspectors. While enriching more uranium than would be needed to produce medical isotopes or generate electricity—the officially declared purposes—the Iranians were also trying to achieve the final stage of a nuclear program: weaponization. That would mean putting together all the components, including fissile material in precisely sized metal spheres, and detonators with high-speed switches.

They were also working on complex calculations of how to detonate a nuclear bomb, and what would be the optimum altitude from which to drop it.

This became clear—to Western officials, undeniably true—when a lap-top computer that contained an incriminating, three-minute Persian-language video found its way to the IAEA. The computer had apparently belonged to an Iranian, who had loaded it with mathematical musings, photos of laboratories and workshops, and details of a mock-up of a warhead on a missile. There was one highly memorable feature: Whenever the video was viewed, it played the music from the Oscar-winning movie *Chariots of Fire*.

The Mossad had procured this smoking gun in 2004 and shared it with other Western intelligence agencies, which passed it to the international inspectors. There were some suspicions that the Mossad might have fabricated the *Chariots of Fire* files, but the CIA considered them genuine.

Equipped with that and other evidence, Western nations managed to per-suade other members of the IAEA to pass a resolution in September 2005 that accused the Iranians of "non-compliance." The official verdict now was that Iran failed to be transparent and refused to obey calls for a halt in uranium enrichment.

The agency then moved its confrontation with Iran to a higher level by referring the non-compliance report to the United Nations Security Council in February 2006. Strong reservations were expressed by China, which bought 15 percent of its oil from Iran, and by Russia, which had strong trade relations and was building an electricity-generating nuclear plant in the Iranian city of Bushehr. But, in December 2006, U.N. sanctions were imposed on Iran.

In the years that followed, more rounds of sanctions were approved. They targeted Iranian military officers, Revolutionary Guard leaders, scientific experts, and corporations associated with the country's nuclear and missile programs. Their travel was banned and bank accounts outside Iran frozen. The world was forbidden to trade with these individuals and companies.

Israeli and American intelligence agencies evaluated the restrictions, how-ever, and determined that they were too soft. The assessment was that only stronger, crippling sanctions might have some effect on Iran's leadership.

It seemed that the kind of steps required would include a ban on buying Iranian crude oil and its byproducts. China and Russia refused to lend a hand to that effort. Sanctions thus were not hobbling the determination of Iran's leaders to keep up their nuclear work.

The Mossad realized that more drastic measures were needed. Dagan's battle plan called next for sabotage. That took various shapes. As early as 2003, the Mossad and the CIA exchanged ideas for damaging utility services and lines feeding Iran's nuclear facilities. Plans were drawn up to place bombs along the electricity grid leading to the uranium-enrichment site at Natanz.

Dagan—keen to tighten intelligence ties with the United States in light of the trauma America had suffered on September 11, 2001—encouraged more joint planning and, eventually, joint operations on the Middle East's clandestine fields of battle.

Another CIA suggestion was to send a physicist, a Russian who had moved to the United States, to Iran to offer his knowledge to the Iranian nuclear program. The caper was ridiculously mishandled when the CIA altered a set of nuclear warhead plans that the physicist was carrying, but neglected to tell him. The Iranians would have received damaging disinformation. Unfortunately for this scheme, the ex-Russian noticed errors and told the Iranians that something was flawed. He simply did not know that the CIA wanted him to keep his mouth shut and pass along the materials.

Despite imperfect penetrations at first, the entire concept of "poisoning" both information and equipment was attractive; and the Mossad, the CIA, and the British kept doing it. These agencies set up front companies that established contact with Iranian purchasing networks. In order to build up trust, they sold Iran some genuine components. But at a later stage, they planted—among the good parts, such as metal tubes and high-speed switches—many bad parts that damaged Iran's program.

The results of this international sabotage began to show. Iran found itself having trouble keeping control of the equipment that it had bought from overseas.

The peak of these damage operations was a brilliantly innovative computer worm that would become known as Stuxnet. Though its origin was never officially announced, Stuxnet was a joint project by the CIA, the Mossad, and Aman's technological unit. The malicious software was specifically designed to disrupt a German-made computerized control system that ran the centrifuges in Natanz.

The project required studying, by reverse engineering, precisely how the control panel and computers worked and what effect they had on the centrifuges. For that purpose, Germany's BND—very friendly to Israel, in part hoping to erase Holocaust memories—arranged the cooperation of Siemens, the German corporation that had sold the system to Iran. The directors of Siemens may have felt pangs of conscience, or were simply reacting to public pressure, as newspapers pointed out that it was Iran's largest trading partner in Germany.

For a better understanding of Iran's enrichment process, old centrifuges—which Israel had obtained many years before—were set up in one of the buildings at Dimona, Israel's not-so-secret nuclear facility in the southern Negev desert. They were nearly identical to the centrifuges that were enriching uranium in Natanz.

The Israelis closely watched what the computer worm could do to an industrial process. The tests, partially conducted also at a U.S. government lab in Idaho, took two years.

Virtual weapons of destruction such as Stuxnet can be e-mailed to the target computer network, or they can be installed in person by plugging in a flash drive. Whether hidden in an electronic message or plugged in by an agent for the Mossad, the virus did get into the Natanz facility's control system sometime in 2009. Stuxnet was in the system for more than a year before it was detected by Iranian cyber-warfare experts. By then, it was giving the centrifuges confusing instructions, which disrupted their precise synchronization. They were no longer spinning in concert, and as the equipment sped up and slowed repeatedly, the rotors that did the spinning were severely damaged.

The true beauty of this computer worm was that the operators of the system had no idea that anything was going wrong. Everything at first seemed normal, and when they noticed the problem it was too late. Nearly 1,000 centrifuges—about one-fifth of those operating at Natanz—were knocked out of commission.

Iranian intelligence and computer experts were shocked. The nuclear program was slowing down, barely advancing, and falling way behind schedule. Stuxnet, more than anything else, made the Iranians realize they were under attack in a shadow war, with hardly any capability to respond.

In late 2011, they announced two more cyber-attacks. One virus, which computer analysts called Duqu, showed signs of being created by the same high-level, sophisticated hackers who authored Stuxnet: U.S. and Israeli intelligence.

If that were not enough, like the Ten Plagues that befell ancient Egypt, the Iranians were hit by yet another blow—this time, a lethal one. Between 2007 and 2011, five top Iranian scientists were assassinated by a variety of methods. One supposedly was felled by carbon monoxide from a heater in his home. Four others were killed by bombs.

Three of the four bombings were accomplished by powerful magnets that held a uniquely shaped charge—a small but powerful bomb that directed all its lethal energy in one direction—when stuck onto a car door. The explosives were placed by fast-moving attackers riding on motorcycles, and motorcycles were practically a trademark of the Mossad's assassination unit.

There was a sixth attempt, using the magnetic method of sticking a bomb on a car door, but almost miraculously that target survived. Fereydoon Abbas-Divani, perhaps because of instincts developed as a Revolutionary Guard, sensed the danger and jumped out of his car. The Iranian regime, to show its defiance—after publicly blaming "the Zionists and America" for the string of attacks—promoted Abbas-Divani to be head of the Iran Atomic Energy Organization.

The common thread was that all the targets were key figures in Iran's nuclear program, at least some of them in the weaponization area. They also were lecturers or researchers in the science departments of top Iranian universities.

All the assassinations took place in the morning, when the targets were on their way to work. The attackers riding motorcycles showed cool-headed steadiness of the highest order. Clearly, these killings were the work of professionals, who had precise information about the home addresses and daily routines of the targeted scientists.

In the midst of all those killings, there was another incident—different, but very large. A massive explosion destroyed much of a missile-testing base near Tehran in December 2011. Dozens of people were killed, including a Revolutionary Guards general in charge of developing long-range missiles that could hit Israel and beyond. Major General Hassan Moghadam was also responsible for liaison with Syria and Hezbollah, and decided what missiles would be shipped by Iran to militants in Lebanon.

As with the assassinations of the scientists, there was no claim of responsibility for the death of the general and the others at the missile development facility. Iran denied that this blast was the result of sabotage, but that contention was probably out of reluctance to admit that a major military base had been infiltrated.

As for wishful thinking on the other side, some anti-ayatollah Iranian exiles claimed that their freedom-seeking brethren inside the country were carrying out these acts of violence. The exiles, frustrated by the endurance of the Islamic regime, wanted to believe that political dissidents had formed an active underground group that could strike the nuclear and missile programs with both courage and accuracy.

The truth, although Israel intended never to confirm it, was that these attacks were the handiwork of the Mossad's long arm. As difficult as the missions were, Israeli intelligence already had a long history of sabotage and targeted bloodshed. The name of the game, as the Book of Proverbs and the agency's motto suggested, was to disrupt the plans of enemy countries.

It was noteworthy, too, that the United States flatly denied any involvement. American officials even went so far as to publicly criticize the unknown killers for spoiling diplomatic hopes, because the chances of negotiations with Iran became slimmer after every attack. The Americans, in private, said that they were chiding Israel.

As for other suspects, while German intelligence was concerned about Iran, this era's set of spies in Berlin thankfully exhibited no taste for murder. And Britain's MI6 got out of the assassination business after the negotiated, if fragile, end of the conflict in Northern Ireland in 1998.

Several journalists suggested that the Mossad was only acting as an assassination contractor in Iran. They guessed that killers were recruited by the Israelis from such Iranian opposition groups as Mujahideen e-Khalq (MEK) or a Sunni Muslim group, Jundallah (Soldiers of God), also known as the People's Resistance Movement of Iran—in that country's Baluchistan province.

It is true that Dagan had drawn up a battle plan that included the use of disaffected minority groups. In a State Department cable from 2007 obtained and released by Wikileaks, the Mossad chief was quoted as telling a senior American official that disaffection among Baluchi, Azeri, and Kurdish minorities could be exploited by the United States and Israel. Dagan also suggested supporting student pro-democracy activists, if only to cause unrest inside Iran.

The official message also said that Dagan felt sure that the U.S. and Israel could "change the ruling regime in Iran and its attitude toward backing terror regimes," and that "we could also get them to delay their nuclear project."

According to the cable, Dagan said, "The economy is hurting, and this is provoking a real crisis among Iran's leaders." The minority groups that the Mossad and CIA could support or exploit are "raising their heads and are tempted to resort to violence."

High unemployment among Iran's young males could be—from a Mossad perspective—extremely useful in recruiting allies, agents who could be trained, or even mercenary or rebel armies.

In the years that followed, clues emerged, indicating that activists in MEK, Jundallah, and a few other dissident groups in Iran served as sources of information for Israel. In addition, when the Mossad wished to plant a tip about Iran in the international media, it frequently fed stories to MEK or another rebel group, which then trumpeted the news. That, in a way, was "laundering" information in order to protect sources and methods of collection.

The Mossad also enjoyed fairly safe passage in and out of Iran by going through nations where the security services were cooperative—including the Kurdish autonomous zone of northern Iraq. Israeli spies had developed excellent relationships with senior Kurds in several countries for decades, traceable back to the minority group appreciating Israel's help against Arabs who kept oppressing them. In the Middle East, the enemy of my enemy is my friend.

But for such a sensitive, dangerous, and daring mission as a series of assassinations in Iran's capital, the Mossad would not depend on hired-gun mercenaries. They would be considered far less trustworthy, and there was hardly any chance that the Mossad would reveal to non-Israelis some of its assassination unit's best methods.

These, in fact, were "blue and white" operations—Israeli intelligence's term for a fully Israeli project, referring to the colors of its nation's flag. From the little that was made public, it was obvious that they were nearly perfect in their execution: daring, innovative, and right out of the office of the Ramsad's playbook.

The Mossad was showing—more than any other Western intelligence organization—its willingness to take drastic measures and risk the lives of its best operatives. In turn, those men and a very few women were displaying their readiness to sacrifice. Clearly, if caught, they would be hanged in a public square in Iran. Israeli spies had come to such tortured ends in the past, sometimes after maintaining double lives in enemy countries for years.

Naturally, no one in Tel Aviv was talking about any operational details of how Israelis entered and left Iran—or where they stayed while inside the Islamic Republic.

There were many possibilities. Obviously, Israeli operatives traveled using the passports of other countries, including both bogus and genuine documents. That fact had been inadvertently revealed several times, over many years. In addition, the Mossad continuously maintained safe houses in Iran, dating back to the pre-1979 years under the Shah. That was an investment in the future, typical for Israeli intelligence.

The Mossad also had a human treasury: Tens of thousands of ex-Iranians now lived in Israel. Iranian Jews had fled, especially just after the 1979 revolution, and many of their children also were well acquainted with the Persian language and customs. Individuals who were brave enough—and then selected and trained by the Mossad—could move back to Iran and secretly serve Israel.

Israeli operatives inside Iran were available for all kinds of espionage and even, if and when the time came, for pinpointing targets for air strikes. The Mossad knew, after all, that the entire Iranian weapons program would not be demolished by assassinations of nuclear scientists and military officers. Those individuals would be replaced.

Yet, any delay at all represented an achievement. Israeli strategic thinking—exercised in Egypt, Iraq, and elsewhere—held that temporary disruptions to an enemy's dangerous projects were sufficient cause for taking significant risks.

This was even truer when it came to killing Iranian specialists, who worked on unique tasks that required years of study. These men were not available in abundant supply, despite Iran's relatively large and advanced technological infrastructure.

The assassinations also had a strong psychological objective: sending a loud and clear message to Iranians and scientists of other nations that working for the nuclear program was dangerous. The Mossad was telling them, in effect: Stay in your classrooms. Do your academic work. Get your research published. Enjoy the university life. But do not help Iran go nuclear. Otherwise, your career could be cut short by a bullet or a bomb.

Indeed, Israeli intelligence noticed that the assassination campaign was paying off, with what it called "white defections": Scientists were worried, many contemplated leaving the program, and some actually did. They did not depart Iran and defect to the other side, but they dissociated themselves from the nuclear program. There were also signs of scientists being reluctant to join the program, despite lucrative terms offered by the regime.

The intimidation campaign definitely showed an impact on foreigners. While in the past, Chinese, Russians, Pakistanis and some others were happily accepting invitations—and high pay—to work in Iran, the only ones who still seemed attracted were North Koreans.

Dagan was pleased by the missions and the "cleanliness" of their execution: no clues, no fingerprints, not even motorcycles left behind. Iranian authorities could only guess who was attacking, in broad daylight, in their capital.

The Israeli intelligence chief's mode of warfare was unusually bold. In addition to the operations inside Iran, he had sent assassins to eliminate Palestinian radicals and the elusive operations chief of the Lebanese Hezbollah party. The new element in the assassinations attributed to the Mossad under Dagan's leadership was that more killings occurred in "target" countries—Lebanon, Syria, Iran, and the United Arab Emirates—than ever before.

Dagan was proud of that change. This was the "dagger between its teeth" that his patron, Sharon, had wanted. In the previous 40 years, with few exceptions, lethal operations had been conducted in safer "base" countries. The Mossad, for instance, had fought a "war of the spooks" against Palestinian militants in the 1970s. Shootings and bombings had turned parts of Europe into a battlefield for Middle Easterners, and the Israelis had a continental headquarters in Paris that moved later to Brussels. Only rarely were murderous incursions made into Arab nations.

As far as Dagan and the Mossad were concerned, assassinations were a legitimate tactic, but not an objective in and of themselves. They had to be considered part of a comprehensive strategy, one of many tools in the multi-pronged battle against Iran.

In a meeting in 2007 with a U.S. official, Dagan did not give details of any acts of violence. But he did urge America to join immediately in a "five-pillar" plan to destabilize the ayatollahs' regime. The pillars were listed as "political approach," "covert measures," "counterproliferation," "sanctions," and "force regime change."

Encouraging the Mossad's research department not to leave high-level analysis to Aman—so that he could hear from what the Bible called a "multitude of counselors"—Dagan engaged his staff in discussion of all the factors to consider.

Dagan was a great believer in the potency of international pressure, especially sanctions. He told Mossad staff members, during analytic discussions, that economic factors in the modern world were powerful. He explained that he carefully studied the motivations of American presidents in formulating foreign policy and realized that the United States went to war in Iraq—twice—because of its energy interests.

Dagan thus reached the conclusion that the U.S. would not allow Iran to have nuclear weapons—not only out of concern that a messianic Shi'ite regime might use the bomb or intimidate Israel—but mainly because Iran would become the most powerful nation among energy producers.

He figured that a nuclear Iran would vastly expand its sphere of influence to the south and west, to envelop Gulf nations such as Saudi Arabia, Iraq, and the United Arab Emirates; and also to the north and east to such secular Muslim countries as Azerbaijan and Turkmenistan.

According to this scenario, Iran could then control 60 percent of the global energy market. The United States, in the world according to Dagan, would not permit that to happen.

In any event, U.S. military capabilities were many times more powerful than Israel's. Dagan favored, and even predicted, a situation where Israel would not need to stand alone. If there was no other way to stop—or keep delaying—

the Iranians, then the best solution to him would be for the huge American military to strike at the nuclear facilities.

After Dagan retired in December 2010, he told the Israeli news media—breaking his years of silence—that if Israel were to attack Iran, it would be "the stupidest thing I've ever heard." Just over a year later, he told CBS's *60 Minutes* that he trusted President Barack Obama. "The military option is on the table, and he is not going to let Iran become a nuclear state," Dagan said on CBS.

Dagan added that the issue "is not an Israeli problem; it's an international problem." He confirmed, too, that if he wanted anyone to attack Iran, "I will always prefer that Americans will do it."

Obama, however, seemed to be delaying any military moves for as long as he possibly could. Yet, in part because he was facing re-election in 2012, the president aligned himself with Israel in declaring that it would be unacceptable for Iran—as an oppressive nation supporting terrorist groups—to possess nuclear weapons.

Although he had personality and policy clashes with Prime Minister Benjamin Netanyahu, when they gave separate speeches to the American Israel Public Affairs Committee (the powerful pro-Israel lobby, AIPAC), in Washington in March 2012, Obama practically echoed the Israeli leader's worrying analysis: that if Iran were to become a nuclear power, other countries in the Middle East would rush to build their own matching arsenals. Turkey, perhaps Egypt, Saudi Arabia, and other Gulf sheikdoms would all want the apparent security of a nuclear umbrella. The most volatile region on Earth would then be replete with mankind's most dangerous weapons.

Obama also said that he was "not bluffing" about possible use of a "military option" against Iran.

American military commanders chose to say little about what could be done against Iran, and leaders at the Pentagon kept insisting that there was "time and space" to try all other options before resorting to armed force.

Israeli officials worked themselves into a rhetorical frenzy of warning that their patience with Iran was running out. Even more urgent, they pointed out, was the fact that Israel had a limited number of missiles, airplanes, and bunker-buster bombs that could penetrate hardened and buried Iranian facilities. That meant that Israel's window of opportunity was rapidly closing in 2012.

Defense Minister Ehud Barak, a former prime minister and before that a commando soldier with plenty of behind-enemy-lines irregular missions, coined the phrase "zone of immunity"—his way of suggesting that if his country waited too long, it would be too late for an Israeli strike on Iran to have much effect.

Barak's and Netanyahu's comments were part of a concerted campaign to keep the American media, politicians, and people highly engaged in this topic, as though to let the notion gain wide credence that *someone* would have to bomb Iran. Sharing intelligence data with their U.S. counterparts, the two

Israeli politicians stressed that even as Iran bought more time by agreeing to negotiations, it was secretly moving forward in uranium enrichment, bomb design, and missile construction.

Wielding some powers of persuasion and helped by the congressional access of the AIPAC lobby, Israelis kept reminding the U.S. that Iran was a growing threat. Israeli leaders were attempting to manipulate public opinion and government decision making, but this could also be seen as urging America to pay attention to something big that might otherwise go unnoticed in the noisy background of Iraq, Afghanistan, terrorism, and economic issues.

The official Israeli message was that Iran's nuclear program endangered American interests all over the Middle East, the shipping lanes for oil, and even targets in Europe that could be reached by Iranian missiles. The Mossad joined in hammering home the message—in Washington—that if Israel did agree to restrain itself and do nothing overt, then the United States should guarantee that America would do everything necessary to take care of the problem.

The pitch was partly aimed at intimidating Iran's leaders, of course, so that they would believe that refusing to stop their nuclear program could trigger devastating attacks. The message was also directed at Europe and especially at Russia and China, which were reluctant to tighten sanctions against Iran. Surely they would not want Israel to take military action, with all the consequences for oil supplies and other disruptions.

The Mossad, even before Dagan's retirement at the end of 2010, helped lead a campaign to leak information about Iran's clandestine nuclear labs and weapons factories. But Dagan felt that Netanyahu and Barak were saying too much in public. It did not seem useful to be extremely alarming, huffing and puffing but perhaps never blowing the enemy's house down.

The Mossad director continued to hope that delay or destruction could be accomplished by sabotage, low-intensity covert warfare, and more efforts to bring down the radical Islamic government in Tehran. He predicted that if Israel were to bomb Iran, the people of that country would "rally around the mullahs," and that would set back hopes of a regime change that could make Iran far more friendly.

Dagan certainly agreed that a nuclear-armed Iran, with a radical Islamic government, would pose a threat to the existence of his country. He always sought to honor the memory of his grandfather and other Holocaust victims by taking a strong stand against enemies of the Jewish people. Yet, along with his analysts at the Mossad, the agency chief concluded that Israel should not find itself standing alone on the front lines in a war against Iran.

He was echoing a repeated dictum of his patron, Sharon: to lower your profile. As highly creative army generals, Sharon and Dagan excelled at hiding their troops until the moment of action arrived.

The truth was that Dagan, as a soldier who had witnessed the horrors of war, was very reluctant to see nations engage in armed conflict. He believed that all-out war, especially against Iran, should be a last resort—only when "the sword is on our neck," he said.

According to Dagan, as Mossad director, covert action against Iran had been highly effective. He refused to elucidate publicly, but the Stuxnet computer worm had done a terrific job. And daring assassinations and sabotage in Teheran were missions accomplished. Dagan estimated that the delays caused in Iran's nuclear program, when totaled, came to between five and seven years.

He was certain that Iran's leaders had intended to have a nuclear bomb by 2005 or 2007, but they continued to be a couple of years away. For Dagan, the greatest achievement of his time as Mossad director was delaying Iran from gate-crashing into the nuclear club.

When he stepped down, somewhat disappointed that Netanyahu did not extend his tenure, Dagan was replaced by one of his former deputies, Tamir Pardo. Pardo was a veteran of many years of Mossad operations, and he was expected to continue Dagan's balance of being careful and attentive, while emphatically active.

Most top commanders of the Israel Defense Forces, including Aman, agreed with Dagan's analysis that an international campaign to put non-violent pressure on Iran should be given more time—though strong sanctions needed to be coupled with as much sabotage as possible inside Iran. And, though without official acknowledgment, sabotage would likely be coupled with carefully selected acts of violence.

The IDF loyally drew up plans to strike Iranian facilities, to be ready in case Israel's political leaders ordered them to strike, but the military had severe doubts about how much damage an Israeli attack could do. They were also concerned about the likely retaliation by Iran and its regional allies, Hezbollah in Lebanon and the Palestinian terrorists of Hamas in Gaza. Life in much of Israel could become a living hell, with missiles raining down as never before if war were to break out.

Although Israeli intelligence's conclusions had, at times, differed from the CIA's, the two allies were by 2012 in agreement on what the Iranians were likely to achieve—and when. Iran might be able to build a nuclear device in 2013, but at most that would be a raw, crude bomb. It would take until 2015 for an Iranian bomb to be made small enough to fit into a warhead on a Shihab missile that could reach Israel.

In other words, Israeli intelligence was telling its political masters that there was still room for a solution without going to war. Mossad experts wanted to see what could be accomplished by tougher sanctions, including a decision by large European nations to stop buying Iranian oil in the summer of 2012, plus more rounds of sabotage by Israel and its covert allies.

Netanyahu and Barak considered the intelligence analysis to be wrong. In speeches, off-the-record briefings with journalists, and interviews, they kept beating war drums. They acted as though they had no doubt about Israel's military capability to smash Iran's nuclear program. But their primary message seemed aimed at the Americans: You had better be on top of this. If you don't act, we will!

Was that a genuine threat or an Israeli bluff? United States officials kept asking for specific plans and to be told in advance of any Israeli attack. Washington yearned not to be surprised. Yet, it appeared that top Israeli politicians wanted America to be left guessing.

The divisions between the Israeli security and political establishments mirrored cracks emerging in Iran. There were signs that the Iranian people were suffering from the sanctions—growing unemployment, cuts in government subsidies, soaring prices, and fuel shortages—and many were blaming their misfortune on the nuclear program.

According to Mossad analysts, Iranian senior echelons were enmeshed in a critical debate. The main issue was the wisdom of pursuing or dropping the military nuclear path.

Iran's leaders wanted nuclear weapons as a tool that would ensure the survival of their regime. They looked at North Korea and saw that by having nuclear weapons, that rogue nation created a cloak of immunity for itself. World powers would not dare attack North Korea, and its dictators—Kim Jong-Il and later his son—got away with almost everything they did.

This Iranian point of view also took note of Muammar Qaddafi's fate. The Libyan dictator had started a nuclear program, but he never built a bomb. He then meekly dismantled his nuclear program in order to reestablish diplomatic relations with the West. Within a few years, however, American and other Western aircraft were supporting a rebellion against him; Qaddafi was overthrown, hunted down like a dog, and ignominiously killed. No bomb equaled no protection. Hard-line Iranians vowed not to make that mistake.

There was another faction in Iran, however, which the Mossad hoped would win the argument. These were senior Iranians among the Muslim clerics, the Revolutionary Guards, and the government who contended that if Israel, America, or both were to attack, it could lead to calamity for the Islamic Republic.

Spotting a possible Iranian rhetorical route for abandoning a nuclear arms program, Mossad analysts noted with great interest that several senior clerics—including the Supreme Leader, Ayatollah Ali Khamenei—issued edicts that such weapons were un-Islamic.

The Israeli experts knew that this could simply be a lie, and also that religious leaders in Iran could decree that exceptional circumstances justified building nuclear bombs. But the analysts held on to the hope that Iranian leaders might reach a less aggressive conclusion: that instead of protecting the regime, building nuclear weapons could hasten its downfall.

Israeli intelligence felt that it had very good and up-to-date information from the inner circle around Khamenei, who ultimately would make the decision. He was the successor to Khomeini, the mystically charismatic founder of the Islamic Republic of Iran. Yet, Khamenei was more of a modern politician, with potentially talkative courtiers all around him in the sacred city of Qom.

The Mossad's nuclear proliferation department believed that Iran's scientists in 2012 would inform Khamenei—and the smug, radically loquacious President Mahmoud Ahmadinejad—that they would soon be ready for a "breakout," a headlong rush to use Iran's enriched uranium to create a bomb. That process might take a year to accomplish, and in the process Iran would almost surely expel international atomic inspectors.

In that sense, Israel and the United States would have some time left for a military attack to disrupt and delay the enemy's fateful move.

The now retired Dagan opined that Iranian leaders were "rational" and could calculate the consequences of their decisions and actions. He and current Israeli intelligence officials fervently hoped—though they could not predict the decisions of Iran's top zealot—that Khamenei would reject the notion that nuclear bombs were the way to guarantee the regime's survival.

The Israeli strategy for a peaceful way out of this crisis was to push Khamenei to embrace the starker point of view: that a breakout would likely trigger a strike on Iran—perhaps a gigantic pounding by America. Instead of securing the Islamic Republic, the breakout could, ironically, trigger the regime's downfall.

The Mossad wanted to keep up the pressure, without all-out war. Pressure already included actions that many other nations' intelligence services would never consider: smuggling Israelis into Iran, targeting individual Iranians for assassination, and in a multitude of ways violating the canons of international law.

To a foreigner, many of these covert activities might have seemed outrageous. But to Israelis in the intelligence community, it all made a lot of sense—in particular, when the alternatives were either bombing Iran, or Iran having the bomb.

Israel's next moves could prove to be more momentous, risky, and potentially damaging than anything the country had faced since declaring independence in 1948.

The actions taken against Iran, so far, bore the unique hallmarks of Israel's espionage agencies. Intelligence gathering, sabotage, assassinations, psychological warfare—and other measures that were kept even more secretive—reflected the modes of operation that were designed, developed, and executed by Israeli security agencies over more than 60 years of trial, error, and success.

The strategies and daring steps of today are rooted in a hidden history. The best way to understand the decisions now being made is to go back as far as 1948 and learn about the motivations and methods of the people inside Israeli intelligence.

CHAPTER TWO

CHILDHOOD DISEASES

D ump him!" That was the order from Isser Harel, the undisputed czar of the Israeli intelligence community.

Several Mossad operatives were sitting in a small office at Sde Dov airfield in northern Tel Aviv near the end of 1954. They were dead tired, having just landed after a four-hour flight in a shaky World War II-era plane. They wanted to go home to their families, but they had a problem. They had just unloaded a corpse, and they did not know what to do with it.

It was the body of Avner Israel. His life, his death, and his disappearance illustrated how almost everything in the country's first years had to be improvised. Whether with a traitor or a spycatcher, you made it up as you went along. Still, all through the history of Israeli intelligence, every failure, every improvised solution, and every stroke of luck was a building block in developing a uniquely successful style.

As for the man whose family name was Israel, he was an immigrant from Bulgaria. In retrospect, his coming from a Communist country should have prompted some attention. Even more troubling should have been the fact that after surviving the Holocaust he moved to British-ruled Palestine for a while, returned to Bulgaria, and then arrived in Israel for good in 1949.

The immigrant's son—Moshe Tziper, himself a colorful character in a small rural community in the Galilee—recounted, more than six decades later, that his father had been married to a Christian woman back in the old country but divorced her. In Israel, he served in the navy and then transferred to the air force.

He was stationed in the north and took part in the first Israeli efforts to develop EW—electronic warfare. This secret work included means of blinding enemies' technology. Israel seemed talented and was promoted to the rank of captain.

In 1953 he married another Jewish immigrant from Bulgaria. "That was my mother," Tziper reminisced with distinctly mixed feelings. "But I know that my father was a philanderer and proved to be a crook."

The couple lived in Haifa, where Israel became romantically entangled with a female secretary at the Italian consulate. The romance seemed to drive him mentally over the edge. He converted to Roman Catholicism in a Jerusalem church and married the woman—without bothering with the bureaucratic niceties of divorcing his wife, Matilda. He did change his name to Alexander Ibor.

Charges filed by the police accused him of pretending to own an apartment—it simply was not his—and selling it for cash to four different buyers. He also posed as a salesman for a foreign refrigerator manufacturer, collected cash deposits from numerous customers, and then disappeared with their money.

Just before a scheduled court appearance in November 1954, he deserted the military and found shelter among the ultra-Orthodox Jews of the Neturei Karta sect in Jerusalem—ironically, or appropriately, a group opposed to the existence of a secular State of Israel.

A Christian priest provided him with false identity documents, and then disguised as a priest himself. Israel/Ibor sailed from Haifa to Italy. Matilda at the time was pregnant with their only child, Moshe.

In Rome, apparently to make some money, he went to the Egyptian embassy and offered to sell Israeli military secrets from his navy and air force work. The Egyptians paid him on the spot. He promised to return with more intelligence, but vanished in an unexpected direction. He bought a ticket on a ship from Spain to South America.

The Mossad became aware of the blatant betrayal. The agency—very successful at penetrating Arab embassies in Europe—received a tip-off about an Israeli officer "named Ibor or Ibon or Ibi" who was peddling classified material.

Amos Manor, who under Harel's authority directed Shin Bet, was quickly made aware of the threat posed by Israel/ Ibor. Manor and Harel decided that there was no way of ignoring the treachery of an Israeli military officer privy to secrets. The turncoat had to be caught.

Almost instantly, they called in the ace kidnapper of Israeli intelligence, Rafi Eitan. A future spymaster who would employ an American, Jonathan Pollard, as an agent in the 1980s, Eitan was one of the leaders of a combined Mossad-Shin Bet operations department.

He put together a surveillance and snatch squad and flew to Italy. In the weeks leading up to Christmas 1954, they commenced a search with highly uncertain prospects.

"Our mission was to find a Bulgarian needle in an Italian haystack," Eitan recounted more than 50 years later. "We didn't know his whereabouts."

Their assumption was that the traitor would try to fly to Egypt. Harel's instructions were: Don't let him get on an airplane. Set up a command post at the airport in Rome. If you see him, grab him physically and injure him if necessary. If all other means fail, shoot him.

This was a green light to kill an Israeli citizen. It was the first and last time that such an order was given.

"We needed a miracle," Eitan recalled, confirming that the search was about to be called off for lack of any results in Italy. All Mossad stations across Europe were instructed to be on alert and to pump all possible agents for any fragment of news about Ibor.

With the reality that it is as valuable to be lucky as good, there was an unexpected break. The wife of an Israeli secret agent in Vienna who worked for another clandestine agency—Nativ, focused on Jewish immigration—happened to be an ex-Bulgarian. And she happened to have a job at the Israeli embassy in Austria.

One day, she told her husband that she had just bumped into an old friend from her childhood in Bulgaria. Amazingly, that friend was none other than Avner Israel.

"Where is he?" the husband asked, calmly as he could. His wife said she would be meeting her childhood friend the next day for lunch.

The Nativ man relayed the information to Mossad headquarters in Tel Aviv, and new orders were issued to Eitan.

The snatch expert rapidly conjured up a simple plan. His Shin Bet team rushed to Vienna and took up positions the very next day, near the restaurant where Ibor/Israel was meeting his old friend. Now it was easy to shadow him.

A few days later, the surveillance target boarded an airplane bound for Paris. Always styling himself a ladies' man, he could not help noticing the pretty woman sitting next to him. He flirted with her, and she reciprocated.

This was a classic, but simple, honey trap. She was a member of the Mossad-Shin Bet operation. In the days to come, she helped keep tabs on Ibor.

Manor himself flew in from Tel Aviv to supervise the surveillance and the capture. Inspired by the army's uniformed senior officers, who prided themselves on being at the dangerous front lines with their troops, leaders of Israeli intelligence often would choose to be at the scene of a highly risky mission.

The capture went smoothly. An armed Israeli team surrounded Ibor and forced him to go to a safe house rented by the Mossad. French authorities noticed nothing.

The turncoat was interrogated and admitted that he had stolen a hundred documents from the air force—about electronic warfare plans and the layout of the Ramat David base in the north—and had offered to sell them to Egypt.

The orders were to return him home for trial, so the team injected Ibor with a tranquilizer to keep him quiet and stuffed him into a wooden box. An old plane belonging to the Israeli air force was waiting at a small airport near Paris.

The human box was loaded on board the plane. An anesthesiologist— Dr. Yonah Elian, a trusted volunteer from a hospital in Israel—administered another injection to keep the captive asleep.

That turned out to be an accidental overdose, fatal in the freezing winds that penetrated the fuselage. Ibor stopped breathing during the flight, and efforts to revive him failed. The captive now was dead. When the plane landed at Tel Aviv's Sde Dov airfield, the Israeli snatch squad was terrified and did not know what to do.

Their calm and experienced commander, Eitan, had remained in Europe for another operation. As he recalled many years later, his underlings waited at the airport for over two hours until Harel surprised them with new instructions: dump the corpse into the Mediterranean.

A fresh flight crew and a new Shin Bet team arrived, and the rickety plane took off again. Ibor's body was dropped to a watery grave from high above.

The original flyers and kidnappers went home, absolutely exhausted "after sleepless nights," according to Eitan, who added: "Why was Isser's order obeyed? Because if Isser told you to do something, you did it without asking questions."

Israeli intelligence did not bother to tell the man's wife anything. Her husband had run off with another woman, anyway.

In 2006, more than half a century after his father vanished, Tziper had a visit from two young intelligence operatives—one from Shin Bet and the other from the Mossad. They told him what seemed, more or less, to be the true story.

Elian, the young doctor who inadvertently killed Tziper's father in 1954, was used by the Mossad and Shin Bet again in at least one foreign escapade: the capture of Nazi war criminal Adolf Eichmann in Argentina in 1960. There, too, the anesthesiologist administered sedatives by injection. On that South American adventure that would find its place in the lore of great intelligence operations, nothing went wrong. Rafi Eitan was also part of that kidnapping.

Elian would commit suicide in June 2011 by suffocating himself with a plastic bag. His clandestine, part-time career may not have played a role in that, but with his death at age 88 his secrets were exposed. Israeli news media discovered that the anesthesiologist moonlighted in Mossad missions and that his experiences had been disturbing to him.

"My father was haunted, all his life, by the tragedy," his son Danny Elian, also a doctor, told Kol Israel radio—referring to the mishandled kidnapping of the spy in the Israeli military whose own name was Israel.

The death and dumping occurred barely six years after the State of Israel declared independence as the British ended their three decades of ruling Palestine. Yet, the fate of Ibor is still considered one of the lowest points in the annals of Israeli intelligence.

"We didn't kill and we didn't torture, and we didn't do anything illegal to Israeli citizens, neither Jews nor Arabs," Manor said many years later.

So what about the death of Avner Israel? "Oh," Manor shrugged. "I am ashamed of this affair. Since then, our intelligence operatives never let even the most dangerous Israeli traitors, who deserved punishment, die in their hands."

The Israeli intelligence community blossomed from a spy service called Shai (an acronym for *Sherut Yediot*, the Hebrew words for "Information Service"). It was the intelligence branch of Haganah, the largest underground organization of the Jewish community in Palestine. The Haganah, and its various units, including the Palmach strike force, battled both the Palestinian Arabs and the British until the latter left on May 14, 1948.

That June 30, half a dozen men dressed in khaki arrived at Shai's office in Tel Aviv. It was a unique group, in a unique situation. In the midst of its first war—as the neighboring Arab states had invaded newborn Israel—they grappled with finding ways to satisfy the country's security and defense requirements while constructing a durable democracy. The men who gathered on that memorably hot, humid day were the founding fathers of the secret agencies that would become the Israeli intelligence community.

They had vast experience in covert operations: spying, smuggling, and gathering information by all means, however ruthless—spearheading the struggle for Zionist independence. Some had been active with British forces in Europe and North Africa, in the name of defeating the Nazis.

But when it came to democracy, they had only been observers and never full participants. They had seen the British at work, as intelligence operatives combating the Jewish underground movements in Palestine and as politicians in the Mother of Democracy back in London. And they liked both.

Their problem, however, was that there was no instant recipe for defending a nation at war without stomping on its democratic values, especially in the Middle East, where Western notions had no natural constituency.

The commander of Shai, Isser Be'eri, cleared his throat for attention. "I have just come from a meeting with *ha-Zaken*"—"the Old Man," he said, a reference to David Ben-Gurion, the charismatic first prime minister of Israel, who was also directing the war as his own defense minister.

The Shai officers unconsciously sat a bit more erect, as an announcement from the white-haired oracle of Israel appeared forthcoming. At the age of 62, Ben-Gurion was the nation's elder statesman and guiding light, bar none.

Ben-Gurion had just finished telling the Shai chief that Israel's defense would have to include intelligence. Not good intelligence, but *great* intelligence.

Shai, the Haganah's intelligence arm, would digest itself and other pre-state Zionist underground groups to produce several agencies in a community. All of them would initially bear names starting with *Shin Mem*—the Hebrew initials for *Sherut Modi'in* (Intelligence Service), followed by a single digit, as in the British style of MI5 and MI6. Formalizing a new structure for the intelligence community would take eight months.

On February 8, 1949, just before the first general election to the Knesset—Israel's parliament—and before the signing of armistice agreements with the Arab nations, Ben-Gurion summoned his top advisors and made official this new division of labor for the security agencies. Military and civilian functions would be separated, and the community was meant to be fitting for a modern state that had won its war of independence. Ben-Gurion's division of labor went as follows:

Military intelligence: Be'eri had announced in June 1948 that he would henceforth head the dominant agency in the new community, then called the Intelligence Department of the army. Known later as Aman, the acronym for *Agaf ha-Modi'in* or "Intelligence Wing," the unit was assigned widespread functions, including collecting information on Arab armies, censoring Israeli newspapers and radio, maintaining security within Israel's army, and a bit of counterespionage.

A domestic secret service: Harel, a Shai veteran, would be director of the agency to be called Shabak—an acronym for *Sherut ha-Bitachon ha-Klali*, or "General Security Service." Later, its letterhead in English would say "Israel Security Agency," but it was typically known worldwide by its first two Hebrew initials, Shin Bet.

Harel was then changing his own name from Isser Halperin. Born in Russia in 1912, he arrived in pre-state Palestine in 1930 and volunteered enthusiastically to be an underground fighter. His specialty in Shai was surveillance of right-wing Jews who rejected the authority of Ben-Gurion and the Haganah. Being the head of Shin Bet suited him well, because he viewed enemies within Israel's borders as just as dangerous as those outside.

The agency was initially assigned broad tasks that including catching foreign spies and spying on Israeli citizens deemed suspicious—mainly the Arab minority. Shin Bet was even put in charge of all prisons for a short time, as well as the security of all government buildings, with a special focus on scientific laboratories and arms factories.

The latter responsibility was transferred a few years later to a security unit within the Ministry of Defense. That unit's existence was not revealed for more than three decades, when it came to light under the name Lakam, an acronym for *Lishka le-Kishrei Mada*, the Science Liaison Bureau. It was Lakam, with Eitan as its chief in the mid-1980s, that handled Pollard and caused extreme tension with Israel's vital ally, America.

A foreign intelligence service: Espionage outside Israel would be in the hands of the Foreign Ministry's Political Department. Two years later, in 1951, it would morph into the Mossad, under the leadership of Reuven Shiloah. A secretive man by nature, he set the priorities that became lasting hallmarks of Israeli intelligence. Shiloah decreed that the Mossad would have to plant operatives in Arab countries, and that Israeli agencies had a duty to serve as Jewish-Zionist protectors of their people all around the world. Shiloah also insisted on developing modern technology, keeping up with the latest in espionage methods by maintaining ties with friendly agencies in Europe and the United States.

A clandestine immigration service: *Ha-Mossad le-Aliyah Bet*, "the Institute for Aliyah B," would continue its role from before Israel's independence. Despite the word Mossad in its name, this institute was not part of the fabled foreign espionage agency.

Aliyah B would, in the early 1950s, be disbanded in a contentious process that saw its functions divided: some for a unit called Bitzur within the new Mossad; and some for a new agency called Nativ. (*See Chapter 13.*)

In its first years, the embryonic intelligence community was inept. This included the only occasion in which an Israeli suspect was intentionally put to death, and it happened on the very day that the intelligence community's outlines were organized: June 30, 1948.

On the instructions of military intelligence chief Be'eri, Captain Meir Toubiansky was accused of spying for the British and the Jordanians. Without any lawyer or real consideration for his denials, Toubiansky was shot by a firing squad. Three intelligence officers were the prosecutors, the judges, and the executioners.

It would take a few years until Ben-Gurion acknowledged the injustice, rehabilitated Toubiansky's reputation, and compensated his family.

The major ineptitudes of this early period also included an absurd episode in which Israel's spies went on strike. In what was called the Revolt of the Spies, employees of the Foreign Ministry's Political Department refused to be shifted to Reuven Shiloah's new Mossad.

Shiloah, with the prime minister's full backing, responded by reorganizing intelligence functions to exclude foreign ministry professionals. Special assignments became the sole purview of Aman, which quickly established a secret military unit to plant agents in Arab countries.

It became clear, however, in less than two years that Shiloah—though brilliant—was not cut out to be an administrator. In September 1952 he was replaced by Harel, who had seemed quite busy with his domestic security duties.

Harel's work ethic and rectitude had impressed the prime minister, who believed that he had found the right man for a task still not fully understood. Given responsibility for both Shin Bet at home and the Mossad abroad, Harel became the supreme chief of Israeli intelligence.

He carried a unique title: the *Memuneh*, the "One in Charge" of the intelligence community. Although Amos Manor became the titular head of Shin Bet, he bowed to Harel's seniority.

In return, the Memuneh displayed boundless loyalty and agreed to undertake almost anything for the government. In truth that included, upon Ben-Gurion's request, using intelligence agencies as political tools for the ruling Mapai party. While Israel's founding fathers believed in democracy, they also had the unbreakable habit of identifying their own political interests with those of the state.

The nation was only beginning its long march away from the clandestine habits of a Jewish underground fighting for independence. Among the vast majority of Israelis, the Mapai party was practically synonymous with the state. Mapai certainly controlled most of its institutions: industrial factories, labor unions, the army hierarchy, and the intelligence community.

Harel was happy to serve the ruling party, but some of his operatives were reluctant to carry out seemingly strange instructions. One day they would be fighting black-market smugglers; on another they would try to locate and arrest subversives; and then they would join Aman's military intelligence officers in opening thousands of letters from abroad—hoping to intercept contraband currency.

In the search for subversion, Ben-Gurion and his Mapai took a simple approach based on the belief that "those who are not with us are against us." Accordingly, Harel ordered Shin Bet operatives to infiltrate Israel's other political parties. Many of them did not care for doing that, either.

Harel was acting more like a Soviet-style secret police, rather than a professional intelligence agency in a democratic state. He spied on right-wing parties and on religious zealots, and he planted microphones in the offices of the leaders of a left-wing party. He interpreted political disagreements—sometimes heated—as subversive and dangerous to the state.

Manor—who had been in Israel for only a few years and spoke Hebrew with the accent of his native Hungary –adapted more to the values of a free country. He ordered Shin Bet agents to stop spying on political entities, and he destroyed archives of gossip and other information about Ben-Gurion's opponents.

It took a while, but Harel went along with making Shin Bet far more professional. The agency became skillful at detecting treason by Israelis, as well as foreign spies planted within Israeli society.

Harel's biggest catch came as an unexpected outgrowth of espionage by Israelis inside the largest of the neighboring Arab countries, Egypt. Aman's actions there were far from glorious and failed to destabilize the land of the pyramids.

In the summer of 1954, an especially secret part of military intelligence that specialized in sabotage, Unit 131, launched a set of missions in Egypt that Israelis would later call *Esek Bish*: the Rotten Affair.

At the heart of it was an effort to create a wedge between the United States, Britain, and France on one side, and Egypt, led by the charismatic President Gamal Abdel Nasser. Israel decided to set off bombs all over Egypt in an attempt to make the country seem like an unstable and unreliable partner for the West. Israel hoped to provoke Britain into re-thinking its decision to withdraw forces from the Suez Canal.

Unit 131 recruited idealistic Egyptian Jewish students who wanted to help Israel and hoped to move there one day. They were instructed to use homemade bombs to attack American and British institutions in Egypt. Aman called this Operation Susannah. The young Egyptians were inept and, falling like dominos, they were quickly arrested one after another. Israel did not acknowledge responsibility. Two of the students were hanged, and several were given long prison terms.

Harel, with a keen sense for disloyalty, strongly suspected that the network had been betrayed by Aman's chief case officer, Avri El-Ad. Harel followed his instincts and determined that El-Ad was hiding out in Germany. The joint Mossad-Shin Bet operations team sprang into action, traveling to El-Ad's location and luring him back to Israel.

El-Ad refused to admit he had betrayed the Egyptian Jews, and, indeed, there was no evidence of that. So, in an Israeli court that ordered total secrecy, he was convicted of having unauthorized contacts with Egyptian intelligence, and he was sentenced to 10 years in prison.

Another important spy caught by Harel was Ze'ev Avni. He arrived from Switzerland during the War of Independence in 1948 and managed to get a job in the foreign ministry with unbelievable ease.

In the mid-1950s Avni was assigned to the Israeli embassy in Belgrade, Yugoslavia. There, he inflicted severe damage to national security by harvesting all the codes used by the foreign ministry and giving them to the KGB.

His employers did not know that Avni was a trained KGB agent, serving his masters in Moscow because of his belief in Communist worldwide fraternity. The Mossad had been ignorant of this, too. In fact, it used Avni occasionally to recruit Yugoslavs and foreigners in Belgrade to do some spying for Israel. Avni then started nudging Mossad chiefs to get him transferred out of the foreign ministry so he could work in espionage full-time.

Harel, constantly surveying personnel rolls with his finely honed counterespionage instincts, found reasons to doubt Avni and his enthusiasm for working overtime.

Clearly, the best way to get Avni to Tel Aviv was to pretend to offer him a job in the Mossad. In April 1956, unaware that he was in trouble, Avni flew home and was arrested by Harel's and Manor's Shin Bet. Under interrogation, the committed Communist at first refused to cooperate. Shin Bet had no evidence against him, so it needed a confession.

As a final desperation move, Manor showed the suspect articles about a secret speech by the Soviet leader, Nikita Khrushchev. Avni did not know that the original text had been obtained, just a few days earlier, by Manor's own men in Eastern Europe—an intelligence coup that delighted the CIA. *(See Chapter 4.)* The speech revealed many of the horrors of Josef Stalin's dictatorship, enough to unsettle all but the most rabid Marxists.

In the end, the Khrushchev speech broke Avni. Shin Bet interrogators could not help but be surprised by Avni's instant disenchantment with Soviet Communism. He confessed everything about his secret career as a KGB agent and named his handlers—a "debriefing" that the Israelis found most useful. Now, Harel knew how the Russians were trying to plant spies in the Jewish state.

Avni was so cooperative that after being sentenced to 15 years in prison, *he* was planted in the jail cell of other suspected traitors as an informer for Shin Bet.

Harel clearly was dealing with highly unusual human beings, both friends and foes. Among his intelligence staffers, he did his best to inspire pride in belonging to an exclusive fraternity. "You are rare creatures in a game reserve," he remarked to his subordinates.

Being all too human, they enjoyed the oddly worded praise. They certainly were not in the espionage game for money. The salaries paid to employees of Shin Bet and the Mossad were in line with those paid to ordinary civil servants in Israel—low by Western standards—but the money was approximately doubled for operatives on foreign assignment. The work was demanding and dangerous, and the hours unending. At the very least, Harel could ensure that his operatives saw themselves as a protected species.

His agents also knew that trips abroad, a rare commodity in those days for Israelis, were among the fringe benefits of their work. Those who toiled in the support division, not normally in the field, were also eligible to enjoy this benefit. From time to time, technicians, mechanics, and secretaries were sent abroad on missions that did not require any specific skill, such as acting as couriers or for guard duty.

In return, Harel demanded total loyalty and utter commitment to their assignments. Harel himself set the example: work, not waste. Rather than lodging in expensive hotels or eating at elegant restaurants, he would choose cheaper and more ascetic alternatives—even as he traveled frequently to Europe, the United States and South America.

The worst sin was to lie. "They train us to lie, to steal, and to cook up schemes against our enemies," a senior operative in the Mossad explained, "but we may not allow these things to corrupt us. We are duty-bound to see to it that our moral standards remain high."

CHAPTER THREE

STRATEGIC ALLIANCE

W e are very interested in having a cooperation agreement with you," David Ben-Gurion said to the director of the Central Intelligence Agency. This was in May 1951, in the original CIA headquarters near the Lincoln Memorial in Washington, DC. The prime minister happened to be in the United States on a mostly unofficial visit, his first after Israel won its war of independence.

Ben-Gurion was helping to raise funds for his country by personally endorsing the first sales of Israel Bonds in the United States. He used the visit for strategic purposes, too.

"The Old Man" met with President Harry Truman, and a secret luncheon was arranged for him with the director of the CIA, General Walter Bedell Smith, and Bedell Smith's assistant, Allen Dulles. Even before Ben-Gurion left Israel, Reuven Shiloah, then still head of the Mossad, suggested that the prime minister propose intelligence cooperation between the two countries.

The process begun on that trip to America's capital would eventually see the United States and Israel inextricably linked in a long series of joint missions, dangerous situations, and policy choices—extending to the challenges of the present day. Enemies of the U.S. and the Jewish state would come to see the two nations, one huge and one tiny, as a single entity. They, in turn, would often fight back together.

At the start of the 1950s, this seemed to be a highly unlikely notion. Israel, ruled by left-wing parties, was considered a socialist state. The kibbutz, the unique Israeli farm cooperative that enshrined the principle of sharing assets among members according to their needs, was regarded as the embodiment of a Marxist dream. The Soviet Union and its Communist puppet countries were early friends of Israel.

In addition, some Israeli actions set off alarm bells in Washington. The newborn nation's operatives were flouting American law while laboring to recruit Arab diplomats on U.S. soil, and the FBI did not like it.

The chief recruiter was Elyashiv Ben-Horin, who was posted in Israel's embassy in Washington with an intelligence role for the Political Department of the Foreign Ministry. One of his targets was Jordan's military attaché, but the Jordanian informed the FBI. Ben-Horin, after pulling out a gun in a restaurant, was expelled from the United States in 1950. The incident was not reported in the press.

The Israeli military attaché—Colonel Chaim Herzog, who later would be head of Aman and eventually president of Israel—also cut short his stay in Washington. Suspicions had been voiced that he was stealing military technology.

Shiloah wanted to change that nasty environment by urging Ben-Gurion to abandon Israel's pro-Soviet orientation and instead form strong ties with America. The Mossad chief's ultimate aim was to negotiate a defense treaty with Washington, and to have Israel join the North Atlantic Treaty Organization. As a first step, he suggested secret contacts between the CIA and the Mossad.

Ben-Gurion and senior government officials did not give Shiloah's proposal much of a chance of being accepted, but they felt that the effort was worth making. The prime minister was surprised when Bedell Smith and Dulles gladly endorsed the idea.

This was not the first encounter between the American general and the Old Man. They had met immediately after World War II, when Ben-Gurion visited Holocaust survivors in the displaced persons camps of Germany. Bedell Smith, then a senior officer in the Allied command, accompanied the Zionist leader on his inspection tour.

The extermination of six million Jews in the Holocaust—and seeing hundreds of thousands of refugees who survived—left an indelible impression on many American soldiers who served in Europe during the war. Israel, for its part, was well aware of how to wring the memory of the Holocaust when emotional manipulation appeared necessary. The sympathy and guilt felt by some Western leaders could be useful when the Jewish state requested political and military aid.

Israeli diplomats stressed, time and again, the necessity of their country being strong, so that there would never be another Holocaust. Coupling that horrible history with requests for military or similar aid bordered on exploitation of the unspeakable crimes of the war era, horrors that remained unique in human history, but it worked. Among those persuaded were Bedell Smith and Dulles. In Washington, Ben-Gurion reached an understanding with the CIA chiefs to begin talks immediately on pressing ahead with cooperation.

Before that, just when the State of Israel was born, American intelligence had not seemed interested. Moe Berg, a retired baseball player—mostly with the Chicago White Sox—was a Jew who worked in the Office of Special Services, the precursor to the CIA. Berg suggested that he be sent to Israel to launch espionage activities as well as liaison. He argued that his religious identity would make it easy to gain the Israelis' trust. His bosses, however, turned down the idea. In fact, Berg later felt very connected with Israel, and he arranged for his ashes to be spread over Jerusalem's Mount Scopus following his death in 1972.

Even without Berg going to bat, the talks with the CIA launched by Ben-Gurion bore fruit in June 1951. Shiloah was sent to Washington to hammer out the final details of a secret understanding. He held long meetings with Bedell Smith, Dulles, and especially James Jesus Angleton.

Angleton was an eccentric but up-and-coming CIA executive, a Christian who had been influenced profoundly by the Holocaust. He was the sort of man who doggedly pursued any subject that interested him. Although his duties were mostly focused on counterespionage—catching foreign spies in the United States—he was fascinated by all things Israeli.

Just after World War II ended, uncovering Fascist spy rings and recruiting informers in Europe, Angleton had found that his best sources of information included Aliyah B agents in Italy who were busy smuggling Jews to the country then called Palestine. One of those agents recalled: "Jim saw in Israel a true ally at a time when belief in a mission had become a rare concept."

Naturally, Angleton was very pleased when the CIA and Shiloah reached their cooperation agreement in 1951. It laid the foundation for the exchange of strategic information between the CIA and the Mossad and committed them to report to each other on matters of mutual interest. Israel and the United States pledged not to spy on each other, and to exchange liaison officers who would be stationed at their respective embassies in Washington and Tel Aviv.

To add flesh to the skeleton agreement, they had to overcome one major obstacle. Angleton had been promoted to the post of counterespionage chief at the CIA, and he was an obsessive opponent of Communism. Despite his admiration for the young Jewish state, he believed that Israel—with its socialist values and its links with the Soviet bloc—could constitute a high security risk.

Angleton was concerned that the emigration of Jews from Eastern Europe would enable Soviet spies to use Israel as a launching pad into the West.

"The admixture of European races in Palestine offers a unique opportunity for Soviet penetration into a highly strategic area," a State Department memorandum declared. The Americans suspected that the Russians were infiltrating Israel's army.

Amos Manor, head of Shin Bet, fit the frightening picture drawn by the suspicious Americans because of his Eastern European origins and meteoric rise after arriving in Israel. The FBI believed he was likely a Soviet plant, and it tried to prevent Manor from visiting the United States on official business.

Israeli officials tried to soothe the Americans' fears, pointing out that Shin Bet was already giving close scrutiny to new Jewish arrivals from behind the Iron Curtain.

What finally persuaded Angleton and the CIA was Israel's contention that "from the bitter could come the sweet," in the words of the Bible—that the new immigrants should not be feared; they should be used. After all, the Jews had come from all walks of life and had intimate knowledge of the Soviet military, science, economics, and politics. Israel thoroughly quizzed them and began feeding such data to the United States.

On the Israeli side, who was in charge of the cooperation with America? Because so much of it involved immigrants arriving in Israel from Eastern Europe, Shin Bet chief Manor was chosen by Ben-Gurion for this task.

Isser Harel strongly disagreed with that decision, and he further suggested that Israeli intelligence should not cooperate with the Americans. They wanted the unilateral transfer of everything learned by Israeli intelligence, he contended, without a genuine bilateral exchange. Harel even suspected that the CIA might organize a coup in Israel, along the lines of the Agency's covert operation in 1953 in Guatemala.

Shiloah, as usual, took a different view. Even after leaving the Mossad and recuperating from a car accident, he was a special adviser to Ben-Gurion on international and regional strategy. Shiloah persuaded the prime minister that for the sake of a broader political alliance with the United States, it was worth paying a price—and providing information to the Americans—until their trust was won.

The CIA, obviously seeing the Israelis as very junior partners, was very demanding. Manor said: "They told me that I had to collect information about the Soviet bloc and transmit it to them. I didn't know exactly what to do, but then I had the idea of giving them the material we had gathered about a year earlier, about the efforts of the Eastern bloc to use Israel to bypass an American trade embargo. We edited the material, made the necessary erasures, and informed them that they should never ask us to identify sources."

The Israelis, despite being treated as inferiors, were sending the CIA what they billed as hot material—even if it was slightly warmed-up leftovers. The Americans displayed "great enthusiasm" at what they received, Manor recalled, "and they asked us to gather more and more material for them."

"Sometimes I didn't understand why they needed us," he continued. "They asked for Romanian cash, telephone directories, maps of cities, and even the price of bread in the Eastern bloc countries." Manor and his liaison team were determined, though, never to give the Americans names of Israelis.

What the CIA did not realize was how easily the Israelis got their information. They conducted "friendly interrogations" of new immigrants, without needing to run expensive undercover operations or plant agents behind enemy lines.

It may have been easy, but the program—code-named Operation Balsam—put Israel in the position of a short-order cook serving up every dish that the CIA ordered. Furthermore, Balsam was compartmentalized. Other parts of the Israeli intelligence community did not know about the program.

The CIA's Angleton came to Israel in April 1952 to see the faces who were feeding him so much information. "I greeted him at the airport, together with Reuven Shiloah," Manor said half a century later. "Jim stayed at the Sharon Hotel in Herzliya, which at the time was the only five-star hotel, but he spent most of the time in my little two-room apartment on Pinsker Street in Tel Aviv.

"Out of seven days, he spent four with me. He would arrive at 11 p.m. and stay until 4 a.m., and then I would drive him back to his hotel. My wife was in the next room, and from time to time she served coffee. He brought a bottle of whiskey with him and drank all the time, but he never got drunk. I didn't understand how a person could drink so much without getting drunk. I myself didn't drink, and he came to terms with that." Angleton seemed to be a fanatic about everything, including his suspicions about Manor.

"Eventually, after maybe 30 years, he told me why he had really come to Israel," Manor said. "He had heard that I, a new immigrant from Romania, was conducting Operation Balsam, and that terrified him. He actually came to examine me. That was the reason why he, the chief of counterintelligence, was in charge of the liaison. They suspected us. But at the end of the visit, I felt that he had a positive impression, and he told Shiloah that he was pleased to have me in charge of the operation."

Manor asked Angleton if he could arrange some training for Israel's counterintelligence officers, and the American agreed. Six Shin Bet men flew to Washington in October 1952, but they did not like the course and complained that it was all "theory."

One might consider it absurd that young Israelis who had never before traveled to America, given the chance to do some tourism and rub shoulders with the mighty CIA, were so grumpy.

To quell their discontent, Manor recalled, "Jim sent me two plane tickets for myself and my wife, so I went to Washington and reassured the guys.

"Jim tried to ensure that I had a pleasant stay," Manor continued. "I met with him a few times at my hotel. He also showed me a new device called a lie detector. I asked him to let one of the students, Zvi Aharoni, into a lie detector course."

Aharoni got together with the inventor in Chicago and returned with a gift arranged by Angleton: the first polygraph in Israel. A decade later, Aharoni would be part of the team that captured Nazi war criminal Adolf Eichmann in Argentina.

Weak in technology, Manor asked Uncle Sam—specifically Uncle Jim—for more gifts. "So they gave us microphones, wiretapping equipment for telephones, and cameras," Manor recalled.

But at this stage, the relationship was still not fully one of trust. Israeli intelligence did not ask the CIA for any raw intelligence, though the Mossad could have used some. Manor said: "We were afraid that they would ask us, in return, for information about the Arab world."

That became an Israeli espionage trait for many years: a reluctance to share material with liaison partners, even the apparently closest allies. The Israelis believed they had the best data in the world and had doubts about where it would go if they shared such gold. America, after all, also made deals with Arab security services and tried to cultivate them with favors.

CIA and other U.S. intelligence officials keenly felt that Israel was not giving as much as it could, and from an American point of view the mindset seemed to change only half a century later—after the terrorism of 9/11 triggered a greater sense of all being in the same boat. Yet senior Mossad operatives felt that they were sharing "almost everything," as one put it, "unless it endangered our sources or some ongoing operations."

Angleton asked the Israelis in 1954 to step up cooperation sharply, and not just pass along tidbits from conversations with new immigrants in Israel. Now the American wanted something a lot more ambitious. He suggested that Israeli intelligence open secret stations in the Communist countries of Eastern Europe.

"With considerable hesitation, we agreed," Manor said. "I personally recruited and briefed a number of people and sent them to be our representatives in Warsaw, Prague, Budapest, Bucharest, and Sofia. But I didn't agree to send people to Moscow, because I was afraid they would be caught there."

The intelligence officers were assigned as diplomats and operated in Israel's embassies under that cover. Manor said: "My instructions to my people were: 'Don't endanger yourselves, look for connections you can make as diplomats, and try to get people to give you political information.' I didn't even dream of military information."

In a way, they were acting as surrogates for the Americans, who knew that intelligence officers at U.S. embassies would be under surveillance and suspicion a lot more than would Israelis. This was a wonderful convenience for America that ended after the 1967 war, when the Communist nations broke their relations with the Jewish state.

The Manor-Angleton connection explains why it fell to Shin Bet—and not, more naturally, to the foreign espionage experts at the Mossad—to run the official liaison with America and even to send operatives abroad. It was all personal. Prime Minister Ben-Gurion, who did not care a whit for bureaucratic titles, saw that Manor was the man forging a relationship with the CIA.

It would be more than 10 years before the Mossad would assert its primacy in friendly foreign ties. Agency chief Meir Amit, after 1963, would insist on a restructuring of the intelligence community—including professional titles.

The separate agency Nativ, which conducted secret ties with Jewish communities in the Soviet-bloc nations and arranged transportation for Jews to Israel, also posted officers at embassies in Eastern Europe under diplomatic cover. Nativ did not avoid the Soviet Union and indeed could not. Israel looked at the millions of Soviet Jews as a reservoir for the future growth of the Jewish state. The pools of immigration from Arab lands were drying up, yet eventually, a huge number of Jews would move to Israel from Russia, Romania, and other ex-Communist countries.

In the 1950s and 1960s, some of those Nativ representatives were arrested and expelled by the host governments, mainly the Soviet regime in Moscow, for what were termed hostile and undiplomatic activities.

When Manor began expanding his personal and professional networking with Angleton, the Israeli was still only the head of the counterespionage department within Shin Bet. Manor was summoned by Harel, who had taken over the Mossad and was the overall "Memuneh" in charge of the entire intelligence community.

Harel surprised Manor by offering him the directorship of Shin Bet in mid-1952. The Memuneh was apparently dissatisfied with the incumbent, his former assistant, Isidore Roth, who had Hebraized his name to the homonym Izzy Dorot.

Dorot moved over to the Mossad and worked with Harel for another 11 years as his right-hand man for special missions. After his retirement, however, Dorot was completely forgotten for four decades. There was no mention of his having been the second director of Shin Bet. Only in the 21st century was his role reinstated, when Shin Bet became slightly more open and featured a brief history of itself on an official website.

As for Manor, he still thought of himself as a new immigrant and thus had never dared to hope that Ben-Gurion would make him one of the chiefs of intelligence. "I was unknown and not a member of Mapai, the ruling party," he recalled. "But I was invited to a meeting with Ben-Gurion, and he quizzed me for three hours and then gave me the job."

Now, with a Harel-Manor team helming a secret relationship with American intelligence, the Israelis consciously reached out to the Western world to prove that they were valuable allies. The CIA and other Western agencies valued Israel's strategic contributions but harbored reservations about the capability of a tiny country. The Jewish state also seemed to be struggling still with its economic and political identity: Was it socialist or capitalist?

Israel's breakthrough into the top echelon of Western intelligence came with a coup scored in the heart of Communism. Manor, Harel, and their boys managed to outrun the CIA's Angleton, the British MI6, the French SDECE, West Germany's BND and all the others who were scurrying around Eastern Europe in search of a speech: a sheaf of papers deemed as valuable as gold.

Chapter Four

FROM WARSAW WITH LOVE

I acted on impulse," said Viktor Grayevsky, the man who boosted the prestige of Israeli intelligence to a new level by handing it one of its most significant successes. That occurred in April 1956, when Grayevsky unknowingly cemented the friendship between Amos Manor and the CIA's James Angleton, giving great pleasure to both and to the governments they served.

In retrospect, what Grayevsky did—a succession of coincidences and lucky breaks upon which espionage agencies capitalize—launched the covert side of a relationship that has continued to bind the United States and Israel in dire, often unexpected circumstances. His place in history also demonstrated the value of well-placed Jews, many of whom have aided Israeli intelligence.

"In hindsight, I know that I was young and foolish," Grayevsky said decades later, a retired man in his 80s, sitting in his small apartment in a suburb south of Tel Aviv. He could barely believe what he had done. "Had the Russians and Poles discovered me, we wouldn't be speaking today. I don't know whether they would have killed me, but I certainly would have sat in prison for many years."

Born in 1925 in Krakow, a once palatial city that was the seat of Poland's kings, his original name was Victor Spielman. As a teenager, he escaped with his family to the Soviet Union at the outbreak of World War II. In 1946 he returned to Poland, joined the Communist Party, studied journalism at a government academy, worked for the official Polish news agency, and made sure to shed his Jewish-sounding name.

The newly minted Viktor Grayevsky rose to the post of senior editor, responsible for the department that covered the Soviet Union and other socialist partner nations.

"It was a position that opened the doors to the party and the government for me," he recalled. In 1949, his parents and his sister emigrated to Israel—part of the efforts coordinated by the secret agency to be later known as Nativ. Grayevsky decided to remain in Poland.

In December 1955, his father contracted a serious illness, and Grayevsky felt he needed to visit him in Israel. To organize the trip and obtain a visa, he met with Yaakov Barmor, ostensibly the first secretary in the Israeli embassy in Warsaw but in fact one of the Shin Bet officers sent abroad by Manor.

"I didn't know he was from intelligence," said Grayevsky. "I thought he was just a diplomat."

The visit to Israel rocked his world view. Grayevsky became a Zionist. He kept that fact to himself, of course, but after returning to Poland he decided to move to Israel. Before potentially ruining his career by filing the necessary application to leave, he kept on working and socializing.

He did not lack for girlfriends in Warsaw, but one in particular had an interesting Jewish background. Lucia Baranowsky had fled from the ghetto in Lvov and joined the anti-Nazi partisans during the war. That was a respectable background for Communists, and she rubbed shoulders with many senior party officials. Her husband was a deputy prime minister, and she worked for the Communist Party's general secretary, Edward Ochab—the leader of Poland.

She was 35 years old, with one son, but her family life was in shambles. Baranowsky and her husband lived in the same apartment, but separately.

"Her marriage was not a success, and she was my girlfriend in every sense," Grayevsky recalled with an old man's pride. At the time of the affair, he was 30.

It was the second week of April 1956, four months after his return from Israel, and he was meeting Lucia for coffee. She was especially busy, so he hung around her desk in the headquarters of the party's Central Committee.

"Everyone knew me. To the guards and the office workers, I was almost a member of the family there. While I was talking with Lucia, I noticed a thick booklet with a red binding, with the words: 'The 20th Party Congress, the speech of Comrade Khrushchev.' In the corner it said: 'Top Secret'."

That was one of the few copies sent by order of the Soviet Politburo to leaders of the Eastern Bloc countries.

"Like other people, I had heard rumors about the speech," Grayevsky added. "We heard that the United States had offered a prize of $1 million to anyone who could obtain the speech. We also knew that all the intelligence services, all the diplomats, and all the journalists in the world wanted to get their hands on the speech.

"Thus, when I saw the red booklet, I immediately understood its importance. It mainly aroused my curiosity as a journalist. I told Lucia: 'I'll take the booklet, go home for an hour or two, and read it.'

"She said, 'Fine, but I go home at 4 p.m., so return it by then, because we have to put it in the safe.'"

Here was Grayevsky, holding the world's most sought-after document, which detailed the crimes of Soviet dictator Josef Stalin. It had just been handed to the Polish journalist as casually as a shopping list.

"I put the booklet under my coat and left the building, without anyone being suspicious or examining me. After all, they all knew me. At home, when I read the speech I was shocked. Such crimes. Stalin, a murderer!"

The document was the text of a speech delivered by the new leader of the Soviet Communist Party, Nikita Khrushchev, to a party congress in Moscow, where he exposed—for the first time—the realities of Stalin's three decades of iron-fisted rule: mass arrests, the torture and killing of political prisoners, people disappearing to the prison camps known as the Gulag, the transfer of entire national populations, forced labor, and megalomaniacal agricultural and industrial projects. These were hidden atrocities that resulted in tens of millions of deaths.

The speech was not only a history lesson, but a message that the new leader in Moscow would be embarking on a new course.

Khrushchev ordered that a limited number of copies be translated and printed, for distribution to the party leaders in each satellite country dominated by the Russians. He did not want the contents known to the rest of the world.

"I felt that I was holding an atom bomb, and since I knew that the entire world was looking for the speech, I understood that if I threw the bomb it would explode," said Grayevsky, explaining his initial decision to do nothing with the text.

"I was going back to return the booklet to Lucia, but on the way I thought about it a lot. Then I decided to go to the embassy, to Yaakov Barmor. Poland hadn't done anything bad to me, but my heart was with Israel, and I wanted to help.

"I went to the embassy and rang the bell. The building was surrounded by Polish soldiers and policemen, and there were cameras all around, checking everyone who entered. I went to Barmor's office and told him: 'Look what I have.'"

As Grayevsky remembered it, the Israeli diplomat literally turned white, and then red—the colors of Poland's flag, as it happened. "Then he changed colors again. He asked to take the booklet for a minute, and he returned to me an hour and a half later. I knew he was photographing it. He came back, gave me the booklet, and said, 'Thank you very much.'"

The senior Polish journalist did his best to remain calm as he walked the speech back to Lucia. She would die in Poland 15 years later. By then, Grayevsky had moved to Israel. "We never spoke about what happened with the speech," he said.

He emphasized that he neither requested nor received any payment or other reward. "I acted out of an impulse that stemmed from my connection to Israel. It was a bouquet from an intended future immigrant to the State of Israel."

A very few days after Grayevsky's visit to the Israeli embassy in Warsaw, Zelig Katz entered the office of Amos Manor at Shin Bet headquarters in Jaffa. It was a Friday afternoon, April 13, 1956.

Before ending his work week and heading home, Manor asked Katz—his principal office assistant—whether anything had arrived from Eastern Europe. He was not expecting anything special—just routine reports from his station chiefs.

"Yes," Katz replied. "Material has arrived from Warsaw."

"Anything interesting?" Manor muttered.

"There's some speech by Khrushchev from the congress," said Katz, clearly having no idea of the weight of his words. Manor practically burst out of his chair. "What!?" he shouted. "Where's the material?"

"In my room," said Katz.

"Well, then, bring it immediately!" his boss thundered.

Katz rushed to his room and returned with 70 photographed pages in Polish. Manor later recalled: "I said to him, 'You're an idiot. You are now holding in your hand one of the most important secrets in the world.'"

Manor's astonishment and anger only increased when he discovered that the speech had been sent from the Shin Bet representative in Warsaw, in a standard Foreign Ministry diplomatic pouch, three days earlier and was not called to his attention. "I told Zelig to call Duvid and tell him to come here at once," he recalled.

Duvid was David Schweitzer, in charge of Shin Bet's photo lab and in his spare time a famous soccer player who later would coach the Israeli national team.

While waiting, Manor asked Katz, who was of Polish origin, to read the document and tell him what it said. "The further he progressed in the translation, the more I cursed," Manor continued. "'My God!' I said to myself."

Within a short time, Schweitzer arrived. "I told him to photograph one copy and develop it as fast as possible so I could bring it to Ben-Gurion." The photo and development took about two hours. While Manor was waiting, his wife Tzipora called. She was used to unconventional work hours and to her husband's absence, and she asked when he was coming home for Sabbath dinner. He told her he would be very late tonight.

At 6 p.m. Manor got into his British-made Vauxhall and drove to the home of the prime minister on Keren Kayemet (today Ben-Gurion) Boulevard in Tel Aviv. "I came to Ben-Gurion and told him, 'We have Khrushchev's speech from the 20th Party Conference. I don't know whether it's authentic. We got the speech from one of our sources in Warsaw, who got it from a woman who worked for the Polish party secretary.'

"I also told Ben-Gurion that I didn't know whether the source was a double agent who had leaked the speech as disinformation, or whether the speech was authentic and had been deliberately leaked to us so that it would reach the West."

Manor told the prime minister that the document seemed authentic, but urged Ben-Gurion—born in Poland and thus quite able to read it—to reach his own conclusions. "I remember that he asked me three times what disinformation meant, and three times I explained it to him. I left him a copy and then I left."

The next morning his home phone rang, and Manor was asked to return to the house on Keren Kayemet. "Ben-Gurion said: 'If it's authentic, it's an historic document, and 30 years from now there will be a liberal regime in Moscow.'" Although prophetic in his pronouncement, the Israeli leader handed the papers back to Manor without telling him what to do with them.

Manor waited until the Sabbath was over, and on Sunday, April 15, from his office, he phoned Isser Harel—the Mossad chief and head of all intelligence matters—and told him about the document from Poland. Despite Ben-Gurion's considering Harel the top official in charge of the intelligence community, Manor had not felt compelled to inform the Memuneh immediately. Manor perceived himself as sufficiently autonomous as head of Shin Bet and the chief liaison with the CIA.

"I told Harel that if it's authentic, it's an atomic bomb," Manor recalled. "And I told him about my conversation with Ben-Gurion, and that I had decided to send the copy immediately to the CIA."

Manor, to maintain the utmost secrecy, chose not to hand it over to the CIA station chief in Tel Aviv. He had a trusted courier fly the text to Izzy Dorot, by now the Harel-appointed intelligence officer at the Israeli embassy in Washington. A written note to Dorot told him to hand the document personally to Angleton. "I emphasized repeatedly that I was not certain about the authenticity of the material, and that they should examine it carefully," said Manor.

Two days later, the document landed on the desk of CIA chief Allen Dulles, who would remember April 17 as the date of one of his greatest accomplishments. Dulles was immediately delighted and quickly informed President Dwight Eisenhower. A few years later, Dulles presented Manor with an autographed copy of his memoir. The handwritten dedication said: "To a true professional."

On the evening of the 17th, Angleton called Amos Manor. "He told me the text was of utmost importance and asked me to identify the source who had provided the speech. I replied: 'Jim, we have an agreement between us that we do not reveal sources of information, and the agreement applies to this case as well.'"

Two weeks later brought another telephone call. Angleton told Manor that America's top Sovietologists had come to the conclusion that the text was authentic. "Jim was in seventh heaven," Manor recalled. "He asked my permission to publish the material. I went again to Ben-Gurion and asked for his opinion. Ben-Gurion told me that he understood the Americans, because this was a document of historic importance, and gave his consent. I informed Jim of the decision, but asked him not to mention us as the source. We didn't want to be involved."

Relations between Israel and the Soviet Union were already very poor, because of Soviet support for Egypt, and the Israeli leadership was concerned about possible backlash: The Jews of the Soviet Union could be punished.

The Khrushchev text was not merely read with great interest at CIA headquarters. The Americans leaked it to *The New York Times* and then had its 26,000 words broadcast in all the languages of the Communist countries over the CIA-financed Radio Free Europe and Radio Liberty. Printed texts were even tied to balloons and flown over the Iron Curtain into the Eastern-bloc nations.

With an aura of brilliance now shining around Israel's name in the halls of the CIA, Angleton felt freer than ever to be Israel's great advocate in U.S. intelligence and defense circles. Given the pro-Arab bias of most of the State Department and Pentagon, and of some CIA personnel, his friendship was an oasis in a Washington desert for the Israelis.

Angleton was even able to counter or distort information from other sources that was liable to harm Israel. When the U.S. military attaché in Tel Aviv sent a report in October 1956 that Israel was planning to attack Egypt, Angleton told his boss that the information was not accurate. Intentionally or not, Israel's great friend in Washington helped to maintain the smoke screen that cloaked the preparations for the Suez invasion.

Cooperation between the CIA and Shin Bet extended from the Eastern bloc to the Western Hemisphere. Nir Baruch, a Bulgarian-born Israeli operative, played his part. First, he joined the Jewish immigration agency Nativ and served as its emissary, under diplomatic cover, in Sofia, Bulgaria. Later, he would join Shin Bet, and in 1961 he was assigned—again, listed as a diplomat—to the Israeli embassy in Havana, Cuba, as deputy chief of mission.

"Manor told me that my main task would be to collect information which would be conveyed to the CIA," he recalled half a century later. "You could say I was an authorized Israeli spy for the CIA." Baruch revealed that he had done the same thing in Bulgaria earlier, photographing military bases; he knew that Manor was giving the photos to the United States.

Baruch arrived in Havana two weeks before the ill-fated, CIA-sponsored Bay of Pigs invasion aimed at toppling Fidel Castro, "so I didn't have enough proper time to fulfill my mission. But after the invasion, I started my secret work. I filmed missile sites. I reported about Russians who arrived on the island. I sent my reports directly to the Mossad representatives working at the Israeli embassy in Washington, DC. They handed it over to Angleton and his people. At a certain stage, the CIA supplied me with a better code machine to speed up my reports. Every few months, I would travel to Washington to meet with Angleton and his assistants. I would brief them in more detail and then return to Cuba.

"A few times, the Americans asked me to serve as a courier and meet one of their agents in Cuba, but I refused. I thought that that was too risky. One of my sources was an aide to Castro, and I convinced Angleton it would be a pity to put my relationship with the aide at risk.

"What impressed me more than anything was Angleton's capacity for drinking. He drank and drank for hours, then would rest on the bed in the hotel room where we met, and after a few minutes he would get up fresh. Of course, I reported all this to Amos Manor."

Manor, as a frequent eyewitness, already knew.

Angleton became truly captivated by the magic of Israeli intelligence, and in Washington he zealously insisted on being the sole handler of the account. Angleton was furious when others in the agency tried to make contact with the Israelis without his knowledge.

"Angleton had one major responsibility other than counterintelligence—Israel—which he traditionally handled in the same totally compartmented fashion as counterintelligence," according to a later CIA director.

Israelis who worked with Angleton admitted that he had an unusual or even "kooky" personality, but they appreciated him for shattering the American wall of suspicion about Israel while paving the way for vital strategic cooperation.

In November 1987, a year after Angleton died, Israel dedicated a memorial corner to its valued American friend. Within sight of the luxurious King David Hotel, where he loved to stay during his dozens of visits to Jerusalem, an inscription on a large stone was carved in Hebrew, English, and Arabic: "In memory of a dear friend, James (Jim) Angleton." It was unveiled at a gathering attended by present and former heads of the Israeli intelligence community.

By investing energy into improving bilateral relations with American and other Western security agencies, Israeli intelligence was also enhancing Israel's posture as an important and unignorable ally in the Middle East. The country was young and tiny, but it could be highly useful as the West pursued its interests in the region: ensuring the flow of oil, supporting conservative regimes, and blocking the pan-Arab nationalism led by Egypt's President Gamal Abdel Nasser.

The Israeli who noticed this helpful reality more than anyone else was the Mossad chief, Reuven Shiloah. He could see that Britain and France wanted to remain relevant in a post-colonial Middle East, and America was trying to establish its own toehold.

To make Israel more valuable, Shiloah launched an almost inconceivable form of outreach. He found that secret contacts could, astonishingly, be established in Arab countries that were officially hostile. The logistical details were difficult, including late-night border crossings and coded communications, but back-channel links with Israel's neighbors could be built—even before Israel was officially born.

As Ben-Gurion's top clandestine diplomat, Shiloah took part in meetings with King Abdullah and other top officials of Transjordan. They reached a tacit understanding whereby the Palestinian state envisioned by the United Nations partition vote of 1947 was aborted well before birth. This, too, was a fateful moment that resulted from intelligence work: an unspoken conspiracy that played out during the war of 1948. Israel overran some of the majority-Arab parts of Palestine after the British left, and Abdullah's army seized the West Bank of the Jordan River—annexing the land and renaming his kingdom Jordan. There was no serious attempt by Transjordan, unlike Egypt and the other Arab countries, to destroy Israel.

King Abdullah became not only an "agent of influence" for Israel in the Arab world—an intelligence catchphrase to describe a person in a foreign country whose political goals fit your own country's—but a paid agent. His Jewish liaisons paid him thousands of dollars for his services. Only Abdullah's assassination by a fellow Muslim in July 1951 prevented his signing a peace treaty with Israel.

In Syria, the army chief of staff, Colonel Hosni Zaim, seized power in March 1949 and offered peace to Israel. Events overtook his seemingly pacific generosity, and no treaty was signed. Only decades later was it revealed that Zaim had been on the payroll of American, French, and even Israeli intelligence agencies. CIA officers actually helped him plot his coup. Israel had other contacts, often based on bribery, within the Egyptian and Iraqi leadership.

Shiloah realized, however, that the ability of Israeli operatives to gain access to Arab leaders could not change the basic political and strategic facts of Middle Eastern life: that Israel's immediate neighbors (known as the "inner circle") would continue to hate the State of Israel and to perpetuate a state of war.

Shiloah also knew there were other geographic and ethnic factors in the region. The inner circle was surrounded by an outer circle, which he called "the periphery" of non-Arab nations; and the Arab states themselves had religious and ethnic minorities. Friendships could be formed with the peripheral nations and with the minority groups.

Any force that opposed or fought Arab nationalism was considered to be a potential ally of Israel: the Maronite minority in Lebanon, the Druze in Syria, the Kurds in Iraq, and the Christians in southern Sudan, who all suffered under the yoke of the Muslim majorities in their countries. Iran and Turkey were always proud to point out that, although Muslim, they were not Arabs.

Thus was born a complex and covert side of Israeli foreign policy, and the Mossad was in charge. This, too, would be a lasting and unique feature of Israeli intelligence. No one, not even an American president, could ever assume that Israel was entirely cut off from anyone. Presidents discovered, in fact, that the Mossad had contacts and assets seemingly everywhere. Even Israeli prime ministers were sometimes surprised.

One of the most significant connections that Shiloah launched was with the Kurds, a stateless people who lived mostly in Iran, Iraq, Syria, and Turkey. The Mossad chief had been in Iraq's Kurdish villages in the 1930s, when he worked for the Jewish Agency in Baghdad, with a cover as a teacher and part-time journalist.

These mountain people were constantly struggling to obtain autonomy, and their most active and direct aid from the Mossad came in the 1960s when Israeli military advisers trained Kurdish guerrillas. The United States and the Shah of Iran supported the project.

Israel benefited from the fact that one of its major enemies—the Iraqi army, which had invaded the newborn Jewish state in 1948—was tied down in a guerrilla conflict. Also, Israel enjoyed the Kurdish fighters' help in smuggling the remnants of the Jewish community from Iraq into Iran, from where they were airlifted to Israel.

The Shah, as leader of a Moslem nation, never established formal diplomatic relations with Israel. But the monarch respected Israel's struggle against its large Arab neighbors, and he supplied oil to Israel and had Iran's national airline fly Jewish refugees to Tel Aviv.

Senior Israeli officials made unannounced visits to Tehran, and a trade office served as an unofficial embassy. The Israeli goal was to encourage the Shah's anti-Arab leanings, and he was easily fed information meant to stoke his suspicions.

Decades later, the opposite held: Israelis would maintain quiet contacts with Arab countries and would try to heighten their suspicions about Iran.

With the blessings of the United States and Britain, the Israeli-Iranian alliance was extended to include another important non-Arab Muslim nation: Turkey.

In June 1958, Turkish and Israeli intelligence officials met. Ben-Gurion entrusted this project to Shiloah, even though the Mossad's first chief had left the agency six years earlier. The talks led to an unannounced visit to Ankara by Ben-Gurion in August, so that he could meet his Turkish counterpart. When journalists noticed an El Al plane at the Turkish capital's airport, the explanation given was: "engine problems that forced an emergency landing."

The concrete result was a formal, but top-secret, agreement for comprehensive cooperation between the Mossad and the Turkish National Security Service, the TNSS. The Mossad agreed on a similar pact, around the same time, with Iran's notorious Savak.

At the end of 1958, the three secret agencies established a formal cooperation network called Trident, which held semiannual gatherings of all three espionage chiefs.

The Mossad found that a plethora of unacknowledged international contacts often required it to play innkeeper, and the agency set up a "guest house" at a highway intersection north of Tel Aviv. Helicopters could land there. Cars could arrive or depart, day or night, without anyone paying any attention; just in case, official press censorship would guarantee no publicity for visits by important but anonymous foreigners.

Within a few years, the area around that guest house—a large, government-owned plot of land—became a training ground for Mossad operatives. Additional buildings were erected, and they formed the core of an academy teaching all the skills of espionage. The Mossad called it the *Midrasha*, a Hebrew word for the kind of intensive religious school where Orthodox Jews ponder the Bible, the Talmud, and other texts that were articles of faith.

The Mossad's secular and secretive Midrasha set high standards and passed them, spy to spy, analyst to analyst, generation to generation, to ensure continued excellence for the agency.

The Mossad would eventually move its entire headquarters to the academy site. This gave the Mossad an entire campus with more space and certainly more seclusion, compared with the two previous sites in Tel Aviv: the original huts in Ben-Gurion's defense compound, the Kirya; and then an American-style office building named Hadar Dafna in a highly trafficked business district.

When censorship prevented any individual or map from identifying the Mossad's location, government officials and journalists would simply speak of "the Midrasha." Some of the privileged few who had been inside the high-security campus described it as surprisingly tastefully designed. It included a sculpture garden, featuring the work of Israel's best known artists. This reflected the Mossad's self-image as a hotbed of creativity. Quite a few of its best staff members were painters or sculptors in their spare time, and when Israelis sought to excel at "the art of espionage," part of the formula was to permit creativity to flourish.

Mossad men and women frequently had some outlandish theories or plans to propose, but they were encouraged to give them voice. Accomplishing the impossible would often have to start with unorthodox approaches.

The unexpected secret alliance that brought the tiny Jewish state of Israel into partnership with two Muslim giants, Iran and Turkey, was based on strong common interests. They were all concerned about the activities of Soviet spies throughout the Middle East, and the three intelligence communities pooled their knowledge of what the Russians were doing.

In addition, Turkey helped the Mossad by sharing information that TNSS agents had collected in Syria, focused on that radical Arab regime's intentions toward Israel. The Mossad trained Turkish secret agents in counterintelligence techniques and the use of technical devices. Similar training took place for the Shah of Iran's secret police, but that abruptly stopped when he was overthrown in 1979.

In eastern Africa, Israel—along with American and British intelligence—found Ethiopia to be of prime strategic importance in the 1950s. The country overlooked the shipping routes leading into the Red Sea and northward toward Israel's port of Eilat and Egypt's Suez Canal.

Ethiopia also seemed pro-Western and fairly stable, under the rule of self-proclaimed emperor Haile Selassie. For over two decades he described himself as a descendant of the ancient Hebrew tribe of Judah. His royal emblem was Judah's majestic lion, and Selassie warmly admired the modern Jewish state.

After an Israeli consulate was opened in Ethiopia, the diplomats were followed by agricultural advisers, by professors who helped establish the University of Addis Ababa, and by the inevitable military advisers and intelligence personnel. Israelis helped the emperor train his security forces. The Mossad was able to maintain a large station, an office fulfilling various covert roles, in the Ethiopian capital.

This corner of the Horn of Africa had a crucial advantage: its location. Just to the north were two Arab countries, Sudan and Egypt, and just across narrow sea lanes were Saudi Arabia and Yemen. For access to many kinds of people and information, Ethiopia and its immediate neighbors were excellent hunting grounds for Israeli intelligence.

The Israelis pioneered a presence in precisely the same locations where the United States would rush to create bases and listening posts after the terrorist attacks of September 11, 2001.

Despite the mushrooming importance of the innovative, unofficial, and non-diplomatic network of connections that Shiloah created, he was quickly and totally forgotten after his death from a sudden heart attack in May 1959. Ironically, he had been preparing for yet another clandestine mission to Turkey and Iran.

No one went to the trouble of keeping Shiloah's memory alive. He had few political allies, quite a few enemies, a tendency to work alone, and no taste for promoting his own importance.

A small group of intelligence operatives and scientists, meantime, worked on a totally secret project: creating a nuclear force for Israel. Their motivation was a belief that the Jewish people should never again be defenseless against armed and more numerous enemies.

CHAPTER FIVE

NUCLEAR MATURITY

I n a private villa in the Paris suburb of Sèvres, Israel took a small step—soon to be a giant leap—toward becoming a mature nuclear power.

There, on October 22, 1956, more than a dozen men from three countries were sitting around a large, impressive wooden table. Among them were two famous Israelis: David Ben-Gurion, in his twin posts as prime minister and minister of defense; and the Israel Defense Forces chief of staff, General Moshe Dayan, who had lost his left eye in 1942 while serving with British troops against the pro-Nazi Vichy French forces in Syria.

Also in attendance was Ben-Gurion's young, ambitious assistant who would go on to carve out his own place in history, Shimon Peres. He was joined, perhaps surprisingly, by the leader of the abortive Revolt of the Spies five years earlier, Asher Ben-Natan—an old hand at secret operations who would later be Israel's first ambassador to Germany and then the ambassador to France.

The French hosts at Sèvres settled into their chairs: Prime Minister Guy Mollet, Defense Minister Maurice Bourgès-Maunoury, Foreign Minister Christian Pineau, and various assistants and advisers. Some were wearing army uniforms and others civilian clothes. Facing them was Selwyn Lloyd, Great Britain's foreign secretary, surrounded by his advisers.

The Sèvres conference was no idle chat. These men were planning a war, to be known in Israel as the Sinai campaign and worldwide simply as "Suez."

France fervently wanted to reassert Anglo-French control of the Suez Canal, which Egypt's President Gamal Abdel Nasser had nationalized. The French were also hoping to stop the spread of Nasserism, because the fiery Egyptian was an inspiration to the FLN—the National Liberation Front in Algeria, which was fighting French occupying forces at the time.

Six months before the meeting at Sèvres, France had begun to arm Israel for the war to come. Starting in April, French cargo planes and ships arrived in the darkness of night and unloaded an abundance of weaponry: tanks, fighter planes, cannons, and ammunition.

Britain had its own war aims, motivated by a visceral hatred of Nasser. The prime minister, Sir Anthony Eden, hoped to humiliate the Egyptian strongman so that he would be toppled from power. Eliminating a radical icon could enable the British to keep their bases at and beyond the Suez Canal. In truth, of course, the sun had begun to set on the British Empire.

As for Israeli goals, the most immediate was to avoid strangulation. Nasser had declared a blockade of the Red Sea, preventing shipping to and from Israel's southern port of Eilat. Israel's wider aim was to eliminate a regional rival—and assistance from big outsiders would be vital in destroying Nasser's Soviet-equipped army.

At the end of the three-day conference, after cementing the war plan, the British delegation left for London. Only then did some French and Israeli officials gather for yet another meeting—even more secretive than the trilateral conspiracy they had just launched.

Now, they were discussing the Israeli wish to acquire a nuclear reactor from France.

No immediate deal was struck. There was no clear memorandum declaring that the Suez war was quid pro quo for an atomic delivery, but that transaction was in the back of everyone's mind. At the end of the meeting, wine glasses were raised. Peres, fluent in French, proposed a toast "to assuring Israel's security forever!" The Gallic hosts clinked glasses with their Jewish guests.

The war plans required close intelligence cooperation. Aman's chief, General Yehoshafat Harkabi, was frequently in Paris for talks with his counterparts in French military and civilian intelligence. To institutionalize the liaison, a permanent Aman representative was stationed in France. Even though Isser Harel insisted that his Mossad should have a monopoly over contacts with civilian intelligence agencies abroad, the Memuneh had to take a back seat while the blueprints for a tripartite invasion were prepared.

A week later, on October 29, Israeli paratroops and ground forces began moving across Egypt's Sinai and toward the Suez Canal. In accordance with the Sèvres plan, France and Britain then issued an ultimatum to the armies of Israel and Egypt, instructing them to freeze their forces in place, several miles from the canal. As prearranged, Israel accepted; Egypt refused. The French and British used the excuse to drop paratroops into the Canal Zone on November 5, taking over the strategic waterway.

The Israeli army, meanwhile, had conquered the Sinai in only four days. It appeared that the Sèvres conference's goal had been achieved, and the many months of planning by military men and intelligence services had borne fruit.

As a military operation, the Sinai campaign—particularly Israel's part—was brilliantly executed. Within days, the entire peninsula, where Jewish former slaves wandered for 40 years and Moses received the Ten Commandments, was captured by Israel. Just as the French and the British had hoped, their forces held the Suez Canal. Nasser's nationalization was negated.

As a political maneuver, however, the campaign was a failure. Israeli, French, and British intelligence had believed that the United States would naturally take their side. That would almost surely have meant the end of Nasser. Instead, President Dwight Eisenhower displayed total contempt for the invasion of Suez and forced the three aggressors to pull back. That proved once and for all that America was a superpower, while France and Britain barely qualified even for the old title of "great powers."

In November, Israeli forces began to withdraw, and the final portions of captured land—Sharm el-Sheikh and Gaza—were handed back to Egypt in March 1957.

Severe damage had been done to Israel's image as a progressive, socialist nation seeking peace. Most of the world judged that Israel had taken part in an ill-advised imperialist plot.

The country's top leaders, in fact, knew precisely what they were doing. They had joined the three-sided Suez conspiracy, above all, because of Ben-Gurion's burning desire to go nuclear. The relationship with France could bring the Israelis nearly everything they needed for this top-priority project.

Nuclear power was a goal cherished by Ben-Gurion from the start of statehood. It would represent true independence in the modern world. Generating electricity without relying on imported coal and oil could be valuable, but developing a nuclear potential was even more important: It would make Israel an unrivaled force in the Middle East. It could be the ultimate guarantee of the Jewish state's continued existence.

Ben-Gurion's cabinet had formed the Israeli Atomic Energy Commission, the IAEC, in 1952. Its chairman was Ernst David Bergman, a brilliant chemist born in Germany in 1903, who moved to Palestine in the early 1930s and founded the science corps of Israel's military. While researching cancer and other matters, Bergman was director of the Defense Ministry's Science Department and a leading supporter of the nuclear option.

At almost every opportunity, Ben-Gurion and his scientific, defense, and political advisers considered the possibilities of purchasing a nuclear reactor—and then the United States sent one for free. In 1955, Eisenhower's Atoms for Peace program provided a small research reactor that was installed at Nahal Sorek, 10 miles south of Tel Aviv. The facility was subject to American inspections, and it was too diminutive to produce anything of potential military use.

That same year, Peres made a series of trips to Paris, where he found that France's socialist government was very sympathetic toward Israel's socialist-led coalition. He started asking about the possibility of purchasing a nuclear reactor, and the answer became affirmative after the collusion of the Suez-Sinai campaign in 1956.

Though just in his 30s and holding only the post of deputy defense minister, Peres had the added clout of being trusted by and close to Ben-Gurion. In October 1957, Peres and top French government ministers signed two top-secret documents: a political pact outlining bilateral scientific cooperation, and a technical agreement to deliver a large, 24-megawatt reactor, with the necessary technicians and know-how. France would construct the reactor in Israel's Negev desert, near the small immigrant town of Dimona.

Ben-Gurion, Peres, and a few senior Israeli scientists were determined from the start that their nation would be far ahead of its Arab neighbors in science and technology. They seriously believed that Israel could be among the top tech powers on Earth, which would guarantee its military supremacy over the much larger nations surrounding it.

Implicit in Ben-Gurion's vision was an Israeli monopoly. Wherever and whenever deemed necessary, Israel would do what was necessary to be the only nuclear-armed power in the Middle East. That unique and unspoken mission would be at the core of crises more than half a century later.

Ben-Gurion's cabinet displayed hardly any enthusiasm, with nearly all ministers considering the project too expensive and diplomatically risky.

Most of the prime minister's scientific advisers also feared that Israel could trigger a dangerous nuclear arms race. They loved research, but not weaponry.

Seven of the eight IAEC members resigned in protest in late 1957. They claimed there was too much emphasis on the possible military side of Israel's budding nuclear potential, and they formed the Committee for the Denuclearization of the Middle East Conflict. There were heated debates behind closed doors, but the subject was shrouded in secrecy so opaque that the arguments never burst into the open. The Israeli press said nothing.

The resignations and dissent did not seem to disturb Ben-Gurion and Peres. They still had Professor Bergman as a one-man IAEC, and they put him in charge of the reactor project's scientific aspects.

If anything, they were pleased that fewer people would now know what Israel was doing. The nuclear program was the ultimate secret of the Jewish state, subject to more security measures than anything in the history of a country where secrecy already abounded.

Peres considered this his own, darling project. He did not ask the intelligence community—as might be expected—to take care of the security and secrecy aspects of the reactor. Instead, he believed that Israel, as a nuclear power, would need a nuclear intelligence agency.

Until then, responsibility for obtaining technical and scientific information from abroad lay with Aman and the Mossad. Peres, however, decided to create a secret agency for nuclear matters in 1957, putting a former Defense Ministry colleague, Binyamin Blumberg, in charge.

"Very little was known about our nuclear program," Peres said almost 50 years later. "And I wanted that even less would be known. I felt that if I were exposed, the press would destroy me and the project. I was politically controversial, known as an unstoppable fantasist. And the program itself looked like a fantasy."

Why Blumberg? "He knew how to keep a secret, so I promoted him," Peres explained. "I trusted him. I believed in him. And he did not disappoint. He did his job in an outstanding way."

When he started his new job, Blumberg moved to a modest office in the Defense Ministry. To conceal his work, he named his new unit the Office of Special Assignments.

He soon renamed the unit Lakam—an acronym for *Lishka le-Kishrei Mada*, Hebrew for Science Liaison Bureau. It would accomplish huge things, but Lakam would also cause one of the worst crises between Israel and the United States.

As the French construction project at Dimona began, fences were erected and roads meant only for crews building the reactor were paved. Israel soldiers manned patrols and easily denoted a secure perimeter.

While physical protection was no special challenge, constructing a conspiracy of silence around the reactor was much more difficult. Thousands of French engineers and technicians were being housed in Dimona and the larger city of Beersheba, 30 miles northwest of the nuclear site. When the construction crews first broke ground, Blumberg and his Israeli security officers delivered group briefings there on what should not be said. They were assisted by some security men from the French companies and the French atomic energy commission.

The major challenge was the foreign workers, living in houses specially built for them in Beersheba. An entire *joie de vivre* industry developed to meet their needs: French-accented restaurants, bars, and brothels. To Blumberg and his lieutenants, those public places were the obvious weak links in a secure chain.

Blumberg and his team would drive from Tel Aviv—about 90 miles each way, several times a week—to the construction site and the residential areas. They felt they had to keep an eye on the entertainment spots; and occasionally they would pull aside individuals who looked like they might be too talkative, if only because their tongues were loosened by liquor. Those men were warned that they might lose their lucrative jobs. In rare cases, the less disciplined were sent home.

The French work contracts spoke of "a warm climate and desert conditions," which did little to mask the location of the nuclear project. Blumberg and French intelligence became concerned about security in the Negev. The French did not fully trust the Israelis, known for their chatty nature, and sent their own agents to preserve secrecy and hunt for leaks.

One spy from Paris posed as a priest and tested the mayor of Beersheba by asking how development was going in the Negev. Proud of how his desert was blooming, in more ways than one, the mayor told the visiting clergyman about the French nuclear reactor being built nearby. The spy-priest, recognizing the original sin of faulty security, sent a highly critical cable back to his headquarters.

Blumberg always felt he had to be on the scene, to make sure that his orders were carried out. He would personally accompany the most important, unmarked shipments of material and equipment that arrived at Israel's main seaport, Haifa, on ships from France or by plane at the international airport near Tel Aviv.

Binyamin Blumberg was born in 1923 at pre-state Palestine's first agricultural school, Mikve Israel. Then, the school was in a rural tract, but now it is a mere six miles east of suburbanized Tel Aviv. It was established late in the 19th century to encourage Jewish pioneers to dirty their hands and cultivate the land. His parents lived and worked there.

After his school years, Blumberg enlisted in the Haganah, the main Jewish underground militia in the decade before Palestine's British rulers departed in 1948. He was assigned to Shai, the Haganah's intelligence wing.

When the fighting was over in 1949, Blumberg joined Shin Bet. The agency's officers were in uniform at the time, and Blumberg was commissioned instantly as a major.

Shin Bet's main office was in an abandoned Arab building near the port of Jaffa, alongside Tel Aviv, very close to a large, old flea market. Shin Bet was divided into eight departments, as an early indicator of the various roles the agency would fulfill.

Blumberg was assigned to Department 5, responsible for security at government ministries, and he was sent specifically to the Ministry of Defense.

"The definition of Blumberg's role sounds very impressive," said Baruch Nir, one of his Shin Bet colleagues of the time, "but all in all, it was a small job. He had two assistants and a secretary, and that's it. What did he have to keep an eye on at the Defense Ministry?"

In 1949 and the early 1950s, not much. The ministry's compound in Tel Aviv contained but a few huts, along with some workshops that much later grew into military industries.

When those larger military enterprises were set up, Blumberg's responsibilities instantly widened. He became the chief security officer at the ministry compound and at new locations constantly being created. As dictated by the times, he Hebraized his family name to Vered for his personal life. At work, he was still known as Blumberg.

"Binyamin was impeccably well-mannered," said one of his former associates. "He never raised his voice, even when he got angry. And he was likeable. But he had no special qualities. He did not have a wide or rich education. Modest. All in all, a typical security officer, effective and hardworking."

More than anything, he was the silent type.

"I remember how he often would walk into my office, drink tea, and say nothing," said another colleague. "There was no small talk with him."

With only two colleagues did he seem comfortable: Amos Manor, who headed Shin Bet under Harel, the boss of all intelligence bosses; and Peres. Blumberg, Manor, and Peres were around the same age, which made it easier for them to find some common ground.

In and around the Dimona project, Blumberg could only hope that everyone would be as silent as he. Quarantining information became increasingly difficult as the months wore on. The last French company departed in 1965, but most of the workers had returned to Europe upon completion of the physical construction of the reactor in 1960. The rumors that had been at a very low level started spreading far and wide.

Questions were going to be asked. Blumberg conceived two cover stories to explain the huge movement of workers, trucks, bulldozers, and heavy equipment. One, that Israel was building a water distillation plant, seemed very odd because those facilities are usually on the edge of a salty sea. The second, more plausible, was that Israel was constructing a huge textile complex to provide employment to the thousands of new immigrants being moved into the Negev.

Supported fully by Peres, Blumberg tried to conceal his agency's existence even from the other branches of the intelligence community—and from Harel.

"Lakam was established behind my back and without my knowledge," Harel recalled angrily. "I had my suspicions. I knew that someone was running around the Ministry of Defense dealing with various matters, and that when he saw anyone from the Mossad he would make a point of crossing to the other side of the street. It was a mysterious body, formed in a conspiratorial manner. Deceptively. Even Ben-Gurion did not know."

Peres felt that he did not need Harel's permission, even though the Memuneh was Ben-Gurion's trusted head of the security services, to set up the special agency for nuclear security. The new reactor from France was, after all, even more secret than any previous hush-hush topics.

Blumberg was not bothered by others' envy or complaints.

While the Lakam chief protected the secret on the ground, a gathering storm came in by air. On a reconnaissance mission in 1960, an American U-2 jet photographed the facility, and U.S. intelligence analysts had no trouble identifying its true purpose. From that moment, American spies sniffed around Dimona, and U.S. political leaders became concerned.

Based on a tip from sources in Washington, the American and British press reported that Israel was developing an atomic bomb.

The United States government demanded the whole truth from the Israelis. The CIA director, Allen Dulles, argued in a meeting with President Eisenhower that Dimona was a "plutonium production plant," and Defense Secretary Thomas Gates went even further: "Our information is that the plant is not for peaceful purposes."

There was also pressure from President Charles de Gaulle in Paris. He decided in May 1960 that France would supply no more uranium to Dimona. The president did not want Israel to produce plutonium at its reactor, because this would be a step toward building an atomic bomb. Peres, the Francophile, continued to be optimistic, for several weeks refusing to admit that the alliance he had built with Paris was becoming very shaky.

The danger to Israel's most clandestine defense project was finally recognized, and Ben-Gurion flew to Paris on short notice to see de Gaulle on June 13, 1960. In his Élysée Palace, the French president asked bluntly, "Why does Israel need a nuclear reactor at all?"

Ben-Gurion answered that it was not a military project, and that no facility for removing weapons-grade plutonium would be added at Dimona. Countries working on nuclear potential have been known to ignore any principle of veracity. As Peres did all he could to leverage his longtime friendships with key officials in France, Israel managed to obtain more nuclear materials.

Before long, the 24-megawatt heavy-water reactor at Dimona—its capacity reportedly expanded with French assistance to 75 megawatts—could produce enough plutonium for at least one Hiroshima-sized 20-kiloton bomb each year.

Foreign pressure kept growing and could not be ignored. Ben-Gurion had no choice but to say something: the first public confirmation that Israel had joined the nuclear age. From the podium of the Knesset on December 21, 1960, he announced that Israel was building a second nuclear research reactor—"designed exclusively for peaceful purposes" such as the needs of "industry, agriculture, health, and science." The prime minister said that Israel would eventually generate electricity, using the atomic facility, and he called reports of a program aimed at building bombs "a deliberate or unwitting untruth."

Ben-Gurion himself, however, engaged in a witting untruth. This was for the sake of a higher cause: ensuring his country's existence in a hostile world, as he saw it, by adding the ultimate defense known in the world as a nuclear arsenal.

A visit to the Dimona reactor by two American physicists helped ease Washington's inquisitiveness, although they were afforded only a superficial view by charming Israeli hosts. They detected no sign of a weapons program at the reactor site, and that greatly mollified the new president, John F. Kennedy, in 1961.

Ben-Gurion, from time to time, confirmed publicly his belief that Israel needed to "build up a deterrent force" to ensure that Egypt would not try to crush the tiny Jewish state. Israeli officials told American counterparts—without saying that his country had a nuclear weapons program—that a priority had to be preventing another Holocaust from ever occurring.

The CIA naturally concluded that Israel had a bomb-making project at Dimona. President Kennedy again started asking questions, and by a wonderful coincidence he found himself quizzing one of the founders of the Israeli nuclear enterprise.

It was April 2, 1963, and Shimon Peres was visiting Washington in his capacity as director-general of the Defense Ministry. Invited by Myer (Mike) Feldman, Kennedy's advisor on Jewish affairs, Peres was strolling through some White House hallways with Feldman. The main subject was to be Israel's purchase of Hawk anti-aircraft missiles, the first significant weapons deal between the two countries.

Apparently just by chance, the president walked by and suggested that they meet in the Oval Office. That conversation lasted 20 minutes, devoted almost entirely to Israel's intentions at Dimona.

According to documents in the JFK Library in Boston, Kennedy told Peres that day that the United States was closely following the development of Israel's nuclear potential. The president wondered what Peres might care to add.

Peres was taken by surprise, but he responded with a policy declaration: "I can tell you clearly that we shall not be the ones to introduce nuclear weapons into the area. We will not be the first to do so."

That was a rhetorical stroke of genius designed to divert Kennedy's pressure and any deterioration of bilateral relations. Israel, at that time, was searching for a new grand ally, because de Gaulle made it clear that he was ending France's special relationship with the Jewish state.

For half a century, successive Israeli governments would continue to use the phrase Peres invented during his chat with Kennedy: They will not be the first to "introduce" nuclear weapons. Some analysts called that an out-and-out falsehood; others posited that Israel might have left all of its nuclear warheads and bombs slightly unfinished, with just a "turn of the screw" needed to make them operational.

Still taking an interest in the subject, right up until his assassination in November 1963, Kennedy insisted that Ben-Gurion and his successor, Levi Eshkol, permit visits to Dimona by American inspectors once or twice a year. It was agreed that the results would be shown to Egypt, to allay Arab concerns about Israel's scientific power.

Blumberg's agency, Lakam, responded with what was reported to be a sophisticated deception and concealment program. The American visitors were escorted at all times, and the Israelis tried to keep close tabs on them.

Because the dates of the visits were set months in advance, the hosts at Dimona had time to build double walls, remove doors, and construct new entrances and control panels—all aimed at fooling the foreigners into believing that only research and industrial projects were underway.

Information that leaked out later indicated that Israel cleverly built the separation plant—where plutonium was produced, to be used in the cores of bombs—deep underground, without leaving any signs on the surface.

The Americans thus saw no evidence of weapons work, but some of them were suspicious and peeled away from their Israeli minders long enough to collect samples of soil, rock, and vegetation from the Dimona area. When they returned to the United States, lab tests on the samples could indicate the telltale radiation of high-level enrichment.

Israeli security chiefs tried to make the sample-collecting process difficult.

John Hadden served as the CIA's station chief in the Tel Aviv embassy through most of the 1960s. He developed a fondness for Israelis but constantly believed that they were lying to him on many issues.

Hadden felt that while politicians described the United States and Israel as friends, that was nothing like true, old chums who played together and went to school together.

The CIA man observed, with admiration, that the founders of the Jewish state could outwit just about anyone. Like other U.S. servicemen in Europe at the end of World War II, he had seen Holocaust survivors as the cleverest refugees: smuggling goods and smuggling themselves to Mediterranean ports to sail to the future state of Israel.

When he arrived in Tel Aviv and settled in, Hadden found that official liaison meetings for the purpose of exchanging intelligence—supposedly a hallmark of cooperation—were unsettling and "crazed."

His prior experiences in such meetings had been in West Germany, where the two sides traded and shared intelligence in a dignified and fairly clear way.

Israeli intelligence men, according to Hadden, would come in "stiff-necked and clutching their files." Instead of offering some data and placing it on the table, "they would stage a parachute drop 20 miles behind our lines"—in the form of 45-minute diatribes on all the terrible challenges to Israel's security, listing all the intelligence and military material they needed for their survival.

"Christ! There you were in your chair," Hadden recalled, "and they were shouting way over behind you. Absolutely outrageous! They were asking for the goddamned moon!"

Eventually, both sides brought their mutual interests into focus and achieved a high degree of sharing.

Hadden also remembered a diplomatic dinner in a private Israeli home in 1963, his first year in Tel Aviv. He was seated across from Colonel David Carmon, the number-two man at Aman. Hadden had started taking private lessons in Hebrew, and he thought he overheard the hostess murmuring something to Carmon about hoping that the American would drink too much and then talk too much.

According to Hadden, he turned to Carmon with a smile and said, "*Nichnas yayin, yotzeh sod!*"—Hebrew for "Wine goes in, a secret comes out!" He enjoyed the look of horror on the colonel's face. The next day, Carmon ordered everyone at Aman not to speak Hebrew around Hadden.

Naturally, the CIA station chief was active in trying to keep up with Israel's most secret project. He traveled to the Negev on occasion, as the CIA wanted photographs and soil samples. He knew that he was under surveillance. Once, when he was driving on a road near the nuclear facility, a military helicopter landed near his car. Security personnel—from Lakam, although Hadden did not know that agency's name—demanded to see his identification. After flashing his

U.S. diplomatic passport, he drove off, fully convinced that there was a lot more going on in Dimona than Israel ever admitted.

He believed in "going native," to the extent of dabbling in some of his host country's passions. He developed an interest in archeology, seeing how Israelis were obsessed with their ties to the ancient land. "When you're in Israel," Hadden said, "you dig."

Digging, in the literal sense, led the CIA man to an extraordinary fortnight of private conversations with none other than Ben-Gurion, now retired. This stroke of luck for U.S. intelligence came in 1965, when Hadden's wife was working on a dig—with some other "embassy wives"—at an ancient Jewish site near the Dead Sea.

Hadden drove three hours from Tel Aviv to visit, which provided a fine pretext to drive fairly close to Dimona.

That night, sitting around a campfire, Mrs. Hadden suffered severe stomach pain. He rushed his wife to a hospital in the Negev desert's largest city, Beersheba, and she underwent surgery on her colon. She was treated very well, and received an unexpected bonus: The lady sharing her semi-private hospital room was none other than Paula Ben-Gurion, the Old Man's wife.

Hadden made a point of driving to the hospital every afternoon, because those were also David Ben-Gurion's visiting hours. The spy and the legendary politician had a lot of long chats during the 14 days that their wives were roommates.

The American did not learn any nuclear secrets from the man who launched the secret Dimona project, but he did understand Zionism and Israeli motivations a lot better. "Imagine two weeks with Churchill!" Hadden enthused, years later. "That's what it was like!"

The visits to Dimona by American nuclear inspectors continued until 1969. They found no incriminating evidence of weapons work. That year, the two governments reached a secret understanding that stopped the visits.

Both capitals, Jerusalem and Washington, had new leaders. Golda Meir had been selected by the Labor Party to replace Eshkol, who had died of illness in February. A month before that, Richard Nixon was sworn in as president and brought in Henry Kissinger as national security advisor.

Kissinger, although not actively Jewish, was always aware that his parents had brought him to America from Germany to escape the Nazi system which took the lives of many of his relatives. He could be tough when negotiating with or lecturing Israeli politicians, but he did feel a strong commitment to the existence of a nation that provided shelter to Jews.

The trio—Golda, Nixon, and Kissinger—agreed that no more inspections of Dimona would be required. The CIA already concluded that Israel had built a few nuclear devices, and fruitless inspections now seemed superfluous. Moreover, the new White House team had apparently concluded that an unquestionably strong Israel would be good for American interests: pushing the Arab countries to negotiate peace by dispelling their dreams that they could, with Soviet assistance, wipe out the Jewish state.

Under Nixon, who did not seem alarmed by or opposed to Israel being a nuclear power, the U.S. government accepted a new formula. It was intended to update and clarify Israel's pledge not to be the first to "introduce" nuclear weapons into the Middle East.

As drafted by the Israeli ambassador in Washington, Yitzhak Rabin, according to officials who spoke about it many years later, it was now understood that nuclear weapons would be perceived as such only if and when they become operational. The key threshold would be a nuclear test explosion.

In effect, Israel was agreeing not to conduct a nuclear test. In return, it was freed from the burden of inconvenient American inspection visits.

Israel, by standing firm but explaining very little, had won the right to be a unique exception to United States policy favoring nuclear non-proliferation. Israeli leaders never agreed to sign international treaties on the subject, yet they continued—time and again—to hope, and even expect, that America would support the unspoken Israeli nuclear monopoly in the Middle East.

Chapter Six

HAREL THE CRUSADER

A lthough Isser Harel was mostly excluded from the nuclear project that Israeli leaders viewed as the nation's ultimate defense, he wielded tremendous authority over all other security matters. After heading Shin Bet from 1948 to 1952, Harel added the Mossad directorship to his responsibilities from 1952 to 1963, a longer tenure than any intelligence chief has had in Israel.

Harel spent a lot of his time and energy unmasking men who were spying on Israel—working either for the Soviet bloc or for an Arab government. He was an excellent detector of disloyalty. His naturally suspicious nature seemed perfect for that part of his job.

Yet he failed, for several years, to discover a Communist-bloc mole buried inside Shin Bet. The man was Levi Levi: a simple name, but one of the most daring spies to penetrate Israeli society.

He was born as Lucjan Levi in Poland in September 1922. Levi was an activist in a Zionist youth movement, and he survived the Holocaust by escaping to the Soviet Union. In 1948 he would move to Israel, which seemed perfectly natural.

Many years later, documents found in Poland's national archives showed that Russian secret police had recruited him during the war, and then he served the Polish authorities by spying on fellow Jews.

"During the period of his collaboration on home territory," one declassified file revealed, "he delivered a lot of valuable and verified information about Zionist activities in Poland."

The Communist government in Warsaw expected Levi to spy inside Israel. Indeed, by showing he had a talent for security work, he got a job at Shin Bet. After a few weeks, he was placed in the Special Unit—the predecessor of what would become the operations team for Shin Bet and the Mossad. The unit had no more than 20 staffers, most veterans of the pre-state Haganah.

Levi was different from his colleagues. His manners and sense of dress, including bow ties, did not match theirs. While they smoked cheap, unfiltered cigarettes, he was smoking American cigarettes, such as Kent. When they would drink inferior rough liquor, he would offer them foreign brand-name brandies and whiskey—certainly a treat in mid-1950s Israel.

Levi flew several times to France, ostensibly to visit relatives. He always carried a small Minox camera with him and would keep taking photographs left and right. He would ask his colleagues to pose for photos, and he even took pictures near the entrance of Shin Bet headquarters in the Jaffa flea market.

The others in the unit thought he was eccentric, but it never occurred to them that it was anything more than that. Not a single warning light flashed in their heads. They were all busy with their work: shadowing foreign diplomats, breaking into their embassies and homes, and planting microphones that were provided by the CIA.

However, in 1957 a large wave of immigration swept in from Poland, and Levi's jig was up. Among the new arrivals debriefed by Shin Bet—as part of Operation Balsam for the CIA—was Jefim Gildiner, who confessed that he had been a captain in Poland's security service. Gildiner also revealed that he was the case officer for a Polish spy inside Israel: Levi Levi.

"We were shocked," Amos Manor recalled. Levi was put under surveillance, but he was very cautious; no evidence that would stand up in court was found.

Still, he was called to the government's manpower office and fired. Astonishingly, Shin Bet allowed him to travel to France—once again to see his "family." Later, it would be learned that he met in Paris with Polish intelligence officers, who debriefed him and ordered him to return to Israel: right back into the Biblically suggestive lion's den.

Polish chutzpa reached a new zenith when Levi flew back to Tel Aviv, met with the chief of the manpower bureau, and demanded that he be reinstated in Shin Bet—or he would sue his employer in court.

Shin Bet decided to go back to shadowing him. This time, Levi was spotted making contact with an intelligence controller in Poland's embassy.

Manor finally had Levi arrested, but he still refused to admit that he was a spy. "We were desperate," the Shin Bet chief recalled. "We knew we had no serious evidence against him, and we were preparing to release him when a miracle happened!" That occurred courtesy of Israel's intelligence liaison with French secret services.

A Polish intelligence colonel, Wladyslav Mroz, had just defected to France. In his debriefings, he revealed some details about a spy from Poland inside Israel's intelligence community.

Manor himself flew to Paris and was handed a dossier by French domestic security, which helped solve the mystery.

Finally, during another round of interrogations supervised by Manor, Levi broke down and confessed. He was tried in secret and sentenced to 10 years in prison. He served seven years, and when freed for good behavior he was put onto a ship out of the country, his eventual fate unknown. It is believed that Levi died in Australia, where he actually did have relatives.

Another bad apple in the clandestine bunch was Mordecai (Motke) Kedar. He had been a petty criminal before being recruited by military intelligence, but he is remembered for the most severe crime committed by an Israeli operative while on an assignment: murdering a Jewish businessman in Argentina who was a *sayan* (a "helper") for the Mossad.

Sayanim, as revealed by a former Mossad cadet, are foreigners who, for personal reasons, are willing to help by making a lot of arrangements that make things easier for Israeli "visitors." The helpers are usually Jewish—but not always—and are not to be told anything about the mission itself, largely for their own safety. Israel has never admitted using Jews as sayanim, and doing so could carry a danger of endangering local Jewish communities.

Born in Poland as Mordecai Kravitzki, Kedar was undergoing a total transformation. He was going to be planted inside Egypt by Aman's Unit 131, the military's plainclothes operations department. For months in Argentina, he was supposed to be developing a "legend," a complete cover story.

The reasons for stabbing his sayan 80 times in 1957 were never clear, and all details were concealed when Kedar was secretly put on trial in Israel and then jailed under a false name.

Within Ramle Prison, he was known only as "X4." In the neighboring cell was Avri El-Ad, the former Unit 131 case officer who was suspected of betraying his colleagues in Egypt. El-Ad wrote later that they played chess, mentally, by tapping out their moves by Morse code on a wall between the cells.

"Don't let them drag you down!" Kedar once tapped. "If you let them demoralize you, you're a broken man."

Kedar refused to confess to any crimes. In prison, he maintained his physical fitness and became a disciple of Ayn Rand. After 17 years in prison—including seven years without a cellmate—this tough guy was released in 1974 and demanded a new hearing. His request was rejected.

When the Aman commander who hired Kedar—Yehoshafat Harkabi, who later would become famous as a professor and peace campaigner—was asked about the obviously horrible personnel choice, he did not rend his clothing in regret. "People who are recruited for these operations are not uncomplicated people," Harkabi said. "There is always some type of story."

After serving his prison term, Kedar left Israel and lived a vagabond life—eventually making his way to Los Angeles, as a yacht operator between the United States and Latin America. Nearly 50 years after his conviction in the secret trial, he told a few reporters that he was innocent, that he had been framed by Harel, and that he would write his memoirs and reveal the whole truth. He never did.

Isser Harel, who arranged Kedar's recall and imprisonment, disclosed that serious consideration had been given simply to killing him so as to cover up the crime. There would then have been less chance of a diplomatic clash with Argentina or any embarrassment to the intelligence community. "I was insistent from the beginning that we cannot take the law into our own hands," Harel wrote. "For this, there are judges and courts."

Harel proudly added: "During my tenure as Memuneh, no traitor was ever executed."

This was narrowly true, although some recalled Avner Israel as nearly an exception. He was the operative who was kidnapped by Harel's snatch squad in 1954 and died during a flight—because of an overdose of sedative—with his corpse unceremoniously dumped into the Mediterranean.

From Harel's viewpoint, the Kedar case supplied further proof for his old argument that running secret agents was too serious to be left to Aman. Harel claimed that the Mossad was the most qualified agency to send Israelis on ultra-sensitive missions abroad.

A deal was struck. Military intelligence retained responsibility for operations inside Arab countries—especially the planting of spies under deep cover. But the Mossad would build up its own core of undercover officers, who would be tasked with missions all around the world. Harel's tiny operations department could now be stretched to global proportions.

The Memuneh got right to the new challenge with his typical, uncompromising vigor. As he had authority over both the Mossad and Shin Bet, he insisted that the new unit be available to both agencies and that it utilize the best human resources of both. It would be bureaucratically based within Shin Bet. Years later, Harel said it was like the "birth" of something new and exciting.

Shin Bet scored a success in 1958 when it spotted Aharon Cohen, an expert on the Middle East for the left-wing Mapam party, having regular meetings with a Soviet diplomat in Tel Aviv who was known to be a spy. Cohen was arrested, but party leaders accused Harel of framing him. They pointed out that Harel had planted microphones in their offices five years earlier. Still, Cohen was convicted and sentenced to five years; Israel's supreme court later cut the prison term in half.

The success in detecting Cohen's cloaked foreign relations was partly due to a new surveillance method honed by the Shin Bet operations unit. The team had undergone a major shake-up after the failure to notice Levi Levi's disloyalty, and among the new tools was a clever trick called "the Comb." It was a method for catching spies by making them come to you.

"We were a small unit," said Yair Racheli, one of Shin Bet's first operatives, joining the agency in the early 1950s. "With our limited resources—dozens of men, just a few cars and insufficient radio communications—we found it hard to shadow the spies of two dozen Soviet-bloc countries. They were professionals and knew how to spot us, how to evade us, and they shook us off."

So Zvi (Peter) Malkin devised new techniques. Instead of following all the Russian, Polish, Czech, and other presumed spies operating under diplomatic cover wherever they might go, Shin Bet's men divvied up Tel Aviv, Jerusalem, Haifa, and some other key cities. When targets of foreign espionage were identified, the Israelis anticipated where the spies were going and waited for them there.

In a basketball sense, this was zone defense rather than man-to-man. Israel in the 1950s and '60s was so small, with fewer than three million people, that it really could be sliced into zones.

"Instead of following them, we were waiting for them at the zone where we believed they were heading," Racheli explained. "A lot was based on improvisation and intuition. Sometimes we were wrong, and they went to another zone. But in the end, the system of combing the cities proved itself and paid off."

The Comb struck gold for a second time in Haifa on a cold evening in March 1960. A Shin Bet operations team was on a training exercise, practicing Malkin's surveillance pattern, when one of its members spotted a car and recognized its license plate as belonging to Czechoslovakia's embassy in Tel Aviv.

The diplomat inside was known to be the station chief of the STB, his nation's intelligence service. He was also known for his clumsiness, carelessness, and laziness—truly the triumvirate of terrible behavior for a spy. The adrenaline started flowing among the Israelis in Haifa, as the unit leader improvised immediately and changed the exercise into a genuine operation.

The diplomat was soon discovered in a nearby restaurant, in the company of an unidentified man.

Shin Bet shadowing teams now focused on the unknown. He left the eatery and strolled to his parked car, which had Swiss license plates from the canton of Zurich. He drove away, and three Shin Bet cars followed him home. The man was readily identified as Professor Kurt Sitta, a scientist from Czechoslovakia who was teaching at the newly established physics department of the Technion—the university in Haifa that was rapidly becoming an Israeli equivalent of MIT.

Sitta was one of the first Soviet-bloc spies to penetrate Israel's scientific community. He had previously taught at Syracuse University and in Brazil, and in 1955 the Technion invited him to lecture there. Sitta found that he liked the school, the country, and the people. Or so he said, as he gladly accepted the post of chairman of the physics department.

Sitta's rare success, as a non-Jewish foreigner in Israel, provided a golden opportunity for the Czechs and their Soviet masters. The intelligence officer at the Czechoslovak embassy in Tel Aviv met frequently with the professor between 1955 and 1960, collecting a mountain of material. It took nearly five years, but with the lucky stroke of a Comb, Shin Bet did finally detect the espionage operation.

The surveillance lasted for three months, from March to June 1960. In addition to meetings with his Czech controller, Sitta proved to be an impressive womanizer. Shin Bet men soon developed a favorite assignment: following and photographing Sitta in the beautiful woods of Mount Carmel overlooking the harbor and the Mediterranean. Once or twice a week, during his lunch break, he would drive his American-made Swiss-numbered car—a rare luxury in then-austere Israeli society—the short distance from his office to the forest with a female student or faculty member. The Israeli surveillance teams were treated to the real-life equivalent of pornography.

On the night of June 16, 1960, two men knocked on the door of Sitta's villa in an exclusive Haifa suburb with a San Francisco-style view of the sea from high above. One of the men was a Shin Bet operative, and the other was in the Special Branch of Israel's national police. They drove Sitta away for arraignment on charges of spying.

At his trial, it emerged that he had been spying on Israel's atomic energy commission. By coincidence or not, Sitta was arrested just two days before Israel's experimental nuclear reactor at Nahal Sorek became operational. Israeli analysts compared his activities with those of Julius and Ethel Rosenberg in the United States and Klaus Fuchs in Britain, who betrayed those countries' atomic secrets to the Soviet bloc.

Sitta was sentenced to five years in prison, but Israel—to head off any embarrassment—quickly paroled him to start a new academic life in West Germany. Senior Israelis said the Czech was only a small fish who dabbled in spying, and Harel insisted that Israel was not badly damaged.

The Comb paid off yet again, in March 1961, when agents spotted Viktor Sokolov, a senior Soviet spy operating under diplomatic cover in Tel Aviv, meeting with an Israeli they thought they recognized. It turned out to be Israel Be'er, a close advisor to Prime Minister Ben-Gurion.

Harel said that he had long suspected Be'er, who was a member of the left-wing Mapam party. Harel found it odd that Be'er kept trying to strike up a friendship with West Germany's BND and its chief, General Reinhard Gehlen.

Gehlen—a consistent friend of Israeli intelligence—stood at the center of the East-versus-West struggle for Europe. The German general had run spies in the Soviet Union during World War II, and now he was reactivating his espionage network in Russia. The Soviets were desperate to find out what Gehlen knew and what he was doing. Be'er—a senior Israeli who could gain the German's trust—might have had a chance of finding out for his true masters in the KGB.

Be'er denied everything stubbornly for days, but Shin Bet interrogators caught him in the kind of little lie that unravels whole cloths of untruth. Be'er claimed that the night he was spotted with the Russian intelligence agent Sokolov, he was actually out purchasing Cinzano, an imported drink he was crazy about, at one of Israel's first supermarkets. Investigators confronted him with the fact that Cinzano was not sold in that store at all. Tripped up by a tiny detail, Be'er broke down.

In the interrogation and in court, Be'er admitted that he had invented his past. He had never received a doctorate in history, as he boasted, nor had he fought in the Spanish civil war. Confusion over who he really was deepened when, in prison, he renounced his courtroom confession and claimed his original autobiography was true.

Even without knowing his real name and background, the Israeli judges found the evidence against Be'er to be incontrovertible, and the Tel Aviv court had ample reason to sentence him to 15 years in prison for espionage. Until his dying day in prison in 1966, he insisted that he was no spy but a genuine patriot seeking only to make Israel non-aligned rather than pro-Western.

The Soviet espionage machine was gargantuan and persistent—forcing Harel to juggle a variety of counterespionage challenges—and these distractions may help explain why Harel ignored an important tip about a top Nazi war criminal. But the case he neglected, for over two years, was that of Adolf Eichmann, and capturing him would become one of the hallmark achievements in the history of Israeli intelligence.

In late 1957 Fritz Bauer, a Jewish lawyer who was the attorney general of the state of Hesse in West Germany, sent a letter to his Israeli counterpart that said Eichmann had been located—living in Argentina. Bauer later was able to supply Eichmann's false name, Ricardo Klement.

Harel sent an agent to Buenos Aires to see the poor suburb where Eichmann was supposedly living, but no definite evidence could be found. The Memuneh and his new operations team could have done a lot more if he really wanted to, but the efforts were only half-hearted.

Chasing Nazis was not a high priority for Harel. Still, every Israeli felt that his nation had a historic responsibility to seek justice for the six million Jews who had been murdered by Nazi Germany. Two of the biggest names on an informal "most wanted list" for Israel were Eichmann, considered the architect of Adolf Hitler's "final solution" for the "Jewish problem"; and Josef Mengele, the German physician who tortured concentration camp prisoners in the name of ghastly experimentation.

Bauer, the German prosecutor, certainly felt motivated to stay on Eichmann's trail. He flew to Israel and complained to the Ministry of Justice that no one was acting on his information. Bauer provided the name of his source, and Harel sent another Israeli operative to follow up.

The tipster turned out to be a half-Jewish blind man, who had fled Germany to Argentina in 1938. His daughter was dating Nicholas Eichmann, who kept spouting anti-Semitic opinions and remained vague about his parents and his home address. Could young Eichmann be the notorious mass murderer's son?

Yes, indeed. The blind man saw things more clearly than the Mossad, which had not bothered to check fully the lead to the Eichmann family's front door.

Simon Wiesenthal, who would gain fame as a solitary, obsessive Nazi-hunter, also sent Israel many tips about Eichmann's whereabouts. Only in 2010, five years after Wiesenthal's death at age 96, was it revealed that he had been working for the Mossad for many decades—as something between a sayan and a paid agent. Assigned the code name Theocrat, Wiesenthal received a small monthly retainer from the Mossad, which helped him set up his research center in Vienna.

Harel did not like Wiesenthal, however, so at times Mossad operatives would be in touch with the Nazi-hunter without telling their boss.

Information about Eichmann was beginning to feel compelling, and, under pressure from Israel's attorney general around the beginning of 1960, Harel decided to move. He sent more men, this time, to Argentina, and they found the German calling himself Klement. He did, indeed, resemble the elusive Eichmann.

Harel informed Ben-Gurion, who had returned to the post of prime minister, and the Old Man immediately gave approval to kidnap Eichmann so he could be put on trial. He was to be brought to Israel—dead or alive, but very preferably alive. Ben-Gurion said it would be a lesson for the world.

Sixty-seven men and women, from both the Mossad and Shin Bet, were chosen for the kidnap team, including support and surveillance roles. No one would be compelled to take part; all would have to volunteer, and they all did. Almost all had lost relatives in the Holocaust and hated Eichmann. Harel cautioned them to control their emotions.

Because of the operational, political, and even personal complexities, the Memuneh himself flew to Paris to set up a staging post for the abduction. Then Harel went on to Argentina to take complete and personal responsibility.

The Mossad's finest forger went to Europe, where he prepared false passports and other documents for the operatives. They made their way to Buenos Aires on separate flights, under names that would never again be used. The forger also flew on to Argentina, with all his special pens and papers, to provide fresh identities for all the Israelis and for Eichmann himself so he could be smuggled out.

At least half a dozen "safe houses" and even more cars were rented in Buenos Aires, in a potential logistical nightmare that was handled with impressive ease.

One member of the team was Moshe Tavor, a genius at logistics who had ice water running through his veins. Born as Moshe Karpovich in Lithuania in 1917, he was taken by his family to Palestine long before the rise of Nazi Germany. He eagerly volunteered for the British army's Jewish Brigade, and he fought in Libya and then in Italy—proud to be killing Nazis.

After the end of World War II, with just over half a dozen friends—including some who later would join Israeli intelligence—Karpovich/Tavor hunted down German officers who had run ghetto round-ups, deportation trains, and death camps.

Tavor and his buddies, acting on information from Holocaust survivors, would stage a rudimentary trial for the Nazi in an isolated field; Tavor then would strangle the man.

Interviewed at age 89, he explained that such killings did not bother him in the slightest. Tavor was chosen as the executioner because of his strong hands, he said, and shooting the Nazi would have left a lot of blood—and that would have led to investigations. The bodies were dropped into lakes.

In Argentina, Tavor—who had become the Mossad's finest safecracker, literally able to open any lock at all—built a metal cart where a folded-up Adolf Eichmann could be secreted. Tavor also prepared secret rooms in the rented safe houses: to store weapons, and to hold Eichmann after capturing him.

Tavor, whose real life was stranger than any Hollywood scriptwriter could imagine, also installed a rotating license plate panel on one of his team's cars—several years before the James Bond movie *Goldfinger* had a similar gimmick—so that the vehicle's identity tag could instantly be changed if the Israelis were spotted.

One side of the panel had a local Buenos Aires license plate. The other had a diplomatic plate, with a number indicating that the car belonged to the embassy of another South American country. The Israelis did flip the plate numbers a few times when they had to pass police roadblocks. "The policeman on duty," Rafi Eitan recalled decades later, "would salute us and let us go on."

Some team members also carried forged diplomatic documents that named them as envoys of that same country.

A female operative was chosen for the traditional role of "housewife," to buy groceries, cook the food, and tidy the residence where the Nazi would be held. She was Yehudit Nessyahu, born in Holland in 1925: highly intelligent, fluent in several languages, described as forgettably plain-looking, and a veteran of clandestine work smuggling Jews out of Morocco. She would rise to be the highest ranking woman in the Mossad, its director of personnel. After her retirement at age 51, she would study law, head the Israeli writers' association, and assiduously avoid cameras for fear that a single snapshot of her could endanger her contacts and agents from many missions abroad.

As a religious woman, Nessyahu prepared only kosher food during the Argentina mission—even for the notorious Nazi. She was disturbed by the fact that she would be nourishing a mass murderer and enemy of the Jewish people.

The honor of physically tackling and grabbing Eichmann on May 11, 1960, went to Rafi Eitan and Avraham Shalom, who would become agency chiefs in the decades to come, along with Malkin—the inventor of the Comb surveillance system.

They tossed the Nazi onto the back seat of their car. The man who posed as Ricardo Klement did not put up a struggle and readily admitted that he was Eichmann.

The abduction had been timed to coincide with the official visit of an Israeli delegation to Argentina, where many foreign guests were taking part in celebrations of the country's 150th year of independence from Spain. An El Al airliner would fly the delegates in on May 19 and would be returning to Tel Aviv late the next night.

Harel and members of his team said later that their most difficult task was feeding and caring for Eichmann for nine days while waiting for their flight to Israel. They interrogated the prisoner and at times simply stared at him in wonderment over how ordinary the personification of evil could appear. The balding man who depended on eyeglasses for his reading meekly signed a statement agreeing to be tried in an Israeli court.

It was chilling, however, for the kidnappers to hear Eichmann switch from German to a prayer in Hebrew, the *Shma*, which had been recited by Jews as they walked to their deaths in the Nazi gas chambers: "Hear O Israel, the Lord is our God, the Lord is One."

According to Harel, Eichmann "told us he was a great friend of the Jews. We were furious. Some of my people started to forget their orders not to touch him. They wanted to kill him. But they didn't, and he started to beg for small favors." The captive also said he would reveal all of Hitler's secrets if the Israelis would spare his life. Harel responded with a promise that Eichmann would get the best lawyer available to defend him at a trial in Jerusalem.

Harel spent little time in the safe house where Eichmann was chained to a bed. The Memuneh instead perfected a secure spycraft technique that could be called the roving headquarters. He told his senior operatives where they could find him at certain hours of the day, and he walked from café to café in the Parisian-style Argentine capital. No stranger was likely to remember seeing him in any particular location.

Sacrificing caution for the sake of on-the-spot control, Harel set up his command post on May 20 in a cafeteria at Ezeiza Airport. He sat at a table with his forger, checking and distributing the identity documents his operatives would need to make a safe and unimpeachable departure from Buenos Aires.

At the safe house, Eichmann and the men who would accompany him were dressed in El Al airline uniforms. The Mossad's chief forger had prepared an Israeli passport, with the name Ze'ev Zichroni, for the VIP prisoner.

A doctor working for Shin Bet—Yonah Elian—the same anesthesiologist who inadvertently overdosed Alexander Israel, whose corpse was then thrown out of an airplane in 1954—did a fine job this time. Elian kept topping off the dose by injecting Eichmann with sedatives. When moving day arrived, the Nazi was transformed into a very sleepy man who could barely walk.

An exhausted or drunk crew member appeared normal to airport officials, late at night, and Eichmann and others in the "El Al" group strolled out of the terminal and onto the Israeli airliner that supposedly had waited there to fly Israeli dignitaries home from the Argentine celebrations.

The genuine El Al pilot was not told about his infamous passenger until after takeoff from Buenos Aires in the first minutes of May 21, and on Harel's recommendation a refueling stop was scheduled in the most out-of-the-way city imaginable. It took every last drop of aviation fuel to reach Dakar, Senegal, but no one in western Africa was making any inquiries about a missing German-Argentinian man.

The special flight carrying the Nazi to meet Jewish justice arrived in Tel Aviv on the morning of May 22.

Ben-Gurion took the rare step of publicly hailing the intelligence community the next day, when the prime minister announced in the Knesset that "the security services of Israel found Adolf Eichmann and ... he will shortly be brought to trial in Israel." The parliament's applause was unanimous.

The judicial proceedings began nearly a year later, on April 11, 1961, with the fullest international press and television coverage that the world of that time could muster. The defendant—dubbed "the man in the glass booth"— listened to witnesses who heartrendingly described his crimes and those of the entire Nazi killing machine. Eichmann claimed he was only following orders as a patriotic German, but he was convicted of crimes against humanity.

He was hanged in Ramle Prison on May 31, 1962—the only defendant put to death by Israel's judicial system.

Eichmann's abduction and the massive public acclaim enjoyed by Israel's intelligence community were surely Harel's finest hour. Until his death in 2003, he had the pleasure of being hailed as "the man who captured Eichmann." The Memuneh's boldest operation was also a pure example of *humint*—the human intelligence skills at which Israel excelled, in this case without any technological gadgets beyond a rotating car license plate.

Harel would later be criticized for grabbing the glory for himself, notably in his best-selling book, *The House on Garibaldi Street*. The critics included some members of the kidnap squad, above all Zvi Aharoni—who later wrote his own book, *Operation Eichmann*, and claimed that Harel had to be pushed into ordering the mission.

Every person involved in the caper seemed to have his own unique memory of who had the good ideas, who had the bad ones, who actually tackled the Nazi, and who got him to confess.

Zvi Malkin, later a New York-based painter and writer, also put his version in a book, *Eichmann in My Hands*, which mentioned a tragicomedy of errors in the months and years before the Nazi was caught.

The Mossad's leading kidnap artist, Rafi Eitan, after he became a garrulous member of parliament in Israel, enjoyed retelling how he had jumped on the war criminal.

Yehudit Nessyahu, the leading female on the team, was among the very few who adhered to their pledge of lifelong secrecy.

Only with the passage of decades did the mixed Mossad-Shin Bet squad tell how close it may have come to capturing an even more notorious Nazi— the death camp doctor Josef Mengele. Malkin wrote that he pressed Eichmann for information by demanding, "Tell us where your friend Mengele is. You must know where he lives." But Eichmann insisted that he did not know. Malkin had to tell Harel, "I tried everything. I believe that he has no idea where Mengele is, or that he is not willing to say a thing."

According to Harel, the medical war criminal moved to Paraguay and later to Brazil.

Some Mossad veterans, however, would complain later that Harel had not taken all the Mengele-related clues seriously. Yet, the attempts to capture him continued. When the Brazilian authorities reported in 1985, after years of rumors, that the Nazi doctor had drowned, the Mossad secretly sent a pathologist to examine the skeleton and confirm that the target atop the manhunt list could be crossed off once and for all.

The list contained the names of 10 notorious Nazis. Among others, the Israelis searched for Hitler's senior aide, Martin Bormann, and for Gestapo chief Heinrich Müller.

Also on the list was Léon Degrelle. A Belgian, Degrelle became an officer in the Waffen SS—the Nazi Party's military unit fighting on the Russian front.

Degrelle, after the war, was a fairly prominent neo-Nazi given shelter by Spain's Fascist government of Francisco Franco. A former Shin Bet man, Zwy (Zvi) Aldouby—hoping for both glory and money—hatched his own plot to capture Degrelle. Aldouby hired a few French mercenaries and approached Yigal Mossinson, a famous Israeli novelist and playwright—giving him the impression that a kidnap mission similar to the Eichmann operation had been authorized by the government.

Hoping eventually to sell the tale as a film script—and having received an advance payment from a major magazine—the oddly concocted team went into action in Spain. They followed Degrelle to his villa near Seville and started to plan his abduction.

After several reconnaissance trips, Aldouby, one French partner, and Mossinson were arrested while crossing from France into Spain on July 14, 1961, for the actual kidnap.

Aldouby and the Frenchman were locked up by the Spanish police, who tortured them and sentenced them to seven years in prison. Mossinson was far luckier—released after just a few hours. Years later, he would be told that because Ben-Gurion liked his writing, The Old Man had phoned Generalissimo Franco and urged him, "Don't touch Mossinson. Please release him."

The next big manhunt after Eichmann was actually a ridiculous boyhunt. Israeli intelligence scoured the globe for a 10-year-old nicknamed Yossele. In late 1959, Yosef Schumacher had been abducted from Israel by his own grandfather, an ultra-Orthodox Jew who feared that the boy's parents were giving him a secular education.

Newspaper editorials were making fun of Ben-Gurion for failing to get the boy back to his mother, and Harel—out of loyalty to the prime minister—vowed to track down the child.

Senior operatives were ordered to drop their other projects, and the entire Shin Bet-Mossad operations team tracked the boy to an apartment in Brooklyn in July 1962.

Word was flashed to the FBI, and Yossele was returned triumphantly to his parents in Israel. It may seem silly, but the secret services were warmly thanked again, and Israel's clandestine defenders basked in the praise.

Harel, however, was developing fresh obsessions, aimed at anti-Semites and anyone who might seek to destroy the Jewish state. The Memuneh specifically began to focus, in the early 1960s, on the ominous arrival of German rocket scientists in Egypt.

President Nasser was hiring the Germans to help him develop ground-to-ground missiles that could be used in a future war against Israel. Harel genuinely saw this as Germans again making a major effort to exterminate Jews.

The Memuneh ordered the start of what he termed Operation Damocles, which would effectively place a sword over the head of every German scientist working for the Egyptians.

Harel's operatives sent booby-trapped letters to the German scientists involved in Nasser's missile project and to their families. Envelopes rigged with explosives were mailed by Israeli agents who were undercover in Egypt on completely separate missions. Harel was willing to put them at risk.

These attacks were coordinated by Yitzhak Yezernitzki, who—before independence in 1948—had been head of the violent and ultra-nationalistic Lehi, or Stern Gang. He later changed his name to Yitzhak Shamir, and in the mid-1980s he would become Israel's prime minister. Short, stocky, and mustached, Shamir operated from Paris, under diplomatic cover, running the Mossad's European operations department.

Back in 1955, Harel had persuaded Ben-Gurion to recruit the most talented members of the former Lehi underground—despite a history of enmity between the right-wingers and the prime minister.

It was a clever move. The former Stern Gangsters needed no basic training. They knew how to set bombs and how to kill. It was no coincidence, however, that they were employed by the Mossad—and not Shin Bet. Despite his newfound openness, Harel still did not trust them fully; he preferred to see them stationed abroad, shadowing or killing the state's enemies far away without wielding weapons and power within Israel.

One exception was Yehoshua Cohen, who in 1948 had been involved in the Stern Gang's murder of a Swedish mediator for the United Nations, Folke Bernadotte. Cohen was assigned to be Ben-Gurion's bodyguard, apparently in the belief that an assassin would know how to outwit assassins—and VIP protection was a Shin Bet function.

German scientists toiling for Egypt's Nasser were often targeted in Europe, where it was generally easier to get to them. This campaign in the early 1960s would set a strong precedent, and not only for spilling blood to affect the behavior of enemies and third parties. These attacks also cemented the Mossad's image as a daring, ruthless, and vindictive spy agency with no parallel.

Certainly more than other Western intelligence operatives, Israel's secret agents were willing to pursue and assassinate targets almost anywhere—if the mission was deemed to be achievable and Israel's political leaders decided that the target deserved the death penalty.

The world, in the decades that followed, would read mostly unconfirmable reports of similar operations: against Palestinian terrorists in the 1970s, Iraqi nuclear technicians in the 1980s, and Iranian nuclear scientists at the volatile dawn of the 21st century.

A high-priority example in 1963 was Hans Kleinwachter, a German electronics expert who had worked on Hitler's V2 rockets and now was employed by Egypt. Two Mossad assassins waited for Kleinwachter's car near his house in a small German village on a freezing February night. They opened fire with at least one silencer-equipped pistol, but the bullet failed to penetrate the scientist's windshield. A more powerful submachine gun hidden under a blanket jammed.

The two luckless Israelis quickly drove away, together with Isser Harel himself. The Memuneh took such a personal interest in the campaign against these Germans that he was on the scene of several attacks.

The sum total of the Israeli violence was a few injuries and much intimidation. The injured, however, included some of Harel's operatives: One Mossad man lost his vision when a bomb he was preparing exploded.

Harel felt his campaign could succeed, but his relations with Ben-Gurion became extremely strained because the prime minister kept urging him not to annoy the West German government. In effect, Ben-Gurion was saying, "Hands off the Germans."

Harel, keeping up his efforts to compel the scientists to leave Egypt, managed to recruit one. Otto Joklik, who was actually Austrian, was a rocket scientist with big ideas and a huge appetite for money. He persuaded Egypt to pay him for advice on building a high-energy cobalt bomb, although he barely did any work on it during his time in Cairo. And then he sold his services to the Mossad.

Joklik was Harel's man on the inside, and after leaving Egypt he flew to Israel to deliver a complete briefing on the clandestine missile project. Joklik warned that the Egyptians were making progress toward the highly dangerous goal of an "ABC" strike force. The initials stood for atomic-biological-chemical, and such weapons of mass destruction could be in warheads atop German-designed missiles. The Austrian's tale dovetailed neatly with Harel's fears.

Largely because of his habit of compartmentalization, laudable among intelligence professionals, Harel told no one else in the defense and security establishment about Joklik's presence in Israel. Still, the deputy defense minister, Shimon Peres, found out from his sources that Harel was secretly holding a man dubbed "the Austrian scientist." Peres insisted on meeting Joklik so that his ministry's top men could question him.

Harel refused. Peres then complained to Ben-Gurion and threatened to resign. The Old Man, as prime minister, ordered Harel to make Joklik available to the defense ministry.

In his other role, as defense minister, Ben-Gurion assigned the interrogation task to Binyamin Blumberg, chief of Lakam. Because his staff included scientists, Blumberg would be in a position to judge Harel's contention that Egypt was close to an ABC-weapons capability that imperiled the existence of Israel. The sense that he had to be judged only made Harel resent Blumberg and Peres more than ever.

Blumberg's analysts rejected Joklik's information on the alleged dangers of the Egyptian missile project. They concluded that the Austrian's scientific credentials were doubtful.

Harel, however, still felt certain that Nasser was plotting the destruction of Israel, and the Memuneh still believed in Joklik. In fact, Harel sent the Austrian—now employed as a Mossad agent—on a mission to Switzerland. He was teamed with an Israeli calling himself Yosef Ben-Gal, whose real name was Baruch Presher, and their goal was intimidation. They approached the daughter of Paul Goercke, one of the German scientists still working in Egypt on Nasser's missile project, and warned of dire consequences if her father did not leave Cairo at once.

Heidi Goercke's reaction took the overconfident Israelis by surprise. She informed the Swiss police of the threats she had just received, and they arrested the two Mossad agents outside a hotel in Basel on March 15, 1963.

Just a few weeks earlier, two Israeli agents had been arrested in Germany, near the home of another of the rocket scientists. The Mossad had been lucky that its warm relations with the BND prompted West German intelligence to arrange the quiet release of the Israelis.

Joklik and Ben-Gal/Presher were not so fortunate in Switzerland. Joklik did, at least, get to testify in open court that he knew of Egypt's plans to develop weapons of mass destruction. In addition, one of the prosecutors spoke with empathy about Ben-Gal's desire to protect his own country from Nasser's dastardly intentions. Still, the defendants were convicted and sent to prison. They served only two months, but the entire incident cast Israel in an embarrassing light.

Harel, clearly a man who never gave up, also launched a campaign in the press. Mossad operatives gave briefings to some foreign reporters. Harel also, for the first and probably only time, used Israeli journalists as agents by sending them to Europe to find out whatever they could about the German scientists.

The articles that appeared caused panic among the Israeli public about the ballistic missile danger from Egypt. Ben-Gurion was furious. He rebuked Harel for leaking to newspapers, and for spoiling good relations with West Germany.

The prime minister demanded that Harel's unauthorized crusade come to an end. Harel refused, and he sought backing from other members of the ruling Mapai party, including Foreign Minister Golda Meir and Finance Minister Levi Eshkol. At the time, the political disputes over the Lavon Affair—cover-ups concerning the sloppy sabotage missions in Egypt—were at their peak of ferocity.

For the first time since 1948, Harel was standing with Ben-Gurion's opponents. He was still hoping to bypass his mentor's veto, so he could renew his holy war against the Nazi scientists. In Ben-Gurion's eyes, however, that was tantamount to treason.

Amos Manor, who said that as Shin Bet chief he always accepted that he was subordinate to Harel, spoke many years later about the Memuneh's obsessions: "Our relationship also soured because of the affair of the German scientists. He began to operate contrary to Ben-Gurion's policy, because The Old Man did not accept his crazy theories. Isser claimed that the German chancellor Konrad Adenauer was playing a double game with Israel, and was presumably helping Nasser to develop atomic weapons. I thought that Adenauer was making every effort to restore Germany to the community of normal nations, and therefore there was no possibility that he would help Nasser attain atomic weapons."

Manor continued: "I saw that Isser had lost all sense of proportion. I told him: 'Ben-Gurion doesn't understand you, and I don't understand you either.'"

The prime minister seemed worried now about all the power he had given to Harel. The issue of the German scientists had torn large holes in the relationship between the two old friends, and flood waters rushed into the breach to sweep away their once-solid trust.

On March 25, 1963, 10 days after Joklik and Ben-Gal were arrested in Switzerland, Harel submitted a letter of resignation. He hoped that Ben-Gurion would reject the letter and would ask him to remain as Memuneh. He had come to believe the myth that he had created about himself. Harel believed that he was indispensable.

Ben-Gurion thought otherwise.

This was the end of an exceedingly busy era. The great crusader had fallen on his own sword.

CHAPTER SEVEN

A MODERN MOSSAD

An army messenger handed a slip of paper to Major General Meir Amit. "Contact the prime minister's office in Tel Aviv immediately," he read, before folding the message neatly and slipping it into the breast pocket of his army uniform. It was March 26, 1963, and Amit was on a tour of military units near the Dead Sea.

About three hours later, he arrived at David Ben-Gurion's office—nominally a mere branch of the main bureau in Jerusalem. It was a two-story, stone building, similar to other unimposing houses with porches along the narrow tree-lined streets of the Kirya, Tel Aviv's military zone.

Ben-Gurion shook Amit's hand and then showed him a copy of a letter sent a few hours earlier to Isser Harel. It was the prime minister's acceptance of the Memuneh's resignation. Not even pausing to ask Amit if he wanted a new job, Ben-Gurion simply said, "You will be the next head of the Mossad."

It was an order. Amit, of course, obeyed.

The general was surprised by the sudden job offer, although he was among the many who believed that it was time for Harel to go after 12 years of wielding extraordinary power.

Another surprise, however, was Ben-Gurion's decision that Amit would not have the same power as Harel. There would never again be a Memuneh in charge of both espionage abroad and counterespionage at home. Responsibility for Shin Bet would go to someone else.

Amit did, in a different way, begin his new duties by wearing two hats. A year earlier, he had been appointed head of Aman—a very sensible post for a respected military man, and the crowning achievement of a long career in uniform. He kept the Aman job for the rest of 1963, while shifting his focus to modernizing the Mossad.

Unlike previous intelligence chiefs, he was not born in Europe. He entered the world as Meir Slutzki in 1926 in Tiberias, in British-ruled Palestine. Brought up as a socialist, Slutzki/Amit joined Kibbutz Alonim in the lower Galilee and enlisted in the Haganah underground army, fighting the British and Palestinian Arabs. He was a company commander in the 1948 War of Independence, and after the victory he felt torn between his lifestyle values and his commitment to defending Israel. Instead of returning to the kibbutz, he chose to remain in the army, the new Israel Defense Forces.

Through the 1950s, Amit commanded infantry and tank units, and he was one of the men who developed the principle of "Follow me!" It became the Israeli army's trademark—that the IDF officer does not remain in the rear but leads his troops into battle, setting an example of courage. Amit became a good friend of General Moshe Dayan and served as his aide-de-camp in the 1956 Suez campaign. Amit took some time off for a liberal arts education, including a degree in economics from New York's Columbia University.

When offered the opportunity to be Aman chief in 1962, perhaps Amit should have thought twice. Harel did not like him and said it was a mistake to choose a man with no intelligence experience. Furthermore, there was no doubt that Aman lived in the huge shadow cast by the Mossad during Harel's years as Memuneh.

Shortly after taking over at Aman headquarters in the Kirya, Amit tried to lessen the hostility and competition between his agency and Harel's Mossad. But tension between the two agency chiefs only intensified.

They did not simply have differences of opinion, but two entirely divergent mentalities. Harel was a virtuoso of operations, while Amit specialized in military strategy. Harel happily scurried around Europe for months searching for little Yossele Schumacher or some other quarry, while sleeping on cots and shivering during street surveillance. Amit's military intelligence officers found the Mossad's methods laughable, because it yielded so little information on the military capabilities of the Arab countries.

Senior army commanders, naturally, expected vastly improved productivity when Amit became the Mossad chief. He was one of their own, and it seemed inevitable that efficiency and coordination would be bolstered by his dual roles at the Mossad and Aman. No one before had held those two posts.

Amit also set a precedent as the highest ranking outsider ever to join the Mossad. A huge negative for him was that most staffers still felt strong allegiance to Harel. At the handover—on the very day that Ben-Gurion sprang his surprise—the fallen Memuneh was "as sour as a lemon," as Amit later recalled. Harel said a few perfunctory words and then simply stood up and left. Harel's three secretaries burst into tears. A legend in his own time had just walked away.

The next day, March 27, a decoded telex message arrived on the new Mossad chief's desk. It expressed alarm at Harel's departure and stressed that "every effort must be made to bring him back." The declaration was signed by the Mossad's most senior operatives in Europe. They used code names so as to observe security precautions in communications, and Amit had to ask his assistants to ascertain that the letter was from Shmuel Toledano, a veteran of Moroccan and South American Jewish adventures; Paris-based operations chief Yitzhak Shamir; and a few others.

They had considered a collective resignation, but in the end decided only to send the one harsh telex. Their protest was less severe than the Revolt of the Spies 22 years earlier, when the foreign ministry's Political Department was reorganized.

Still, Amit had no sympathy or patience for letter writers and petition signers. He came from a different tradition, where the military chain of command was respected. If a commander falls in battle or departs for any other reason, he can and must be replaced.

The new Mossad chief shot back a strong response aimed at quelling the discontent. "I do not accept your behavior," Amit wrote. "I am not accustomed to collective protests."

The bad blood within the secret service prompted Amit to order that Harel's sabotage operations against the German scientists in Egypt be investigated. A special committee of cabinet ministers mounted an inquiry, and Harel was given access to the Mossad's files before reluctantly testifying before the panel.

The clash of styles and personalities was never settled. The mutual repulsion between Amit and Harel gained strength with each passing year.

Huge changes in Israel's government, ironically, helped reduce tensions. In June 1963, three months after Ben-Gurion forced Harel to quit, the Old Man himself resigned as prime minister. He was tired of the internal power struggles of the Mapai party over the Lavon Affair, which ate away at Ben-Gurion and finally toppled him nine years after the sabotage ring was arrested.

Ben-Gurion stalked off to found a new, centrist political party, Rafi, with his supporters Moshe Dayan and Shimon Peres. Still controlling a majority of Knesset seats, Mapai chose Levi Eshkol as the new prime minister.

Eshkol showed great interest in intelligence. He was awed by the work of the Mossad. From time to time, he would compliment Amit on the work of his agents. Amit would then make sure that Eshkol, who had been the minister of finance and understood government purse strings, enlarged the Mossad's budget. This enabled Amit to hire some of his own men and women and accelerate his reform of the secret agency.

During the nine months he ran both agencies, just a few houses apart in the Kirya, Amit transferred military intelligence's élite operations arm, Unit 131, from Aman to the Mossad. The move clearly helped Unit 131, which had seen its reputation sullied by the Lavon Affair. It now was integrated with two small operations units in Mossad, and the new entity was code-named Caesarea. Its operatives would be called, in Mossad parlance, *lochamim* ("combatants" or "warriors"): a morale-boosting name that also made them feel distinct from the men and women working at headquarters.

Yitzhak Shamir did not like the change and resigned. Within two years, all the senior field operatives who had signed the protest telex to Amit left the Mossad.

As replacements, Amit installed his own top operatives. He brought several of them from Aman, including Colonel Yosef Yariv, who was made the new operations chief at Caesarea.

Amit aimed to transform the Mossad into a serious, up-to-date intelligence organization focusing on what he considered its primary task: the collection of military and political data on the Arab states.

He regarded the Mossad as mainly an information-gathering body that would henceforth eschew show-off operations, which he viewed as a waste of resources. There would probably be no more risky and expensive kidnapping of Nazis, and no international hunts for missing Yosseles. Influenced by the economics and business courses he took in the United States, Amit wished to imitate that country's corporate mentality and style of management.

It was Amit who moved the Mossad's headquarters into new, corporate-style premises, in the Hadar Dafna office building in the center of Tel Aviv—escaping from the modest huts of the Kirya. The agency chief granted himself an American-style office—plush, by Israeli standards of the 1960s, with wood paneling and stylish new furniture. Even from the domestic design point of view, the austere-monkish era of Isser Harel was over. Amit was out to modernize the Mossad, and fresh new quarters were part of the plan.

Amit also changed the Mossad's methods of recruitment. Rather than relying on recommendations by friends, along the lines of a British "old-boy network," he preferred to use more systematic techniques. He made an effort to spot potential candidates, not only in the army, but in universities, in the business world, and among new immigrants.

Still, there were no Mossad women regularly going out into "the field" to fight for their country. Females were employed almost exclusively in administrative capacities. "A woman cannot gather information in the Arab world," one of the senior men in the Mossad explained. "The different way in which women are treated in Arab society prevents us from employing women as operatives or case officers. Arab agents wouldn't accept them. They would see a woman like that and jump out the window."

The changes in the agency under Amit did lead to some improvement in opportunities for women, though. The new boss's demand for proficiency and professionalism gave women a fairer chance to be appointed to run "desks" covering specific regions or subjects. These were women who had slowly made their way up through the ranks, until they were finally made responsible for a single area of expertise.

Only when a specific mission required women would a female be sent on an overseas assignment, and that was decided after all other avenues were explored and dismissed. For example, when a Caesarea combatant in a dangerous field assignment needed a female companion to improve his cover story, he would be escorted by a Mossad female who was especially trained for the mission.

There was also a slightly increased use of women in action for purposes of sexual entrapment, but very reluctantly. "It was rarely expected of them to use sex as one of many weapons in the field," said Hesi Carmel, who was Amit's chief of staff. "If sexual blackmail or entrapment was to be an integral part of the mission, we often employed prostitutes, and they could be Israelis or foreigners. We were surprised how some of Israel's streetwalking law-breakers proved to be surprisingly patriotic, although the secret agency did not tell them any details of the operation or even the identity of the men whom they were ordered to bed."

There was less hesitation in sending the men of Mossad abroad to exploit—as part of their official missions—the sexual hunting grounds. Carefully selected, with handsomeness a key attribute, these Israeli operatives are expected to befriend—and usually to become intimate with—an international array of targets. Lovers and pillow talkers can provide much valuable information about the diplomats, airports, and cities of the Arab world and other countries.

Most of the Mossad structure and characteristics of today were developed during Amit's years.

The most important sections of the Mossad were the Collection Department (known as Tsomet—Hebrew for "Junction"), two operational departments (Caesarea being one; the other, founded in 1966, called Keshet—which means "Arc" or "Rainbow," specializing in surveillance and break-ins), the Research Department, and the Department of Political Action and Liaison (known as Tevel, meaning "Universe," in charge of contacts with foreign agencies).

There are also support functions done by the Training, Finance and Manpower, Technology, and Technical Operations departments. The effectiveness of this corporate structure, with its foundations laid during Amit's time, can be seen in the fact that it barely changed over the next 50 years.

The Collection, Research, and Political-Liaison departments were organized on both regional and functional bases, and they are highly specialized: to deal only with southeast Asia, or to think about only weapons of mass destruction. The Mossad had a virtual monopoly on the collection of intelligence outside Israel, with the exception of certain military targets—usually not far from Israel's borders—on which Aman could spy.

Mossad's reliance on human intelligence expertise—*humint*—shifted with the passage of time and personalities. Harel had been a great believer in the power of people's instincts. His own were excellent, if imperfect; he preferred unexplained, but well practiced, inspiration over dependence on cold, unfeeling technology.

Harel did not hide his scorn for electronic gadgets, even though Israel was home to some of the world's greatest inventors. He was always proud of the fact that his Mossad, unlike other espionage agencies in the West, was an organization that relied on human resources and human intelligence. As such, it was almost universally acknowledged by experts as the world's finest example of humint.

The Mossad, under Amit, continued to be primarily humint-oriented, but other strengths were also stressed. Advanced computers were introduced to the agency in large numbers, and a great deal of effort and resources were channeled toward improving the Mossad's technological capabilities.

Above all, however, Amit is credited with refocusing the Mossad on the traditional role of an intelligence body: to collect information by all means about enemies, to eliminate miscellaneous and often meaningless tiny operations, and to look for broader horizons so as to develop a better understanding of the world—foes and friends alike.

The well-organized Mossad would never forget that its customer—the consumer of the intelligence—was the nation's elected leadership, hungry for knowledge to help its efforts to pursue peace and prevent war.

If and when Israel were attacked, or Israel felt it had no choice but to initiate violent action, the Mossad's job was to make sure that the military had the best intelligence to win the war.

Amit's Mossad planted more quality combatants in the Arab world than before. It upgraded relations with friendly secret services around the globe. It established secret ties with Arab leaders and engaged in more clandestine efforts aimed at avoiding war.

To achieve these goals, Amit departed dramatically from Harel's traditions and trends. But the new Mossad chief, despite his personal preference, could not stop the hunt for Nazi war criminals. The sense of historic duty was unavoidable—even for such a modern and practical agency director as Amit.

In 1964, he ordered the Caesarea department's chief Yosef Yariv to find and kill Herbert Cukurs, known as "The Butcher of Riga" for all the murders of Jews he ordered in Latvia's capital during World War II. Cukurs was on the "most wanted Nazis" list prepared in the 1950s by the Mossad.

Amit recalled decades later: "I and Prime Minister Eshkol, who approved the operation, reached the conclusion that after the dramatic impression which the Eichmann trial in Jerusalem made on us and the world, having one more trial of a Nazi war criminal would not create the same impact. It was more effective and less complicated to kill him."

Born in 1900, Cukurs had become a hero in the small republics along the Baltic Sea because of his pioneering long-distance flights to West Africa and to-and-from Tokyo. He was called "the Latvian Charles Lindbergh." After the Germans occupied Latvia and its neighbors in 1941, Cukurs enthusiastically became a general in the Arajs Kommando, a regiment of murderous collaborators that later was blamed for killing half of Latvia's more than 60,000 Jews.

After Germany's defeat, Cukurs managed to escape to Brazil, where he prospered as a tour operator and owner of small airplanes.

Israel's political purpose in deciding to kill him was to send a message to the governments of Europe, and above all Germany. They were halting their pursuit and prosecution of Nazi war criminals. An assassination by the Mossad would be a way of telling the Europeans that if they did not take action through their legal channels, then they would have to face the young Jewish state's settling of scores in its own fashion.

The mission went into motion in February 1965. The Caesarea Department operative chosen to make first contact was an experienced man, with some ideas and a cover story that might penetrate the closed social circle around the suspicious Cukurs. The Israeli posed as a wealthy Austrian businessman, and he used some local Jews and Israelis living in Brazil as sayanim to help him navigate through Cukurs's neighborhood.

The operative was able to befriend the Latvian pilot, then 65 years old, gaining his trust and persuading him to take a business trip to Montevideo, the capital of neighboring Uruguay.

The Mossad had already rented a house there, where Yariv and three other combatants were waiting. Their plan was to stage a miniature "trial," in which Cukurs would be declared guilty of murdering 30,000 Jewish men, women, and children. A sentence of death would be immediately carried out by the judge, jury, and executioners from Israel.

When Cukurs entered the Montevideo villa, he sensed something was wrong. He fought back, bit Yariv's hand, and nearly grabbed Yariv's pistol. The Israelis felt no choice but to shoot him, on the spot, using guns equipped with silencers.

The next day, yet another Mossad operative—part of a new unit for "psychological warfare," tasked with spreading disinformation and fanning rumors—phoned a news agency in Montevideo to report that there was a body in the villa. The Israelis hoped that European and South American governments would realize that Zionist justice was real and potent; instilling some fear in Nazi war criminals would probably be a good thing, too.

Yet, nothing happened. A few days passed, and not a word appeared in the Uruguayan or other news media.

Amit ordered that another call be placed, and this time the killing did hit the headlines. Major dailies and magazines around the world told of police finding the body of the formerly flashy Latvian aviation hero, covered with blood, in a large box inside the house. A note was attached to Cukurs's chest, declaring that he had been convicted of mass murder of Jews and was punished for his crimes "by those who would never forget."

The long-distance execution mission achieved its purpose. West Germany's government cancelled its plan to declare a statute of limitations on the prosecution of Nazis.

Although Amit had doubts about spending time, money, and resources on this hunt, he felt encouraged by the success in Brazil and Uruguay. Mossad men, even assassins from the Caesarea Department, could act with apparent impunity in two more South American countries.

Amit told Caesarea to pursue more names on the decade-old list of targets. Efforts were made, yet again, to locate Dr. Josef Mengele, but they led nowhere.

The closest the Mossad got to yet another Nazi war criminal was in 1967, when some strong leads were developed on Heinrich Müller, the brutal head of the Gestapo secret police in Hitler's Germany. A member of Yariv's operations team, Yair Racheli, recalled: "We believed that we were getting close to Müller. We located the address of his wife. The plan was to break into her apartment in Munich, to find letters and photographs—which, presumably, if he was alive, he was sending to his wife. We thought that from the letters we would find his whereabouts."

Racheli and a partner arrived at the building and started climbing the stairs. But they were spotted by suspicious neighbors, who called the police. The two Israelis were arrested and later sentenced to six months in jail—but they never broke down to authorities and stuck to their cover story that they were British businessmen. West German intelligence suspected that they were Mossad men but chose to turn a blind eye, in the spirit of goodwill that the new Germany's security officials generally displayed toward the Jewish state.

Eshkol and Amit did eventually phone their counterparts to tell the truth and ask that the two Israelis be released. They were set free, after serving three months behind bars.

Müller was never found. Some investigators believe he died in or near the bunker in Berlin where Hitler committed suicide in April 1945.

Cukurs was the last and—by officially sanctioned action—the only Nazi liquidated by Mossad hit men.

Despite the failure of the break-in in Munich, and what Yariv discovered to be another abortive attempt just before that in the same city, the Mossad was working hard on new, even elaborate, methods for penetrating what were called "still objects."

The chief innovator was Zvi Malkin, one of Adolf Eichmann's kidnappers in Argentina. He helped create the operational unit Keshet in 1966 and moved to Europe to replace Avraham Shalom—the future Shin Bet chief who would be caught up in a scandal over the 1984 killing of two bus hijackers. *(See Chapter 19.)*

One member of Keshet who took part in many break-ins reminisced: "Zvi completely changed our operational thinking. Under Shalom, the operations department was afraid of taking risks. Thus, we didn't dare break in to embassies or offices, only to hotel rooms in Western Europe, where the targets were usually Arab officials and military personnel." That was occasional work, only when a targeted Arab was visiting. But when methods were perfected to get inside buildings, "there started to be an operation almost every night."

The standard Keshet team consisted of two burglars, who were masters at picking or otherwise opening locks, plus one photographer. Another one or two Mossad operatives would be outside the building as look-outs in case Arabs who worked there, curious neighbors, passersby, or—even worse—the police might notice and approach.

One of the burglars would usually be fluent in Arabic, so that he could quickly sort through the documents found and thus instruct the photographer as to which ones were important.

One such Israeli would gain, within the halls of the Mossad, the reputation of a living legend. Nothing could stop Yaacov Barda, and no mission was impossible for him. Posing with incredible nerve as an Arab businessman, Barda specialized in befriending security guards. He would entertain them at bars and clubs, thus getting them out of the way for a while, as well as learning details of the buildings' security arrangements.

Twenty years later, in the mid-1980s, Barda would have diplomatic cover in London until being declared persona non grata by the British government. He was expelled because, as a Mossad case officer, he was running a Palestinian agent in a PLO cell that murdered a Kuwaiti political cartoonist in London.

Veterans of the Keshet operations unit remembered Barda's managing to persuade all three guards—at Egypt's embassy in a Western European country—to leave their shift for a night of drinks, gambling, and prostitutes. Barda's colleagues could then easily gain access to the building, take photographs, and plant microphones and transmitters.

On another continent, a Keshet team had an easier task. An Israeli contractor built an office building in which an Arab government located its embassy. Even before construction was completed, the contractor contacted the Mossad and invited it to take advantage of the situation. A Keshet team was sent with sophisticated microphones. The team waited until the workers at the site left for home at night and then planted bugging devices in the walls.

These operations and many others had one principal purpose: to collect as much data as possible and improve Israel's understanding of the Arab nations' capabilities and intentions. As this was before the rise of Palestinian terrorism, Israeli intelligence focused on two countries: Egypt and Syria.

Keshet and its burglars were not the only Mossad operatives who contributed to the goal. No less important were the relations cultivated by members of the Tevel department.

Under Amit, the Mossad became an alternative foreign ministry—to the chagrin of Foreign Minister Abba Eban and his diplomats. Tevel personnel did highly valuable work by expanding liaison ties with steady allies: the CIA, the West German BND, and the British MI6. In Washington, Bonn, London, and also in Paris and Rome, the Israelis exchanged ideas and shared information with each country's intelligence agency.

Many of those liaison partners had the ability to send intelligence agents to Arab countries, because their nations had diplomatic representation in places where Israelis were still officially banned. There were many opportunities for Israel to request, and to receive, assistance in those hard-to-reach areas.

This was one of the areas of action where the Mossad's relations with West Germany—specifically, the BND, led by General Gehlen—were especially useful.

The Mossad became expert at "false flag recruitment," in which a paid agent—such as an Arab, perhaps shuttling frequently between his home country and Europe—would agree to help an espionage project in many ways. The agent, though, would never know that he was working for Israel. The Mossad case officer would typically let the recruit believe that the money and instructions came from Washington, London, Brussels, or Madrid.

A false flag was the key to recruiting, for instance, Jack Leon Thomas. He was a highly educated Armenian who grew up in Cairo and moved to West Germany in early 1958 so he could try his hand at various commercial enterprises. This Israeli approach occurred while Harel was the Memuneh, but the method would be used under Amit and his successors—and continues apace today.

Thomas, while frequenting bars in Bonn and Cologne, kept bumping into a friendly Lebanese man named Emil. The party never stopped for young Emil, and he was obviously wealthy because he would always pick up the tab. They talked about business and women, and when the chat drifted into politics Thomas did not hide his hatred for Egypt's President Nasser.

One evening, Emil offered Jack a huge amount of money and suggested that he return to Egypt to help overthrow the corrupt dictator. Thomas was told he would be working for one of the NATO countries.

In a small apartment in Cologne, anonymous people taught him the basics of espionage: photographing documents and developing the film; hiding negatives in toothpaste tubes, shoe boxes, or books; writing with invisible ink; and passing coded messages by leaving them in "dead letter drops" for unknown accomplices.

Full of enthusiasm, Thomas returned to Cairo in July 1958 and began recruiting informers into his network. From time to time, he would travel to West Germany for meetings with his operators, who continued to pose as "senior officials in NATO." In return for the military information Thomas brought with him, his case officers gave him money and new orders.

Thomas was tasked with recruiting his own agents in Cairo—a kind of clandestine subcontracting. He tried to recruit an Egyptian army officer, but that officer reported the approach and had Thomas arrested. His apartment was found to have a treasure trove of espionage gear: five cameras, a suitcase with a false bottom, an electric shaver with a secret compartment for hiding documents, a hollow cigarette lighter for hiding film negatives, and a sophisticated two-way radio. He never even knew that it had all come from the Mossad.

An Egyptian military court convicted Thomas and two of his recruits of espionage and treason, and the three men were hanged in December 1962.

The Mossad was encouraged, at that time, by the CIA to penetrate the awakening continent of Africa. While the United States might be rejected by newly independent black nations, suspicious of superpower imperialism, Israel was seen as an imaginative and progressive success with a lot to offer. Israeli experts in agriculture, construction, and military training were welcome guests.

The CIA secretly underwrote some of these projects, occasionally with money funnelled through labor unions and the AFL-CIO.

The Mossad's leading force in Africa in the 1960s was David Kimche. Under various guises and names, he worked all over the continent. His preferred legend was that of a journalist. That was relatively easy, since Kimche, an immigrant from England, had been a night editor for *The Jerusalem Post* before he joined the Mossad in 1953. His elder brother Jon was also a journalist and editor of the *Jewish Observer and Middle East Review*, published in London, and he was happy to help David by providing press credentials to him and other "journalists" from the Mossad.

David Kimche leveraged those "media" operations to launch the Mossad's psychological warfare activities. As he saw it, a key role was to befriend journalists all over the world and to provide them with tips on hot stories—usually highly speculative, and only partially factual. False information that might hurt Israel's enemies could be planted, as could other stories that might help Israel gauge the likely reactions to some step Israel was considering.

"It worked very well," Kimche recalled years later, "and we didn't have any problems getting our stories into major, respectable daily newspapers and weeklies."

Veiled by Israel's image—then considered friendly, fresh, and innocent in Africa—the Mossad would occasionally conspire against regimes that were clearly hostile to Western countries. A case in point was Zanzibar, a small island off the east African coast. Until 1964, it was ruled by a sultan whose senior courtiers were descendants of Arabian slave traders. The black majority rebelled against the sultan and seized power. Kimche "happened" to be in Zanzibar on the day of the revolution, and on behalf of the Mossad he offered the rebels further assistance. Israel was happy to see the elimination of at least one government where Arabs had heavy influence in Africa.

Just to the north, the Mossad had a large presence in Kenya's capital, Nairobi. Tevel formed very close relations with a Scotsman named Bruce McKenzie, a farmer who was a confidant of President Jomo Kenyatta and was the only white man in his cabinet.

The Mossad-McKenzie channel would prove its value a decade later, when preparatory work had to be hurriedly done for Israeli commando forces to rescue hijacked air passengers from Entebbe in Uganda on July 4, 1976. Kenya was cooperative with Israel in every, usually unacknowledged, way possible. (*See Chapter 12 for more on the historic Entebbe operation.*)

In neighboring Sudan, Mossad operatives were helping the South Sudanese Liberation Army in its struggle for independence from the Muslim-dominated central government in Khartoum. Sudan's government was an ally of Egypt, which was then Israel's most formidable enemy.

Looking across from the Horn of Africa, where Israeli secret agents were often active, the countries of Arabia were just on the other side of the Gulf of Aden. The Mossad had a role in Yemen, where the monarchy was toppled in 1962 and a civil war ensued. Egypt's army and air force rushed to help the rebels hold on to power, and Cairo's assistance included brutal bombing raids.

A strange coalition of bedfellows took action to counter Egyptian President Nasser's incursion: Saudi Arabia's royal military, the Mossad, and the British MI6, with additional support from a private security firm led by Colonel David Stirling, a legend from fighting the Germans in North Africa in World War II. Stirling created the potent and feared SAS, Britain's Special Air Service commandos.

This coalition helped the Yemen's monarchists. The British trained them, the Saudis sent foot soldiers, and Mossad agents coordinated drops of ammunition by the Israeli air force.

Israel did not really care who ruled either South Yemen or North Yemen. Israel's interest was to make the Egyptian Army bleed in the treacherous terrain of Yemen, keeping Nasser at bay and busy, far away from the Israeli border.

The Mossad's globetrotting extended into Southeast Asia, when Amit's assistant, Hesi Carmel, was sent to be the Mossad station chief in one of the small countries of that region. From that base, he had the sensitive task of forging secret relations with the largest Muslim nation on earth—Indonesia. Officially, Jakarta was hostile toward Israel. This was expressed in part by Indonesia being the birthplace in 1955 of the Non-Aligned Movement, which refused to be part of the Western or Soviet blocs but was unfriendly toward Israel.

In secret, however, Indonesia agreed to buy weapons from the Jewish state, and its military was trained by Israeli experts. The connection could be useful for Israel in many ways, certainly including the cash input from the arms and training contracts. This was yet another fruit of the Mossad's alternative diplomacy.

Especially in the immediate vicinity of the Middle East, the fundamental principle that guided these hectic activities was this: The enemy of my enemy is my friend. That dictum, put into practice again and again by Israel, was supplemented by Mossad founder Reuven Shiloah's "peripheral" notion: that Israel should make friends with non-Arab minorities, with Muslim non-Arab states, and even with moderate pro-Western Arab leaders.

As a prime example, Jordan's King Hussein agreed to meet Israeli prime ministers, foreign ministers, and generals. The first encounters were at the home of Emanuel Herbert, a prestigious Harley Street physician in London who was the king's Jewish doctor and a good friend of the Israelis, too.

After 1967, the meetings would take place closer to home, at secret spots near the long Israeli-Jordanian border. One of the main goals, from Israel's point of view, was to keep Jordan out of the Nasser camp.

To achieve a nearly complete encirclement of Egypt, the Mossad managed to gain access to another Muslim country: the North African kingdom of Morocco. The Mossad thus had good information along a strategic coastline and in part of the Sahara Desert. In exchange, Israeli intelligence officers trained the Moroccan secret police.

The relationship led to unexpected dilemmas. The Moroccans demanded that the Mossad help them hunt for Mehdi Ben Barka, a charismatic opposition leader who tried to stir up a revolution in his country and was forced into exile in Switzerland. The head of the secret police, General Mohammed Oufkir, then explicitly asked Amit to have Ben Barka killed.

The Mossad chief hesitated. He knew that rejecting the request might imperil a very valuable relationship. Yet, he also knew that it would be wrong, on many levels, to turn his Caesarea operatives into a mercenary force—Murder Incorporated, Mafia-style—in the service of a foreign regime.

Amit consulted with Eshkol, and they decided on a compromise. The Mossad would give non-lethal assistance, helping the Moroccans locate Ben Barka and persuading him to come to Paris—but that would be all.

Mossad operatives, posing as a film crew, found the Moroccan dissident in October 1965 and invited him to meet them in a fashionable café on the Left Bank. General Oufkir was waiting there, with a team that included Moroccan agents and French mercenaries.

Oufkir's men spirited away Ben Barka and tortured him in a villa. He was then either shot or stabbed, reportedly by Oufkir himself. A senior Mossad man based in Paris was apparently nearby, maintaining contact out of some strange sense of courtesy.

The corpse was never found, but over the years a few details of the murder emerged. In Israel, military censorship prevented anything about the Mossad being mentioned in the press, but people close to Israeli intelligence whispered about an unusual lethal mission that was beyond the Mossad's control.

Unluckily for Amit, Harel had returned to government service as a special advisor to Eshkol, and this gave the ex-Memuneh an opportunity to blame his successor for the Morocco misjudgment: a terrible idea that was hatched behind the prime minister's back. Eshkol and Amit knew the truth, however: that both of them had decided to give Morocco's Oufkir the help he was demanding.

They together quashed Harel's attacks on Amit, underlining that if this became an open, international scandal like the fiasco in Cairo—the Lavon Affair, a decade earlier—it would cause damage to Israel and specifically to Eshkol's government.

Yet the Mossad and Israel did not escape unpunished. Furious and proud, President Charles de Gaulle ordered that the large and important Mossad station in Paris be shut down.

Again and again through Israel's history, its operatives learned that partnerships with foreigners could be tactically useful, but that it would be a reckless abandonment of Israel's principles and sovereignty to depend mostly on others. Self-reliance, in crises large and small, would be a hallmark of the intelligence community.

CHAPTER EIGHT

SPYING WAR ON THE HORIZON

I knew that as head of Aman and then the Mossad, history would judge me based on two metrics," said Meir Amit, almost half a century after his heyday in the 1960s. "One would be the prevention of war, and the second on providing the best intelligence, analysis, and understanding of our enemies' capabilities and intentions."

Amit and his Aman and Mossad people worked simultaneously on both fronts. Supported by the dovish Prime Minister Levi Eshkol, a higher priority was often placed on preventing war. Amit optimistically believed that if he could just establish contact with Egypt's top echelon—and above all with its belligerent President Gamal Nasser—some basis for compromise could be found.

Amit sought channels—or, to use an intelligence term, "levers"—that could be manipulated to help achieve the goal of reaching the Egyptian leadership. Surprisingly, he found them in Otto Skorzeny, a Nazi war hero.

Surely this was a sensational double standard, gilded in hypocrisy. Israel was born from the ashes of the Holocaust, and its intelligence operatives were in hot pursuit of Nazi war criminals. Yet, at the same time, Israeli espionage agencies never missed an opportunity to use Nazis when finding them valuable for a mission—as Harel and Amit did with Skorzeny.

During World War II, he had proudly worn the uniform of the Waffen SS—the Nazi Party's most loyal soldiers. Marred but also somehow glorified by having a stereotypical scar on his face, Skorzeny proved to be more than just a true believer. He was also a charismatic, creative, and clever warrior.

In Italy, he rose to Nazi fame after commanding a daring rescue mission in July 1943 that freed the deposed dictator Benito Mussolini from captivity. Three months later, Skorzeny commanded the failed Long Jump operation intended to assassinate the Big Three leaders—Winston Churchill, Josef Stalin and Franklin Roosevelt—during their summit meeting in Tehran.

A year later, he was in charge of an ambitious deception plan, in which he disguised more than a hundred German soldiers in captured American and British uniforms and sent them in captured jeeps to infiltrate Allied lines. This was a violation of internationally recognized rules of war, and Skorzeny later was put on trial as a "war criminal." The tribunal in Dachau found him not guilty, however, after a British Special Forces officer testified that he also had dressed his own men as the enemy—in German uniforms and insignia.

Skorzeny was next held in a de-Nazification camp, but he escaped in 1948: first to France, and then Spain. He was soon back in the shadowy world of conspiracies and excitement.

He set up an engineering company, which served as a front for smuggling his ex-SS comrades to South America by providing them with false documents. In this capacity, Skorzeny was the Spanish coordinator of a route known as the Rat Lines, believed to be part of an organization of former Nazi officers calling itself Odessa.

That was not the only thrill in Skorzeny's new life. He also reestablished relations with General Gehlen, the Nazi spymaster who was now heading West Germany's BND spy agency. Gehlen had a knack for playing many sides: the darling of the newborn CIA, cooperating with the Mossad, but also occasionally helping Arab regimes.

After the revolution in Egypt that toppled King Farouk in 1952 and eventually brought Colonel Nasser to power, Gehlen sent some German professionals to help the new government in Cairo. Among them was the ex-SS colonel from Spain, Skorzeny, who was assigned to train Nasser's bodyguards.

German aid to Egypt was coordinated by the CIA's Archibald Roosevelt Jr., a grandson of President Theodore Roosevelt and a renowned linguist who served as an intelligence officer in many countries under diplomatic cover. Known as Archie, he truly had a long love affair with the Arab world. With disgust, he wrote that Israelis viewed Arabs as "alien, threatening, hateful, and inferior ... a people with whom they have nothing in common." He maintained that that explained what he considered the failures of Israeli intelligence.

American Arabists, including some in the CIA and the State Department, hoped in vain that Nasser would become a friend of America. The CIA certainly turned a blind eye to Skorzeny's Nazi past.

His activities and contacts in Egypt certainly did not go unnoticed by the Mossad. One day in the summer of 1962, when Skorzeny was at his office in Madrid, he had a visit from two mysterious men—one short, the other tall and solidly built, both in their late 30s. They introduced themselves as businessmen from a European country but soon revealed their true identity: representatives of the Israeli government.

This was three months after Adolf Eichmann was hanged in Israel. Senior Nazis in hideouts all over the world lived in fear that the "long arm" of the Israelis—the new and vengeful Jews—would reach out and grab them at any moment. As bold and adventurous as Skorzeny was, he is said to have thought to himself for a quick second: They found me. This is the end.

But this pair of Israelis did not come to kill him. They were out to seal a deal. The Mossad had found Skorzeny via his former second wife, who ran a metals trading business in Spain with a Jewish partner. The partner happened to be a sayan for the Mossad, and he persuaded Skorzeny's ex to facilitate a series of meetings.

After hearing that Skorzeny—when promised immunity from prosecution or assassination—would be willing to help Israel, intelligence chiefs sent the two operatives to Madrid. The short man was Rafi Eitan, the kidnapping expert who had become a multi-purpose all-rounder for the joint operations department of Shin Bet and the Mossad. The tall guy was Avraham Ahituv, who years later would be head of Shin Bet.

They were a bit surprised that Skorzeny did not ask for money. The ex-SS officer instead made an unexpected, self-aggrandizing request: that the Mossad help arrange for his memoirs to be published in Israel. The Israeli secret agents agreed.

Did the Nazi war hero know that, in exchange for a book deal, he might be fingering a group of former colleagues for assassination? In any event, within a few weeks, Skorzeny honored his side of the bargain. He contacted a former Waffen SS subordinate, who now was the security officer for the Germans, working in Egypt's secret weapons programs. The security officer treated the message from Skorzeny as an order from his commander and promptly sent back a list of German scientists, engineers, and technicians in Egypt.

This was a sudden bonanza for Isser Harel's collection of obsessions. The Memuneh sincerely believed that the Germans were helping Egypt to pursue what the Nazis did not accomplish: finishing off the Jewish race.

However, there were conflicting arguments made by military intelligence men under Amit's command. They felt that Harel was crying wolf, that Egypt was far from threatening Israel with missiles and weapons of mass destruction. Six months later, Harel was out of office, and Amit became the undisputed czar of the Israeli intelligence community.

One of the strongest traits of intelligence work is the phenomenal institutional memory: the seemingly minor, marginal details that are stored and never forgotten. Thus, a few years later, when Amit was exploring the possibility of peace with Egypt, he again thought of Skorzeny.

Once an intelligence asset, always an asset. Skorzeny was asked to facilitate a meeting between Amit and a senior Egyptian intelligence officer. The ex-Nazi delivered yet again. He arranged a meeting in Paris in 1966 with Mahmoud Khalil, a colonel in Egypt's air force intelligence who was in charge of a secret program to develop an indigenous Egyptian fighter plane with armaments. The program eventually failed, but Khalil remained a close confidant of the defense minister, Field Marshal Abdel Hakim Amr—the number-two man in Nasser's regime.

At the meeting in Paris, Amit offered to travel secretly to Cairo to meet Amr. "My plan was to reduce the tension between the two countries and prevent us from slipping into a war," Amit recalled many years later. "I wanted to offer a package deal to the Egyptian leadership: Israel and world Jewry would provide Egypt with financial support. In return, Egypt would ease the Arab economic boycott on Israel and allow the free movement of goods via the Suez Canal to Israel."

The meeting took place in good spirits, and Amit got the impression that his offer to visit Cairo might be welcome in the Egyptian capital. It certainly was clear that Khalil was acting on higher orders, not meeting on his own with Israel's intelligence chief.

Yet, when Amit returned home, he found that the indefatigable Harel had plotted behind his back. The ex-Memuneh convinced Prime Minister Eshkol not to allow Amit to go to Cairo, as it might be a trap. Harel painted a picture of a Mossad chief being arrested, tortured, and forced to spill state secrets to the enemy.

Angry, disappointed, and somewhat desperate, Amit felt that a great opportunity for lessening tension was being lost. Yet, he had no choice but to focus solely on the other high-priority task of the intelligence community: preparing his nation and its military for another round of hostilities with its Arab neighbors. An increasing rate of border clashes in the first half of the 1960s made a war seem inevitable.

Under Amit's prior command, Aman had begun to expand and refocus itself with high professionalism. The organization was tightly run, as might be expected from a military body.

Aman was comprised of four departments. One of them, Collection, was responsible for gathering information by two classic methods: humint, based on running networks of agents and informers outside the borders of Israel; and sigint, excelling at the interception of signals, such as military radio exchanges and telephone calls inside Arab countries.

The second department was known as *Mem-Mem*, the Hebrew initials for *Mivtza'im Meyuchadim* (Special Operations). It directed the army's finest commando force. Military officials always cloaked its missions in secrecy, even as Israelis took part in secretive border crossings. Soldiers went behind enemy lines to plant electronic bugs, or perhaps to kidnap or assassinate Israel's enemies.

Listening devices and transmitters were designed by the third major department of Aman: the Technological Directorate, which was nicknamed "the Toy Factory." The designers there produced silencers for guns, luggage with concealed compartments and hidden cameras, and innovative communications gear.

The fourth department—where all intelligence gathered was brought together—was a research team known as Production. This was the largest unit, and by early in the 21st century almost 5,000 of the 9,000 men and women in Aman worked in this department. Its central task was to classify, store, and analyze all the information that Aman collected.

Once a year, the director of the agency would use the data to write the National Intelligence Estimate. This small book—officially aimed at the prime minister, the defense minister, and the army chief of staff—often contained some bold predictions. The Aman commander's task was to review developments in the neighboring Middle East countries, blend in military, political, and economic analysis, and add all that up to yield the outlook for war or peace.

The agency adopted the name IDI, Israel Defense Intelligence, for its relationships with foreign countries—foremost among them the United States. Israel shifted its purchasing patterns in the 1960s so as to acquire the vast majority of its military hardware from America. First, there was a deal in 1962 for anti-aircraft Hawk missiles, and later for some warplanes: Skyhawks and, later, F-4 Phantom fighters.

That was the overt face of the growing military ties between the two countries. There was also a covert aspect: the growing trade in intelligence equipment. Aman began buying state-of-the-art systems from such manufacturers as Texas Instruments. This was the start of a new era of Israel-U.S. military and strategic cooperation.

Israel's intelligence community was among the first to introduce computers, though large and clunky, in the early 1950s. As links with the United States intensified, Amit and his successor at Aman, Major-General Aharon Yariv, wanted their agency's small high technology Unit 848 (later re-numbered 8200) to be modeled on America's stunningly powerful but clandestine National Security Agency. For many years, some of the staffers at NSA headquarters at Fort Meade, Maryland, were said to have joked that their employer's initials stood for No Such Agency. That kind of secrecy sounded terrific to Aman.

The designation 848 or 8200 had no particular meaning. In fact, the original eavesdropping unit in the 1948-49 War of Independence was a small team known as Intelligence Service Number 2. It came up with ways to plug in to Arab telephone lines and to glean important information on the movement of fighters in the field.

The unit had a valuable injection of fresh blood in the mid-1950s thanks to the success of "Jewish intelligence" projects: the arrival of bilingual Arabic- and English-speaking radio operators who had worked in the formerly British Iraqi railroad company. Those new immigrants were recruited to work in the unit as "listeners."

Amit and Yariv wanted to modernize and build a formidable central collection unit. It would be equipped with sophisticated sensors, listening devices, antennas, and cameras. Decades later, the seeds sown by the two generals would bear massive fruits. Unit 8200 would turn into an intelligence empire. It would have outposts—including radio dishes and antenna farms that tourists sometimes notice—in Israel's north, south, and east, on high terrain where the equipment looks out over the borders. The Unit is headquartered north of Tel Aviv, next to the Mossad's compound.

The main concerns of the unit are sigint and what intelligence jargon dubs "elint" (electronic intelligence). In everyday language, that means listening in to telephone, fax, radio, and other communications; deciphering coded messages; and using large reception dishes to detect telemetry from military maneuvers, such as missile launches.

Dozens of high-tech companies, both in Israel and in California's Silicon Valley, owe their existence to Israeli military veterans who were in 8200. They learned their craft in that intelligence unit, whether in the mandatory three years of national service or during a longer stint, and then many used their experience to create companies.

In the late 1950s and early '60s, however, the beginning of what would become Israel's ears and eyes was modest.

Amit knew that without creativity and the human touch the equipment would be worth nothing: just wires, switches, and future scrap metal and plastic. To operate all that was acquired, Aman and the Mossad needed Israel's best talents: the crème de la crème—mathematicians, programmers, code breakers, polyglots, and brave soldiers.

This kind of thinking led to the birth of an élite fighting unit, Sayeret Matkal. *Sayeret* is the word for reconnaissance, and *Matkal* is the Hebrew acronym for the military's General Staff. This unit, with a rarely mentioned numerical designator, 269, was created solely to serve the intelligence community. It was put under the direct command of the chief of staff and the head of Aman.

Before Sayeret Matkal was formed, the idea of highly trained, armed, and usually uniformed soldiers in "a shadow unit of ghosts" was bouncing around in the mid-1950s. The founder—a notable and practical dreamer—was Lieutenant Colonel Avraham Arnan, who was inspired by reading about Britain's glamorous Special Air Service (SAS). He kept pressing for creation of a unit that could be sent consistently into enemy territories to carry out top-secret intelligence gathering.

Sayeret Matkal uses a Hebrew motto that is basically identical to SAS's: "Who Dares Wins." Four words characterize the spirit of the Israeli unit: disguise, deception, cunning, and courage. Its fighters are trained in a variety of methods and know how to track quarries through deserts as nomadic Bedouin do. These Israeli soldiers are experts at using all sorts of weapons, including knives, as well as explosives and night vision equipment. They are exceptional specimens of physical fitness, training often with long runs or marches while carrying heavy equipment.

The unit happened to be established a year after the formation of Israel's first helicopter squadron. These flying machines gave Sayeret Matkal its favorite mode of transportation. Sayeret soldiers pioneered the military advantage of being ferried by helicopter under the dark cloak of night. Israeli infiltration teams could stay especially deep, and for a long time, inside hostile Arab countries.

As secret as the unit was supposed to be—just like Britain's SAS—Sayeret Matkal could not completely avoid making headlines. When, for example, its men rescued hostages from a hijacked airplane on the ground at Tel Aviv's international airport in 1972, the commandos garnered public recognition and a sky-high reputation.

Yet, their first and foremost mission was to sneak behind enemy lines and plant bugging devices.

From 1962 to 1972, when Generals Amit and Yariv led Aman, the Sayeret proved to be a potent addition to Israel's special forces capabilities. Many future combatants in the Mossad's operations units would come from the ranks of Sayeret Matkal.

Israeli intelligence was developing into a three-dimensional shadowy powerhouse. In the skies above, the Israeli Air Force acquired new types of aircraft from the United States and came up with innovations to prepare for battle. On land, Sayeret Matkal infiltration teams greatly expanded Aman's monitoring capabilities. Mossad agents, also on the ground but in highly unexpected locales, gathered information about Arab military capabilities.

The triple threat was a synchronized effort that transformed Arab armies and political leadership into an open book for Israeli intelligence.

This admirable blend of technology and human creativity reached its zenith in 1965, when the secret agencies filled an important gap in Israel's military knowledge base. As often occurs, success stemmed from a charismatic senior leader putting his fondest wish into words—for his wish literally becomes someone's command.

It was General Ezer Weizman, head of the air force and a future president of Israel, who told Amit: "If you get me a MiG-21, I promise we will easily defeat all of our neighbors' armies. All of them."

Russian aircraft factories had started churning out that fighter plane in 1959, and the Soviet Union exported many of them to its Communist puppet states and friendly countries. Israel and the rest of the West had never been able to take a close look at it, however. The CIA and the militaries of many American allies yearned to examine the latest example of Soviet technology, capable of flying at twice the speed of sound. The MiG-21 was a potent threat.

Amit's military intelligence planners considered a wide array of ideas for getting their hands on a MiG-21. One proposal, apparently hatched by someone who watched too many action movies, would have had a helicopter-borne Sayeret Matkal unit infiltrate an Egyptian airbase in the Sinai Peninsula. A smart Israeli pilot, perhaps one who reads Russian, would travel with the commandos. They would steal the MiG fighter jet, and he would fly it to Israel.

Another plan would have had an Israeli pilot pose as a South American purchasing agent, who would travel to Communist Poland and claim an interest in buying planes. He would ask for the aerial equivalent of a test drive, then would fly away in the MiG-21.

Eventually, a practical scheme was designed. The Mossad station in Tehran was ordered to find a pilot in neighboring Iraq who might be ready to defect. With a MiG-21.

The prevailing opinion was that, while difficult, this avenue offered Israel its best chance of success. Aman and the Mossad had already amassed a tremendous amount of information on the air forces of Egypt, Jordan, Syria, and Iraq. Israeli intelligence dossiers recorded every scrap of information on the enemy pilots, organized and stored by Aman using Amit's new computers.

The information was so comprehensive that those in charge of the files felt as if they personally knew hundreds of Arab pilots. One was an Egyptian captain, Abbas Hilmi, but they had no reason to think that he would surprise them one day. Yet Hilmi did just that, in January 1964, and even Israeli air defenses did not notice his low-altitude flight to a base southeast of Tel Aviv. He was defecting with his Russian-made airplane, but Aman was disappointed to see that it was an uninteresting Yak-11.

The motives behind his defection were also far from inspiring. Hilmi had been having an affair with his Egyptian commander's wife, and he was fleeing for his own safety.

The Israelis did give him a warm welcome, however, and for propaganda purposes—or as the Israelis privately termed it, psychological warfare—they had Hilmi speak in public about how Egypt was massacring fellow Arabs in Yemen's civil war.

The Egyptian turncoat was offered a new identity and a good job in Israel, but he was unable to acclimatize himself to life in the Jewish state. Rejecting strong advice from his intelligence handlers in Tel Aviv, Hilmi decided to move to South America. The Mossad furnished him with yet another set of false identity documents and gave him a large sum of cash to begin a new life in Argentina.

He made some fatal errors in Buenos Aires, however, drinking and talking too much while socializing with Egyptian expatriates. He was found dead in his apartment, and it was unclear whether he fell victim to the long arm of Egyptian secret police or to a drinking pal who saw Hilmi as a traitor.

Disappointed by Hilmi and his Yak, Israeli intelligence leaders pushed harder to get their hands on a MiG-21. The long search for a high-level Arab pilot continued, with Iraq still looking like fertile ground. Finally, a potential candidate was singled out. Years later, an Israeli journalist, influenced by James Bond movies, invented a sexy code name for the operation: "007." Officially, it was codenamed "Diamond."

The selected MiG provider was Munir Redfa, a member of a wealthy Maronite Christian family in Iraq, where non-Muslims generally suffered discrimination. Trained by the Soviets, he was a pilot in a squadron of MiG-21s.

The Israelis—thanks to newspaper clippings, Iraqi communications they intercepted, and agents on the ground in Baghdad—had an almost complete picture of Redfa's life. They learned that he had been upset about his air force's bombing and strafing raids on Kurdish villages in the north, as part of the suppression of that minority. The Mossad developed a psychological profile of the man, and that report suggested several conversational gambits and lines of approach.

Additional Mossad operatives flew into Tehran, and from there they crossed into Iraq. Contact was established with Redfa, and any concerns that the pilot might be resistant to Israelis—or report the contact to Iraqi security—were quickly assuaged. Redfa agreed to use his upcoming vacation to fly to Athens.

He honored his commitment by making a rendezvous with Mossad case officers in the Greek capital. Once in, Redfa was in all the way, and he accepted their invitation to fly on to Israel. They gave him a false passport, and the Iraqi—officially an enemy of the Jewish state—was a passenger on an El Al flight to Tel Aviv.

In Israel, he was taken on a tour of an air force base. That was where he met senior officers of the Mossad, Aman, and the air force to finalize a defection deal. He agreed to fly a MiG-21 to Israel. A navigational route was designed. Code words for radio communication were agreed.

There was one major obstacle, however. Redfa would, of course, receive a lifetime pension, but he made an additional thorny demand: that Israel extract his family, so they could be together. The Mossad felt it had no choice, and the pledge was made.

Redfa returned to Iraq via Athens. The Mossad's Tehran station needed a few months to arrange a smooth and invisible exit for Redfa's wife and children. They were flown to Israel, bearing false names and documents.

Redfa's next step turned out to be relatively easy. During a routine exercise in August 1966, he steered his Soviet-made airplane away from the other Iraqi pilots, and Redfa just kept on going, heading West.

He flew over Jordan and into the narrow airspace of Israel. He descended, made a smooth landing, and received a hero's welcome at an Israeli airbase. Within a few hours, Redfa had radically changed his own life, while altering also the strategic balance of the Middle East.

This was the first time a sophisticated Soviet warplane had reached the West. Decades later, the air forces of the United States and its NATO allies remained impressed by the feat accomplished by Israeli intelligence that day. Among Western military people, the acquisition of a MiG in full working order was one of the key events in building the Mossad's image into unassailable mythology.

Among intelligence people—in the West, the East, or straddling the two great power camps—Israel was now respected as a master of humint methods. Operation Diamond was truly a gem.

While plotting the successful acquisition, or theft, of the airplane from Iraq, Amit had to cope with the disastrous end of wonderful successes in both Syria and Egypt. The Mossad's two most senior agents in the two most important Arab capitals were both lost in a five-week period in 1965: Eli Cohen in Damascus, and Wolfgang Lotz in Cairo.

Until they were captured, Cohen and Lotz supplied Israeli intelligence with information from the very heart of the Arab political and military power centers. Highly capable men, trained and talented in the art of lying, they penetrated the highest ranks of the leadership in their respective espionage posts. Cohen became a personal confidant of Syria's president, while Lotz befriended senior officers in Egypt's army.

They were sent there on long-term, deep-cover missions. As difficult it might be to imagine, the Mossad would continue—for many decades—to find patriotic, brave Israelis who were willing to give up their personal lives so as to bury themselves in enemy countries as spies.

The chief role for Cohen, Lotz, and their still anonymous successors is to serve as "warning agents": to report with urgency and clarity if the target country intended to go to war against Israel.

Cohen and Lotz found ways to achieve high social status in Damascus and Cairo, respectively—no easy task for foreigners. That gave a window into the top echelons of the two capitals.

Their stories have been told and re-told, their places in the pantheon of Israeli intelligence cemented. Yet, they also committed one of the most heinous sins in espionage: over-activity. They were both so good, and so effective, that their handlers in Tel Aviv could not resist swamping them with demands for more work and more data.

Eliyahu (Eli) Cohen was born in Alexandria, Egypt, in 1924. He clandestinely helped other Egyptian Jews move to Israel and then took part in the ill-fated Israeli espionage network that was smashed by the Egyptian authorities in 1954. He, like the others, was arrested; but the police found no evidence in his apartment, so he was freed.

He stayed in Egypt until just after the 1956 Suez war. Only then did he move to Israel, where he happily joined Aman. Being fluent in Arabic, French, and Hebrew, he was a translator for military intelligence. He declined offers to be transferred into Unit 131, stained by its failures in Egypt but still in charge of espionage in Israel's neighboring Arab countries.

The intelligence community let Cohen go on with his life—which included a wife, children, and his comfortable and safe desk job—until border tensions with Syria erupted in May 1960. Now, the espionage team at Unit 188 (a renamed and better run 131) urgently required a spy in Damascus and had an ambitious plan for preparing and planting an undercover Israeli there. Cohen was the man for the job.

Even with a sense of immediate need, his training took over half a year. A small but significant part was a vigorous course in Quran studies in Israel so as to be conversant with "fellow Muslims" when he got into Syria.

In February 1961, he arrived in the "base" country, Argentina—by now a favorite, if out-of-the-way choice for building a spy's cover story—carrying the passport of a European country. It bore what was, for him, a temporary name.

Three and a half months later, a Unit 188 courier arrived in Buenos Aires and handed Eli Cohen his new identity as Kamel Amin Taabeth, a Syrian businessman born in Lebanon. Taabeth had been invented by Aman, and his avatar as a rich man would make this a high-budget operation for Israel's frugal military. For a year, Cohen blended in with the many Arab entrepreneurs in South America, and he was dazzlingly successful at meeting rich and influential members of the Syrian community abroad.

At the start of 1962, he was ready to move to the "target" country. First came a flight to Lebanon, and then a long taxi ride across the border into Syria—with a sophisticated, high-speed radio transmitter hidden in his luggage. Cohen/Taabeth was also carrying genuine letters of introduction, penned by Syrians in South America. These were the fruits of his smooth socializing labors.

In Damascus, he was instantly the fascinating new man in town, having been recommended by everyone who was anyone in Buenos Aires. Before long, one of his best friends from Argentina, Major Amin al-Hafez, became the president of Syria.

While running an import-export business, Cohen/Taabeth cultivated his political contacts. He arranged lavish parties at his home, with pretty women—some of them paid to be intimately entertaining for his powerful new friends. This was expensive. The Israeli spy had to have plenty of cash, as well as nerves of steel. But it paid off.

He was regularly invited to military facilities, and he drove with senior officers all along Syria's Golan Heights, looking down at the vulnerable farms and roadways of Israel down below. Cohen made a point, of course, of memorizing the location of all the Syrian bunkers and artillery pieces. He was able to describe troop deployments along the border in detail, and he focused on the tank traps that could prevent Israeli forces from climbing the heights if war were to break out. He also furnished a list of all the Syrian pilots and accurate sketches of the weapons mounted on their warplanes.

The data he sent to Tel Aviv, mainly by tapping Morse Code dots and dashes on his telegraph key, covered all areas of life in Syria. Israeli intelligence was able to get a remarkably complete picture of an enemy country that had seemed impenetrable.

Ironically, one of the communications officers who handled the coded messages to and from Damascus was Cohen's own brother Maurice. For years, each brother did not know that the other was working for Israeli intelligence. Eli had told Maurice that he was traveling abroad procuring computer parts for the Defense Ministry.

The true clandestine mission, meantime, was transferred from Aman to the Mossad: part of Amit's move to the Mossad.

If Cohen and his Israeli controllers had only been more cautious, his chances of survival would have been much better. In November 1964, he was on leave in Israel—shedding his Taabeth identity, and trying to be a normal husband and father at home—awaiting the birth of his third child. He always pined for his family and had taken to sending them indirect greetings through his Israeli handlers, without revealing where he was.

Cohen kept extending his leave and hinted that, after nearly four years abroad, he might want to come in from the cold. He mentioned that he felt danger from Colonel Ahmed Suedani, head of the intelligence branch of the Syrian army.

Unfortunately, Cohen's case officers did not pay attention to the warning signs. They were too focused on preparing for conflict, because there was another bout of tension on the border. One could not be certain, but war seemed to be on the horizon. It was vital to have reliable intelligence from Damascus, and the Mossad applied pressure on Cohen to return to his espionage post as soon as possible.

In the last two months of 1964, Cohen forgot the rules of prudence. His broadcasts became more frequent, and in the space of five weeks he sent 31 radio transmissions. His case officers in Tel Aviv should have restrained him, but none did. The material he was sending was just too good to stop.

Apparently guided by radio direction-finding equipment, most likely operated by Soviet advisers, Colonel Suedani's intelligence men broke into Cohen's apartment on January 18, 1965, and caught him red-handed, tapping his telegraph key in the middle of a transmission.

A day later, rumors of the sensational arrest of a highly placed Syrian named Taabeth in Damascus reached Israel. The information was brought by a third-country citizen who did some work in Syria, while moonlighting for the Mossad.

The State of Israel immediately went into action, hoping against hope to get Eli Cohen out of Syria—or, at least, to keep him alive. The government quietly hired a prominent French lawyer, who arranged official appeals to European governments and to the Pope.

Syria turned a deaf ear. A court in Damascus sentenced Cohen to death, and he was hanged in a public square—to the cheers of a large crowd—on May 18, 1965. The Syrians did allow the spy to send a final written message to his family. "I am writing to you these last words, a few minutes before my end," he wrote. "I request you, dear Nadia, to pardon me and take care of yourself and our children. Don't deprive them or yourself of anything. You can get remarried, in order not to deprive the children of a father."

He also asked his wife "not to spend your time weeping about something already done," adding that she should "look forward for a better future!"

To this day, Cohen's family has waged a public campaign for Syria to return his body for burial in Israel. The Israeli government brought up the subject indirectly through third-party envoys. The Mossad tried to locate the grave. But Bashar al-Assad's dictatorship may well have been sincere in declaring privately that no one in Syria knew where Cohen was buried.

A new clue as to why this Israeli hero was caught by the Syrians came from another operative, Masoud Buton. He was planted inside Lebanon from 1958 to 1962, when he quit over a financial dispute with Mossad headquarters and moved to France. His memoirs declare that he created the Taabeth identity during his time in Beirut.

Buton was born in 1923 in Jerusalem to a Jewish family which had already been there, under Turkish and then British rule, for eight generations. After fighting in Israel's war of independence and rising to the rank of major, he was recruited by Aman. He used his Arabic-language fluency to live in French-ruled Algiers in the mid-1950s and to create his own false identity there, while also spying on senior members of the Algerian nationalist movement. Israel shared that information, including Buton's photos, with French intelligence.

As an "Algerian businessman" named Tallab, representing a British company, he moved to Beirut in 1958 and managed to befriend senior Lebanese officials. He acted the part of a devout Muslim and attended a mosque at least once a day.

Buton/Tallab occasionally crossed into Syria, where he was able to photograph army bases. In Lebanon, he obtained plans and drawings of Beirut International Airport, and that would help Israeli commando troops many years later.

He was ordered, in 1962, to procure identity documents for a "Lebanese-born businessman of Syrian extraction." Buton managed to do that and sent the papers for a Kamel Taabeth to Aman's Unit 131, but later he sent a warning that the documentation might be compromised in some way. Still, he writes, the identity was provided to Eli Cohen: a mistake, Buton claims, because Syrian officials eventually became suspicious.

Mossad chief Amit strongly rejected Buton's claim that, by ignoring his warning about the papers, the agency somehow contributed to Cohen's downfall. But Cohen's wife and family have said that they believe Buton.

Considering that the Israelis had an intelligence asset so well placed as Cohen, it is all the more impressive that they had yet another at the same time: Wolfgang Lotz, in Egypt.

Lotz was born in Mannheim, Germany, in 1921. His mother was a Jewish actress, his father a Christian who managed a theater in Berlin. For his own perilous espionage act, it was lucky that Lotz was not circumcised.

After his parents divorced and Adolf Hitler rose to power, the young Lotz was brought by his mother to Palestine in search of a safe life as Jews. Wolfgang changed his name to Ze'ev Gur-Arie, *ze'ev* being the Hebrew word for "wolf."

Lotz/Gur-Arie joined the Haganah underground in 1937 and fought for the British in World War II, infiltrating German lines in North Africa. He mastered Arabic and English, as well as German and Hebrew.

He served as an officer in the Israeli army, and in the late 1950s he was recruited by Unit 131 of Aman to be planted in Egypt.

According to the "legend" given to him, Lotz had been a German army officer and had fought under Rommel in the North African deserts. After the war, he supposedly moved to Australia and became rich from breeding horses. His ostensible ambition in Egypt was to establish a large ranch for the same purpose.

Lotz was one of the few secret agents ever to work using his real name, with his own genuine papers.

As Unit 131 was transferred to the Mossad, the German-born operative was known affectionately there as "Wolfie." His official code name would be "Shimshon" (Samson).

He underwent a battery of tests, known to Israeli intelligence as "stations": psychological, psychiatric, handwriting analysis, and field-operation techniques. One of the testers wrote that Lotz/Gur-Arie was a "self-loving type," was "vulnerable to pain and threats," would not likely "stand up to suffering," and would have "problems in overcoming passion for women and wine."

His other ratings, however, were highly positive, so Gur-Arie was accepted for the mission. "He had nerves of steel," his handler, Yaakov Nahmias, said. "He could look the Angel of Death in the eyes, invite him to a drink, and raise a glass to him."

Gur-Arie/Lotz was, however, a bit apprehensive about going to Egypt, in part because someone might recognize him from his service with British forces there. The commander of Unit 131, Yosef Yariv, suggested a few warm-up trips, including Libya, Damascus for three weeks, and then Cairo for five weeks to scout around and learn about Arabian horses. When Lotz got back to Israel, Yariv said many years later, "he was brimming with confidence."

His initial operational order from June 1960 and his contract are preserved in Gur-Arie's personal file in the Mossad archive. The contract for the gutsy move to Egypt stipulated that he would be employed for five years with the option of an extension or cancellation upon one month's notification. In addition to his modest government salary, he received an expense account of $350 a month plus one British pound per day as compensation for residing in an "enemy country."

Now, as Lotz, the spy enthusiastically hit the Egyptian ground running at the start of 1961. A convivial and charismatic man, he seemed the happy host of parties for senior army officers, for a police commander who became a best friend, and for many of the right people in wealthy Cairo high society. He smoked hashish with them and encouraged them to talk about their defense-related work.

Using a tiny radio hidden in the heel of a riding boot, and later a larger radio in a clothing drawer, he telegraphed detailed reports to Tel Aviv.

Lotz's operational order was radically altered when he was told to join Isser Harel's ill-fated campaign against the German scientists in Egypt. The new instruction from Tel Aviv stated: "You are to get close to the circle of scientists consisting of Paul Goercke, Wolfgang Pilz, and Hans Kleinwachter. The goal is to liquidate them."

Unruffled by being converted into an assassin, Lotz turned to the new mission with his usual willingness to serve. His handlers sent him explosives hidden in Yardley soaps. Lotz inserted the materials and trigger mechanisms into envelopes, which he mailed from Cairo to the scientists. Unfortunately one of the envelopes was opened by the secretary of the rocket scientist Pilz, and the explosion left her blind.

More errors followed. Every few months, the spy went to Europe to report to an Aman or Mossad case officer. On a night train from Paris to Germany in June 1961, Lotz met a tall, curvaceous blonde who was a dozen years younger than he. They quite simply fell in love. Just two weeks later, Wolfgang married Waltraud.

The only problem was that he was already married. He and his Israeli wife Rivka had a son, Oded, who was then 12, and they lived in Paris under the supervision of the Mossad's substantial station there.

Lotz's bosses in Tel Aviv learned of his bigamy only by chance. "One day we received a letter from him," Yariv related. "The envelope had a black lining, to prevent others from reading it. We noticed that the lining, which was a bit torn, contained an incomplete address, and we were able to identify the words 'Mrs. and Mr. Lotz.'"

Mrs.? What Mrs.?

The Mossad immediately summoned "Shimshon" to Israel to explain. Once they were face to face, Yariv asked, as though offhandedly, "How's the wife?"

Lotz replied quickly, "Fine, thanks." The spy was too self-confident to follow that with an immediate "oops." According to Yariv, Lotz tended to conceal things, but when presented with the facts he immediately confirmed them. And so it was, as he discussed his two simultaneous spouses with his bosses.

The spy chiefs considered aborting the entire mission and bringing "Shimshon" back to Israel—perhaps for punishment—but he was so successful that the Mossad did not want to lose him. It was decided to leave everything as it was, and not to tell Rivka about her husband's other wife. A Mossad psychologist observed that they always knew Lotz could not resist young, pretty women.

"It was a cardinal error to let him live a true double life," one of the spymasters admitted years later. "His personality thus became even more fragmented, with two families: one in Paris and the other in Cairo."

Lotz did tell Waltraud, his second and simultaneous wife, that he was a spy—but not that he was working for Israel. She apparently thought that

West Germany was his employer, and, perhaps adding to the excitement of their relationship, she agreed to cooperate. Yariv said Waltraud Lotz "was an extraordinary success, which helped him in his work."

Lotz/Gur-Arie also told his son, in Paris, more than he should have. Oded recalled, more than 40 years later, that his father revealed that he was a spy—and they enjoyed going to a James Bond movie together. The elder Gur-Arie remarked that real-life espionage was even more exciting than the film. The secret was a difficult burden for a teenage boy, but his father must have figured that Oded would be more careful about what he said if he understood some of what was at stake.

Only in 2007 did Oded Gur-Arie, an entrepreneur and a professor of business administration who lives in the United States, agree to speak publicly about his suffering and about how his father betrayed him and his mother.

The younger Gur-Arie distinctly remembered the morning of February 27, 1965. He left his home on Pierre Guerin Street in the 16th Arrondissement of Paris. As he did every Saturday, he walked to the local kiosk to buy the *International Herald Tribune*. "I took the paper and started to walk home," Gur-Arie recalled, "and, as always, I glanced at the main headline."

That was the shock of his life. The front page said that six West Germans had disappeared in Egypt, among them Wolfgang Lotz and his wife, Waltraud. The headline knocked him for a double loop. First, "because I knew Dad was a spy and it was obvious to me that he hadn't 'disappeared,' but had been caught by the Egyptians. I was sure they would discover that he was an Israeli. That would be the end of the story. They would kill him."

The second shock came, he said, "when I asked myself who this Waltraud was. His wife? My mother was his wife! How could he have another wife? And what was I going to tell my mother in a few minutes? I understood that the story was getting complicated."

He went upstairs and into the family apartment. "I told my mother that Dad had disappeared in Cairo. She grabbed the paper and read the report quickly. She remained unruffled and went to the phone. She called our liaison in the Mossad.

"Apparently because it was Shabbat [the Jewish Sabbath], the Mossad people hadn't woken up that morning," he remarked caustically. "At that moment they didn't know that Dad had been arrested. I imagine that within minutes all the Mossad agents in Europe rushed out to buy the *Herald Tribune* in order to be updated. The fact that the Mossad didn't know that Dad had been caught and that they heard it from my mother, who heard it from me after I had read about it in the paper, was another breaking point for me.

"Until then, I was certain that the Mossad was omnipotent, that they had resources and that they always knew everything. As a youngster, the reality came as a great disappointment to me."

On several levels, the Mossad suffered a harsh blow when Lotz was arrested—with the German wife—by Egyptian secret police who burst into their Cairo apartment on February 22. To this day, the Mossad does not know with certainty how "Shimshon" was discovered.

One theory for what occurred—which Yariv did not rule out—held that Lotz was caught by accident: pure, dumb luck for the Egyptians. The prevailing explanation, however, is that a Soviet counterespionage team, training the locals on how to tighten their security, detected Lotz's radio transmitter. That would be similar to the process that doomed Eli Cohen in Syria.

There were clear differences between the Lotz and Cohen cases, however. Whereas torture forced Cohen to admit he was an Israeli spy and he was hanged, Lotz tenaciously clung to the contention that he was a non-Jewish German who had helped Israel just to earn some money.

Immediately upon Lotz's arrest, Amit contacted West Germany's General Gehlen and told him about the arrest of the Israeli operative. Gehlen agreed to Amit's request that he take the Israeli spy under his wing and present him to the Egyptian authorities as Germany's spy in Cairo. To prevent the possibility that someone in Israel would recognize Lotz and blab about it, the Mossad obtained equipment to jam the reception of Egyptian television broadcasts in Israel during the trial.

The Egyptians, too, preferred to portray Lotz as a German spy. That would not be nearly so embarrassing as being penetrated by a Zionist agent.

Wolfgang and Waltraud were convicted by an Egyptian court. He was sentenced to life imprisonment with hard labor, and she was to serve three years. Both were freed after three years, part of an Israeli-Egyptian prisoner swap seven months after the Six-Day War.

Lotz/Gur-Arie and his wife were flown to Germany and then to Israel. The Mossad helped Lotz rehabilitate himself, a process that included his running a horse ranch near Tel Aviv. Rivka divorced him, but that only strengthened his image as a *bon vivant* and a national hero.

The former spy, having just gotten out of a bad prison cell, was invited to showy receptions and fabulous parties. He was back on the champagne circuit, and he tried to maintain a far higher standard of living than was possible on his Mossad pension. Lotz's equine business collapsed, and his condition deteriorated even further after the premature death of Waltraud in 1971, as a result of torture she underwent in the Cairo prison.

Her death, Oded said, utterly broke his father's heart. Later he would marry for a third time, divorce, and marry yet again. He moved to California to pursue his dream of producing a movie about his own life. That never led anywhere, and with great frustration he left for Germany. He lived there until his death in 1993 at age 73. This is a sad story, with a lesson: Old spies are rarely happy.

Israel was fortunate to have a few more warning agents planted in Egypt by the Mossad. Decades later, officials refused to allow details to be published, just in case similar methods would have to be used again—perhaps even in the same locations, in some unforeseeable future.

Another key to the success of Israeli intelligence, in the run-up to the 1967 war, was an evolving and well practiced expertise in the use of double agents.

Handling agents is at the heart of espionage work. The handler must often behave like father and mother to his agent. He must be a social worker and a psychologist. He must groom his agent, but remain wary of him. Massage his ego, encourage him, reward him, be a shoulder to lean on and a good listener, but also be prepared to scold.

When the person being manipulated is a *double* agent, the challenges are multiplied. The art of espionage requires many delicate tasks—from shaking surveillance pursuers, to planting bombs—but none is more sensitive than the craft of "doubling" an enemy operative so that he will work for your side.

"You can never fully know and trust such an agent," Amit explained. "You cannot be sure to whom his final loyalty is given."

The double agent moves in a twilight zone between the two sides, crossing lines back and forth. He must be very cautious and sly, lest his actions and true status be exposed. He assumes and discards identities. He presents a false façade of loyalty to one side—or is it false to both sides?—and he must guile-fully gain the trust of each.

Two important double agents, run by the Mossad during the Amit era, fed disinformation aimed at deceiving Egypt. One was Victor Grayevsky, who already had done so much for Israel by supplying Shin Bet with a copy of Nikita Khrushchev's secret speech in 1956.

Grayevsky moved to Israel from Poland in January 1957. The head of Shin Bet, Amos Manor, helped arrange a rental apartment and a job for him. In fact, two employers welcomed the new arrival: the Eastern Europe department of the Foreign Ministry, and the Polish-language broadcasts of Kol Israel—the Voice of Israel shortwave radio station.

He was also sent to a Hebrew language class, and that is where he got to know two of his classmates who were both Soviet diplomats. When they learned that Grayevsky worked at the Foreign Ministry, their interest grew and they invited him out to a lavish meal with plenty of vodka.

Grayevsky did not mind the eating and drinking, and he loyally reported all this to Manor. The Shin Bet chief recognized an opportunity, and he instructed Grayevsky to continue meeting with his Soviet friends. Manor assigned an experienced case officer to back up Grayevsky, who got to consume a lot of alcohol in the line of duty.

As is standard in such approaches, the two Soviets told Grayevsky that they were going abroad on vacation but would like to introduce him to a man who would be filling in.

Following the guidance of his Shin Bet handlers, Grayevsky readily agreed. The replacement was Viktor Kaloyev, ostensibly an administrator of the Russian Orthodox Church, who lived on the church grounds in Jerusalem's Russian Compound. In reality, Kaloyev was another Soviet intelligence officer.

For over a decade, ending in 1971, Grayevsky held hundreds of meetings with KGB officers. The Russians gave him a hundred dollars, sometimes more, at each meeting. Grayevsky dutifully passed on the money to Shin Bet, so, unknowingly, Soviet spies were financing Israeli intelligence.

Every few years his Soviet handlers changed, and four decades after it all stopped he could not remember all of their names. What he did remember is how the vodka flowed like water at these meetings. As a proud ex-Pole, Grayevsky was far from troubled by that. "I never got drunk. I outdrank them," he declared with a smile.

Most of the meetings took place in a Russian Compound apartment. Priests also attended these meetings, as "diplomats," for they were all espionage agents for the Soviet Union. Israel was never naïve about any of this, but here was a golden opportunity to have Grayevsky feed false information to the Soviets—knowing that some of it, at least, would reach Arab governments.

"The information was prepared and tailored by all three branches of our intelligence community," Amit revealed years later. "Shin Bet, we at the Mossad, and most importantly Aman were all involved. This was aimed at deceiving the Arabs about our war plans, and the order of battle if war should break out."

Grayevsky's most important meeting with the Russians took place in May 1967. Nasser had just moved his army into the Sinai, subsequently closing the Straits of Tiran so as to paralyze all the shipping at Israel's southern port Eilat.

Israel found itself in the crisis that led to the Six-Day War. But the Jewish state was trying to prevent the war.

Israeli intelligence chiefs instructed Grayevsky to activate, for the first time, an emergency contact signal that the Russians had given him. He met them the next day on a small road in the hills near Jerusalem. This time, his task was to feed genuine information to the Soviets.

Grayevsky recalled: "A guy I never met before came to this rendezvous. He seemed to be around my age, in his 40s. He held a briefcase and looked like a clerk from a government office. But he was a very sharp fellow. I told him that Israel wouldn't be able to just sit by and ignore the closure of the Straits, and that it would go to war against Nasser. He asked me how I knew this. Using the story that Shin Bet had concocted for me, I told him that as a journalist and radio broadcaster, I'd been invited to the prime minister's office and I'd heard a briefing there to this effect from a senior IDF officer."

Grayevsky heard differing accounts regarding the information that he provided, on what turned out to be the eve of war. One version said the KGB never told the top Soviet leadership that Israel was chillingly serious about using force to break Nasser's sea siege. Another version, endorsed by some historians, said the information reached the Kremlin but, for various reasons, was not conveyed to Nasser.

Although the Soviet Union and its Communist allies broke diplomatic relations with Israel just after the Six-Day War, the spy-priests remained in the Red Church compound in Jerusalem, and Grayevsky continued to meet with them for another four years. During a final conversation, his KGB handler told him that he had done a terrific job and was being awarded the Order of Lenin. The Soviets said they would hold the medal in Moscow for him.

In fact, Grayevsky was fervently loyal to Israel.

An extremely important double agent was known by his Israeli handlers as Yated, the Hebrew word for stake or peg. He was an Egyptian intelligence operative who was doubled—turned—by the Israelis, and his story was a truly remarkable deception.

Egypt's spy services, never ranked among the world's best, did what they could to penetrate Israeli society. They hired a few of Israel's Arab citizens—a far from ideal choice, as they were naturally under suspicion by Israeli authorities—and occasionally would send agents into the Jewish state posing as tourists.

The man who would become Yated was recruited by the Egyptians for something far more ambitious. In fact, the mission was a mirror image of the Mossad's modus operandi. An Egyptian would attempt to learn precisely how to pose as a Jew and would move to Israel as an immigrant, unnoticed in a multitude of new and welcomed Jewish arrivals.

The man with that plan was Rifaat al-Gamal, a petty criminal who was recruited by Egypt's intelligence services in 1954 by making him an offer he could hardly refuse: avoid going to prison by becoming a spy. Al-Gamal agreed, underwent training, and then was furnished with a false identity—as an Egyptian Jew named Jacques Biton. Now he immersed himself in Jewish life and even made contacts with the community by spending time at Egyptian synagogues.

In early 1955, Gamal/Biton sailed from Alexandria to Italy. He remained in Italy for quite a while and even worked there, hoping to make his cover story more credible. He eventually approached the Jewish Agency, and with its assistance he joined the wave of *aliyah*, or immigration to the Holy Land. According to the ambitious scenario his handlers in Cairo drew up, he was to get himself fully integrated into Israeli society. For that, he was given a respectable sum of money that he invested in a partnership with an Israeli. Together they opened a travel agency in Tel Aviv.

Gamal/Biton did not know that the partner, Dr. Imre Fried, was actually working for Israeli intelligence. It turned out that Shin Bet was quietly but seriously suspicious of the new immigrant from Egypt and Italy.

Espionage can make strange bedfellows, but consider these circumstances: Biton's half of the investment came from Cairo, while Fried's cash was from Shin Bet.

Biton was placed under surveillance, and with the help of a Mossad team his movements were also monitored abroad, where he was seen meeting with his Egyptian handler.

Upon his return to Israel from one such trip, he was arrested by Shin Bet and given two options: either sit in jail for decades for espionage, or agree to serve as a double agent whose ultimate loyalty would be to Israel.

The choice between prison and espionage was familiar to Gamal/Biton by now, and he chose the latter option.

The Israeli who most closely handled Biton, now codenamed Yated, was David Ronen. He eventually rose to the post of Shin Bet deputy director. In the 1990s, he wrote a novel in Hebrew called *The Sting of the Wasp (The Story of a Double Agent)*, and that was loosely based on Operation Yated.

To maintain his credibility with his Egyptian handlers, Biton photographed—but only under Ronen's close supervision—Israel Defense Forces bases, soldiers at hitchhiking posts, and army unit tags. The Egyptians considered Gamal/Biton one of their top spies.

He married a German woman, and they had a son in Israel—even celebrating his bar mitzvah at the Western Wall in Jerusalem after it was captured from Jordan in the Six-Day War. For Egyptian intelligence, this all seemed like a fantastic coup.

From an Israeli point of view, Operation Yated's crowning achievement was the transfer of false information to Egypt in the spring of 1967, on the eve of the war. Biton told the Egyptians that according to the war plan he had obtained from his sources, Israel would begin with ground operations. That was a deception of the highest order. It could even be likened to Operation Mincemeat, wherein British intelligence during World War II brilliantly fooled the Germans regarding the site of the Allied landing in northern France in June 1944.

Biton's misleading information was one of the reasons the Egyptians were so relaxed and careless in leaving their fighter planes out in the open. Israeli pilots had an easy time swooping in and destroying the aircraft on the ground. Thus, the Six-Day War was truly won in the opening three hours.

"He spared us a great deal of blood, and using him was equal to the strength of a division," Shin Bet veteran Avraham Ahituv said about Biton.

After the war, Israel had no more need for Biton. He had grown increasingly stressed by the daily tensions of his clandestine double life. In light of his mounting complaints to Ronen and growing demands for monetary compensation, Shin Bet decided to let him go—but first to rehabilitate him for a normal life somewhere.

People in the Defense Ministry arranged business opportunities for Biton, including an oil-related partnership with an Italian businessman. But that was not enough for the ex-double agent. He demanded millions of dollars to compensate for his 12 years of service to Israel. Senior Shin Bet officers no longer liked him at all.

Biton had the misfortune of being diagnosed with cancer. He could not shake the fear that Shin Bet would try to poison him in a hospital room, so he demanded to be transferred to Europe for treatment. Israel paid for all that, but it did not last long. He was hospitalized in Germany, and he died there in 1982.

A lingering mystery is why he was buried in Egypt. A few years after he died, an author in Cairo published a long story about a daring and talented Egyptian spy who had penetrated the heart of the "Zionist enemy." He did not publish the spy's real name. The story was then adapted for television and became a popular series viewed all around the Arab world. The protagonist was called Rif'at al-Haggan.

Eventually, al-Gamal's real name was published in Egypt, and a city square in Cairo was named after him. Egypt clearly enjoyed hailing heroes. Harel, the Memuneh who guided Israeli intelligence during much of the Yated operation, shrugged dismissively when asked about the Egyptian claim that Gamal/Biton was definitely their guy.

"If it makes them happy," said the retired Harel, "let them continue to believe their tall tale."

The literally smashing air blitz that marked the beginning of combat, on the morning of June 5, 1967, was much discussed beforehand by top Israeli leaders who felt they had to consider how the United States and the Soviet Union would react.

The man who took Washington, DC's temperature, reporting to official Jerusalem that President Lyndon Johnson would not be opposed to a preemptive strike by Israel, was Amit. Eshkol sent the Mossad chief to deliver a three-part message to CIA headquarters: that war was inevitable, that Nasser started it by trying to strangle Israel, and that Israel was so outnumbered that it would have to launch the first attack—or the Jewish state might not survive.

The CIA director, Richard Helms, listened to Amit. So did President Johnson. They did not explicitly endorse going to war, but they did not object to the notion of a preemptive attack by Israel.

The understanding shown by Johnson and by Helms could be considered a kind of reciprocation for the giant favors that Israeli intelligence had done for the United States: procuring an advanced Soviet MiG fighter by persuading a pilot to defect from Iraq, and obtaining the Khrushchev speech. Amit's international intelligence links were paying off. The air force and the army had to do the rest, and they made quick work of it. Unfortunately there was no serious planning for the day after the war.

CHAPTER NINE

MEET THE NEIGHBORS

The bed was still warm, the sheets and blankets lay strewn all over the floor, the water boiled over in the kettle, and the tea in the cups was still hot, but the man known as Abu Ammar was not to be found. A few seconds before Israeli troops and security men broke into the three-story house in Ramallah, on the West Bank, the leader of the Palestine Liberation Organization—who would become world-famous as Yasser Arafat—had fled.

From his second-floor hiding place, Arafat—with amazing instincts honed by danger—heard the voices of the Israelis as they surrounded the villa. Arafat leaped from a window and hid in a car parked nearby. When the men who were after his scalp had left, he hurried eastward and crossed the Jordan River. For the next quarter of a century he did not set foot in the West Bank.

Time and again, the Israelis would try to catch him by land, air, and sea, and still Arafat eluded them. For the Israeli security services, he became their Phantom of the Opera—elusive, unpredictable, and lucky.

After the failed raid in Ramallah, Shin Bet agents took some of Arafat's personal belongings—even that once-warm bed—to their Jerusalem District Headquarters as souvenirs and as a reminder of their unfinished job.

This was in mid-December 1967, six months after Israel captured the West Bank from Jordan, the Gaza Strip and the Sinai Peninsula from Egypt, and the Golan Heights from Syria.

The six-day victory over Arab enemies on three sides was perhaps the biggest event in Israel's history. Foreigners marveled at a small country's ability to wage and win a war cleverly and quickly. Seen nearly half a century later, however, the triumph could be considered pyrrhic.

Having given themselves the burden of ruling over their Palestinian Arab neighbors, the IDF and the security agencies were forced into learning more than they ever knew about the people who insistently pursued their own claim on the same historic Holy Land. Eventually, over the decades that unfolded, Israelis would try to make peace with the Palestinians but would then find the efforts frustrating.

The so-called peace process, launched a quarter of a century after the Six-Day War, would go on to a kind of paralysis; and it would not seem nearly as urgent as crises involving Iran and its Shi'ite Muslim allies in Lebanon.

At the very least, from the start, the victory in 1967 presented new challenges in the area of internal and external security—and thus an entirely new era for Shin Bet. Yosef Harmelin, a veteran Shin Bet operative, had replaced Amos Manor as director upon the latter's retirement in 1964.

No one had a better poker face than Harmelin. He was an impressively tall man, but the ability to maintain an expressionless countenance was his most memorable quality and an excellent attribute for an intelligence operative. He was probably born with the talent when he entered the world in Vienna in 1923.

After Nazi Germany annexed Austria in 1938, Harmelin's parents escaped the approaching Holocaust by moving to Mexico. The teenaged Yosef, more Zionist than his parents, moved to Palestine instead. Like Harel and Amit, Harmelin moved onto a kibbutz before enlisting in the British army in World War II. After the war, he joined the Haganah, where he met Harel; and a few years after Israel's independence, Harmelin was recruited by Shin Bet. He gradually worked his way up to the top.

Harmelin inherited an agency that was small and self-contained, working in virtually total anonymity. The public hardly ever heard of Shin Bet by name, details of its operations were censored out of the press, and it was illegal to identify any of its personnel. The entire force numbered around 500 people, and the atmosphere within was that of a close family in which everyone knew everyone else. Family secrets were never divulged to outsiders.

It was also, however, a lackluster agency that had always been overshadowed by the Mossad and by Aman. Only rarely were a few crumbs of excitement tossed to Shin Bet by the operations department, which it shared with the Mossad. Shin Bet's main task was the usually unglamorous business of watching vigilantly for foreign spies and domestic subversives. Naturally, the Arab minority in Israel had always constituted the main pool of suspects.

The Arab citizens of the Jewish state—in the 1960s making up around 15 percent of Israel's population—enjoyed the right to vote for Knesset members, but they had not been governed by the same civilian systems as Jewish-dominated areas. There had been military governors for the Arab-populated sectors, mainly the Galilee and Wadi Ara regions in northern Israel, and the residents had been closely watched also by Shin Bet.

Immediately after the establishment of the State of Israel, the Shin Bet and the army assigned "case officers" or "military governors" to each Arab village and community. They were part of a large system that aimed to control every daily routine of the Israeli Arabs. The system was not something of which to be proud in a free country, but the reason was the suspicion that Israeli Arabs might be a "fifth column": Their true loyalty might be with their Arab brethren in countries that had declared themselves enemies of Israel.

The case officers were usually Jews from Arab nations who spoke Arabic and understood Arab and Muslim cultures. They were trained to run networks of local informers, collaborators, and agents who fed data of all sorts to Shin Bet. As with most intelligence collection, some of the information was vital and some of it banal.

Four years after independence, distrust had grown to the point that this system sought a deeper penetration into the Arab psyche. In 1952, Shin Bet formed a highly secret unit of young Jews who were trained to behave as Arabs and live in Arab towns and neighborhoods in Israel.

They were given fake identities and planted in such places as Nazareth and Jaffa to be the eyes and ears of the Shin Bet. Their bosses called them "*mista'arvim*," coining a new word by combining *mistavim* (Hebrew for "masqueraders") and *Aravim* (the word for "Arabs").

One of the main goals was to have trusted Israelis on the inside, in case a war were to break out and Israeli Arabs were to join the enemy.

Shmuel "Sami" Moriah, a senior Shin Bet officer who came to Israel from Iraq and had plenty of experience smuggling Jews out of his native country, led the unit. He recruited 10 other Iraqi-born men for this highly demanding mission.

With detailed cover stories about returning to Palestine after fleeing abroad in the 1948 war, they were sent into Arab villages and cities. Their genuine parents, siblings, and friends in Israel were kept in the dark about their whereabouts and activities.

These Shin Bet agents became so integrated in community life that it was fully expected by neighbors and village elders that they would get married— and most of them did.

Moriah said that he left the decision to each man, but "it seemed suspicious that young vigorous men would stay alone, without a spouse. When we sent them on the mission we didn't order them to marry, but it was clear to both sides that there is such an expectation, and that it would help the job they were doing."

The elders introduced them to eligible young Arab women. They had the brief courtship typical in conservative Arab societies. And most of the 10 men married, not ever telling their wives that they were Jewish Israelis.

As time passed, the intelligence from this daring deception proved to be almost worthless. Shin Bet wanted to call off the mission. But now Shin Bet had a tough problem.

"The double life they were living cost them a lot, emotionally," said Manor, who created this project but then backed away after seven years. "I saw that the price is not worth it and decided to put an end to it."

The unit was disbanded by 1959, but the ramifications haunted Shin Bet for years. The Muslim wives were informed that their husbands were actually Jewish—and, perhaps even worse, government agents—and then the women were given a choice of being sent to an Arab country, to avoid any local retaliation, or being resettled with their husbands in Jewish communities in Israel.

Almost all chose to stay with their husbands, even in the very changed circumstances. Some of the wives needed and got psychological counseling.

"Problems started surfacing," the project commander Moriah recalled a few decades later with a grimace. "We tried to rehabilitate the people involved, but we weren't really successful. The agents' kids experienced serious trauma. They tried to recover, to forget their past, where they come from, but they couldn't. A few of the kids succeeded in life, but most of them were left behind. They still suffer from problems."

In 1965 the Israeli government decided to end the military administration of majority-Arab areas, but for the sake of security Shin Bet was asked to step up its observation of those cities and villages.

Two years later, after Israel's grand victory at war brought more than a million additional Arabs in the West Bank and Gaza under Israeli rule, Shin Bet was tasked with spotting and quashing dangers in the newly occupied territories.

The intelligence community formed a task force—made up of Shin Bet and Aman men, plus the Mossad's David Kimche—to explore the politics of the local inhabitants.

"The Palestinians were in a state of shock," Kimche reminisced. "We thought Israel should exploit the situation by being generous and offering the Palestinians a noble solution that they could live with." Kimche, with long experience as a clandestine diplomat and honestly trying to pursue diplomatic solutions, proposed granting a form of autonomy to the Palestinians—with a view toward creating a separate state for them. The intelligence men on the task force endorsed that far-sighted vision.

Most Israelis, however, were immersed in a euphoric mood—a shock of victory coupled with a huge sense of relief—that did not foster experimental or generous gestures. Prime Minister Levi Eshkol and his cabinet ignored the task force's advice.

Israel's leadership seemed focused only on the here and now, while the immense changes in the Middle East called for complex analysis. A unique opportunity to resolve the heart-rending dispute between Jews and Arabs in Palestine was neglected. Almost half a century later, the Israel Defense Forces—a people's army, thanks to the almost universal military service by Jews—was still stuck as an occupying force in the West Bank. The dilemmas, clashes, roadblocks, settlements, and patrols all threatened the fragile fabric of Israel as a Jewish and democratic country.

Within two months of the transformative Six-Day War, Kimche himself was moving on. The Mossad sent him to Khartoum, the capital of Sudan in northeast Africa, in August 1967. Kimche's cover, on a brief visit to that Arab nation, exploited his impeccable English accent and manners. He posed as a British journalist at an important Arab summit. The leaders of eight nations convened to discuss the humiliating defeat of Egypt, Syria, and Jordan by the Israelis.

Their public declaration was simple, summarized and immortalized as "The Three No's." The summit's final document declared that there would be no recognition of Israel, no negotiations with Israel, and no peace with Israel.

This was one of the bases for Foreign Minister Abba Eban's observation that Arab leaders "never miss an opportunity to miss an opportunity" for peace. That seemed true enough at the time of Khartoum, but the same accusation could be directed at Israel, the United States, the United Nations, and a host of other parties with interests but few insights in the Middle East.

The Mossad's Kimche got to see all this in person, and he reported the details—including observations of Arab leaders and delegates—to headquarters. Intelligence analysts had plenty to analyze, but they could not change the reality. Israel had scored a major military victory in June 1967, and perhaps even had saved itself from total disaster, but there was not a single step forward toward peace.

In Kimche's words, "The events of the two months after the war were dramatic and marked by a historic opportunity missed by both sides—but especially by us, the victorious Israelis."

The victors naturally felt that they were both brilliant and lucky, but immediate challenges raised doubts as to whether the brilliance and the luck would hold out. It could fairly be said that most Israelis enjoyed—even reveled in—the fact that Jerusalem was reunited, and Jews could again pray at the iconic Western Wall of King Solomon's holy Temple. Many also derived deep satisfaction from returning to locales in the West Bank that were an authentic part of Biblical history. Yet hardly anyone with a scintilla of sensitivity enjoyed being an occupier: unable to avoid the friction and inequalities between Jews with power and Arabs who had just lost their dignity.

On the Arab side, Arafat's PLO could easily blame the six-day humiliation on the political leaders of governments that never truly cared about the Palestinians. The PLO was hatching its own ambitious plans, calling on Palestinians to rise up against the Israeli-Zionist occupation. This nationalist rhetoric was reminiscent of the Vietcong, then successfully confronting the powerful American armed forces in Southeast Asia, and of the FLN, which had driven France out of Algeria.

The essence of the strategy was to make the occupied territories ungovernable for the Israelis. The PLO hoped to control daily life in the 500 towns and villages of the West Bank and Gaza, and left-wing theorists among the guerrillas believed a Palestinian revolutionary government would be inevitable.

The PLO borrowed not only foreign concepts, but also operational tactics. Deriving additional inspiration from China's Mao Zedong and Cuba's Fidel Castro, the Palestinians also had active assistance from Colonel Ahmed Suedani, the head of Syrian military intelligence who was credited with catching Eli Cohen in Damascus. Suedani was known as an enthusiastic supporter of "popular struggle" throughout the Middle East—everywhere, that is, except in Syria.

Palestinian militant cells mounted hit-and-run operations against Israeli army vehicles and patrols. They managed to execute ambushes on the narrow streets of West Bank towns.

In Israel itself, Palestinians detonated bombs in markets, movie theaters, bus stations, and restaurants. One of the most publicized events took place in October 1967 inside the Zion Cinema in the heart of the overwhelmingly Jewish western part of Jerusalem. During a screening of Howard Hawks's *El Dorado*, two Arab sisters placed a bag of explosives, wired to a clock, on the floor near their seats and hastily left. The bomb failed to go off and the attackers were arrested, but the thought of a large blast in a crowded, enclosed hall was alarming to Israelis.

The PLO soon realized the importance of the news media. "If you strike, it means you exist," became the Palestinian leadership's tactical philosophy.

The notion was broadened when Palestinians found that they did not actually have to act. They merely had to claim. Thus, for many years, accidents and natural disasters were attributed to "our brave Palestinian fighters."

However baseless the propaganda, it was effective. One of the first such ploys followed an accident that befell Defense Minister Moshe Dayan. He was an amateur archeologist who showed no regard for regulations governing where and where not to dig. In 1968, during an excavation, he was trapped by a cave-in and suffered injuries to his back and ribs. The PLO claimed it had sent a commando unit to assassinate Dayan, and that was why he was nearly buried.

Nonsense of that kind occasionally made the claimants, at least, feel a bit better.

The Israeli government started to cope with issues that would be more fateful than anyone realized at the time. What was the legal status of the territories captured in the 1967 war? Were they "liberated" portions of the ancient Land of Israel, thus rightfully under Jewish control eternally? Or "occupied" acreage that belonged to the Arab residents?

In the absence of a clear and considered decision by Israeli politicians, the intelligence and security agencies were forced to enact an administrative policy. They developed a "carrot and stick" approach, designed to preserve the status quo while maintaining order as the highest priority. In an attempt to drive a wedge between the majority of the Palestinians and a dangerous minority, the Israeli chiefs decided that almost all inhabitants would be permitted to conduct their lives normally. That was the carrot.

The stick was a policy of punishing, strongly and surely, anyone participating in subversion or outright violence. Palestinians who aided guerrilla groups were clamped into prison, and their houses were flattened—usually by dynamite, in almost flamboyant explosions meant to serve as an example to others.

Losing one's home was serious punishment, but for many Arabs the most severe penalty would be separation from one's land, family farm, or vineyard.

Thus, Shin Bet turned to expulsion as a major stick. Palestinians believed to have ties with PLO terrorists were escorted across the bridges into Jordan and banned from returning. More than anyone else, this policy was identified with Dayan.

Transforming the carrot-and-stick theory into practice was no simple task. Shin Bet officers were not prepared for it. The new territories in Israel's hands were *terra incognita* to them: an unknown land where the agency had no men in the field and did not know the population. Shin Bet had to start from scratch.

As a first step, Harmelin's operatives, with the help of Aharon Yariv's military intelligence staff, used psychological warfare by spreading rumors of how tough the Israeli hard line would be. These were not so much accurate as they were chilling.

After it was clear that Israel's determination to remain in the territories was known to their inhabitants, Shin Bet turned to the second and major stage: preventing any attempted Palestinian uprising and combating terrorism.

In no time flat, Shin Bet licked the immediate problem. Palestinians were unable to organize a broad uprising, because the Israelis were quickly able to install networks of informers and secret agents all over the West Bank and Gaza Strip. Arabs in the territories were recruited, either by monetary payments or by various forms of intimidation. The agents often gave Shin Bet advance information of attacks planned by guerrillas.

Israeli officers, acting on tip-offs, were able to swoop down on subversive meetings and lay ambushes to capture Palestinian squads on their way to attacks. The system that permitted these successes became known as "preventive intelligence," which is the greatest desire of every internal security service that has to deal with violence and terrorism. The ultimate aim is to avoid having to search for perpetrators after an act of violence. Instead, they should be prevented from carrying it out in the first place.

By December 1967, Shin Bet had chalked up an amazing record of triumph: Most of the PLO cells collapsed, and their headquarters within the West Bank were forced to retreat to Jordan. Two hundred Palestinian guerrillas were killed in battles with army and Shin Bet units, and more than a thousand were arrested.

The failure of the attempted Palestinian uprising in 1967 was not, however, due solely to the efficiency of the Israeli secret services. Credit should be shared with the Palestinian militants for being so poor at developing professional skills.

They did not adhere to the practice of compartmental-ization that is so basic in spycraft and underground movements. Instead, they organized in relatively large groups, knew one another by genuine names, and relied on local Arabs not to turn them in to the authorities. Arafat himself and his senior commanders, completely disregarding the rules of a good conspiracy, knew most of the members of the cells. Their communications system was primitive, and their codes were simple. No escape routes were planned. Their "safe houses" were not really safe. Nor were the members of guerrilla squads prepared to withstand interrogation when captured. As soon as they were picked up by Shin Bet, they would tell everything they knew.

Their codes were broken, and their weapons and explosives were confiscated. Like dominoes, the cells fell one after another. Failing to live up to Mao's dictum that a guerrilla fighter must have the support of the population and feel "like a fish in the water," the Palestinian fighters could not "swim" unnoticed among their neighbors, who pursued favors from the Israelis by sweeping guerrillas to the Shin Bet shore.

Motivated by Israeli carrots and sticks, the local populace shunned any armed uprising and preferred peace, quiet, and prosperity.

Full credit was given to Shin Bet. The importance of Harmelin's agency within the intelligence community was growing, and its case officers became known as the "kings of the territories." Almost as in a feudal regime, each Israeli operative was given his own region, generally a village or a group of villages. He had to be Israel's eyes and ears, knowing everything that happened in his fiefdom. The officer would typically know most of the villagers by name, while they knew him only by an alias—usually an invented Arabic name, such as Abu Musa, "Father of Moses."

If a Palestinian wanted a building permit, the military government in the occupied territories would first check with the local Shin Bet case officer. An Arab merchant who wished to export his citrus crop from Gaza or his olive oil from the West Bank was able to obtain the necessary licenses only with the assent of Shin Bet.

Palestinians felt compelled to make deals, morning, noon, and night. They would supply information, and in return Israel delivered security and fringe benefits such as jobs and travel permits.

Shin Bet's success came at a price, however. As the years and decades went by, Israeli society was increasingly judged in the outside world by its security policies. While potential rebellions were crushed, Israel's goodwill around the world was being squandered. Instead of continuing to be an admired favorite of international public opinion—as it was in most of the Western world's press in June 1967—the Jewish state became the Ugly Israel.

All the good the country had done was swept aside by negative headlines. The underdog of the crisis that led up to the Six-Day War was now seen as a brutal occupier of another people's land.

Shin Bet became the security service of an occupying power, self-confident and even arrogant. Having to cover a lot more ground, perfectionism and meticulous work gave way to hasty and often inequitable improvisation.

With Shin Bet's growing intelligence networks, there was an urgent need to expand its manpower. A new and modern complex of buildings was built in a northern suburb of Tel Aviv to house Shin Bet headquarters, replacing the old one in Jaffa near the flea market. The recruiting criteria were made less demanding, playing down old-fashioned high standards.

Everything was done in a hurry, and the social profile of Shin Bet's personnel changed. Arabic speakers were essential, so new staff members hired were from the Oriental, Sephardic sector of the Jewish populace. As in many Israeli institutions, that was a change from the initial domination of the European, Ashkenazic Jews filling positions of leadership.

The changed nature of the work also dictated new methods. At a time when thousands of Arabs were being detained for questioning, when booby-trapped cars were exploding, and when hotels and airliners were terrorist targets, it was felt essential to extract information as quickly as possible. The time factor became the most important element of Israel's preventive intelligence. Fast action sometimes seemed to require brutality, without pausing for a second thought.

At first, Shin Bet found it difficult to adjust to this new reality. Harmelin once saw one of his young interrogators slap the face of a Palestinian suspect, and the agency chief fired his employee on the spot. Harmelin did not agree that physical violence was necessary as a shortcut to information.

Shin Bet operatives learned the hard way what the occupation meant. Theirs was dirty work in the service of a perhaps noble cause. Harmelin and his deputy, Avraham Ahituv—who would be the next head of the agency in 1974—did manage to suppress terrorism, but they had to do it by introducing what their men called "the System."

The security methods were indeed systematic in creating a double standard of justice. One, democratic by nature, applied to Israeli citizens; an entirely different one, operating in the gray area between the permissible and the forbidden, was used against Palestinian troublemakers and suspects in the territories.

The System and its double standard created a new frontier that could be dubbed "Shin Bet Country." In Shin Bet Country, the agency had its own detention centers for Palestinian detainees. The police and national prisons authority never took a look at what was occurring in the cells behind those walls.

Arabs accused of terrorism faced coercive interrogation. Physical blows were rare, but there were other forms of harsh treatment that left no marks. Once the gates of Shin Bet closed behind a Palestinian prisoner, he typically had his head covered by a black sack, and then he would be left, exposed to the hot Israeli sun or winter cold, waiting for the interrogators. The questioning then went on for hours. Suspects were usually deprived of sleep and sometimes soaked with freezing water.

After failing to ignite an uprising in the territories, Palestinian militants shifted their battle to other locales. Israeli intelligence received fragmentary reports in 1968, from friendly secret services in Europe, indicating stepped-up efforts by Palestinian groups to attract volunteers from radical left-wing circles in Europe. Most of the recruiting was done by George Habash, who led a

Marxist-Leninist wing of the PLO known as the Popular Front for the Liberation of Palestine.

Peripatetic emissaries—on behalf of Arafat, Habash, and others—hopscotched across Italy, Holland, France, and West Germany, using ideological comradeship and financial incentives to persuade young Europeans to come to the Middle East and fight "the Zionist occupation" and "its imperialist allies." Dozens of highly motivated volunteers answered the PLO call. They were brought to Jordan and Lebanon, trained in guerrilla camps, and in some cases went on to hijack airplanes and stage other attacks against Israel.

Even as Israeli intelligence tried to figure out what the Palestinians had in mind by being so active outside the Middle East, Habash's radicals sprang a surprise by targeting Israel's national airline. In July 1968, three Arabs hijacked an El Al airliner on a flight from Rome to Tel Aviv and forced the plane to land in Algeria.

The passengers and crew were held prisoner in Algiers for three weeks, and only when Israel agreed to free a dozen wounded guerrillas from jail did the first Palestinian hijacking end with the release of the hostages.

That was the last successful hijacking of an Israeli airliner. Israeli decision makers quickly drew lessons from the humiliation of succumbing to blackmail. They vowed never again to surrender to the demands of terrorists, but the Israelis also knew that defiant statements of intent are insufficient in such matters. Rather than words alone, they would need a new and muscular art: counterterrorism.

Palestinian gunmen and bombmakers, however, seemed to have seized the initiative. In December 1968, two PFLP men threw hand grenades and opened fire at an El Al airplane at Athens airport, killing one Israeli passenger and wounding two female flight attendants. An almost identical attack took place at Zurich airport the following February, when four PFLP gunmen killed an El Al pilot and wounded five passengers. Other airlines flying to Israel became targets of hijackings and bombings, as the entire Earth seemed to be transformed into a global terrorist village. No target, especially if connected to Israel or Jews, was off limits.

It took a while for Shin Bet to get fully up to speed, but the agency was close on the Palestinian militants' heels when they moved abroad. This sparked some interagency rivalry in the intelligence community, as the Mossad preferred to protect its near monopoly over foreign operations. The Mossad did, however, acknowledge that Shin Bet had the legal and professional responsibility to expand its activities abroad in the hot pursuit of terrorism.

Shin Bet officers were either attached—on loan—to Mossad stations, or were assigned to Europe independently by Shin Bet. In what became an undercover, no-holds-barred war fought with innovation and improvisation, Israeli operatives played a deadly game of cat and mouse with the Palestinians.

Shin Bet's responsibilities also focused on developing anti-terrorist defenses. The agency had to build, from nothing, an effective and sophisticated system to protect such Israeli interests abroad as embassies, banks, tourism offices, and the national airline. Not only the fleet of airplanes, but ground facilities, too, had become terrorist targets. El Al's check-in counters and offices in all airports abroad had their defenses "hardened" and were assigned armed guards.

Israel introduced a radically new type of security setup by posting armed sky marshals on every flight. They sat in ordinary seats in the guise of routine travelers in plainclothes. These were young men who had served in élite army units and had learned to be quick on the draw.

The assumption was—and all experience had shown—that hijackers would want to stay alive, land the plane somewhere, and hold hostages. But as early as 1973, Israel was aware that there could be a major change: Intelligence intercepts indicated that terrorists might hijack an airliner and crash it into a building.

The United States and almost all other countries generally ignored Israel's aviation security knowhow, methods, and preparations for worst-case scenarios. This was mainly for budgetary reasons. Only after the terrorism of September 11, 2001, would they follow in Shin Bet's footsteps to protect their own respective airlines.

Yet, Israeli security was not perfect. Whether best described by clichés about shutting barn doors after horses bolt, or about fighting the last war, the fact is that Israeli procedures—as good as they are—generally have been reactive to attacks mounted by terrorists. It was impossible to predict where, when, and how violent enemies determined to shock the world would strike next.

Chapter Ten

MORE THAN VENGEANCE

I n 1968 Meir Amit was replaced as director of the Mossad. No offense was intended by Prime Minister Levi Eshkol, and none was taken. Everyone involved with these appointments seemed to agree that an 11-year tenure—the time Isser Harel wielded his outsized power—was too long. Amit's five years, marked by impressive modernization, felt honorably sufficient.

As was then standard practice, the name of the new director was not announced to the public, but he was Zvi Zamir. One army general was replacing another, and the new chief was a soft-spoken man who was always willing to work hard. For better or for worse, he was never a headline maker during his long military career.

As the head of Israel's foreign espionage, however, he would see the most imaginably exciting events unfold. And Zamir would be compelled to refocus his country's covert war against its enemies—in ways that would have a lasting impact, even on the Mossad's eventual secret war against Iran.

Why was someone so colorless selected for one of the most important jobs in Israel? Because leaders of the Labor Party considered Zamir "one of us." Similar to many Labor politicians, he was born in Poland in 1925. He arrived in Palestine in his parents' arms, at the age of seven months, and the family name then was Zarzevsky.

Zamir joined the underground fighters of the Palmach at age 18, fought in the 1948 War of Independence, and chose to stay in the Israel Defense Forces. He attained the rank of major general, was placed in charge of the Southern Command, and served in London as the military attaché at the Israeli embassy.

His post in Britain meant that he missed the Six-Day War and the limelight of glory cast upon other IDF generals. He truly lacked glamour and seemed to be an expressionless military bureaucrat.

From Eshkol's point of view, Zamir's strength could be found in his weakness. After two decades of strong, overconfident spymasters, the prime minister wanted to appoint a completely different type of character. Zamir fit the bill.

He immediately threw himself into cooperation with Shin Bet's Yosef Harmelin in the fight against growing Palestinian terrorism. These joint efforts brought the ostensibly domestic security agency into foreign battlefields more than ever before.

When the PLO began to attack Israeli embassies and diplomats in Europe and Asia, Shin Bet was ready to respond. The embassies and consular offices were transformed into fortresses. Double-thick steel doors protected entrances, television cameras scrutinized all visitors, building perimeters were surrounded by electronic sensors, and Shin Bet guards were assigned to keep watch over buildings and their staff. The expanded "protective security" department of Shin Bet did everything possible to defend Israeli facilities abroad, but the intelligence chiefs realized that to deter terrorism they needed stronger measures.

Dissatisfied by passive defense, Israeli intelligence moved full speed ahead into *active* defense. More accurately, it was offensive action.

IDF special forces—led by Sayeret Matkal, which had infiltration into enemy territory as its specialty—suddenly landed in helicopters at the international airport near Beirut, Lebanon, on December 28, 1968. Two days earlier, terrorists had attacked an El Al airliner in Athens, Greece.

Almost casually engaging in a gun battle with Lebanese troops, the Israeli commandos blew up 13 empty civilian aircraft belonging to Arab airlines.

The world was shocked by the audacity of the move. Some critics condemned an act of "state terrorism" and found it hypocritical that now the Israelis were attacking civil aviation. The United Nations Security Council voted, 15 to 0, to condemn Israel's raid on Beirut. Israeli leaders would feel, over the decades that followed, that the U.N. always voted against them; and that sending a strong message that terrorists and their supporters were subject to attack was more important than winning votes in New York.

Behind the condemnations, the world had to admire Israel's military prowess. The Beirut raid was a clear sign that Israel could strike with astonishing accuracy at the heart of the Arab world. Excellent intelligence, built up over many years, made such freedom of action a reality.

A vicious circle of violence and retaliation reached its peak at the Olympic Games in Munich on September 5, 1972. Under the cover of the shadowy Black September group—named for the month in 1970 when Jordan's King Hussein crushed the PLO—eight Palestinian terrorists seized 11 Israeli athletes and coaches in the Olympic village. Two Israelis were shot dead, while fighting back.

Though Black September pretended to be autonomous, it was actually a front for the PLO.

As in other hostage incidents, the terrorists at the Olympics demanded that Israel free their comrades from prison—in this case, 250 jailed Palestinians. The Israeli government, true to its firm policy, refused.

As the world's media broadcast the siege into homes around the globe, there were two simultaneous, perhaps contradictory, impacts. The live TV coverage publicized the demands of the Palestinians, and it also generated sympathy for Jewish victims suffering again on German soil.

In Jerusalem, Prime Minister Golda Meir handed responsibility for the Munich crisis to the Mossad director. Zamir immediately flew to Munich and held urgent discussions with West German security officials. He was accompanied by Victor Cohen, a veteran Shin Bet interrogator who had gotten Israel

Be'er and other spies to break. Cohen was fluent in Arabic, and that could be helpful if negotiations were to commence with the Palestinian terrorists.

Under Prime Minister Meir's direct orders, and armed with the experience of rescuing the hijacked passengers of a Belgian Sabena airliner in Tel Aviv only four months earlier, Zamir pleaded with the West Germans to permit a specially trained Israeli commando unit to deal with the siege. The country's Chancellor, Willy Brandt, probably would have agreed, but the German federal constitution left the decision in the hands of local state officials. And they refused.

Zamir and Cohen, therefore, could only watch helplessly from the control tower of Munich's military airport—where the terrorists by then had taken the hostages—as inexperienced and ill-equipped German sharpshooters opened fire. They failed to kill all the terrorists in the first volley, and the three who were still alive slaughtered the nine Israeli hostages by firing machine guns and tossing hand grenades into two helicopters in which the athletes were sitting.

The head of the Mossad had the searing experience of seeing Israelis shot, burned alive, and blown to pieces. The level of frustration could not be overstated, as leaders of the Jewish state have always been determined not to depend on other countries for Israel's security. The lessons of Munich were being drawn at a sickeningly rapid pace.

Waves of shock reverberated around the world. The massacre was seen as both a human tragedy and a warning that terrorism was growing out of control.

In Israel, an inquiry committee decided that the head of Shin Bet's protective security department, who had been responsible for guarding the Olympic athletes, should be dismissed. Agency chief Harmelin, however, argued passionately against pinning the blame on the department head, and for the only time in his career Harmelin threatened to resign. Prime Minister Meir insisted that the dismissal was a cheap bureaucratic price to pay, and Harmelin reluctantly fired his subordinate.

Only five days after the Munich murders, the PLO/Black September struck again. A Shin Bet officer, on loan to the Mossad and listed as first secretary at his embassy in Brussels, was shot at point-blank range at a café. Zadok Ofir suffered wounds to his head, abdomen, and chest. Miraculously, he survived.

Ofir admitted later that he knew his assailant and had mishandled him. The terrorist was part of a clever plot by the PLO to identify and attack Israeli case officers in Europe. The Arab first made contact by writing a letter to the Israeli embassy from a prison in the Netherlands, where he was serving time for theft. He claimed he was a Moroccan revolutionary who now wanted to work with Israeli intelligence.

The Mossad turned to its Dutch liaison, asking that the man be released, but that was refused. Ofir found some pretext to visit the man in jail, claiming he was a relative. The inmate left a good impression on Ofir. The man seemed valuable, and it was agreed that he would get in touch when his prison term was over.

A year later, the telephone call arrived at Ofir's desk. They agreed to meet in the café where Ofir was shot. He did not have any bodyguard, although an armed observer is usually assigned to such a meeting. The Arab gunman fled to Paris, where a PLO representative—Mahmoud Hamshari—helped him vanish.

The Palestinians probably knew that Brussels was the center of Israeli espionage activity in Europe. The Belgian capital gained that status after Charles de Gaulle expelled the Mossad from Paris: a reaction to Israelis helping Moroccan security men there kill the dissident Ben Barka in 1965. (*See Chapter 7.*)

The Brussels shooting should have kindled huge warning lights in the Mossad and Shin Bet headquarters. For the first time, an Israeli intelligence officer on active duty abroad had been shot. The massacre at Munich, however, was overshadowing all other incidents and considerations. Even Zvi Zamir, returning from Munich, did not recognize the importance of the attack on Ofir.

The Mossad chief hurried from Lod Airport to Jerusalem, where he told the prime minister of the disaster he had witnessed in Germany. There were tears in Meir's eyes. She was a tough politician, but nevertheless a sensitive woman who tried to be the entire nation's "Jewish mother."

Now she felt torn between calm logic and an angry desire to avenge the lives of her murdered "boys." Meir wanted to get some cool-headed advice on what could and should be done to hit the Palestinian killers most effectively. She created a new post, the prime minister's adviser on counter-terrorism, and chose General Aharon Yariv for the job. He had just retired after eight years as Aman director, his place in history assured by the six-day victory of 1967.

Terrorism became an obsession for Meir, Yariv, and Zamir. It also became a magnet for curiosity all around the world, as reports mounted of a clandestine tit-for-tat war in the shadows between Israel and Arab extremists. The body count was also mounting, and soon it became clear that most of the casualties were Palestinian radicals. A mythology of Mossad vengeance missions grew quickly and would persist for decades.

The central myth—disseminated by books and at least two movies—was that Israel embarked on a worldwide, murderous manhunt for the sake of striking back for the Munich Olympics massacre. Yes, the Mossad sent gunmen and bombers who killed Palestinian terrorists in Europe and elsewhere. But the motives were more nuanced than mere revenge.

The popular tale has been bolstered by the secondary myth of a top-secret Committee X created by Meir and Moshe Dayan. The image suggested that with great drama and formality this tribunal decreed that any Black September member involved in planning, assisting, or executing the attack at the Olympics should be killed by the Mossad.

What truly occurred was that Israel's leaders decided to step up their war against the PLO. As the Palestinians were turning Europe into a battlefield, the Mossad would join the bloody battle and win it there. The Munich massacre—followed by the shooting of the Shin Bet man in Belgium—made Meir and her advisors realize that the Jewish state was under attack beyond the country's borders, and that passivity would lead only to more losses.

For the sake, then, of going on the offensive, Zamir created a team that would specialize in finding and liquidating terrorists. He assigned Mike Harari to be the "project manager," a dry title for a violent job. His selection was only natural, as Harari had taken over from Yosef Yariv as head of Caesarea—the operations department that sometimes called itself Metsada.

Harari never publicly revealed his life story, but he was born in 1927 and fought in the pre-state Palmach strike force. He worked on Aliyah B clandestine immigration projects, then became a leading figure in the joint operations unit of Shin Bet and the Mossad. He tended to be wherever the action was for Israeli secret agents.

Harari looked like a tough guy, and indeed he was. To show how small and intermingled Israeli society tends to be, however, it may be noteworthy that his wife was a senior administrator at Tel Aviv University; his sister-in-law, Dorit Beinish, was later the president of Israel's supreme court. Those institutions celebrate openness, freedom of speech, and the rule of law: qualities that seem totally at odds with the Mossad's image. Yet Israel's covert combatants would contend that they fight to preserve those democratic values.

Ordered to spearhead the Israeli response to the Munich massacre, Harari handpicked a team of operatives, both men and women, and established a command post in Paris. He personally adopted several false identities. Harari and Mossad officer Avraham Gehmer, whose cover job was as first secretary of the Israeli embassy in Paris, were in charge of the planning.

From this modest beginning would emerge one of the most notorious yet admired units in the worldwide business of espionage: an élite squad to become known as Kidon, the Hebrew word for "Bayonet." It would handle the extreme end of special operations, including but not limited to assassinations, kidnappings, and sabotage.

Kidon members would be recruited from special forces units of the military, mainly from Sayeret Matkal. Kidon would administratively be part of Caesarea-Metsada. But if the "action teams" of Caesarea were a kind of Mossad within the Mossad, Kidon could be considered a separate, self-sustaining planet on its own. (*See Chapter 22.*)

In launching the post-Munich campaign, Harari ignored the PLO's attempt to distance itself from violence by using the cover identity of Black September. He and Zamir decided to go after key Palestinians who were managing the PLO's terrorist activities in Europe. That was surely in the spirit of what Golda Meir intended.

The first assassination, in October 1972, was that of Adel Wael Zwaiter, a Palestinian intellectual in Rome who worked as a translator for the Libyan embassy but was a senior coordinator of the PLO/Black September infrastructure. Zwaiter, according to the Mossad's information, was involved in a failed plot to blow up an El Al airliner.

Harari's team shot him more than a dozen times inside his apartment building in the Italian capital.

Within nine months, Harari's men and women took the lives of six Palestinians in Rome, Paris, Cyprus, and Athens. Among them was the PLO's Mahmoud Hamshari in Paris.

Some might ask: only six? A legend grew that the Israeli hit team eliminated dozens of PLO men, as though the Munich tragedy led to a bloodbath. Stories spread about innovative bombs set off by pressure switches and high-pitch tones transmitted through phone lines, while shadowy gunmen expertly aimed silencers at the heads of Palestinian foes. Yet in Europe, in that time frame, there were only six.

While Israeli intelligence continued with assassinations, another form of warfare was introduced. The Mossad was sending letter bombs to PLO officials in Beirut. One was killed, and another scarred for life.

The PLO/Black September could see that something new was going on. Some of its top men were being killed. The PLO fought back, mailing letter bombs to Israeli diplomats in Europe. An attaché in Israel's embassy in London was killed by one blast. The battle on European turf became a two-way affair, later dubbed "the war of the spooks."

On January 26, 1973, Israeli businessman Hanan Yishai was shot dead as he stood in a doorway on Madrid's main boulevard. After his death, it was revealed that his real name was Baruch Cohen, and that he had come to Spain on a mission for Israeli intelligence. Like Zadok Ofir in Brussels, Cohen was a Shin Bet case officer—on loan to the Mossad—running a network of Palestinian agents.

One of his Arab operatives was a double agent, whose ultimate loyalty turned out to be to the PLO. Cohen became the first and only Israeli intelligence operative in Europe killed by a Palestinian.

Some members of Cohen's family claimed later that his death could have been prevented. In violation of security precautions, his photograph had been published—ironically, in an official army album celebrating the 1967 victory—and the snapshot showed Baruch Cohen in military uniform with his best friend, Zadok Ofir, also in uniform. Arab intelligence services collect such clippings, and it is considered vital that Israeli operatives never show their faces. Even though Cohen concealed his identity when operating his Palestinian network, that photograph may have given him away.

The war raged on and morphed into new shapes. In April 1973, the PLO attacked an Israeli civilian plane in Nicosia, Cyprus, and the nearby home of the Israeli ambassador.

The Jewish state seemed to be retaliating the very next night—although the timing was probably pure coincidence, as this was a major operation on territory much more treacherous than Rome or Paris. The Israelis would now take the battle to PLO headquarters in Lebanon, an enemy country. They had concluded that liquidating Palestinian operatives and coordinators in Europe was not sufficient. Leading the way into the lion's den, this time, would be army commandos. The Mossad would play a support role.

The assassins were members of Sayeret Matkal, wearing civilian clothes. At least one of them, the future prime minister Ehud Barak, wore a wig and was dressed as a woman. In the middle of bustling Beirut, using vehicles and routes provided by the Mossad, the well-trained soldiers killed two organizers of PLO violence in their apartments and also shot dead the group's spokesman. The intelligence about where they lived, and that they would be home, was perfect. So was the entry and exit plan by way of a Lebanese beach.

After a few years, Israel did not bother to deny this invasion of a neighboring country, and its code name *Aviv Ne'urim* (Spring of Youth) appears on official Israeli military websites as a notable and laudable event.

When Palestinian terrorists and activists were liquidated, relatives of dead Israelis were informed that a blow had been struck in tribute to their loved ones. The families, however, generally derived little joy from the fact that Arabs also had fatherless children now attending funerals.

Baruch Cohen's widow Nurit revealed: "Occasionally service officers would come to visit me and ask, 'Have you read in the newspaper that this-and-that guy has been killed or this-and-that guy has been blown up?' What could I say, that it consoled me?"

All of these glorious missions of the Mossad and the military would come to a sharp, if temporary, halt—only nine months after the start of the post-Munich campaign—because of a startling failure in a town called Lillehammer.

At the beginning of July 1973, Mike Harari brought members of his "project"—some, chosen for their experience in meting out death, others only for their expertise in Scandinavia—to that small skiing town in northern Norway. The Israelis were assembling for their most important mission in the post-Munich campaign of killing, because the victim was to be the operations chief of the Black September front organization: Ali Hassan Salameh, who had been nicknamed "the Red Prince."

They had been hearing about Salameh for a few years, as a talented terror operator who was very close to Yasser Arafat, and the Mossad believed he was one of the masterminds of the attack on the Israelis at the Munich Olympics.

This clever and highly violent Palestinian was not busying himself only with the shadowy, but ultimately bogus, Black September. In reality, he was the commander of Force 17, the PLO unit responsible for the protection of Arafat. The 17 was simply its telephone extension number at PLO headquarters.

The Israelis saw the connection as conclusive proof that Arafat himself was ordering attacks on athletes in Munich, tourists waiting for flights to Israel, and other civilians in many locations. But the PLO chief would usually distance himself from distasteful operations, providing himself with plausible deniability while depending on Salameh and others to do the dirty work.

Salameh knew that he was in danger and took precautions—often surrounded by bodyguards—but he also was addicted to the bright lights of wealth and glamour. Believing he deserved nothing but the best, in 1978 he married a gorgeous Lebanese Christian, Georgina Rizk, who in Miami Beach had been crowned Miss Universe. The year before their wedding, they vacationed in the United States: at Disney World and in Hawaii.

A Palestinian guerrilla leader, living it up in America? The CIA reportedly arranged safe passage to Mickey Mouse and the luaus, and even paid for the trip. That was because the Agency was wooing Salameh to be a fully employed agent.

He was the PLO's secret contact man for talks with the CIA—as early as 1969, in the years before the PLO foreswore terrorism and earned official recognition from Washington. Salameh arranged a guarantee that American diplomats would not be attacked.

It is not clear when Israeli intelligence became aware of the CIA's special link with Salameh, but the Israelis had their own accounts to settle with the Red Prince and were not going to let his American connection stop them.

He was, however, often very difficult to locate. A breakthrough came in July 1973, when Mossad informants in northern Europe felt certain that they had spotted Salameh. Harari's gunslingers headed to Norway with great enthusiasm.

Within days, they were joined by Zamir. The head of the Mossad himself, adhering to the Israeli military tradition of a commander taking risks at the front with his soldiers, would supervise this significant assassination. This Palestinian was not just one more target. Zamir had personally seen the death and destruction caused by Salameh's colleagues at Munich the previous September. Killing him would be a significant win in the shadowy post-Munich war.

Equipped with photos of Salameh, the support members of Harari's team tailed the man they had pinpointed for several hours. At least three assassins then were delivered by car. They pumped around a dozen bullets into the man, by the side of a road where he and a woman had been walking.

The gunmen drove off toward pre-set escape routes out of Norway, and before long the rest of the Israeli team was hiding in safe houses in Oslo. Lillehammer had just had its first murder in 40 years.

Only the next day did the Israeli agents discover that they had made a terrible mistake. They had killed the wrong man, a Moroccan waiter named Ahmed Bouchiki, who was married to a Norwegian—the pregnant woman with whom he had been strolling. It would take more than 20 years for Israel to pay compensation to her and her child, though still without admitting legal responsibility.

A junior member of the Mossad team had been right, it turned out. While watching the man reputed to be Salameh, Marianne Gladnikoff had told other members of Harari's squad that the man's face seemed different from Salameh's. They would not listen to her. To them, she was merely a Shin Bet secretary who had been added to Harari's team only because of her Swedish passport and Scandinavian language skills.

The Israelis might have gotten away with murder—keeping their error an absolute secret—had it not been for the stupid behavior of the Israeli support agents, the men and women who did the surveillance and some of the planning. They made every conceivable mistake and left police a clear trail at every step. They drove around Lillehammer in cars they themselves had rented, rather than using go-betweens who would never know the true nature of the murder mission. In trailing Bouchiki, they had been as graceful as a herd of elephants in a china shop. They did not observe the rules of compartmentalization, but instead knew who and where everyone was.

The unfortunate waiter's neighbors reported a license-plate number to the police, and two of the Israeli operatives were arrested as they returned their rented car to Oslo's airport. Traveling as Gladnikoff and Dan Ert, they both admitted they were working for Israel and provided the address of an apartment used by the Mossad. The police found two more members of the hit team there.

Norwegian investigators were amazed at the amateurism displayed by the espionage agency considered to be the world's best. The Israelis fell into the hands of the police, one after another, like overripe fruit off a tree. Harari himself managed to flee, but Gehmer and five other Mossad operatives were arrested.

Zamir, the head of the Mossad, luckily had arranged his own escape route. An occasional helper in Norway, a sayan, had approached a Jewish textiles manufacturer—a survivor of Nazi death camps who had strong sentiments toward Israel—to ask if his yacht could be borrowed. The rich man was given to understand that he should not ask many questions, as this loan would be for the good of the Jewish state of Israel.

By saying yes, the yacht owner was also a sayan. Israeli intelligence already had a well established pattern of gently establishing relationships with people who could be helpful in almost every nation on the planet. Most were Jewish, but many were not. Some were wealthy, and many were not.

The rich helpers might have private airplanes, boats, and country houses that could be borrowed for clandestine meetings. Yet, a high income was not a prerequisite for renting cars, leaving an apartment door unlocked, or providing some useful information.

The sayanim (helpers) unknowingly were part of an outer perimeter, in case of problems or a need for standby escape routes. The Mossad, as a rule, took care not to ask local Jews to spy on anyone—just to make arrangements.

Zamir wisely chose to avoid Norway's airports and, after making his way to a port, he was whisked to nearby Sweden on the new sayan's yacht.

Those left behind said far too much to Norwegian police interrogators. For the first time, some of the *modus operandi* of the post-Munich assassinations was thus exposed. One of the Mossad men was carrying a key to an apartment in Paris, where the French secret service found keys to even more safe houses used by Israeli operatives. Evidence was found that connected the Israelis with the unsolved killings of Palestinians in several countries.

The most talkative of those captured was Ert, a Danish-born veteran of many Mossad missions whose apparently genuine Hebrew name was Dan Aerbel. As soon as the Norwegians placed him alone in a dark room, he began to tell them everything. The interrogators were barely able to conceal their amazement when Ert/Aerbel blurted out that he suffered from claustrophobia, a definite handicap for a secret agent. In return for being moved to a larger cell, he was willing to confess.

Another Israeli arrested in Norway was Sylvia Raphael, but she was far more professional than Ert/Aerbel. She did not break. She stuck to her cover story: that her name was Patricia Roxborough and she was a news photographer with a Canadian passport.

In fact, Raphael was using forged travel documents and had been doing so for a long time.

She was born in 1937 in Cape Town, South Africa, to a Christian mother and a Jewish father. She fell in love with Israel while in her 20s. She volunteered at a kibbutz named Ramat HaKovesh, and being pretty, smart, and easily suited to a terrific cover story, she was spotted by Israeli intelligence. In the early 1960s, the military intelligence unit specializing in penetration of Arab countries hired and trained her.

Her personal instructor was Gehmer, who would be arrested in Lillehammer with her. Ten years prior to that, he sent her to Canada to build up professional qualifications as a cover. Later, the entire Aman unit was transferred to the Mossad as part of the new Caesarea operations department.

Fully trained as a combatant, she repeatedly used the Roxborough cover as a way to reach any place where journalists might go. She conducted espionage in Egypt, and even reportedly in Palestinian refugee camps where Arafat was putting together his PLO.

Her case in Norway had a happy ending, at least, because she fell in love with Annaeus Schjodt, her Norwegian defense attorney, and married him after her release from 11 months in prison. Their romance was first noticed by an eight-year-old, the daughter of Israeli ambassador Eliezer Palmor. Raphael was permitted to stay at his house in Oslo during holiday breaks from her cell— generously approved by Norway's government—for Passover and for Rosh HaShana. During a dinner, the girl ran to her mother to report that Sylvia and her lawyer were "secretly touching" under the table, so "they must be in love." Their cover was blown.

The couple became celebrities in Oslo and was invited to social events, where many Norwegians wanted to chat amiably with a Mossad assassin. It was as though Israel had produced yet another champagne spy.

In the 1980s, the Mossad uncovered a PLO plot to assassinate Roxborough/Raphael. The Tevel department, in charge of foreign liaisons, sent a detailed message to the Norwegian secret service—because clandestine relations were back to normal within a few years after the mistaken murder. The Norwegian government, a great supporter of the Palestinian cause, privately warned Arafat that if Raphael were killed, then he would be held responsible.

Five of the Mossad operatives had to spend time in a Norwegian prison, with terms ranging from two to five-and-a-half years. Yet, the sentences were reduced for all of them.

Raphael did not return to the Mossad, at least not in life. She and her husband lived in Norway for a while and then in South Africa, where she died of leukemia in 2005 at age 67. The Mossad arranged to bring her body to Israel for a hero's funeral at her kibbutz, surrounded by the scent of citrus flowers from nearby groves. Clandestine colleagues attended the moving ceremony, and her own words are carved on her gravestone: "I love my country wholeheartedly."

In an unprecedented move, the Mossad agreed to open parts of its secret archives to publicize Raphael's heroic service. One of her trainers in espionage tradecraft, Motti Kfir, was permitted to take part in writing a biography titled *Sylvia*.

The Mossad was lucky that Norway did not press very hard in its investigation of the complicated Lillehammer case, clearly preferring not to add public humiliation to Israel's embarrassment. Despite incriminating information that emerged at the trials in Norway, the French and Italian security services also displayed a great deal of solidarity with the Mossad. They ignored the PLO's demands to renew investigations into the violent deaths of Palestinians in those countries.

This was, of course, not simply the result of dumb luck. The seeds sown by the Tevel department were bearing fruit. Western secret services respected the Jewish state's willingness to show the world an alternative to appeasement and submission in the war against terrorism. Most European governments thus did not look intensively into things they would rather not know.

This was small consolation for Israel. The Mossad could not be satisfied until it finally caught up with Salameh. Yet, there was a six-year halt in counterterrorism killings. Lillehammer made it seem that the danger of exposure was too great, and assassinations not worthwhile.

Finding Salameh remained a high priority. That would happen under a new Mossad director and a new—and very different—Israeli government.

In 1977, for the first time in the 29-year history of the nation, the Labor Party lost an election. The leader of the right-wing Likud bloc, Menachem Begin, became prime minister.

Begin had been a leader of the Irgun, an underground movement that battled Arabs and the British before statehood in 1948. Irgun attitudes were more unbending and its methods generally more violent than those of Ben-Gurion's mainstream Jewish fighters. Shifting from opposition leader to prime minister, Begin was now enchanted by the excitement of Israel's intelligence community. He always believed in Jews being able to fight—and now, in fascinatingly innovative ways, they really could fight!

General Yitzhak Hofi had already taken over the Mossad from Zamir in 1974, and Begin was giving Hofi a free hand in almost everything. The prime minister enthusiastically approved finishing the job that was frustratingly incomplete: finding and eliminating Ali Hassan Salameh.

The Red Prince was known to be spending almost all of his time in Beirut, where his boss, Arafat, ran a mini-state within the nation of Lebanon. Reaching him there was certainly a possibility, as Israeli spies, assassins, and commandos had operated there before. But it was never easy.

This time, the key figure in the operation would be Erika Chambers. She was born in 1948 in London, where her father was a famous racing car driver. Her mother, a Czech Jew who grew up in Vienna, exposed Erika to Jewish culture and history.

She studied hydrology, first in England and then in Canberra, Australia. In 1972, she flew to Israel to do some field work in the Negev desert, continuing her studies at the Hebrew University in Jerusalem.

Then, one day, she disappeared. She had joined Harari's special operations department, Caesarea. She underwent training in all the relevant arts, including the use of explosives, and prepared herself to be planted undercover in enemy territory for a Kidon assassination mission.

Chambers first spent a long period in Germany establishing a legend, making sure to leave a trail of home addresses. Then she did some work for a children's charity in Geneva, where she volunteered to be its representative in Lebanon. Soon Chambers was renting an apartment in Beirut, and she chose a location along the route where Salameh drove to and from his home every day.

She told her neighbors her name was Penelope, and they would see her feeding street cats and painting on an easel she set up on her balcony. That was a wonderful vantage point for looking down to spot approaching cars.

She also visited Palestinian orphanages, and her target—Salameh himself—was among the PLO officials she befriended.

In January 1979, she subtly made contact with at least two more Mossad combatants who had entered Lebanon using British and Canadian passports. These were the committed, seemingly emotionless, trained killers of Kidon. Using material that other Israeli agents had pre-positioned, they were able to fill a vehicle with explosives and a reliable radio-controlled detonator.

On January 22, they parked it along Salameh's habitual driving route. When the Red Prince came up that road, one of the Mossad operatives pressed a button. The powerful bomb exploded. This particular elusive enemy of Israel was vaporized, his car mangled and charred. His four bodyguards and four bystanders—including a German nun and a British visitor—were also killed.

The Israeli assassination squad quickly fled. Yet for some reason, probably haste and uncharacteristic sloppiness, "Penelope" left behind her authentic British passport—identifying her as Erika Chambers—in her Beirut apartment.

Her return to the Mossad's bosom came at sea. Harari personally waited for her and the other combatants on a navy missile boat, in the Mediterranean north of Israel's territorial waters. Israeli naval commandos used motorized rubber craft to pick up the assassination team, after rendezvousing with them on a Lebanese beach.

Chambers received a hero's welcome at Mossad headquarters. She was assigned to desk work—boring, of course, after her heart-pounding covert experiences. She took part in some lectures and training within the Mossad's secret educational compound, but quite quickly Chambers retired and practically ceased to exist.

She changed her name and told her British parents and brother nothing, but she did regularly mail them holiday cards with Israeli stamps on the envelope. Here, then, was a woman from England—inspired by a partially Jewish upbringing and a short time in Israel to take daring and drastic action on behalf of the Mossad—then willing to give up her entire genuine life for the cause. Israeli intelligence was lucky to have more than a few other women and men who did much the same.

The Kidon unit's achievement in 1979, erasing Ali Hassan Salameh, felt like good news in Israel. But the publicly exposed failure in Norway in 1973 continued to haunt Israeli intelligence. Many in the community referred to Lillehammer, in an unhappy pun, as *Leyl-ha-Mar*, Hebrew for "the Night of Bitterness." Every time it was mentioned, Israeli secret operatives cringed. They all agreed that killing the wrong man—and then getting caught—added up to their greatest operational failure.

It could be argued that a post-Munich obsession with escalating the shadow war of assassinations prompted the intelligence agencies to misplace their keen judgment. Some senior officials complained that it was a mistake to be drawn into becoming a branch of Murder Incorporated. They claimed that Mossad resources, even after the massacre at the Olympics, should have been devoted far more heavily to tracking the military capabilities of Israel's Arab neighbors.

The internal dissenters claimed that Israel was exaggerating the importance of Palestinian terrorism, for in the final analysis it was not this that would imperil the country's existence. At worst, it was like a pesky insect annoying Israel without posing a huge threat. Others stressed that there was no use in wiping out the heads of Palestinian guerrilla groups, because there was no guarantee that their replacements would be more moderate or less able.

Some of the dissidents within Israeli intelligence further charged that the Lillehammer debacle did not lead to sufficiently harsh consequences. Mike Harari offered his resignation, but it was rejected by Zamir and Meir. The tenor of the times did not require individuals to bear responsibility for their failures. The Israeli public and the media still fully trusted the government.

Harari resumed his operations job in Tel Aviv for a few more years.

Zamir, as Mossad chief, was comfortable with the post-Munich focus on bringing the fight to the Palestinian enemy. His analysts concluded that PLO activists, rather than devoting their energies to terrorist planning, were now spending a lot of time and trouble looking over their shoulders—fearing that they themselves were about to be attacked.

Zamir broke his silence only three decades later, because of outrage over a movie. In an interview, his version of events was more complex than the oft-told tale of Prime Minister Meir demanding revenge against the individual Palestinians who organized the Olympics massacre.

The occasion that provoked Zamir to talk was the release of *Munich*, Steven Spielberg's film based on a book, *Vengeance: The True Story of an Israeli Counter-Terrorist Team*, by Canadian journalist George Jonas. Jonas's information came mainly from Juval Aviv, a New York-based private detective who claimed that he had led the Mossad's post-Munich hit team.

Spielberg said he, too, had a chance to meet with "Avner," the name used by Aviv. The famous filmmaker felt that he gained an understanding of the deep doubts supposedly felt by hit-team members—and, in the end, the uselessness of waging a war on terrorism.

Zamir was furious at the way the movie depicted the post-Olympics massacre events. "The film is a kind of Western, but with no connection to reality," he said, then making a point of adding: "Aviv was never in the Mossad. He is an imposter."

Explaining the true motivations of the Mossad and Meir, Zamir insisted that myth is not truth. "We didn't go on a vengeance mission," he said. "The Mossad was not and is not a Mafia organization. Golda did not instruct me to take revenge."

He did agree that the 1972 massacre led to a huge change in Israel's response to attacks. Zamir said: "Until Munich, our policy was guided by the assumption that European nations would not allow Palestinian terror to operate on their soil or to stage a wave of hijackings. That meant that there was no need for us, the Mossad, to operate against the terrorists on European soil. Indeed, we avoided doing so."

The PLO kept attacking Israelis in Europe, and in Tel Aviv and Jerusalem a faction arose that wanted a stronger, lethal reaction. "We—the intelligence and military chiefs—tried to persuade Golda that the European governments were soft on terrorists," Zamir recalled. "And when they did arrest them, after a while they were released." The Mossad chief concluded that Israel would have to mete out justice.

A dramatic dilemma developed in the highly eventful year, 1973. On February 21, a Libyan airliner on a routine flight from Benghazi to Cairo made a navigational error, overshooting the Egyptian capital and flying into Israeli-controlled airspace over the Sinai Peninsula. Israeli fighter planes were scrambled, but a political or senior military decision would be needed on how to respond to what appeared to be a civilian plane that was simply off course.

Unfortunately, only a few weeks before that, Israel's intelligence community received a tip that an Arab terrorist group planned to hijack a passenger plane and crash it into either the Dimona nuclear reactor or the Shalom Tower in Tel Aviv, the country's tallest building.

The Libyan pilot did not respond to radio calls from the Israelis or to such internationally recognized signals as flapping wings attempted by the fighter pilots. With only a few minutes remaining until a target building might be hit, the military chief of staff—General David (Dado) Elazar—issued an order that the Libyan airliner be shot down. Out of 112 passengers and crew, 105 were killed. News coverage of the wreckage and of the bodies of victims, scattered over the sands of the Sinai, made Israel look awful.

Libya's dictator, Colonel Muammar Qaddafi, was livid. To take revenge against the Jewish state, he insisted on immediate and extreme use of a Libyan-Egyptian political-military alliance then in effect. He had heard that the British ocean liner, the *Queen Elizabeth 2*, would be visiting the Israeli port of Ashdod in May to mark the 25th anniversary of Israel's independence. Qaddafi insisted that an Egyptian navy submarine sink the *QE2*.

Luckily, cooler heads prevailed in Cairo. President Anwar Sadat blocked any such order to his navy, regardless of the shared authority that Qaddafi supposedly wielded. The dictator was to be told that the submarine could not locate the cruise ship.

One of Sadat's motivations was that he had already started planning a surprise attack, for October 1973, in the hope that it would force the Israelis out of the Sinai Peninsula. Torpedoing Britain's gem of the ocean could well torpedo Sadat's more significant plan.

Qaddafi—who had seized power in a military coup four years earlier and was only beginning to earn his eventual nickname of "Mad Dog of the Middle East"—insisted on revenge for the downing of the Libyan airliner. According to Israeli officials, Sadat gave in and agreed to a more modest operation that might seem fitting: downing an El Al airliner as it approached Rome's Fiumicino Airport for a landing.

Egypt's intelligence agency agreed to provide Soviet-made SAM-7 Strela missiles to a team of PLO guerrillas, who would fire them. The coordinator of the plot was Ashraf Marwan, a young and ambitious chemist who was a significant character in Cairo for three reasons: His father was a senior Egyptian officer; he himself was the husband of Mona, daughter of the late President Nasser; and he was a close aide to President Sadat.

Two Strela missiles, with their launchers, were packed into boxes bearing Mona's name, and they were sent from Cairo to Rome as legally unsearchable diplomatic mail. The addressee was an Egyptian arts center in Italy.

Marwan picked up the parcels, wrapped the missiles and launchers in a large carpet, and personally delivered them to the Palestinian terrorists at an elegant shoe store on Via Veneto, near the United States embassy. Marwan then flew to London to await the results.

The plot failed. Italy's security services and police arrested some of the terrorists and seized their missiles. What the Libyan, Egyptian, and Palestinian conspirators never knew was the secret about Marwan: He was a paid agent for the Mossad, one of the best Israel ever had.

Zamir knew what was happening, every step of the way. He knew about Qaddafi's drive for revenge, his pressure on Egypt, and Sadat's approval of a plan to shoot down innocents on an Israeli airliner.

Zamir had flown to Rome, to supervise Mossad operatives who kept the Palestinian plotters under surveillance. Zamir, waiting until he knew that they had the missiles with them, personally informed his Italian counterpart.

Frustration for the Mossad came, however, when the five Palestinians who were arrested—despite being sentenced to long terms by a judge at their trial— were released by Italy after only a few months.

The release was forced upon Italy by a PLO method that became increasingly routine. Palestinians hijacked an Italian civilian airliner, and they refused to release the plane and a large number of hostages until the five prisoners in Rome were set free.

What filmmaker Spielberg and countless publications did not comprehend fully was the logic behind the Mossad's post-Munich assassinations. European governments were repeatedly giving in to blackmail and releasing Arabs who clearly were guilty of terrorism. Israel wanted its enemies to be neutralized. It would have settled for seeing them jailed for long terms. But because Europe was releasing them, Israel decided that it would have to remove them from the scene.

Finding it impractical to take the extra risks to kidnap and imprison known terrorists in distant lands, the Mossad would kill them.

In addition, there was a desire for psychological impact. Despite the fact that there were barely 10 killings in this campaign, a deterrent effect was surely achieved. Israel was perceived as a country with a very long arm and the memory of an elephant.

More than 30 years later, in light of Hollywood's distorted take on the post-Munich killings, Zamir felt compelled to clarify the nuanced reasons for the Mossad sending out assassins—even to friendly countries where police and politicians were unhappy about playing host to bloodshed. He insisted that the killings were tactical, part of a war.

Zamir said: "Munich was a shock to all of us, a turning point. Yet, Golda didn't order us to avenge the slaughter of our athletes, as the world has assumed.

Our decision was to disrupt the PLO's operational infrastructure in Europe: their offices, couriers, representatives, and routes.

"Golda left the decision whom to kill, and where, to us. Our attitude was that in order to defend ourselves, we have to go on the attack. And I believe we succeeded in our campaign. Those who accuse us of being motivated simply by revenge are talking nonsense. We didn't wage a vendetta campaign against individuals. It was a war against an organization, aiming to halt and prevent concrete terrorist plans.

"Yes, those who were involved in Munich deserved death. But we didn't deal with the past. We concentrated on what was expected to happen."

Zamir also refuted the myth of Committee X. "There was no such committee," he said. "The system worked differently. At headquarters, the heads of the operational and research units collected data on the most active PLO representatives and agents in Europe. Based on that information, a list was compiled, and that was shown to a small group of senior Mossad managers.

"That was the forum that decided whom to kill, and where and when, if operational circumstances allowed that to be carried out."

The process was far more informal, in a sense more Israeli, than having a stodgy committee labeled X. Zamir did, indeed, go to Prime Minister Meir with the list of recommended targets, and she consulted with a small group of cabinet members: Moshe Dayan, Foreign Minister Abba Eban, Yigal Allon, and Yisrael Galili. Her counterterrorism advisor, Aharon Yariv, was also part of the consultation process—focused on the danger that the intended target might pose if he continued to be alive and active. They also considered what the damage might be to Israel's relations with the country where the assassination would take place.

Last, but surely not least, the prime minister and her advisors—in a pattern that became a fixture of Israeli behavior—wanted to know about collateral damage. The Israelis believe they are different from, and, indeed, morally superior to, their Middle East counterparts. The Mossad targeted only the suspects and tried to avoid killing innocent people, though occasionally some deaths and injuries did occur.

In the end, it was Golda Meir herself who gave Zamir the final green light for any "elimination mission." A planned assassination, by the foreign intelligence agency of a modern democratic country, was considered something for which the highest elected authority in the land should take responsibility.

Murdering individuals was and remains a rarely used weapon for Israeli intelligence, but it would continue to be a very important tool: to eliminate the person or persons gunned down or blown up, and to send a message to others who might think of joining or replacing those killed.

Israeli leaders kept their focus on terrorism, probably to an exaggerated degree. They almost ignored the fact that military build-ups by Arab armies would pose much more of a danger than the ambitions of a "Red Prince" Salameh or Arafat.

CHAPTER ELEVEN

FORBIDDEN ARMS

In the first half of the 1960s, Israel managed to repel pressure from the United States and France to slow down or fully reveal its embryonic nuclear program. Side-stepping pressure from powerful foreigners gave the Israelis who were privy to the secret an energizing sense of confidence. They realized that producing nuclear bombs would be doable. No one would stop Israel.

Yet the project would require raw materials, know-how, and the right technology and equipment.

Entrusted with nurturing, protecting, and zealously hiding a weapon that Israel was intent on developing—but hoped never to use—Binyamin Blumberg continued toiling in anonymity. And he toiled even harder.

His Science Liaison Bureau, Lakam, moved out of the Defense Ministry compound, where it might have been noticed. He opened his office in an ordinary civilian building on Tel Aviv's Carlebach Street, very close to the large *Ma'ariv* building, but no one at that newspaper seemed to know about him and his unmentionable mission.

Prime Minister Ben-Gurion's desire for a nuclear option, to put tiny Israel in the big league with the United States and other great powers, remained strong in the hearts of top Israeli leaders. Shimon Peres made sure that funding and facilities were always available, as needed; their budgets usually were hidden in those of other defense projects.

Blumberg in 1957 had begun to procure everything Israel needed to build a nuclear bomb, and all through the 1960s he stepped up the effort. He correctly believed that official French assistance could not be counted on forever, and he realized that no open source of help would be found.

President John F. Kennedy, and even his friendly successor, Lyndon Johnson, would never provide supplies for this project. Other Western governments either danced to the American tune or feared the reactions of Arab countries.

Blumberg concluded that Lakam would have to operate outside the borders of Israel, effectively on a worldwide scale, so he knew he would need help from other secret agencies.

First, he would have to make the effort to heal old wounds and rivalries within the Israeli intelligence community.

"I was suspicious of Blumberg and his people," Meir Amit admitted—unknowingly echoing the words of his own rival, Isser Harel, who a few years earlier held almost identical sentiments about Lakam. Still, a project that the nation's leaders saw as a high priority demanded the attention of the secret agencies. Although suspicions never fully evaporated, amicable cooperation developed between Lakam and Amit's Mossad.

Blumberg also managed to overcome a bureaucratic battle with the Foreign Ministry and got authorization to send his own scientific attachés to Israeli embassies abroad. Carefully selected from a pool of engineers, physicists, and chemists with security clearance, many of them had worked at the Israel Atomic Energy Commission or in military-related research. They were ordered to pay close attention to any new scientific development, to buy all the journals and professional publications, and to establish friendly contacts with scientists in their countries of residence.

Lakam officers also mapped the wide terrain of Israeli academia, pinpointing professors and researchers who were heading abroad for exchange programs and major conferences. If they were considered trustworthy, they were approached and were asked to do the government some favors. Very few refused.

The requests were usually tiny, involving technical information from open sources such as magazines. There were, however, cases in which academics were asked to steal scientific materials—including blueprints and studies—from research centers where they were spending sabbaticals.

At times, the scientific attachés at embassies abroad were clearly not professional spy handlers. They were protected, however, by diplomatic immunity, so at least they would not end up in prison.

One senior Israeli scientist, who was studying at a prestigious German institute, secretly photocopied various documents on a regular basis. He brought the copies home, and once a week the science attaché of the Israeli embassy would come to pick them up. The attaché, a Lakam man, displayed an unconscionable lack of responsibility, however. He often arrived late for meetings and sometimes did not show up at all. The two Israelis were lucky that the host country suspected nothing.

It was actually harder for Israelis to commit such deeds in America. From the late 1960s onward, America's intelligence community kept tabs on nearly every Israeli scientist who visited the United States. The Federal Bureau of Investigation simply assumed that Israel, as a young and ambitious country, was engaged in espionage ceaselessly and everywhere.

Professor Yuval Ne'eman, who had developed a host of useful gadgets and technical systems for Aman and also served as a senior member of the IAEC, saw the suspicion up close in the 1960s after arriving at Caltech in Pasadena for a semester of physics research.

"Professor, I am from the department," an unfamiliar voice on the telephone announced. "Can we meet?"

Ne'eman assumed that the person speaking was a member of the university faculty. To his consternation, the man who arrived for the appointment introduced himself instead as an investigator for the U.S. Department of Justice. "Are you Colonel Ne'eman?" the American asked.

"Yes," Ne'eman replied, somewhat surprised to be addressed by his military rank and realizing that the investigator was in fact an FBI special agent. The Israeli explained that he was no longer in his country's military intelligence; he had left, and now worked at Tel Aviv University.

"But we know that you are still involved in spying," said the American. "I'd advise you to stop immediately."

Ne'eman vehemently denied the allegation, and the conversation ended abruptly. This had obviously been an attempt to intimidate him, probably in reaction to a visit Ne'eman had just made to the federal nuclear research center in Livermore, east of San Francisco. Considering what the United States was starting to figure out about Israel's Dimona facilities, a tour of Lawrence Livermore National Laboratory seemed important.

A few weeks later, Ne'eman moved to the University of Texas at Austin, where another Justice Department official paid a visit—this time demanding that Ne'eman register as a "foreign agent" of the Israeli government.

Doing so would have harmed Ne'eman's reputation as a physicist, and his travel would have been restricted by U.S. authorities; but the U.S.-Israel intelligence connection was able to help him. The liaison officer representing Mossad's Tevel department in Washington lodged a direct appeal with the CIA, which was able to cancel the requirement that the Israeli register as an agent.

These incidents should have alarmed Blumberg and his assistants, yet the Israeli fishing expeditions in America continued. Years later, in the 1980s, such sloppiness would lead to exposure and a life sentence for Jonathan Pollard, an American naval analyst spying for Israel, who was run by Lakam. (*See Chapter 18.*)

The entirely anonymous agency also turned, in the 1960s, to a small but growing network of Israelis who did business overseas. One of the pillars of Lakam's risky operation was Eliyahu Sakharov, a successful businessman with a strong streak of patriotism.

Born in Jerusalem in 1914 to a wealthy family of Jewish traders, he joined the Haganah during the pre-state years and became a personal assistant to Shaul Avigur, the head of the illegal immigration agency Aliya B.

When Israel declared its independence, Sakharov was sent by the organization to Czechoslovakia to arrange the purchase of German-made warplanes. The sale by a Communist country was approved by Stalin, as a way of helping Israel so that it, too, would become a Soviet satellite.

Sakharov would be dispatched later to the United States to arrange more weapons smuggling from America, Mexico, and Latin American countries—on occasion with the help of gangsters, including notorious Jews such as Mickey Cohen and Bugsy Siegel.

After reaching the rank of lieutenant general in the IDF, Sakharov joined the family business as a leading importer of lumber and timber for the furniture industry. One day in the early 1960s, he was on a flight home from West Germany, on one of his frequent business trips to buy machinery, and was seated next to one of his old friends, Amos Manor.

Sakharov mentioned to the Shin Bet chief that he had just met with German industrialists involved in the chemicals trade. Manor was highly interested and said that he would get in touch with him soon about something.

Instead, it was Binyamin Blumberg who phoned Sakharov a few days later. They met at Blumberg's office. The security chief asked Sakharov if he would volunteer to approach the German businessmen and try to cajole them into procuring materials that Israel needed for a sensitive and secret project. Sakharov said he would try.

Though offered reimbursement for his expenses, Sakharov declined and paid for his travel and efforts out of his own pocket.

It turned out that the West Germans he would approach were former Nazis. On several occasions and on disparate subjects, Israeli intelligence showed no inhibitions or bad conscience about working with men of such background.

The West Germans had a company, Asmara Chemie, named for the capital of Eritrea, then part of Ethiopia, where one of the partners had gotten his postwar start in business. The company was wheeling and dealing in chemicals, weapons, and most anything it could buy and sell for cash. Its main office was in Wiesbaden, West Germany.

Sakharov's principal contact there was Herbert Schulzen, a veteran of the Nazi air force who was wounded when he crashed his plane in Denmark. Schulzen was a colorful extrovert, as well as a shrewd businessman, and had close contacts with West Germany's army and atomic energy commission.

Sakharov made a point of purchasing glues from Asmara for his timber business and then invited Schulzen to Israel. The ex-Luftwaffe officer, still convalescing from his wartime injuries, decided to come—attracted by the prospect of great medical care. He had a lot of time for socializing, too.

Sakharov introduced him to Blumberg and other officials of the defense ministry. The Israelis referred to him as "the Nazi pilot," and they went out drinking together in Tel Aviv. Schulzen enjoyed the feeling that the Jews did not hate him and in fact needed him. He decided to help them.

An Israeli who was close to the operation, when asked why former Nazis would help a Jewish state, pondered before replying: "Some of them did it out of sympathy for Israel; others, for financial gain. In any case, we knew how to play on their guilt feeling, as Germans, toward us Jews. We took advantage of it."

The Blumberg-Sakharov project needed calcium, a material used in treating sensitive metals. It is also used on "yellowcake"—uranium hexafluoride—a material necessary for the production of a nuclear bomb. At that time, the appropriate form of calcium was produced by Degussa, a German company that made gold bars and industrial metals. Degussa had profiteered during the war from gold teeth and other metal items stolen from murdered Jews.

Before long, Sakharov was unofficially Lakam's "case officer," running a network of agents whom he and Bloomberg dubbed with Biblical code names: Giv'on, Ayalon, Shemesh, and Yare'ach (the latter two being the Hebrew words for sun and moon, alluding to the tale of Joshua stopping the sun over a place called Giv'on and the moon in the valley of Ayalon).

Schulzen's Asmara served as a front for the purchases by Israel, in exchange for hefty commissions. Shipments of chemicals, metals, and other materials for the Dimona nuclear project began to arrive from Degussa, usually via other European ports, disguised as cargo for Sakharov's lumber and wood-processing businesses.

Schulzen probably did not know this had anything to do with nuclear weapons, but he had to know he was part of something clandestine and important to the Jewish state.

The acquisition chain almost came to an abrupt end in 1966. A shipment of calcium was loaded in barrels aboard an Israeli vessel named *Tsefat*, owned by Zim—then Israel's government-run shipping company.

The *Tsefat* sailed from West Germany to Rotterdam, in the Netherlands, to pick up more cargo. While anchored at Europe's busiest port, a fire broke out aboard the ship. The local Dutch fire department extinguished the blaze by flooding the storage spaces of the *Tsefat*. The contact between water and the calcium caused an effervescent chemical reaction, and the falsely labeled barrels jumped into the air. Television crews and photographers took plenty of pictures of a wondrous scene of smoke, steam, and leaping barrels.

The cargo calmed itself, but the crew of the ship fled, and other ships refused to tie up near the Israeli vessel. Confusion, embarrassment, and attention compounded.

Sakharov flew from Tel Aviv to Rotterdam, via Paris, to see how he could help. While in Paris, he heard from Blumberg that atomic energy experts believed the situation could be dangerous—that perhaps they should advise the mayor of Rotterdam to evacuate residential neighborhoods near the port.

Sakharov refused to follow that advice, deciding that he would do everything he could to save the precious cargo for Israel. After all, a lot of clandestine efforts had been invested in obtaining those chemicals.

When he got to the port, he introduced himself as the cargo owner and insisted that it was not hazardous. He said the contents were needed for special glue for his furniture factory's planks and boards in Israel, but he declined to identify the precise chemicals. He claimed that the formula was an industrial secret.

Sakharov boarded the *Tsefat* to show that it was not dangerous.

Finally, after he mollified the port officials by paying extra fees, everyone was persuaded to forget about the furor. He managed to summon another

Israeli ship to pick up the cargo. Everything was taken away, including empty barrels and some material that spilled into the harbor.

The most important and precious element for Dimona was uranium, the fuel to run the reactor. France did keep its promise to deliver uranium, but when relations became strained Israel's atomic energy officials feared they would run out of fuel. Blumberg was instructed to find alternative sources.

In the almost six decades after the construction of the reactor, Israeli scientists and Lakam's acquisition teams secured four providers. France was first, then came some European and American companies, followed by South Africa in the 1970s. The fourth source was Israel itself, as rich reservoirs of chemicals were mined and extracted from the Negev desert.

There was an American man in the nuclear business who clearly helped Israel, but in ways that no one was willing to explain fully. Zalman Shapiro was the founder of Numec—the Nuclear Materials and Equipment Corporation—in Apollo, Pennsylvania, a tiny town northeast of Pittsburgh

Born in Ohio in 1921, the son of an Orthodox rabbi, Shapiro lost many relatives in the Holocaust and himself faced anti-Semitism even while earning his Ph.D. in chemistry in 1948. The founding of the State of Israel that same year clearly inspired him, as he joined Zionist organizations including Friends of the Technion, which raised funds for Israel's top technological university.

His company supplied uranium to nuclear reactors in the United States, but in the early 1960s, Numec seemed to have an inordinate number of foreign visitors. They came mainly from France and Israel.

America's Atomic Energy Commission, the AEC, also noticed that Numec's records showed significant quantities of enriched uranium missing. No proof of any crime was found, but in 15 years of investigations, the AEC reported that 587 pounds of uranium had mysteriously vanished—enough, in theory, to make at least 11 atomic bombs.

FBI investigators focused on Shapiro's ties with Israel, but could not arrive at any clear conclusion. They tapped his phone calls and questioned him, yet he denied ever diverting anything to anyone. Still, the FBI and the CIA believed that he had somehow gotten weapons-grade uranium to Israel.

Investigators said that Shapiro did admit to having meetings with Avraham Hermoni, the scientific counselor at the Israeli embassy in Washington. Hermoni, in secret, was the Lakam station chief.

While the CIA was not aware of the existence of Lakam within the Defense Ministry, it did know that Israeli intelligence was deeply involved in industrial espionage aimed at helping military projects. A classified booklet written by the CIA in 1976, *Israel: Foreign Intelligence and Security Services Survey*, makes no mention of Lakam or of Binyamin Blumberg.

Investigations of Shapiro and Numec, as well as probes into other nuclear-related matters, caused a great deal of concern in Israel. The Mossad's best friend in the CIA, James Angleton, had shielded Israeli projects from scrutiny, but his influence diminished by the late 1960s. A new CIA director, Richard Helms, was notably suspicious about Israeli motives and actions.

To explore the situation in Washington and in Pennsylvania, four Israelis—including Hermoni; the Mossad's kidnapping expert, Rafi Eitan; and future Shin Bet director Avraham Bendor (who later changed his surname to Shalom)—dropped in on Shapiro's Numec plant in September 1968. Although Eitan and Bendor were certainly not scientists by vocation, they listed themselves as "chemists for the Defense Ministry" in an application for U.S. government clearance to visit the nuclear facility.

When they returned home from their damage assessment mission, Eitan and Bendor/Shalom reported that Israel was still enjoying the benefit of any doubt and could get away with quiet uranium procurement.

By 1976, American suspicions grew with a further twist.

The CIA's deputy director for science and technology, Carl Duckett, told selected members of the U.S. Nuclear Regulatory Commission what he had concluded—largely based on consultations with Edward Teller, a Hungarian Jew who grew up to be hailed as "the father of America's hydrogen bomb" and visited Israeli atomic scientists as Yuval Ne'eman's guest. The conventional understanding among researchers is that Duckett told the meeting that Israel at that point, in 1976, already had possessed nuclear bombs for about eight years.

Yet, one of the members of the NRC who heard Duckett gave a completely different account in 2004. Victor Gilinsky wrote that the CIA science chief's purpose had been "to deal with rumors about a deeper secret in the CIA reports, one that had an even bigger potential for political disaster, and one that I believe was the real reason for the hyper-secrecy."

Gilinsky continued: "What Duckett confirmed, to everyone's astonishment, was that the CIA believed that the nuclear explosives in Israel's first several bombs, about 100 kilograms of bomb-grade uranium in all, came from material that was missing" from Numec, which "had exceptionally close and suspicious ties to Israel. The firm's sloppy material accounting could have masked the removal of the bomb-grade uranium. After numerous investigations and reinvestigations, the facts remain unclear."

It may be mere coincidence, but in the 1990s the philanthropic Shapiro was listed as a prominent contributor to the Israel Intelligence Heritage and Commemoration Center, a non-profit group hoping to build a museum in Israel, closely linked with the intelligence community. Its founder and first president was Meir Amit, succeeded by another former Mossad director, Efraim Halevy. Considered a brilliant inventor, Shapiro clearly knew a lot and made friends with some of the most important people in Israel's clandestine defense system.

Blumberg's Lakam certainly kept working with the Mossad and Sakharov's German network, executing stunningly innovative missions to acquire materials for Israel's secret weapon. One of the most complicated, successful, and daring capers—stretching from Africa to Europe, to the high seas of the Mediterranean—became known as the Plumbat Affair.

This imaginative gem of spycraft would be the inspiration for a thriller by Ken Follett, *Triple*, and in real life a reminder to authorities of the kind of smuggling that could deceive customs officials and nuclear inspectors everywhere and anytime.

In essence, Israel managed in 1968 to purchase a huge quantity of radioactive "yellowcake" in sealed oil drums mislabeled "plumbat"—meaning that they contained lead. The sale was made by a Belgian company, and the cargo was shipped illegally under the nose of Euratom—the nuclear regulatory body for Europe—and then vanished, as far as official shipping records were concerned.

It all began in December 1965, when Sakharov wrote a letter to top officials at Israel's defense ministry. He said that one of his business acquaintances in Belgium had told him about a surplus of uranium simply waiting for a buyer. Most ministry officials were skeptical, but Blumberg had high faith in Sakharov's ability and asked the clever volunteer to coordinate the entire effort.

It would take nearly three years to design the almost perfect plot. When all seemed ready, Sakharov asked his German friend Schulzen—always happy to earn fat commissions—to have the Asmara company place the order to purchase the uranium.

It had been mined in the former Belgian Congo, the same African source that provided uranium for the first American atomic bombs. A company in Belgium, Société Générale de Minerais (SGM), had been sitting on the material for years and was happy to sell it—around 200 tons of yellowcake—for a total of four million dollars.

Asmara's office in Germany told SGM and Euratom that the uranium would be part of a chemical process for producing colored fabrics. The end user was to be Saica, an Italian company in Milan specializing in textile dyes. Saica's chief executive was a good friend of Schulzen. Euratom approved the transaction, as the radioactive materials would simply be going from one European country to another for an industrial purpose—and the regulators did not even think about the absurdity of Saica, practically bankrupt and lacking any proper facilities, using uranium.

Meantime, Sakharov worked with Rafi Eitan, then head of Mossad operations in Europe, to register a shipping company in Switzerland by the name of Biscayne Trading Corporation. Using a mysterious Turkish maritime intermediary and a Norwegian ship broker, the corporation purchased a small and unimpressive cargo ship called *Scheersberg A*, built in Germany and flying Liberia's flag of convenience.

The owner of the corporation was Dan Ert-Aerbel, who five years later would be arrested in Norway for his involvement in the Mossad's mistaken assassination of a waiter. The Danish-born Israeli had been working for the Mossad, on and off, since 1962. In 1973, after mistakenly revealing his claustrophobia, he told Norwegian interrogators everything: not only about the murder in Lillehammer, but also, "I was the owner of the uranium ship."

The Plumbat plot, though complicated, went off without a hitch. The uranium was packed into 560 drums by the Belgian vendor in November 1968, then transported by train to the port of Antwerp and loaded onto the *Scheersberg A*. The ship's captain, a trusted officer in the Israeli navy, wrote in its log book that the destination would be Genoa, but it never got to Italy.

He changed course in the Mediterranean and rendezvoused with another Israeli merchant vessel that was being guarded by two missile boats. Eitan and Sakharov had also purchased this ship, and its captain was Itai Be'eri—a neat bit of historical irony, as his late father Isser had been the first commander of military intelligence, fired for ordering a wrongful execution in 1948 and for being too rough on other suspects. The young Be'eri now got to restore some family honor.

Within a few hours, the drums containing radioactive yellowcake were winched from one ship to the other, which then sailed to the new Israeli port of Ashdod. Blumberg and Sakharov waited for it on the piers and witnessed the unloading of the cargo. Trucks then took the drums to the nuclear bomb factory in Dimona.

The *Scheersberg A*, two weeks after it was due in Italy, instead docked at a port in eastern Turkey. The ship was empty, and the captain and crew immediately disappeared. Several books were written about this controversial, impressive, and never acknowledged achievement by Israeli intelligence. But neither Blumberg nor Sakharov was mentioned at all.

Israel pulled off another coup on the water on Christmas Eve in 1969, when navy personnel—with the tacit cooperation of some French officers— took control of five missile boats that Israel had purchased from France and sailed them out of the harbor at Cherbourg. President de Gaulle, punishing Israel for the 1967 war, had imposed an arms embargo. He was livid that the Israelis now, as he saw it, were behaving like thieves in the night.

Lakam and the Mossad helped the navy by providing yet another cargo vessel—purchased by phony companies in Norway and Panama—to refuel the missile boats on their voyage to Israel. Those small but potent attack vessels would become very important to Israel, first in the October 1973 war and even beyond that, as government-owned Israel Aircraft Industries (IAI) was able to adapt the French model and built even better missile boats.

Sakharov's friendships proved valuable again, when the entire network built around Asmara Chemie came under scrutiny. Germany's domestic security service started investigating illegal activities by Asmara. Prime Minister Golda Meir was made aware of the threat, and she was concerned. Sakharov rushed to Germany to coordinate cover stories with Schulzen, but the probe continued.

He then went to see another former Nazi pilot, now an industrialist in Zurich, Switzerland. Their bond was not business, but a shared passion for music. The industrialist had another friend, Horst Ehmke, who was the West German cabinet minister overseeing his country's intelligence agencies. Sakharov pointed out that the German government could fall if everything about Asmara were revealed. The ex-pilot contacted Ehmke, and the investigation was dropped.

Lakam's next coup was in Switzerland. Israeli operatives penetrated a company that manufactured engines for France's Mirage warplane, using the classic intelligence technique of looking for a weak link in the staff. They identified a Swiss engineer, Alfred Frauenknecht, who had several promising attributes: his resentment of the company, his need for cash to afford having a mistress, and his positive feelings for Israel after the Six-Day War.

He was rather easy to persuade to provide something of immense value to Israel: a complete set of blueprints for the Mirage jet. Frauenknecht accepted cash, but made sure to point out that he was acting mainly out of personal commitment.

The engineer got his nephew to help him make copies and deliver them to a truck driver. The documents were then driven to the Israeli military attaché in Rome.

Swiss authorities became suspicious and tried to arrest the driver, but he managed to escape and called his Israeli controller for instructions. The controller told him to drive to Germany, and one of the Asmara Chemie executives then helped get the precious documents to the Israeli embassy in Bonn.

The driver was then smuggled to Belgium, where Eitan sheltered him for a while and then sent him safely to Israel. The driver was not Israeli, but he was safe.

Frauenknecht, however, was arrested; and Swiss interrogators persuaded him to confess. He said the Israelis had promised him a million dollars for the Mirage plans, and so far he had received $200,000. A Swiss court in 1971 found him guilty of espionage, but the judges seemed to respect his motives— as he still stressed his affection toward Israel, rather than greed—and the convicted spy spent only one year in prison.

That same year, Israel's air force started flying a new, domestically-produced warplane: the Nesher (Eagle). It was obviously a copy of France's Mirage 5.

IAI added modifications to make an even better jet fighter, the Kfir (Cub), which was proudly unveiled in April 1975. The Kfir also bore an uncanny resemblance to the Mirage, and the man responsible for that—Frauenknecht— made his first visit to Israel to see the inaugural flight, looking up and knowing he had something to do with that silver streak across the Mediterranean sky.

Israeli intelligence chiefs were ambivalent, however, in their attitude toward the man who was caught and served time. The Israeli government did not even pay his airfare from Switzerland, and he felt abandoned by his operators.

While the Swiss spy was bitter, Blumberg's reputation within the intelligence community grew to mythic proportions. Few knew exactly what he did, but senior operatives and defense staffers knew he was good at it. Only the highest officials linked Blumberg with Dimona and atomic weapons.

Another pillar supporting the nuclear project and working closely with Blumberg was a young, ambitious Israeli—Arnon Milchan—who, years later, would be one of Hollywood's wealthiest movie producers.

Born in 1945, Milchan inherited a small chemical and fertilizers business from his father and expanded it in the 1960s and '70s by winning licenses to represent such global giants as America's DuPont. He also brokered deals for defense contractors and was paid sizeable fees.

In the late 1960s, Milchan had a key role in doing the CIA a favor in pre-revolutionary Iran. The Americans were hoping to build a large listening post there. The Shah was among the regional players extremely impressed by Israel's swift victory over Nasser and Arab nationalism in 1967. Thus, he was receptive to a request by Milchan and other Israelis to allow the CIA to build its listening post on Iranian soil: a billion-dollar collection of dishes, antennas, and computers to harvest electronic intelligence (elint) from the nearby Soviet Union. As part of the deal, the facility would occasionally help the Shah by turning its "ears" toward Iran's neighbors—Pakistan and Iraq.

Milchan, who was in his early 20s, also earned commissions from American companies providing the elint equipment.

His "recruiter" for Israel's nuclear project was Peres, who introduced Milchan to Blumberg. Despite a generation gap between the latter two and their different personalities—Milchan was funny and talkative, while Blumberg was quiet and monkish—they struck up a friendship. "The only times I have ever seen Blumberg smile," said another Lakam operative, "was when he was with Milchan."

They also got a lot of secret business done. In 1972, guided precisely by Blumberg and Israel's atomic commission, Milchan was tasked with purchasing blueprints for centrifuges. Israeli scientists wanted to build their own devices for spinning uranium to weapons-grade potency.

That would give Israel another avenue, enriching uranium—and not only the reactor route—for making nuclear arms.

The Dimona project was mostly based around the reactor, which Israeli engineers had made much more powerful since the French initially built it. The reactor turned uranium in fuel rods into more radioactive and volatile plutonium. Plutonium bombs were typically smaller—requiring less than five kilograms of fissile material each, compared with over 25 kilograms for enriched uranium bombs. Plutonium devices were more apt to be miniaturized, to be the warheads on missiles.

Milchan was instructed to befriend a corrupt scientist at Urenco, a joint British-Dutch-German consortium that produced the centrifuges. With his charm and a lavish offer of $250,000, Milchan was successful.

As agreed, the scientist brought the blueprints to his home for a weekend and left his back door unlocked. Israelis from the Caesarea operations department subtly surrounded the house, and Mossad photographers copied the thousands of documents in a matter of hours. The scientist and his wife returned home, and on Monday he returned the documents to his office without arousing any suspicions.

Based on the drawings, Israel was able to design and build gas centrifuges. They were installed in Dimona and soon started enriching gaseous uranium hexafluoride, to produce fissile material for bombs.

Only two years later, Abdul Qader Khan would steal the very same blueprints. He was a Pakistani nuclear scientist, carrying out research at the Urenco consortium. A.Q. Khan returned home, built centrifuges, plotted the procurement of uranium, and was hailed there as "the father of the Pakistani nuclear bomb." He is even more notorious as the driving force behind notions of "an Islamic bomb," and Khan rightly became known as the world's biggest nuclear proliferator. He sold his knowledge to Iran, Libya, and perhaps other countries in the late 1990s.

Israel, in the meantime, kept upgrading and improving the centrifuges at Dimona to make them more efficient.

Yet, the old ones also proved to be of great value. In 2008, they would serve as a test bed for the computer worm invented by a joint Mossad-Aman-CIA operation: the malicious Stuxnet virus planted inside Iran's computers, which were controlling a Urenco-type centrifuge array. The Iranian machinery would be severely damaged, and that would be a significant setback to an enemy's program seen as highly threatening. (*See Chapter 1.*)

In appreciation of Milchan's success in getting Israel its own centrifuges, he was one of the very few Israelis—outside a tight circle of cabinet ministers, selected members of parliament, and senior military personnel—to be honored with a tour of the Dimona facility.

In 1973, Milchan launched a chain of business decisions that would bring Israel sophisticated triggers for nuclear bombs. These were krytrons: a type of high-speed switch, resembling the kind of cathode tubes old radios had, costing only $75 each but requiring a U.S. government license to be exported.

Milchan persuaded an engineer at Rockwell, the American defense contractor, to start a company in California. Milchan promised Richard Smyth that the new firm, Milco, would get plenty of orders. Milchan and his friends in Tel Aviv would see to that. For years, Lakam sent Milco lists—often using codewords for nuclear-related items—and Smyth was earning handsome commissions for shipping the parts to Israel.

In 1985, federal agents raided Milco and charged Smyth with illegally exporting more than 800 krytrons to Israel. Milchan, despite obvious ties to Milco, was not charged; apparently, that was because Peres, his longtime patron, persuaded Reagan administration officials not to prosecute Milchan.

Milchan told two authors, writing a book about him, that he had not violated any American laws. He added that he had been "ordered" to cut off all contact with Smyth, who fled to Europe and could never get Milchan or Lakam to return his phone calls. Israel's defense ministry did send Smyth money for several years.

Smyth, after almost 15 years, was located by U.S. authorities and extradited from Spain. He was sentenced to 40 months in prison, and in 2010—when he was 80—the two authors found him, practically broke, living in a trailer park in California.

Milchan continued to do very well. He produced many hit movies, dividing his time between Los Angeles and Tel Aviv and unceasingly helping Israel with its secret intelligence and defense requirements.

Similar to Sakharov, he refused to accept any payment from Israel for his assignments on behalf of Lakam, but many of his missions were indirectly rewarding. Peres, Blumberg, and Moshe Dayan introduced Milchan to international leaders and key security officials, and he was able to make highly profitable deals with monarchist Iran, the isolated government of Taiwan, and the doomed apartheid regime of South Africa. He invested in various enterprises in Iran, which he wisely sold about a year before the Shah's downfall in 1979.

When deals involved products delivered to Israel, Milchan put the commissions into a huge slush fund: millions in cash that Israeli intelligence could use for special assignments. Milchan controlled the checkbook.

Patriots who donated their time and energies to the cause, such as Milchan and Sakharov, helped Israel acquire what it needed to be an undeclared nuclear power.

The scientific and technical breakthroughs that made it possible for Israel to build an atomic bomb came—by coincidence—just before the Six-Day War of June 1967. Only a few people knew that the Jewish state became the sixth country to achieve nuclear weapons capability, joining the United States, the Soviet Union, France, Britain, and China in that exclusive club.

Israel's undeclared status nearly came into play during the three-week crisis that led up to the outbreak of war on June 5.

Israeli political leaders and military chiefs were very concerned by the expulsion of United Nations peacekeepers from Egypt's Sinai Peninsula. It was also impossible to dismiss Cairo's raucous psychological campaign that claimed Arab armies would smash Israel and throw the Jews into the sea. Fears of another Holocaust were fueled by the fact that Egypt's military had just used chemical weapons in Yemen's civil war.

Against that background, some defense ministry officials and scientists in Tel Aviv deliberated over nuclear strategy. Ben-Gurion had insisted on developing the world's most dangerous weapons, but no one had clearly decided when they might be used. Forty-five years later, the results of these discussions continue to be secret and, according to sources close to the participants, surprisingly ambiguous.

The emerging picture is that Rafael, the official Israeli company for developing armaments, mobilized all of its top engineers and technicians during the weeks of crisis in 1967. According to Lt. General Tzvi Tzur, a former IDF chief of staff who was then a special adviser to the defense ministry, those men and women "worked around the clock and neared total collapse" to assemble Israel's first nuclear device.

Tzur told oral historians: "A committee of two was set up, in the days leading to the war, to connect a few wires." This was a big bomb, not ready to be fit into a missile or even dropped from an airplane.

Around the same time, the commander of the Sayeret Matkal commando unit, Lt. Colonel Dov Tamari, was summoned to headquarters for a meeting with a general. Tamari was ordered to prepare a team of Sayeret soldiers to fly by helicopter into the Sinai. They would be carrying "a thing," which the general did not specify.

The mission sketched out would have the troops place Israel's first nuclear bomb and some kind of detonation mechanism on a high peak—probably for maximal psychological effect choosing Mount Sinai, where the Bible says Moses received the Ten Commandments. If Egypt's army, already massing in the Sinai, were to cross into Israel and threaten Tel Aviv or other major cities, the Israelis would shock the invaders by turning the mountain into little more than rubble under a mushroom cloud.

The plan was dropped, in large part because Israel won the June 1967 war so easily.

In fact, even as Israel secretly built nuclear weapons, it did not test any of them until 1979. Scientists and engineers did not feel the need to conduct a test explosion, largely because Blumberg's Lakam obtained from "assets" in France the full results of French nuclear tests. The Israelis were able to use the measurements and observations to calculate the quantities, components, and bomb structure that would yield a viable nuclear device that could be stored and transported safely.

As technology advanced, Israel was able to test its nuclear bombs, in a sense, by using computer simulations—the method generally used by the United States to examine and update its huge arsenal.

In September 1979, according to American government scientists whose monitoring equipment detected a flash and electromagnetic signals emitted by a nuclear explosion, Israel did conduct a test—over the Atlantic Ocean, just west of South Africa. Israeli officials stubbornly refused ever to confirm publicly that they worked with South Africa's all-white regime on the test; but Blumberg's Lakam would have been in charge of providing secure transport for an Israeli bomb to a South African naval base, arranging for IAEC members to be present, and taking steps to prevent public knowledge of the test.

Nuclear cooperation was the zenith of the secret military ties between two unlikely bedfellows: Israel, the homeland for Jews who suffered anti-Semitism and racism, working together with a government based on white supremacist apartheid. The unholy alliance prompted worldwide condemnation. Israel justified the policy as a national-security necessity.

When the 1979 test took place, Israel already had missiles with nuclear warheads. These were Jericho ground-to-ground missiles, an Israeli product based on models sold by France in the late 1950s.

Yet, the precise art of fitting a nuclear warhead onto a Jericho came from the United States. Lakam's agents and Israeli air force personnel on training trips to America managed to obtain or steal details of the warhead structure for the U.S.-made medium-range Pershing 2 missile. The Israelis used that as a model.

Lakam tried, on occasion, to expand its horizons. Thus, Blumberg gathered a few nuclear scientists in the mid-1970s to form his own research department. He asked them to study India's nuclear program, using almost entirely open sources. The report had some interesting observations about proliferation and about weapons development by a nation with widespread poverty, but nothing that would affect Israeli decision making.

The Lakam research department did not last long, largely because other Israeli intelligence agencies felt that it was wasting resources by writing reports on topics already well covered.

Lakam, for the few who knew its true business, could not really escape the fact that its main mission was to be a theft contractor for all of the Israeli government's military, technical, and science requirements.

Blumberg would object to the label, but he was Israel's master thief. Israel's perception of its own needs constantly prompted planning for getting things done through secrecy and deception, and nowhere was this truer than in the nuclear program.

Based on a prevailing sentiment that never expired, Israel took what it felt it needed whenever purchase or negotiation failed to do the trick. Lakam's acquisitive business flourished, bordering on the illegal or even crossing that border.

As the 20th century gave way to the 21st, Binyamin Blumberg was still secretive about the work he had done for Israel's security. Old and poor, alone in his fourth-floor walk-up near Tel Aviv's City Hall, he wondered how he had been abandoned. His health deteriorated as he reached his late 80s, and he rarely left his austere apartment, but it was apparent that he used to be a handsome, tall man.

The name on his building's mailbox said Vered, and the people who knew him as Blumberg—who had worked with him on Israel's most sensitive and secretive projects—hardly ever got in touch any more. Perhaps on major Jewish holidays, a few might call and ask him how he was doing. Yet the monkish bureaucrat always kept his private life to himself. He rarely had friends over to his home and hardly ever socialized.

When occasionally invited to his old headquarters at the defense ministry for a courtesy briefing or to fete a new senior official, he rarely uttered a word. His name—whether Vered or Blumberg—hardly ever appeared in the hyperactive Israeli newspapers, let alone the international media.

He did grant one interview, in 2012, in which he complained about his poverty and stunningly declared: "I regret that I sacrificed my life for the security of the state."

Blumberg also revealed that, in his heyday, he used to keep a cyanide pill handy. If he were captured by an enemy and was likely to be interrogated, he took his job and the attendant secrets so seriously that he would have committed suicide. After all, for nearly three decades, he was playing a key role in the Jewish state's most covert project: building up its technological, scientific, military, and nuclear power.

His colleagues insisted that Blumberg seemed ordinary in every way; or, to borrow an Austrian novel's title, he appeared to be *A Man Without Qualities*. Yet, Blumberg had grasped in his hands unprecedented power. He stood at the junction of all the crucial decisions that shaped Israel's defense doctrine and capabilities.

What did he lack in his old age? More than anything else, Blumberg/Vered would have liked some recognition: respect from Israeli officials in acknowledgement of his contributions. Yet, a man who kept himself silent and invisible throughout his career should not have been surprised when no one noticed him.

CHAPTER TWELVE

SURPRISES OF WAR AND PEACE

T he Yom Kippur War stands as one of the most famous surprise attacks in history. Israelis were sleeping or praying, and apparently unprepared to defend their nation, on the holiest day on the Jewish calendar. Yet, there were many reasons why Israel should not have been caught unawares when the Egyptian and Syrian armies commenced shelling and advancing on the afternoon of October 6, 1973.

Those reasons took the form of agents—authentic gems of human intelligence (humint)—in both Egypt and Syria.

Three of the agents were particularly good: a foreign diplomat in Cairo who was secretly an Israeli, an Egyptian seaport worker, and a close advisor to Egypt's president. In addition, there was an Arab monarch who shared his impressions and information with Israel.

All of them were assets—with excellent access to innermost Arab secrets—recruited and run by the devoted case officers of Mossad's Tsomet and Caesarea departments. Yet, the spies and their Israeli handlers were almost totally ignored at headquarters in Tel Aviv.

These were cardinal errors, which Israel's intelligence community would take great care to avoid repeating after 1973—in the Lebanon wars of 1982 and 2006, the many uprisings and violent incidents in between, and the confrontation against Iran, which required that excellent intelligence be processed promptly and diligently.

Before that fateful Yom Kippur, there was top-notch espionage work that provided warnings of war, but they were simply not heeded. The clues and facts that were gathered stood no chance in the face of three complacent figures who ran the country in those days: Prime Minister Golda Meir; Defense Minister Moshe Dayan; and the Aman commander, Eli Zeira.

General Zeira was born in 1928 in Haifa and, naturally, fought in the 1948 War of Independence. He stayed in the military and, among other experiences, gained an impressive understanding of the United States by taking courses at army schools in America.

After joining military intelligence, Zeira spent some time as commander of a secretive combat unit known as Mem-Mem (the Hebrew initials for *Mivtza'im Meyuchadim*, meaning "Special Operations"). Later, he was posted to Washington as the Israeli intelligence attaché. Zeira was brought back home to take the top job at Aman when General Aharon Yariv retired in 1972.

The most formative experience Zeira had was probably his two-year run as bureau chief for Dayan when he was chief of staff of the IDF. Dayan, in effect, tutored Zeira in the dark arts of despising fellow officers, manipulating politicians, and exercising his natural arrogance.

By the autumn of 1973, Zeira had probably earned the right to feel confident. His agency, after all, had made possible the triumph of the Six-Day War six years earlier; and Aman seemed to be a good, solid organization, thanks to upgrades by Meir Amit and Yariv.

Zeira, time and again, clashed personally and professionally with the Mossad director, Zvi Zamir. They were, after all, worlds apart. Zeira was outgoing and handsome, proudly wearing the red beret of the IDF paratroopers. Zamir was soft spoken, looking like a lanky European intellectual obsessively burrowed in files about his war against Palestinian terrorists.

Lacking a significant research department in the Mossad, Zamir—like the rest of Israel's leadership—depended on Aman to assess the capabilities and intentions of the neighboring enemy countries. In the early 1970s, the National Intelligence Estimate authored by Zeira declared that Arab armies would not attack Israel because they were incapable of doing so.

That was the key statement—the memorably grand error of the decade for Israel.

If Zamir strongly disagreed with Zeira's optimistic analysis, the Mossad chief did not bother to confront him. He would be depending on reports from the field, funneled through the case officers in his Tsomet department, which ran agents in Syria, Egypt, and Jordan. The Mossad's human sources were "warning agents," whose main purpose in undercover life was to provide Israel with early alerts of danger on the horizon.

The Mossad had drawn lessons from the arrests of Wolfgang Lotz and Eli Cohen (in Egypt and Syria, respectively) by limiting the demands made of secret agents in dangerous places. They all could be asked for information of great potential value, but that could divert them from their main mission and expose them to unnecessary risks.

Each of the three agents who did issue warnings in the weeks before Yom Kippur in 1973 had a fascinating personal history.

A., an Israeli man whose family insists he not be identified, was born in a South American country where he was highly active in a Zionist youth movement. Carried away by pride when Israel scored its stunning six-day victory in 1967, he migrated to the Jewish state.

After a while, he was spotted by recruiters for the Caesarea (operations) department, who took an interest in Israelis who had lived abroad and possessed foreign passports and a knack for learning new things. A. was offered a job in his adopted nation's intelligence service and, as a newly minted patriot, he readily agreed.

"Serving in the Mossad was a big honor for him," one of his controllers recalled. He was clearly willing to take on a notably dangerous assignment: living, under a false identity, in an enemy country. His destination would be Egypt.

He underwent an intensive course to learn the crafts needed to be an intelligence officer. That was the usual stuff taught to dozens of Israelis as they prepared to vanish into enemy lands. Unusual in his case was the cover story.

Thanks to especially warm relations with a small nation, the leader of which was a true friend of Israel, the Mossad arranged that A. would go to Egypt as a diplomat of that country. Only the country's leader and three of his top officials were privy to the secret.

Before A. left Israel, the head of Caesarea, Mike Harari, tried unsuccessfully to persuade A.'s girlfriend to marry him and tag along on the adventure in Cairo. A married couple was considered safer—far less likely to be harassed or blackmailed—than a 30-year-old bachelor. Even worse, when Wolfgang Lotz went to Egypt without his wife, he ended up marrying a second woman.

A. was very successful, from the Mossad's point of view. He quickly became a prominent member of the diplomatic circuit in Cairo, hosting parties and mingling with the Egyptian elites, including army officers.

He sent his information and observations in coded messages to Tel Aviv, using a transmitter hidden in the posh villa he rented in one of Cairo's most prestigious neighborhoods. Some reports were sent in the mail to post office boxes rented by the Mossad in Europe.

When circumstances permitted, he traveled to European capitals for face-to-face meetings with his controllers, because then he could freely add details and respond to questions. He used some of those trips to fly to Israel for brief visits with his girlfriend.

Mossad headquarters began to realize that the fears about sending a bachelor were materializing. Several women in Cairo, notably the daughter of a European diplomat, were attracted by A., and he went out on dates with some of them.

His loneliness manifested itself in personal messages that he transmitted—along with his official espionage reports—asking that "birthday wishes" to his friends and regards to his girlfriend be passed along by the Mossad communications desk. His handlers, including Harari, found that to be excessive and reprimanded him; but they also grew increasingly concerned about his state of mind.

Still unable to persuade A.'s girlfriend to join him in Egypt, Harari decided—for the sake of the important mission—to "marry him off." The Israeli spy was instructed to fly to Europe on "vacation," where he would meet a pretty young woman and bring her to Cairo. Harari sent a female combatant, whose first initial was M., to meet A., and they were "married" in Europe by virtue of documents she brought with her from the Mossad's forgers.

Before their flight to Egypt, they lavished a lot of Israeli government cash on new furniture, bed linens, and tableware—just as any newlyweds might do.

Now the Mossad had two spies in Cairo. A. and M. worked in concert and helped each other achieve more than one person could. In the months leading to the October 1973 war, A. was able to photograph the military build-up from Cairo all the way to the Suez Canal.

A. reported that Egypt was preparing for war. Military intelligence analysts in Tel Aviv were not moved by his reports. They were sticking to their conclusion that Egypt's President Anwar Sadat was not ready for a new war.

A. and M. would remain in Cairo during the war and had the strange experience of seeing the entire city rejoicing at setbacks for Israeli troops. This, frankly, was frustrating for two Jews in the middle of a crowded Arab country, however well trained they might have been to act dispassionate.

They stayed in Egypt for another two years. The Caesarea department decided in 1976 to remove the "couple," after consulting with the Mossad chief who took over in 1974, General Yitzhak Hofi. A. was offered a new job as an instructor at the Midrasha, as he would have many experiences to share with up-and-coming Mossad field personnel. But he declined and decided to leave the agency.

M., meantime, had actually fallen in love with A. and wanted to marry him. Harari, in a cruel manner, told her that even if A. were willing, the Mossad would not allow that to happen. "You were sent on a specific mission," Harari told her, "which now comes to an end—not to falling in love."

A. was not interested in marrying her. A series of quarrels ensued, and M. telephoned him several times, yelling at him and insisting that some of the household assets were hers.

A. instead married his longtime sweetheart, who had loyally waited for seven years. They had an ostensibly normal life, including two children. But his espionage years were bothering him. The Mossad's "rehabilitation" effort, routinely offered to operatives who returned home after a long mission, seemed to have failed.

He was haunted by the secret life he had lived. A. could not help but be suspicious of everyone as a potential attacker or assassin.

On the other hand, in business, he genuinely was cheated by partners when trying to set up a plastics company. That failure depressed him. An even more scarring tragedy occurred when A.'s car struck and killed a pedestrian.

He asked the Mossad to help him with the obvious legal complications, but the agency refused to do anything for the former undercover employee. Feeling disappointed and bitter, A. left his wife and children and abruptly moved to his original homeland.

He did some odd jobs there, living hand to mouth. His life story was reminiscent of that of Wolfgang Lotz, who also became a lost soul after his secret years in Egypt. But in this case, the story had an even sadder ending. Sitting in a city park one day, A. committed suicide.

In his tale is further proof that very rarely did any spy who worked under deep cover return home as a happy, well-adjusted person.

During the months before the 1973 war, the observations transmitted by A. and M. from Cairo were helpful but not sufficient.

Israeli intelligence needed more specific information on the structure of the Egyptian army and its order of battle. The Mossad and Aman liked to have the names of unit commanders and information on their habits and weaknesses. The names and sizes of brigades and details of their equipment would also be highly valued.

The best way to get that data would be to pay an agent inside the Egyptian army. The Mossad assigned a *katsa* (a Hebrew acronym for *k'tsin isuf,* meaning collection officer) to pinpoint an officer who might be traveling abroad on a study or purchasing mission.

In 1969 the katsa found, approached, and recruited an Egyptian brigadier-general who became one of Israel's best sources. For four years, in return for a growing bank account, he provided the Mossad with solid information about military movements and exercises on the Egyptian side of the Suez Canal.

The general, codenamed Koret (a Hebrew word for "woodcutter"), proved to be an especially productive agent from the summer of 1973 until the outbreak of war on October 6. His reports were received, put into storage—and, like many other pieces of information, wrongly interpreted.

Even more worrisome was the treatment of a report sent by another Egyptian agent. He was a seaport worker in Alexandria, the country's second largest city. Recruited a few years earlier, as he responded enthusiastically to Israeli cash, he was instructed from time to time to supply information about the movement of military ships in and out of the port.

His major mission was to provide an early warning in case of war. But he couldn't know that war was looming—that was the role of Aman's research department. The analysts there had compiled a checklist of dozens of "war indicators." These were events for which to watch out. The belief was that if two or more of those events took place, it could be assumed that the enemy was preparing for war.

The list was flexible, with changes made as circumstances warranted. But, always on the list, was the ports indicator: If the entire Egyptian fleet was leaving, that meant war was expected.

This was adopted because of lessons learned in the Six-Day War. In June 1967, Israeli naval commandos surprised Egypt by placing mines on ships anchored in ports. Now, it could be assumed, if Egypt were planning to go to war, it would move its ships out to the open sea first.

The Mossad thus tried to recruit an agent in every major Egyptian port. The port worker in Alexandria seemed outstanding, and he sent his coded observations to Tel Aviv regularly, as required. The flow was interrupted, however, in the spring of 1973, when he had a meeting with his Israeli handler in

Europe. The Mossad man told the Egyptian to maintain complete silence for a while—basically to go underground until further instruction—because there was reason to believe that the Egyptian secret police were on his trail.

In mid-September, three weeks before war broke out, a seemingly innocent postcard arrived at Mossad headquarters in the Hadar Dafna building. The card was sent from a European address. Mossad mail processors essentially ignored it for two days, but then a junior desk officer found it intriguing.

It had been written by the port worker—the spy in Alexandria—violating his instructions to remain silent and communicating in such a risky way.

The message he penned was only personal regards to an invented person, but there was one sentence that seemed to be out of context. The junior officer realized that the phrase contained the agreed code for the "war indicator." The Egyptian was reporting that his country's fleet had just left its base in Alexandria.

The Mossad informed Aman, but senior military analysts were unimpressed. All they did was hand the report to the intelligence branch of the navy, which meant relegating it to a lower level.

"We have to prepare for war!" the head of naval intelligence said to officers of his and other branches. But this small unit was habitually ignored by the rest of the IDF, and the army's top commanders stuck to their preconceived notion that Egypt was unable to attack Israel.

What can be said about a warning personally delivered by King Hussein, the pro-Western monarch of Israel's eastern neighbor, Jordan?

His nation, an artificial creation by Britain in 1921, may not have been the most powerful. But, as a great survivor squeezed between the conflicts and contradictions of Israel, the Palestinians, Iraq, Syria, and Saudi Arabia, Hussein had his finger on the pulse of the entire region.

The CIA considered him an agent of influence and put him on the Agency's payroll in the late 1950s. In 1963, he started to have frequent, but secret, meetings with Israeli officials.

The king was not an Israeli agent, though. His grandfather, King Abdullah, had taken money from the Zionists, and he was assassinated for that relationship in 1951. Hussein's loyalties were not to Israel, but to his own kingdom and the Hashemite royal family. It was all about survival, and that would continue to be his son Abdullah II's priority after Hussein's death in 1999.

Hussein made a huge mistake by joining Egypt's Nasser in what became the Six-Day War against Israel. Jordan thus lost the holy sites in Jerusalem and all of the West Bank. Hoping that by talking he could regain territory and prestige, the king stepped up his encounters with top Israelis.

As arranged by the Mossad's Tevel department, in charge of foreign liaison relationships, Hussein met eight times with Prime Minister Meir—usually on the Israeli side of the border, but occasionally aboard the royal yacht in the Gulf of Aqaba in the northern Red Sea.

On September 23, 1973—when Israel's leadership insisted on being bliss-fully unaware of looming dangers—King Hussein requested an urgent meeting with Meir. Two days later, Israeli helicopters flew him to the Mossad's guest house, north of Tel Aviv, for his ninth rendezvous with the so-called "Old Lady," who had become prime minister in 1969 at age 70.

Now she was 75, and the king was 37 years old. Perhaps there was a genera-tion gap or a credibility gap, but Meir simply did not believe what he was saying.

Here was an Arab king, going well out of his way—in fact, risking his life—to tell the leader of the Jewish state that Egypt and Syria were going to attack Israel in the near future. The king did not specify any date for the attack, but he revealed that he had met recently with President Hafez Assad of Syria and Egypt's Sadat, and he got the impression that both were fed up with the long impasse in Middle East diplomacy.

In the Arab leaders' view, Hussein explained, they could no longer accept the limbo of no war and no peace, which they believed was good only for Israel.

Mossad analysts were, of course, listening to the conversation in a fully wired room in their agency's guest house. But they were not buying what the king was saying.

He surprisingly volunteered the information that he was not only giving Meir his personal impressions. He felt very certain about Syria drawing up a war plan for sometime soon, revealing that the information was substantiated by a "good source" in that country. The Mossad would later learn that the source was a Syrian general, who had been recruited by Jordanian intelligence as a spy in Damascus.

This was an amazing intervention, probably unprecedented in modern international relations. A leader of an enemy country—officially, Israel and Jordan had reached only a 1967 ceasefire deal through mediators—was warn-ing of an imminent attack by his allies.

The Israeli political and military leadership—like the famous three mon-keys—did not want to see, hear, or speak about the danger. They chose not to believe the intelligence data that were mounting up, preferring instead to adhere to their self-deluding detachment from reality.

It seemed that everyone had their brains manacled by what strategic experts in Israel called *ha-Konseptzia*—"the Concept." This informal but force-ful doctrine developed rapidly in the euphoria that followed the stunning vic-tory of 1967. It held that the Arabs would never launch an all-out war, since it was so clear that they could not win.

The Concept went on to say that if the Arabs decided, despite everything, to start a war, it would have to be a joint effort. It seemed certain that neither Egypt nor Syria would dare go to war alone; the chances of them joining forces was deemed to be very, very slim.

In the unlikely event of war, the Israelis were utterly convinced that they could smash the enemy—as they did in 1967—and march on the Egyptian and Syrian capitals, Cairo and Damascus.

A non-stop stream of verbal hostility from those two capitals continued. President Sadat, on September 28—the third anniversary of his predecessor Nasser's death—told his nation that "liberating" the Sinai from Israel was his top priority. Not unreasonably, Zeira and his Aman analysts had decided long before to ignore the flood of hyperbole heard from Arab politicians.

But should they have ignored what an Israeli intelligence officer reported, on October 1, from the IDF's Southern Command? Lieutenant Binyamin Siman-Tov's detailed report of attack preparations on the Egyptian side of the Suez Canal would be remembered as a key clue that was stupidly neglected.

The Concept was in the driver's seat, and the Concept decreed that any military activities by Arab armies near the borders or ceasefire lines were meaningless exercises. At most, Egypt or Syria might be perpetrating a hoax aimed at prodding Israel into ordering an expensive and disruptive mobilization of IDF reserves.

The Concept was convenient and reassuring, and it spread up and down the military, intelligence, and political chains of command.

Only 12 hours before the actual invasion did Israel's intelligence chiefs accept that a coordinated attack on their country was imminent.

The eureka moment occurred after midnight on October 6 in London, at the apartment of the Mossad station chief. Zvi Zamir had flown to England for the precise purpose of hearing the latest information from Egypt—from the best "warning agent" the Mossad ever had.

The grim expressions on the faces of Zamir and his colleagues told the whole story. Sitting on soft sofas and armchairs were four Israelis: the top spymaster, the London station chief, a very accomplished katsa (case officer) identifiable only by his first name Dubi, and Zvi Malkin, who 13 years after kidnapping Adolf Eichmann was in charge of Zamir's personal security.

All of them now realized how they—actually the entire intelligence-military establishment and, above them, the political echelon—had failed to understand what now seemed clear. But there was no time for soul searching.

Zamir now had to get to business. It was 2:30 a.m. in Israel on the most somber and quiet Jewish holy day, but prayers and atonement would have to wait. He telephoned his chief of staff in Tel Aviv, Freddy Eini, who naturally sounded sleepy.

"Put your leg in cold water!" Zamir ordered, meaning that Eini should make certain he was fully awake.

The Mossad chief then recited a short message he had just inscribed on a piece of paper, so as to be careful about what he said and did not say. Zamir used a few code words which he knew that Eini would understand: "the angel" and "chemicals."

Angel was one of the codenames used by the Mossad for Ashraf Marwan, the agency's supreme source in Cairo. He was married to one of the late President Nasser's daughters and was an advisor to President Sadat. He had a Ph.D. in economics, but because his bachelor's degree was in chemistry his code word for an imminent attack was "chemicals."

Marwan was a highly ambitious man, born in 1944 to a well-off family in Cairo. His grandfather was the president of Egypt's main Sharia (religious) tribunal. His father was a general in the army. Ashraf's success at the Science University meant that he started in the army as a first lieutenant.

Everything in his life was going smoothly. A tall, handsome, and educated bachelor was sure to have a great time in the Cairo of the mid-1960s. He went to glamorous parties and played tennis at a prestigious sports club, where he met Nasser's daughter, Mona.

Their wedding was huge, with Egypt's most famous singers performing. His father-in-law did not seem to like him, yet Marwan was able to get a job in the president's personal bureau, where he was privy to a huge amount of gossip—plus a wealth of political, military, and economic information. His government salary, however, was low.

The young couple moved to London in 1968, after the gloomy depression of the six-day defeat had made Cairo an unpleasant place. The swinging British capital seemed perfect for Marwan's tastes.

He became a regular at the Playboy Club and other casinos, although he could barely afford the drinks and the gambling. Word filtered back to Cairo, where President Nasser shouted that his daughter should divorce him. She refused, but an arrangement was reached that had her living with her baby in Egypt, while Marwan would travel back and forth to continue his economics studies in Britain.

During one of those trips in 1969, he stepped into one of London's famous red phone booths and placed a call to the Israeli embassy, which was located in a mansion near Kensington Palace.

The receptionist at the embassy later remembered hearing a man, in accented English, asking to speak "to someone from the intelligence." For the receptionist, this was not so strange. Israeli embassies frequently get such calls, and the instructions are to transfer the calls to either a military attaché or to one of the officials at the "prime minister's extension"—the term for the Mossad stations inside embassies.

Marwan found himself speaking to an attaché. He introduced himself by name and said that he was interested in working for Israeli intelligence. He left his hotel's phone number and mentioned that he would be in London for the next 24 hours.

By pure chance, Shmuel Goren—the head of Tsomet, the agent-running department of the Mossad—was in London at the same time. He was told about Marwan's phone call, recognized the man's name, and became quite excited. Breaking the usual rule of doing a background check before having any face-to-face contact, he phoned the Egyptian at his hotel and made a date at a café. He and the station chief decided to send Dubi, then a young katsa, to the meeting.

The first chat went very well, but the Mossad could not eliminate all its suspicions. A walk-in volunteer could easily be a trap, or someone who will feed disinformation. Walk-ins are respected but also suspected. The Israelis were never certain about all of Marwan's reasons for betraying his country. Getting back at his father-in-law? Needing money? His belief, perhaps, that he actually was helping Egypt by changing the course of history?

Zamir and other Mossad executives debated whether to work with this walk-in and decided that the opportunity was irresistible. They assigned Dubi, the original contact man, as the case officer.

The initial communication system had Marwan calling phone numbers belonging to "Anglo-Jewish Zionist" women: friends of Israel who were willing to jot down the few coded words that an unknown caller said. The women then had to call a phone number at the Israeli embassy and pass on the coded message. This was an oral version of a well-known espionage technique, the "dead drop," a pre-set location where messages could be left between agent and handler.

The calls would invariably set the time and location for Marwan to meet Dubi. Their relationship would go on for almost 30 years, well past the peace treaty between Israel and Egypt signed in 1979. Marwan was paid a total of around a million dollars, and he was a huge part of Dubi's life. Most any katsa wants to run an interesting agent, and that was certainly Dubi's privilege.

Marwan cut off ties with the Mossad in 1998 when the Israelis tried to change handlers. A new policy aimed at preventing a katsa from becoming too close to a source. Marwan, however, had already declared that he would not work with any other Israeli—trusting only the man he had first met as "Misha." While the walk-in agent never concealed his real name, Dubi did hide his.

Their meetings took place in London, Paris, or Rome, and in public the only nouns that an eavesdropper ever could hear were chemistry terms. Yet, in the privacy of closed-door talks, Marwan was able to provide information and unique insights on military and political topics. Thanks to him, Israel felt it was very well informed on what Soviet military advisors were doing in Egypt until their expulsion by Sadat in 1972.

Sadat had Marwan in his inner circle, and thus the Mossad was also told about the Egyptian leader's sincere determination to launch a war if Israel refused to withdraw from occupied Sinai. Marwan was also able to provide details of the Egyptian army's order of battle, a fairly specific outline of how Israeli forces in the Sinai would be attacked when the fateful day came.

On Thursday, October 4, two days before Yom Kippur, the Mossad received a message through the Englishwomen's dead-drop telephone link. It said that Marwan wanted to meet with the "general"—which could only mean Zamir himself—in London the next day to discuss "chemicals." That got the Mossad's attention.

Zamir flew to London from Tel Aviv. Dubi was already in England. Marwan arrived at the Friday night rendezvous, explaining that the previous day he had been in Paris with an Egyptian delegation and could not say anything substantive until now. He told Zamir, in so many words, that the very next day Israel would be attacked by both Egypt and Syria.

Zamir immediately telephoned the IDF chief of staff—keeping in mind that the Yom Kippur holy day had already begun, staffing levels at most every job were at minimal levels. Many Israelis had just been at Kol Nidrei prayers and were preparing for more synagogue time on Saturday.

Aman analysts were immediately informed, and they were told that the high-level Egyptian source did not know what time the attack would commence. They had reason to guess that it would occur at sundown, because they had intelligence about Egyptian and Syrian officers discussing that matter in theory some time earlier.

Word went out to the Northern and Southern Commands, at about 4:30 a.m. on Yom Kippur morning, that enemies were expected to attack at 6:00 in the evening. A general mobilization would require at least two or three days, but forces at the frontiers were able to brace for an attack.

The Mossad and Aman did not know that, just a few weeks earlier, Egyptian and Syrian military planners had moved what they called H-hour to 2:00 in the afternoon.

The standard Israeli playbook, exemplified by the success of June 1967, would have had the air force staging preemptive strikes as soon as possible on that day. For political reasons, however, Prime Minister Meir decided not to attack first. She made sure to inform the United States government of that decision, believing that would win her some points with Richard Nixon's administration, but only after first checking with Moshe Dayan to ascertain that Israeli troops could absorb a first blow by the enemy.

The coordinated attacks on Israel's forces did, indeed, begin at 2:05 that day. The results were misery, blood, and an unaccustomed retreat.

The four-hour difference between the actual H-hour and the guess based on Marwan's tip was enough to cause a deep division within Israeli intelligence.

The Aman commander, Eli Zeira, accused the principal Egyptian source—not naming him at the time—of misleading his Israeli handlers by telling them of the October 6 attack plan so late. Zeira and other intelligence officers in an emerging anti-Marwan camp further charged that the Egyptian let the Israelis think that the attack would come at dusk, and thus the 2:05 surprise was worse than it might have been with an accurate warning.

Almost twenty years after the war, Zeira made a point of meeting foreign journalists and researchers and telling them that Nasser's son-in-law had been a double agent who deceived Israel. Many who met with Zeira were shocked that he was exposing the Egyptian. His obvious goal was to cleanse himself and Aman from responsibility for failing to act on a series of intelligence warnings in the weeks before Yom Kippur.

Instead of studying and adequately considering the observations sent in by sources so painstakingly planted by Israeli intelligence over the years, Zeira—at a meeting as late as October 3 with senior officials—had dismissed the notion of an Egypt attack with two laconic words: "low probability."

In the years after the 1973 war, Zeira also sought to blame his rival, Zamir, for the intelligence failure. After all, it was the Mossad that was running Ashraf Marwan.

The debate was renewed in 2007, when Marwan was found dead in London. He had plunged from the balcony of his elegant apartment, and some witnesses thought they had seen other men on the balcony looking down after the Egyptian fell. There was no reason to think that he would have committed suicide, at age 63. A manuscript he was believed to be writing—his tell-all memoir—vanished on the day of his death.

Were the Egyptians homicidally angry at him? Perhaps they learned of his disloyalty only because Zeira had named him? There was certainly no public sign of anger, as Marwan's funeral in Cairo was attended by very senior Egyptian officials. They all spoke of the marvelous services rendered clandestinely by Marwan over the years.

Did the Mossad conclude that he was a double-crosser, and Israeli assassins settled a score by throwing him off his balcony? Myth-makers in Egypt and Europe propagated such tales, but most intelligence officials in Israel showed no sign of feeling they were betrayed by Marwan.

The strongest clues might be in his chosen career: as a high-level weapons dealer, buying and selling on behalf of various Arab governments. He might have made some murderous enemies over the years, and Egyptian sources said they suspected that Libya's Colonel Muammar Qaddafi was angry over a deal and ordered Marwan's murder.

In Mossad headquarters, however, analysts reached the conclusion that Egyptian intelligence probably killed him to avenge his betrayal. It was supposed to look like suicide, and British police simply left this in a file full of unsolved cold cases.

The Mossad analysts, with great bluntness, believed that Zeira's big mouth led to the demise of the best agent they ever had in Egypt. Never in the annals of Israeli intelligence had the identity of an agent been deliberately revealed, and by no less than the chief of military intelligence. Some officials called for Zeira to be prosecuted, and Israeli legal authorities said for several years that they were investigating the matter.

In the Yom Kippur War, IDF foot soldiers and tank crews had to pay with life and limb for the mistakes made by their country's intelligence services and political leaders. Israelis lost ground on the Golan Heights, captured from Syria in 1967, and on the eastern side of the Suez Canal in Sinai.

Dayan, one of the heroes of the 1967 war, panicked. On the third day of the 1973 war, he muttered darkly about the possible destruction of "the Third Temple" of Israel. Jewish history tells of a first holy temple in Jerusalem that was destroyed by the Babylonians in 586 BC, and a second temple that was demolished by the Romans in 70 AD. The third temple was the contemporary State of Israel, and Dayan rated its chances of survival as very low.

There was talk among Israeli generals and political leaders of using "unconventional" weapons. Serious consideration was given that week, for the first time, to the possible use of Israel's nuclear bombs as a last act of almost suicidal defense. On Dayan's orders, Jericho missiles and special bomb racks on Phantom aircraft were prepared for the possible launch of atomic weapons.

The defense minister's despair weighed heavily on Meir's spirit. She seemed to be considering suicide, as her secretary and confidante Lou Kaddar recalled: "I never saw her so gray, her face as in mourning. She told me, 'Dayan wants us to discuss terms of surrender.' I thought that a woman such as she would never want to live in such circumstances. So I prepared it for both of us. I went to see a doctor, a friend of mine who would agree to give me the necessary pills so that she and I—we both would go."

Meir pulled herself together; and with her army chief of staff, Lieutenant General David (Dado) Elazar, who was strong as a rock, she directed the counterattacks that eventually helped Israel to stop the Egyptian advance and to defeat the Syrians. The short-term damage from the 20-day war represented an extremely heavy price for Israel: 2,700 soldiers killed—equivalent, by proportion of population, to 170,000 dead Americans. In a nation of just over three million people, the loss was traumatic.

The long-term damage was that the entire State of Israel lost confidence in its once legendary intelligence community. It was not just a feeling. It was in writing. Prime Minister Meir reluctantly commissioned an official inquiry into the Yom Kippur War and the *Mechdal*, or "Neglect"—the instantly coined euphemism for the intelligence blunder that made the war a near-total surprise.

The commission, led by the chief justice of Israel's supreme court, Shimon Agranat, cleared Meir and Dayan of "direct responsibility" for the Mechdal. It criticized senior IDF generals and scathingly destroyed the careers of Aman commander Zeira and three of his assistants.

They were instantly replaced, and Major General Shlomo Gazit became the head of military intelligence. He created a small new unit within Aman named the Revision Department—which staff members dubbed the Devil's Advocate Department. They were tasked with questioning and doubting the assumptions and consensus beliefs of other intelligence analysts. The unit's top officer was given the unusual right to send his reports directly to the prime minister and a key parliamentary committee.

Meir and Dayan technically survived the Agranat Commission's findings, but they could not take the heat of sharp public criticism. In April 1974, they both resigned.

Yitzhak Rabin became Israel's new leader. As the army chief of staff in the 1967 war and then ambassador to Washington, Rabin was no stranger to intelligence reports. In fact, he constantly asked Aman and the Mossad for extremely detailed raw data and seemed to worry that something important may have been missed.

He did have his pick as head of the Mossad. Zvi Zamir felt absolutely fine about retiring in 1974, after five years marked by the Munich Olympics massacre, a new tactic of fighting back with assassinations, and the humiliation of not doing enough to warn before the Yom Kippur War.

The new Mossad director was Yitzhak (Haka) Hofi, a major general whom Rabin knew and trusted.

One notable emergency that suddenly erupted was handled with great skill and good fortune. On June 27, 1976, a mixed band of Arab and German hijackers took over an Air France Airbus 300 flying from Athens to Paris. Because the flight had originated in Tel Aviv, many Israelis and Jews were among the 248 passengers.

The hijackers, announcing that they were with the Popular Front for the Liberation of Palestine, forced the plane to fly to Entebbe airport in Uganda, where the mercurial, violent, and reputedly cannibalistic dictator—Idi Amin— sided with the pirates.

Chillingly, Jewish and Israeli passengers were separated from the others. The non-Jews were released. In Paris, they were questioned by French and Israeli intelligence officers who learned as much as possible about the hijackers and where the remaining hostages were being held.

The Mossad quickly explored options for taking action, even at that great distance from Israel. Invisible relationships in neighboring Kenya helped with reconnaissance efforts, and a Mossad operative was able to fly a private Kenyan plane over Entebbe to photograph the layout of the buildings and runways there. Thanks to David Kimche and other "alternative diplomats" who had advanced Israel's cause in Africa, Nairobi was consistently a center of cooperation for projects both overt and covert.

Uniformed commandos of Sayeret Matkal executed the rescue mission on July 4 with stunning speed and courage. Large transport planes landed in near silence, Israeli soldiers and vehicles that rolled out of them gave the impression that they were Ugandans as they approached the terminal, and the assault itself resulted in a quick gun battle that left all seven hijackers dead. At least 30 of Idi Amin's soldiers were also killed.

Entebbe was a glorious success, but there were casualties on the Israeli side: Four hostages lost their lives, as did the commander of the operation. He was

Yoni Netanyahu, the younger brother of the future prime minister who himself would serve in the Sayeret unit.

Israelis never felt better than that evening, when military transport planes delivered the rescued hostages to Tel Aviv. The world admired what Israel was able to accomplish, and that it had the courage not to surrender to hijackers.

Yitzhak Hofi would lead the Mossad until 1982, but Rabin was long gone by then. In the election of May 1977, Israeli voters rejected the Labor Party, which had led the country since independence. The right-wing Likud bloc won the election, and the new prime minister was Menachem Begin.

Begin was a completely new figure: a member of the right-wing pre-state underground movements opposed to David Ben-Gurion, never an army general, an ideologue who could barely tolerate Israel having friendly relations with ex-Nazis in West Germany, and a man seemingly opposed to any concessions to Arabs.

At the Mossad, Hofi offered to resign. So did the Shin Bet chief, Avraham Ahituv. But Begin told them to stay. He liked the job they were doing. In fact, he loved hearing a lot of details of intelligence work, as it reminded him of his days in the militant Irgun underground.

Begin was out to change history, and he was going to use Israeli intelligence to do it. To defy his critics, who branded him a warmonger, Begin was determined to be a great peacemaker. One step was to make Dayan, a Labor stalwart, his foreign minister. Another step was to send Hofi on a secret mission to Morocco.

That North African country was, for an Arab nation, fairly friendly to Israel. King Hassan, when asked by Hofi to arrange a meeting for him with senior Egyptians, was only too happy to oblige.

Two senior officials from Egypt flew to Morocco in the summer of 1977, showing that Sadat—after restoring some of his nation's pride during the 1973 war—was ready for a transformation. Hofi and the Egyptians, with a minimum of disagreement or drama, spoke of their sincere desire to end the long conflict between their countries.

Dayan had a follow-up meeting in Morocco with a senior aide to Sadat, and they agreed that future meetings should not be in secret.

President Sadat, delighted by developments, went on CBS television to tell Walter Cronkite that if he were invited by Begin, he would go to Jerusalem and address the Knesset—Israel's parliament—to show that he wanted no more war. Begin immediately told CBS that he was inviting Sadat.

History was made—no, *shattered*—on Saturday night, November 19, 1977, when Egypt's president stepped out of his official jet at Ben-Gurion Airport, near Tel Aviv.

Within 17 months, Begin and Sadat were signing a peace treaty on the White House lawn, with President Jimmy Carter—who had worked very hard to mediate the deal—as the smiling godfather.

The truth is that Israel's intelligence community was again taken by surprise. It did not predict that the election of a hard-line prime minister in Israel would provoke a peace offer from the country's biggest enemy.

Even when contacts began, intelligence analysts were skeptical about Sadat's sincerity. They had misread him before the 1973 war, and they now misread him again.

A lasting lesson for the Mossad, Aman, and smart political leaders in Israel was to be open to the possibility of genuine surprises. For a country as small as Israel, with many enemies all around, many unknowns could constitute dangerous threats; but others might offer pleasant opportunities.

Israeli leaders tended to emphasize the negative possibilities, often because they contended that their country was too small to permit errors. In light of the Holocaust—and Begin often invoked its memory—prime ministers felt that it was their job to protect the entire Jewish people from calamities.

That sense of duty, though always weighed against the realities of domestic and international politics, continued to be a powerful factor in determining what Israel and its intelligence community would do.

CHAPTER THIRTEEN

JEWISH INTELLIGENCE

This was my finest hour" was a phrase used often by almost every head of the Mossad, reflecting back on the exciting times of his professional career. More than any other achievement, they spoke of the help they were able to give to fellow Jews.

"Of all the operations and activities that I was responsible for, the strongest and most exciting experiences were saving our Jewish brethren from countries of oppression and bringing them over here," Zvi Zamir reminisced. "It was a great humane deed."

The intelligence community—which, from the beginning, included units devoted to facilitating immigration to Israel—executed clever and often dangerous operations to get people out of Iran, Syria, Ethiopia, Sudan, Yemen, the Soviet Union, and other far-flung Jewish communities that were hopelessly isolated. That was after an initial flurry of immigration from Iraq, Egypt, Morocco, and other Arab countries where Jews were made to feel unwelcome by anti-Jewish and anti-Israel governments.

The whole notion of "Jewish intelligence," intent on ensuring the safety and success of millions of Jews around the world, was a self-appointed mission. The individual communities only rarely requested assistance. Israeli envoys came to them, helped them, and generally got them out. Many moved to Israel, but others chose to go to America, Europe, or Australia. The main intent was to get them to safety.

The founding fathers of the Jewish state—and its intelligence community—believed that those projects were an almost mystical calling: important steps toward reversing the ancient exile that had turned a once-united people into a Diaspora.

These were highly sensitive missions, however. Jews scattered around the world were not Israeli citizens. Their home countries could object very strongly to interference in the lives of their nationals. The Jews receiving uninvited aid could suffer from a kind of split personality—as well as accusations of dual loyalty hurled by the non-Jewish majorities all around them.

As unique and touchy as it was, Jewish intelligence seemed natural. Israel calls itself the Jewish homeland, and it has a Law of Return that grants automatic citizenship to any Jew who reaches its soil and asks for it.

Israel also had a powerful strategic motive. Immigration represented a chance rapidly to make the new state stronger and, in population terms, bigger.

If more people meant greater national security, the intelligence community was sure to be involved.

The launching pad for action in this sphere was the pre-state clandestine agency that focused on illegal immigration, *ha-Mossad le-Aliyah Bet*, "the Institute for Aliyah B." Its original work focused on sneaking Jews into British-ruled Palestine. Similar work continued and even expanded after Israel was born in 1948.

While 6,000 Israelis, mostly young, were losing their lives on the battlefields of the 1948-49 War of Independence, the secret operatives of Aliyah B were setting up bogus companies to arrange flights for Jews out of Iraq and Yemen—two of the Arab countries whose armies had invaded the newborn Israel. The agent in charge of this network of clandestine travel was Shlomo Hillel, who would rise in the next three decades to be a cabinet minister and speaker of the Knesset.

Posing as fictitious British businessman Richard Armstrong, Hillel chartered airplanes from an obscure American airline to extract, in 1949, almost every single one of the 50,000 Jews of Yemen. This operation, code-named "Magic Carpet," was relatively easy.

For the Iraqi operation, Hillel/Armstrong had help from a sayan, a British Jew working in the aviation industry. They made sure to give a maintenance contract to the Iraqi prime minister's son, and things went remarkably smoothly after that indirect bribe—known in the Middle East as *baksheesh*, and a truly quotidian expense for Israeli intelligence.

The Shah of Iran, ruler of the neighboring country, was happy to cooperate by facilitating travel arrangements. From May 1950 to January 1952, Hillel's exit route managed to bring nearly 150,000 Iraqi Jews to Israel by air. The direct flights were known as "Operation Ezra and Nehemiah," named for the two Jewish leaders who led their people back to the Holy Land from exile in Iraq—then called Mesopotamia—23 centuries earlier.

Thanks to the secret agents of Aliyah B, the population of Israel nearly doubled—to more than one million Jews—in the first four years after independence.

Aliyah B was an economic empire and an operational masterpiece. No nation has had anything like it: a huge organization involved in the global conveyance of Israel's most important asset, people. Built around a massive undercover travel agency, Aliyah B owned over 60 ships and airplanes and countless cars and trucks. Their movements were well coordinated by a world-wide network of quasi-legal radio transmitters.

Aliyah B agents formed direct relationships with political leaders, often in nominally hostile nations: not only Iraqi prime ministers, but also Hungarian, Bulgarian, Polish and Romanian politicians. Contacts at the highest levels were tapped to explore routes for the safe passage of Jews to Israel.

Some of the airplanes became the first El Al airliners. Aliyah B refugee boats helped form the core of Israel's national shipping company, Zim. The experience acquired by operatives worldwide helped Israel's new navy. Aliyah B also had some of Israel's finest forgers and field agents, whom the Mossad would later put to good use.

The masterpiece was torn to bits, as part of modernizing Israel's intelligence structure. Aliyah B was disbanded in March 1952, and its missions were divided into two. One part was given to a newly established intelligence unit, Nativ ("Path"), which stood outside the major agencies. The other assignments were tasked to a unit—given the name Bitzur ("Fortification")—inside the newly established Mossad.

Successive prime ministers and policymakers understood that immigration was contributing to the Jewish state's strength and national security. So, while intelligence structures and units altered their names and changed management through the years, this covert work—unique to Israel—continued apace.

Israeli secret agents, under diplomatic cover or posing as foreigners, were sent to nations where Jews lived in difficult circumstances. They set up dummy corporations, opened bank accounts, recruited corrupt or sympathetic local officials, befriended border-crossing guards and airport and seaport managers, and bribed key government figures.

As with Aliya B, these missions were supplemented by financial assistance from Jewish philanthropists and strong support from many community organizations. Towering above them all was the American Jewish Joint Distribution Committee (the JDC, often called "the Joint"), a ubiquitous and often secretive welfare organization.

When needed, Nativ and Bitzur—with the Joint's assistance—mobilized international public opinion to apply pressure on Arab governments, the Soviet Union, and Russian-controlled regimes in Eastern Europe to allow Jews to emigrate. They rallied the support of Western governments, labor unions, human rights organizations, and the media. Gaining enthusiastic backing from American Jewish organizations, it became fashionable to chant slogans on behalf of freedom for Soviet Jewry.

The division of labor was clear. Bitzur, acting from within the Mossad, was tasked with bringing Jews from Arab and Muslim countries, as well as organizing defensive tactics against anti-Semitic violence—even providing self-protection plans to Jews in Europe and South America.

Nativ's territory was the Communist bloc, and it occupied itself only with immigration issues and gathering intelligence that could help sneak Jews out. The issue of self-defense in these countries, with their authoritarian regimes, was considered too risky.

Nativ's director was Shaul Avigur, the longtime head of the former Aliyah B. He began by sending operatives into the Soviet Union, which had the world's second-largest Jewish community: three million strong, second only to the six million of the United States. Elie Wiesel, the educator and activist, called his brethren in Russia "The Jews of Silence," making that the title of his book on the issue.

Avigur's first aim was to establish contact with the key Jewish communities spread all over the vast republics of the Soviet Union. Nativ would then try to awaken Jewish culture and religion—hoping later to turn the wave from simple Judaism to Zionism—the desire to migrate to Israel. Nativ's diplomats' and agents' work included slipping pocket-sized Jewish calendars and Hebrew-Russian dictionaries into the jackets of Jews in synagogues. They also distributed prayer books, Bibles, newspapers, and books in Hebrew, even though they knew that the Soviet authorities considered these to be "anti-state propaganda."

Avigur chose his envoys carefully. They had to be volunteers who demonstrated "high Zionist motivation." And they had to know Jewish traditions and customs.

It would be best, he felt, if they were young married couples with children. Youthful strength would help them tolerate long and uncomfortable train rides across Russia. Single men were not preferred, because Soviet authorities might try to ensnare them in sexual temptation and blackmail—the classic "honey trap" of intelligence agencies.

There was a major change just after the Six-Day War of 1967. After the Soviet clients, Egypt and Syria, were soundly defeated, Moscow showed its anger at Israel by cutting diplomatic relations. They were not reestablished until the dissolution of the Soviet Union 23 years later.

One Communist country in Europe continued to have full diplomatic and trade relations with Israel, and that was Romania. Its leader was a megalomaniac, Nicolae Ceausescu, but Israeli intelligence knew how to play him like a virtuoso's violin.

Most important for Nativ was that he agreed to allow several thousand Romanian Jews to leave for Israel each year. But Israel had to pay a kind of head tax for each and every Jew. The price per capita varied, depending on education, location, and the person's importance to the authorities. The payments were disguised as "compensation" to Romania for the investment the nation had made in these citizens. It was truly a simple trade: people, in exchange for ransom.

Ceausescu played an interesting double game when it came to Palestinian terrorist groups. He offered shelter to the notorious Abu Nidal and his murderous gang, even providing training and light weapons. At the same time, Romania spied on them and collected valuable information about the radicals' travels and plans.

The Nativ operative entrusted with "the Ceausescu account" was Yeshayahu (Shaike) Trachtenberg-Dan, a former Aliyah B man whose first covert work was for the British army, parachuting behind Nazi lines in Europe. Born back in 1910 and remembered as "Shaike Dan," this white-haired peripatetic immigration spy in the 1960s, '70s, and '80s went to Bucharest, Romania's capital, twice a year with a suitcase full of cash. On the way, he would stop in Vienna and hand a substantial sum to a Romanian diplomat who happened to be one of Ceausescu's relatives. Only then would Dan receive a visa to proceed.

In Bucharest, he would meet with Romanian officials and give them the rest of the money. The corruption was barely hidden, and for Nativ it was a fact of life rather than cause to be offended. Americans who worked for the Joint often helped to set up Dan's meetings with the right people.

In this way, nearly all of the 200,000 Jews of Romania emigrated to Israel from the mid-1960s until the collapse of Ceausescu and his regime in late 1989. Israel paid around $400 million, half of it to the dictator, his family, and cronies. That worked out to $2,000 per Jew, and Israeli intelligence had no regrets about it.

In the Soviet Union, the end of formal diplomatic ties made Nativ's work more difficult. There were no more cover jobs in an Israeli embassy in Moscow, and no diplomatic immunity should an Israeli operative get into trouble.

On the other hand, there was a dramatic increase in the religious and Zionist consciousness of Soviet Jews: an awakening prompted by Israel's exciting six-day victory over the Arabs. Many more Jews started defying the law by listening to news and commentary, in Russian, from Kol Israel (the Voice of Israel) on their shortwave radios.

Nativ saw an opportunity for success in towns where nothing good had been happening for many years. Unable to send in many Israelis, Nativ helped arrange visits to the Soviet Union by Zionist youth activists from North America and Western Europe. They entered as tourists, but in their suitcases were Hebrew dictionaries and Jewish prayer books.

No one epitomized the sea change more than a young Russian student who was a proud Jew—not something safe or wise to be in the decades of Communist rule—and practically shouted that fact to the skies.

His courageous tale began in mid-February 1967, when he dared to approach the front gates of the Israeli embassy in Moscow. A Soviet policeman tried to block his path, but the young man told him to shut up and rushed into the Israeli compound.

One of the diplomats invited him into the building, all the while suspecting that the entire incident might be a provocation by the KGB. He asked the student what he wanted.

"To go to Israel," he replied.

"Who are you?" the diplomat asked.

"My name is Yasha Kazakov, and I am a 19-year-old Jewish student at the Moscow Transportation Institute."

Kazakov, who eventually would move to Israel and change his name to Yaakov Kedmi, recalled: "They at the embassy clearly did not know how to behave toward me. The diplomat said, 'If you're serious, come back in a week.' "

When Kazakov left the embassy, KGB officers were waiting for him. "They asked what I was looking for in the embassy, and I invented the excuse that

I was looking for information about my grandfather, who had disappeared during the war."

Four months later, when the Soviet Union announced that it was severing relations with Israel, Kazakov walked to the United States embassy and—using his already tested technique—rushed inside. "It was a little more difficult," he recalled, "because security was tighter and it was a longer run."

The American consul agreed to see him. "I told him my story and gave him a letter of protest to pass on to the United Nations Human Rights Commission. When I left, a large contingent of KGB men was waiting, and I was taken away for interrogation.

"They stripped me and threatened they would break my bones. I answered them with a chutzpah that came from faith: 'Try, we'll see who'll break whose bones.' I wanted to make them angry, but I knew that as long as they were interrogating me and talking to me, they wouldn't beat me up. That went on for a few hours. They threatened to send me to prison for disturbing the peace. I explained that I went into the embassy just to ask who was representing Israel.

"They didn't know what to make of me, and because of the Soviet bureaucracy—and this is the best thing I can say about it—no one wanted to take responsibility."

Before long, however, the KGB decided to discipline Kazakov by having him drafted into the Soviet army. "I threw the draft notice in the garbage," he recounted. "During another KGB interrogation and a talk with the Soviet youth organization of which I was a member, I told them that Israel was my homeland—and if I served in any army, it would only be the Israel Defense Forces."

Luckily for this particular non-conformist, the Red Army did not pursue the conscription of young Kazakov. He thought that it could be because the Soviet military was distracted by its invasion of Czechoslovakia, in August 1968, to quell a pro-freedom movement.

He was even more fortunate to be told, in February 1969, that he could leave the Soviet Union—in fact, that he *had* to leave within two weeks. He took a train to Vienna and then flew to Israel.

Taking on his new, Hebrew name of Kedmi, he was instantly invited for a talk with the heads of Nativ.

"They were in shock," he said. "Here I was, a bachelor with no family in Israel and who didn't speak Yiddish, allowed to come to Israel. It couldn't be! 'Something was wrong,' they thought. They warned me not to speak to reporters, so as not to anger Soviet authorities."

Years later, Kedmi realized that Nativ used military censorship to prevent the publication of articles that Israeli journalists were writing about him. The conspiracy of silence did not last. Some Knesset members from opposition parties publicly hailed his arrival, and that plainly annoyed Prime Minister Meir. The right-wing Likud took him under its wing, and he quickly became a darling of the media.

To the chagrin of Nativ's managers, Kedmi was invited to lecture in Jewish communities in the United States. In New York in 1970, he joined another recent emigré in a nine-day hunger strike in front of United Nations headquarters, demanding that their parents be allowed to move from Russia to Israel.

Public reaction compelled Golda Meir to agree that Nativ's campaign could go public. The Israeli agency, although still not publicly using its name, helped sponsor hundreds of events at which crowds were encouraged to echo the Biblical exodus from Egypt by chanting, "Let my people go!"

After Likud came to power in 1977, Prime Minister Begin himself invited Kedmi to join Nativ, and by the late 1990s Kedmi was in charge of it.

In 1991, he happened to be accompanying Nahum Admoni, who had been director of the Mossad during most of the 1980s, on a private tour of Moscow. Kedmi arranged a visit to Vladimir Kryuchkov, who had been the last director of the KGB before the Soviet Union was dissolved.

During the chat between the two former adversaries, Admoni told his host: "I want to share a little secret with you. We in the Mossad never spied against you."

Admoni's small talk was technically accurate. Israel obtained its information on Soviet life mainly by debriefing immigrants from there, and that work had been done by Amos Manor's Shin Bet. Admoni was also evading the fact that there had been espionage activity in Russia and the other republics—not by his famous Mossad, but by Nativ agents.

The KGB, not concerned about Israeli bureaucratic labels, considered Nativ personnel to be spies, put them under surveillance, and tried to make their lives extremely difficult.

Israel, without doubt, achieved its goal. One million Jews left the Soviet Union, and most of them moved to the Jewish state. Similar to previous waves of immigration, this was a fresh injection of blood into Israeli economic, cultural, and security veins. The principal reasons were the historic changes that shattered a Communist empire, but Nativ must be credited with being in the right place at the right moment to guide those Jews to their growing homeland.

By the year 2000, it became clear that Nativ was no longer needed. The agency was stripped of its status as a member of the intelligence community, but then Israel's typically chaotic bureaucracy—rather than making a decision about Nativ—let it die by depriving it of funding and gradually firing its employees.

On the other battlefield of clandestine immigration, the Arab lands of the Middle East, Israeli operatives had equally difficult challenges that demanded unique solutions. Morocco became an extremely difficult field of play when French colonial rule ended in March 1956. The French had allowed Moroccan Jews to come and go, but the new government under King Mohammed V stopped the outflow. The king believed, as did other Arab rulers, that anyone who moved to Israel would become a soldier and strengthen the Jewish state.

The Mossad organized a team of Israelis, all able to speak Arabic and French, to devise ways of extracting the remaining 100,000 Jews in Morocco. The Bitzur unit organized self-defense for them—part of an operation called *Misgeret* (Framework), designed by longtime operative Shmuel Toledano.

Misgeret arranged taxis and trucks to take Jews out of Morocco, with the Israelis making sure to pay bribes to all manner of uniformed officers along the route. A favorite route out was through Tangier, at the time an international city, and from that port on to Israel.

Later, two towns in Spain were used as bases for the project, which had the full cooperation of Generalissimo Francisco Franco—acting, so the Mossad believed, out of guilt feelings over his ties with Hitler and even over the expulsion of Spanish Jews in 1492.

The Mossad also purchased a former army camp along the southern coast of Spain, actually located inside the British colony of Gibraltar. The grounds and barracks were converted into a transfer facility for Jews exiting from Morocco.

Tragedy struck on January 10, 1961. A fishing boat named *Pisces*, packed with clandestine Jewish refugees, capsized in a storm between the Moroccan coast and Gibraltar. Forty-two men, women, and children, together with a Mossad radio operator, drowned. The disaster aroused some sympathy abroad, but it also triggered a sharp response from the Moroccan authorities. They uncovered the underground network, arrested scores of Zionist activists, and jeopardized the entire operation.

Luckily for Israel, in March of that year there was a change in tone at the highest level in Morocco. Mohammed V died a somewhat mysterious death at age 51, and his son Hassan II succeeded to the throne. He was highly interested in gaining Western support, and being kind to the Jewish minority was excellent for his image. He let them leave, if they wished to do so; he found that many Jews whose ancestors had long been important advisors to royalty decided to stay.

France was remarkably cooperative at the time, and French warships transported around a thousand Jews out of another North African country, Tunisia.

Shmuel Toledano—the head of the Mossad operation in Morocco, credited with bringing 80,000 Jews to Israel—was given a new assignment. Isser Harel was sending him to South America.

There was a crisis for the half-million Jews in Argentina, largely as backlash after Israel kidnapped Adolf Eichmann there in 1960. Harel felt somewhat responsible for a new wave of anti-Semitic attacks organized by a fascist group that had support from military and police officers.

In July 1962, fascists abducted a Jewish student and tatooed a Nazi swastika on her breast. Argentine Jews were terrified, and Israeli newspapers published editorials urging their government to send assistance to "our Jewish brethren" in South America. Harel hardly needed any encouragement.

He instructed Toledano and the Mossad's Bitzur unit to construct another Misgeret (Framework), inspired by the work done in North Africa. Jews would be trained to defend themselves.

In Argentina, a highly willing volunteer quickly made himself known: a self-described *gaucho judio*, a "Jewish cowboy," named Leo Gleser. Telling his tale almost half a century later in Israel—his tall, solidly built frame clothed in jeans, a denim shirt, and custom-made leather boots—Gleser recalled his exciting endeavors as a young socialist-Zionist. He was born in Argentina in 1949, keenly aware that his Jewish grandparents had fled Russia after a pogrom in 1903. They made their new home on farmland owned by a Jewish foundation.

"I was a strong, blond boy, very impressive," Gleser reminisced. "There wasn't a tree I couldn't climb. I was like a cat. I fished in the river and hunted animals. I specialized in hunting iguanas. I would lie in ambush for them for hours by a hole in the ground, and when the lizard emerged from the opening, I would hit it with a stick and kill it."

When Gleser was nine, his father ran off with a younger woman. Leo's mother took him to a new home in Buenos Aires.

Life in the capital city changed him. The wild nature boy became an urban street fighter, molded by the militancy of a left-wing Jewish youth movement, *Ha-Shomer Ha-Tza'ir* (The Young Guard). "In Buenos Aires, I encountered anti-Semitism that was not just religious. It had economic, social, and political dimensions."

When Mossad personnel and Israeli soldiers in civilian garb flew in and offered training to Gleser and his pals, "everything smelled of secrecy in the style of a French thriller,." he said. There was also a paradox. Isser Harel, who did not trust the left within Israel, was relying heavily on young idealistic leftists in Argentina to be the protectors of the community.

The Israelis ran a camp where they taught martial arts, intelligence-gathering surveillance, navigation, and other skills. The fact that Gleser had known, from his youth, how to shoot a hunting rifle made him one of the top campers. Once they were trained, the volunteers were assigned various security tasks.

"We guarded Jewish buildings, and after meetings we would escort the boys and girls home, so that they would not be attacked in the street," Gleser recalled.

Another former Framework member gave a more aggressive description, saying members of this Argentine underground "initiated deterrence operations, beat up local anti-Jewish hooligans, destroyed places where they met, and sabotaged printing presses where anti-Semitic material was produced."

Gleser's Zionist organization sent him to Israel in 1967 for more elaborate training at a kibbutz—but not yet for aliyah (immigration). He got to witness the patriotic fervor of a victorious Israel, as the stunning Six-Day War changed the Jewish state forever.

Returning to Argentina in 1968, Gleser was given a leadership role in the self-defense movement. "The studies and training in Israel gave me tremendous strength and confidence," he recalled. "I was a kid of 19 without commitments to a family, and without any sentiments. Now I became a proud Jew fighting for his people. I felt I was the representative of a small, powerful nation."

A few months later, however, Gleser was arrested just after one of his operations. He and his team had set fire to a printing plant that was producing anti-Jewish literature. A few days in jail were bad enough, and Gleser left Argentina for good. He spent a little time in the United States, then sailed to Israel. He settled there and became a successful consultant on private security.

Ambitious, secret missions to protect Jewish communities worldwide continued in the decades that followed. Immigration projects relied still on the partnership of the Mossad's Bitzur unit with the New York-based Joint, often with the help of sympathetic Western governments.

In this way, in the 1970s, the remnants of the ancient community in Iraq—around 3,000 Jews—were extracted with the help of Kurdish rebels and the Shah of Iran. Israeli operatives said, years later, that some of the cash they and the Joint brought along for bribery went to an Iraqi deputy prime minister named Saddam Hussein.

Around the same time, Jews were also smuggled out of Syria, the Arab country most hostile to Israel. Bitzur men and some Jewish sayanim (helpers) from various nations engaged with the small Jewish communities in Syria and coordinated an exit plan with them. In small groups they were driven to Lebanon. Then, like Israeli secret agents in the past, they headed for the Mediterranean shore, where small boats ferried them out to Israeli navy ships.

Seeing the Syrian Jews sail into the port of Haifa was what triggered Mossad chief Zamir to remark that no espionage mission could possibly be so exciting and satisfying. As a bonus, the sayanim were able to smuggle out some old, precious Torah scrolls that no one in Syria would ever have read again.

In the 1990s, the few Jews who remained in Yemen were able to leave for Israel. This was similar to the Iraq mission, with Bitzur, the Joint, and lavish bribes working together to perfection.

The Mossad also had to operate inside Iran, which was exceedingly difficult after the Islamic Revolution of 1979, to help Jews escape—often leaving vast properties behind—through a variety of routes that Israel insisted on keeping secret.

The most significant Bitzur operation took place, in several stages, in the Horn of Africa. Israelis had always known that some of the black inhabitants of Ethiopia claimed to be Jewish. Their story was ignored by successive governments in Jerusalem, but Prime Minister Begin believed them—not deterred in any way by the color of their skin, unlike many of his countrymen. Begin ordered the Mossad chief, Hofi, to find a way to bring the black Jews "home" to Israel.

Bitzur operatives infiltrated Ethiopia, which was beset and distracted by civil war and famine, in the late 1970s. They made contact with the "Beta

Israel" (House of Israel) communities, helped them with food, medicine, and enticing conversations about life in the actual State of Israel. The Mossad people spread the message that the Jews should move to neighboring Sudan.

After uncomfortable truck rides and, more typically, exceedingly long treks with all their belongings, the Jews were placed in refugee camps run by international humanitarian organizations. The Mossad knew that this arrangement was temporary, at best. A cover story for some sort of processing facility in Sudan, which was an Arab country, would have to be created.

The Israeli spies set up a travel agency in Europe and purchased a small beach resort on the Red Sea coast of northeastern Sudan. The hotel staff and the diving instructors were Mossad operatives, who entertained genuine European customers with a smile by day—and then, by night and in the off-season, became secret agents delivering Jews to the shoreline. The Ethiopians who would soon be Israelis were taken by truck to the beach, where small boats would ferry them to Israeli navy vessels. The boats headed to the Israeli port of Eilat, where instant citizenship was bestowed upon them.

The process, however, was slow and required too many steps. The number of immigrants who got to Israel was relatively low.

Prime Minister Begin ordered Hofi to find a better method. The Mossad gingerly approached Sudan's dictator, Gaafar Nimeiri, and his security chief, General Omar el-Tayeb, and a deal was clinched. The Jews from Ethiopia could be bused to the international airport in Khartoum, the Sudanese capital, and a Belgian charter airline—usually used to fly Muslim pilgrims to Mecca for the *hajj* (pilgrimage)—would fly the Jews to freedom.

Israel would raise substantial sums of money from Jewish contributors around the world to finance the operation, and a significant part of that would go into bank accounts belonging to Nimeiri and Tayeb.

The Israeli role would be kept hidden, and at Nimeiri's insistence all flights had to go to Europe—and not directly to the Jewish state.

To the Mossad's pleasure, the CIA was more than happy to help coordinate this modern-day Exodus. The plan had plainly touched the hearts of many officials in Ronald Reagan's administration. Foremost among them was a former CIA director, Vice President George H.W. Bush.

The CIA station chief in Khartoum was Milt Bearden. He recalled years later that Bush had personally asked Nimeiri to facilitate the rescue of the starving Jews from Ethiopia. Sudan's president consented, apparently not mentioning that the Israelis had already started making the necessary bank transfers.

The operation began in 1983, and Bearden recalled meeting in Sudan with Efraim Halevy, the Bitzur director who would become the head of the Mossad 15 years later. The conveyor belt for the refugees changed yet again, as Bearden helped organize a fleet of American military transport planes—apparently Vice President Bush's idea—to take the Jews from a desert airstrip directly to Israel. It was an uncomfortable trip for a few thousand Ethiopians, waiting their turn to be crammed into aircraft not designed for passengers; but the new arrangement avoided bringing them into an unstable and unpredictable Arab capital.

Matters became more complicated when Nimeiri, while visiting the United States in 1985, was overthrown by Sudanese officers who had help from Libya. They immediately declared that the president and his secret police chief, Tayeb, were guilty of collaborating with the Mossad and the CIA in exchange for millions of dollars in bribes. This was a rare case in which claims broadcast by rebels were precisely correct.

Now the Sudanese authorities were searching for the Israelis and Americans who were involved in such perfidy. Bearden, over 20 years later, recounted how three Mossad men individually made their way—as was prearranged—to his house in Khartoum as their emergency shelter.

Bearden's wife, Marie-Catherine, heard a knock on the door. "A young man stood there and told her: 'I am French and I want to talk your husband,'" Bearden said. "My wife smiled at him and answered: 'You are not French. I am French. But I know who you are. Come in and go to the second floor.'"

A month later, Bearden and his CIA colleagues felt it was safe to fly the Mossad operatives out of Sudan.

In all, from 1977 to 1985, an estimated 20,000 Jews left their villages in Ethiopia in search of food, safety, comfort, and spiritual fulfillment. As many as 4,000 died on the way, and even as a new dark-skinned minority group joined the kaleidoscope of Israeli society, the sacrifice made by parents and grandparents to move future generations to the Promised Land of ancient times was never forgotten.

After the biggest immigration projects undertaken in the name of Jewish intelligence were complete, there were growing calls—even within the Mossad—to shut down the Bitzur unit. The separate agency Nativ, after all, had withered and vanished. Perhaps Israel could now move on to protecting its own citizens at home.

A decision was made to keep Bitzur open as a small unit, as two Mossad officers put it in simple terms: "just in case," and "for a rainy day." Unpleasant precipitation arrived after 9/11, when Israel noticed an upsurge of anti-Semitism in many countries. A historic synagogue in Tunisia was bombed; and other Jewish sites were targeted by terrorists who seemed to believe that Jews and Americans all constituted the same enemy, which Islam needed to wipe out.

Bitzur operatives were assigned to perform their traditional task of helping to organize self-defense for Jewish communities around the globe. This time, however, the task was almost always performed in conjunction with local police forces.

Israel's intelligence community could never abandon completely the duty it saw to protect Jews and guarantee a safe shelter to them. That, after all, was why the Jewish state existed.

Chapter Fourteen

NORTHERN EXPOSURE

No one needed the best intelligence in the world to know that Israel was poised to attack the PLO infrastructure in Lebanon in 1982.

Menachem Begin's intentions became clear after his reelection in 1981. With a measure of reluctance and a whirlwind of controversy, Begin elevated Ariel Sharon to the post of defense minister. The feisty and ambitious retired general had a reputation as a man of action who believed in using a glove of iron—rather than velvet—in dealing with Arabs.

Another cabinet minister remarked—only half-jokingly—that if Sharon got that job, one day tanks would surround the prime minister's office in a coup d'état. Yet Sharon, as a hero of the Yom Kippur War against Egypt, had many admirers and lobbied vigorously for the defense ministry. Begin lavished praise on Sharon as a modern-day Judah the Maccabee, but also feared Sharon as a charismatic figure who could cause trouble.

What did occur, and quickly, was that Sharon began planning an invasion of Lebanon. Military planners codenamed it "Big Pine." The concept, in truth, also fit Begin's strategy. The prime minister was feeling remorse over his offer of Palestinian autonomy in the West Bank and Gaza—part of his peace treaty with Egypt's President Sadat in 1979. Begin now was concerned that autonomy would lead to an independent Palestinian state, which he opposed. The most effective way to derail that would be to smash the organization that embodied the Palestinians' aspirations, the PLO.

In public, Begin kept warning that Palestinian terrorists—after being expelled from Jordan in 1971—had built a state within a state in Lebanon as a launching pad for attacks southward into Israel. He even dehumanized the enemy by referring to PLO chairman Yasser Arafat as "this man with hair on his face," and to the PLO as "two-legged beasts."

Even for the large circle of Israelis who were privy to the secret war plans, it was a surprise to see how trigger-happy Begin and his defense minister were when news broke in April 1982 that two Israelis had been murdered in the Bois de Boulogne park in Paris. Sharon called Begin, and suggested that this would be the opportunity to execute the pre-cooked plan to invade Lebanon.

It turned out that the corpses in Paris were those of Israeli criminals, killed in an organized crime clash. They were not victims of Palestinian terrorism.

Tranquility reigned for only two months. Late on a Thursday night, the third of June, the Israeli ambassador in London—Shlomo Argov—was shot in the head, and crippled for life, while leaving the elegant Dorchester Hotel after a banquet.

The next morning in Jerusalem, Begin's cabinet convened for an urgent meeting. Researchers from Aman explained that the three Palestinian attackers, arrested by efficient British police, belonged to a renegade wing of the PLO named for its leader: the Abu Nidal organization. The army chief of staff, General Rafael (Raful) Eitan, immediately jumped up and said: "Abu Nidal, Abu Shmidal, they all are the same." (The IDF's top officer was not related to the intelligence operative, Rafi Eitan.)

The cabinet approved a limited penetration by Israeli forces into Lebanon, to smash PLO positions. Begin told parliamentarians in the Knesset—in Biblical terms—that the IDF operation would bring the Jewish state 40 years of peace and quiet, in which "the children of Israel will happily go to school and joyfully return home."

On Sunday, June 6, the mighty Israeli military invaded Lebanon by land, sea, and air. Things went well, at first. Palestinian guerrilla fighters were no match for the fully trained and equipped IDF. Within six days, the Israelis encircled the sprawling capital city, Beirut.

Along the way, as tanks advanced northward from the border, the Israelis were welcomed by Druze villagers, Maronite Christians, and even Shi'ite Muslims who showered the invaders with the traditional greeting of handfuls of rice. They saw the Israelis as liberators from an oppressive PLO-Sunni Muslim coalition backed by Syria.

But the honeymoon did not last long.

The promises made by Begin and Sharon, and supported by General Eitan, for a quick victory turned out to be hollow. The invaders went far beyond the 40 kilometers (25 miles) declared by Begin as the war plan. Sharon had a grander strategy, intent upon forcing the Palestinians to leave Lebanon and make their way back to Jordan—the country he wanted to be the permanent solution for the Palestinian problem.

That was not the way events played out. Very soon, the Israelis were perceived by most of Lebanon's factions as an occupying force. The IDF became the target of attacks by Palestinians and by a new force: Hezbollah, or Party of God, created by the new Islamic regime in Iran to empower their Shi'ite brethren.

The major breakdown of Sharon's strategy occurred that September. Just after being elected president of Lebanon, Bashir Gemayel—whose family had a long history of secret cooperation with Israeli intelligence—was assassinated by Syrian agents. Syria felt it had to crush the obvious alliance between Israel and Maronite Christians, including the Gemayels.

Retaliation followed swiftly, and it was bloody and history-changing. Either encouraged or malevolently ignored by the Israeli military, Christian militiamen entered the Sabra and Shatila refugee camps in Beirut and massacred 800 Palestinian men, women, and children.

Israel sank even deeper into the mud of Lebanese politics: a complex and fractured mosaic of rival and often violent ethnic groups.

American, French, and Italian forces intervened, intending to stabilize the failed state of Lebanon, but they themselves became the targets of a new form of terrorism: suicidal attacks by Hezbollah. The organization glorified the Shi'ite Muslim tradition of martyrdom: giving your life for a holy cause, wiping out Islam's enemies, while guaranteeing yourself a place in Paradise where 72 virgins would await you.

The worst attack of all was the truck bombing that brought down the United States Marines barracks, killing over 240 servicemen in October 1983. A simultaneous suicide bombing in Beirut killed 58 French paratroopers.

Israel found small comfort in the mass departure of PLO fighters, led by Arafat. Ships brought them from Beirut's harbor to their new headquarters, far to the west in Tunisia. Israeli snipers had Arafat in the crosshairs of their gunsights, and a junior intelligence officer felt this could be an opportunity to get rid of the man viewed by Israel as a terrorist chief. Restraint prevailed, because of a ceasefire an American envoy had negotiated, so Begin and Sharon did not approve taking the shot.

The PLO left, but Israel was stuck for another 17 years in its own Vietnam.

An Israeli inquiry commission forced Sharon to resign. Begin's mental condition deteriorated, as he felt severe pangs of conscience for the more-than 600 Israelis who ultimately were killed in the Lebanon war. The prime minister retreated into seclusion, becoming a prisoner in his official residence.

Both politicians and the Mossad were pilloried for the nation's quagmire.

Inside Mossad headquarters at the Glilot junction, the finger-pointing was directed at Menachem (Nahik) Navot. Even 27 years after the start of the war, Navot—now retired—was perceived as the intelligence mastermind behind Israel's conspiracies in Lebanon. "Have you seen the movie, *Waltz With Bashir*?" Navot was asked by a senior female colleague from the 1980s.

She was referring to the 2008 Oscar-nominated Israeli film that depicted the Lebanon war's horrors from the point of view of director Ari Folman, who had been a tank crewman. She asked the question before a private screening of the animated film was arranged for Mossad employees.

After the movie, Navot lectured the crowd: "A lot of people think that I am responsible for the war. When you talk about the war in Lebanon, unfortunately, they bring up my name. That is the image that was stuck on me and the Mossad."

Before and during the war, Navot was Mossad's deputy director and was in charge of the Tevel liaison department. His job was to cultivate a clandestine relationship with the Christians' armed Phalangist party in Lebanon.

In 1952, at age 21, Navot joined Shin Bet and became a bodyguard to Prime Minister Ben-Gurion. He later moved to the operations department, which was shared with the Mossad, and eventually worked on foreign intelligence projects. He worked in the Shah's Iran and facilitated Israeli military assistance to the Kurds inside Iraq. In the mid-1970s, he was the Mossad's primary representative in Washington.

Back in Tel Aviv, he and his boss, General Yitzhak Hofi, followed in the footsteps of Reuven Shiloah, the first Mossad director, whose brainchild was the peripheral-alliance strategy. In Lebanon, the chief partners were the Christian Maronites.

The small country just to the north was not a significant threat to Israel, and an oft-told joke was that if a war broke out the IDF would send its military orchestra to the front. But Lebanon was a crossroads for infiltrations in all directions, particularly into and out of Syria. Being a relatively open and permissive society with casinos and brothels, Lebanon attracted influential élites from the Arab world. Thus, it served as a convenient field of play for collecting intelligence.

Since the 1950s, Aman case officers from Unit 154 (later 504) had Lebanese agents who spied on all kinds of people passing through. These agents also provided safe houses and transportation for Israeli operatives, when necessary.

As part of the spycraft of that era, even for the simplest tasks an agent would be needed. Some of the Lebanese then on the Israeli payroll had to endanger themselves, almost every day, for such mundane tasks as bringing Beirut's newspapers south to the border and handing them to Israeli intelligence analysts. There was no internet. There was no embassy in Beirut. And open-source information has always been a vital part of espionage.

In addition, Israelis frequently went undercover into Lebanon. Unit 154 men developed close relationships with the two leading Christian families, the Chamouns and the Gemayels.

The patriarchs of the two families met secretly with Israeli leaders. One of the Lebanese, Camille Chamoun served as president of his country. Here was a head of state of an Arab country who had no hesitation in mutually beneficial cooperation with the Jewish state. Senior Israelis were friendly with Pierre Gemayel despite his sympathy with fascism, as his own Phalange militia had been formed based on Mussolini's template. As in the cases when tactics called for cooperation with ex-Nazis served Israel's needs, Israeli intelligence had no compunctions against cooperating with Phalangists.

Responsibility for maintaining contact with the Lebanese minorities eventually was transferred from military intelligence to the Mossad's Tevel unit. The secret liaison advanced further in the 1970s, against the background of a vicious civil war in Lebanon, when the Mossad started coordinating the supply of weapons to Phalangist militiamen—and Israel created the South Lebanese Army.

The growing cooperation, however, blasted cracks within the Israeli intelligence community. Prime Minister Yitzhak Rabin, who met with both the Chamoun and Gemayel clans, decided that the role of Israel should be limited to helping the Christians to support themselves. After Begin's election in 1977, that approach began to change. With his Holocaust obsession, Begin believed that the Christian minority in Lebanon was facing possible destruction by the majority Muslims and Palestinians.

Sharon saw the Christian story as one more element in his strategy to install a compliant government in Lebanon on the sharp points of Israeli bayonets. Military intelligence analysts at Aman opposed his grand schemes and believed that the Phalangists aimed to drag the Israelis deeper into Lebanon: to manipulate Israel into fighting their wars for them.

In the Mossad itself there were divisions. Hofi believed in Rabin's concept of limited aid. His lieutenants, Navot and David Kimche, favored widening the Israeli role—and they did so.

Eventually, Kimche's deep involvement in Lebanon and his belief in the alliance with the Christians led to his downfall. Hofi, who suspected that Kimche was operating behind his back, forced Kimche to resign—ending, after 30 years, the British-born spy's aspirations of becoming the agency director.

Lebanon also brought down Hofi's designated successor, Yekutiel (Kuti) Adam, a decorated army general and an experienced agent-runner as head of the Mossad's Tsomet department. Just before the invasion in 1982, Begin selected Adam to be the next Mossad director. As the tanks rolled in, in June, Adam rushed to the front—motivated by little more than the excitement of combat—and the unlucky general was killed by a Palestinian ambush.

The partial blindness of some Mossad operatives such as Navot and Kimche could be explained by the excessive warmth of their reception by Lebanese Christians—fine restaurants and nightclubs, at beauty spots along the Mediterranean coast. The Mossad seemed not to see the dark side of the alliance. The agency helped the Phalangists and the SLA restructure themselves along Israeli lines: with combat strategies, shadowy prisons, and interrogation teams. The added Lebanese elements included torture and executions without trial.

Outrageous behavior by Christian allies, more than once, backfired on Israel. Phalangists at a roadblock during the 1982 war kidnapped four Iranians, including three diplomats, and then murdered them and dumped their bodies. (Years later, when Israel wanted to arrange a swap with Hezbollah—of prisoners and corpses of soldiers—negotiations were prolonged by a demand that Israel deliver the remains of the four Iranians. Israel responded that it had no way of doing so, as a building had been constructed on the suspected burial site.)

However, Navot saw the entire drama in a very different, insider's context. "I was sitting with Hofi and his chief of staff in Mossad headquarters, when the news about the assassination of the Israeli ambassador in London reached us. All of us said, '*Oy va voy* [oh, woe!], we are going into a war!'"

Navot feared that Lebanese Christians would not be reliable allies when fighting began. "We knew that the Christian Phalangists wanted us to conquer all of Lebanon for their sake," Navot reminisced.

When their leader Bashir Gemayel—Israel's great hope—was killed by a Syrian bomb planted in his office, Navot took it hard and took it personally. He rushed to the scene. "People were searching for Bashir and did not find his body. I met one of Bashir's advisors there, who asked me, seriously, 'Have you abducted him?' Later I went with Bashir's widow to the hospital, and there we identified his body."

There were many more corpses and tons of destruction, as Israel remained in southern Lebanon until the year 2000. The involvement of the intelligence community deepened and widened. It was not only the Mossad there, but also Aman and increasingly Shin Bet. Israel's domestic security agency, with its counter-terrorism specialty, started running more Lebanese agents than ever, arresting and interrogating suspects, and getting to know the territory as though settling in for a long occupation.

Lebanon instantly became the biggest focus for all three Israeli agencies, consuming resources budgeted for other projects. Case officers, interrogators, and researchers were taken off their projects and relocated to Lebanon. A notable example of someone who had to move was Dubi, the same katsa who was busy running an extremely important agent in Cairo: Ashraf Marwan, the Mossad's best eyes and ears in Egypt.

Lebanon was a dangerous place that required extra guards and defenses when going to meetings with sources and agents. Ambushes and roadside bombs were frighteningly common. A thin organization, such as the Mossad, where personnel liked to move around invisibly, instead wound up in heavily armed convoys. For Aman's Unit 504, which specialized in running agents and interrogations, Lebanon was its biggest field of play ever.

Using all three major agencies in a relatively small territory did not make sense. There was a question of organizational ego, leading to inevitable turf fights and a lack of proper division of labor. Unnecessary duplication was evident in the absurdity of the three agencies' often running the very same agents, hiding their identities and information from the other Israelis.

Worse than that, they depended on well-established drug dealers as sources of information. Lebanon was known for decades as a hotbed for growing poppies and hashish and producing opium and cocaine, to be smuggled out of the country—often via Syria and Jordan into Egypt in one direction, and to European markets in the other.

The illegal but thriving drug trade first attracted Lebanese politicians and generals, then powerful Syrians as their country's influence in Lebanon grew. This trend eventually generated a class of professional drug traffickers, often as a family tradition. These criminal clans learned to cooperate with every power: with the central Lebanese government; with the Syrians; and now, acknowledging their new masters, with the Israeli forces in southern Lebanon.

The Israelis welcomed those families and gangs and started using them. Part of the deal was that the agencies turned a blind eye to their business.

Israeli intelligence did not notice what impression all of this would make on local residents, who became aware of the foreigners' extending their protection to drug smugglers. The Biro family was a case in point. Muhammad Biro, the father of the family, was a Lebanese customs officer at a border crossing with Syria in the 1950s, but his real business was selling drugs.

In a 20-year period, he became one of the biggest drug traffickers in the Middle East. Biro's business extended from Lebanon into Syria, Jordan, Egypt, and Europe. He was moving tons of drugs by land and sea to supply an unending demand. By becoming rich, he also became respectable. The Israelis started paying their respects to him and his heirs.

When Israel's defense minister, Moshe Arens, visited the area, he accepted an invitation to dine with the Biro family. He did not know the family's true business, and Aman's case officers who handled Biro did not tell Arens. It was no surprise that ridiculous rumors spread across Lebanon that Arens and Biro were drug-smuggling partners.

In any contacts with Arab drug smugglers, one key rule was imposed on them: If you sell to Israeli drug dealers, you have to inform on them and testify in court. The dealers, however, believed in free trade and globalization—before that term was coined—and for them there were no borders.

Ramzi Nahara, another giant in the Lebanese drug trade, cooperated with Israeli intelligence officers. While making a fortune, he furnished information to Israeli police; but he also smuggled more of his inventory into Israel behind the backs of the cops—until, one day, they decided that enough was enough and arrested him.

He was put on trial and sentenced to a long stay in an Israeli prison. Nahara continued to run his drugs business from a prison cell. He also managed to smuggle out a message to the emerging power of Lebanon—Hezbollah—telling them that he was severing his ties with Israel and now would be on their side. This would be significant in the future.

Starting in the 1990s, Israeli intelligence considered whether to dismantle Unit 504, with its checkered history. The proposal was to merge it with the Mossad, to put the art of running agents under one roof. But top military commanders had doubts about the wisdom of such a move, arguing that Unit 504 case officers and agents were providing tactical intelligence that was necessary for the troops in the field. They doubted that the Mossad, with its international and strategic outlook, would be interested in filling that role so well.

Hezbollah's birth stemmed from a long history of Shi'ite Muslim suffering, the facts of local Lebanese politics, and the Iranian Islamic revolution of February 1979. Its emergence also coincided with the Israeli invasion. The longer Israel remained in Lebanon, and the wider its activities there, the stronger Hezbollah became.

The Israeli presence gave the Shi'ite Party of God a focal point for its passion, fueled by resentment and hatred. Its first spiritual leader was Muhammad

Fadlallah, a Muslim cleric who studied in the Shi'ite holy city of Najaf in Iraq. Returning to Lebanon in 1966, he immersed himself in religious and educational concerns, even establishing an orphanage.

His work sowed the first seeds of Shi'ite pride in the country. For generations, his community in Lebanon and other majority Sunni Muslim countries suffered from discrimination and a lack of resources. In 1979 and 1980, with the rise of Ayatollah Ruhollah Khomeini in Iran, Shi'ites around the world were energized by the establishment of the first Shi'ite government in modern history.

From Iran's perspective, Lebanon was important because of the Shi'ite community—but also as a bridgehead to the Mediterranean and beyond to Europe. It could be a key base for a holy war against Israel and Western interests.

As in the French and Russian revolutions, the activists who took power quickly sought to export their ideals. The Iranians started sending emissaries to establish ties with other Shi'ite communities, and Lebanon was an obvious destination.

Iran's point man for the Lebanese community was Ali Akbar Mohtashemi, the Iranian ambassador in Syria. He found that Lebanese Shi'ites had already been spiritually inspired by Fadlallah, and now the envoy from Iran would add a large measure of political power. And money. And arms.

The day after the Israeli invasion of Lebanon in June 1982, an Iranian military delegation arrived in Damascus and discussed how to stir up resistance against the Israelis. The group was led by Iran's defense minister and by the head of the Revolutionary Guard Corps, joined by Ambassador Mohtashemi. It was agreed to send Iranian volunteers into Lebanon, and that was the start of a significant Iranian presence in the country. The volunteers were mostly Revolutionary Guards and intelligence officers.

With the help of the Iranian professionals, Hezbollah began to organize itself on three fronts: as a Lebanese political entity, as a religious and social organization, and as a military force. They called themselves resistance fighters. The Israelis and the West labeled them terrorists.

As well as turning their guns on Israelis, they also targeted Westerners. Americans, Britons, and other foreigners working in Lebanon were kidnapped. An American TWA airliner was hijacked to Beirut in June 1985, enabling the whole world to get acquainted with a young Lebanese Shi'ite by the name of Imad Mughniyeh. The 22-year-old had just defected from the PLO to the fast growing Hezbollah, and later he would become the world's most wanted terrorist—until the arrival of Osama Bin Laden.

A veiled war between the United States and Lebanese Shi'ite radicals had already begun. The CIA found no alternative to violence—not only because of the attack that killed sleeping U.S. Marines in their barracks in October 1983, but also the loss of the CIA's top case officer for the Middle East, Robert Ames, the previous April, when the United States embassy in Beirut was leveled by a car bomb. Those blows at American interests would also be blamed on Mughniyeh. The CIA retaliated, in a most unorthodox and bloody way: with a massive car bomb.

That may have seemed a fitting weapon in the Middle East, land of "an eye for an eye," but unless the explosives are sized and tailored with great expertise—as the Mossad has done repeatedly in enemy capitals—the casualties are almost sure to include many non-combatant civilians.

So it was in the southern Shi'ite district of Beirut on March 8, 1985. The target was Muhammad Fadlallah, the cleric who established Hezbollah. William Casey, then the director of the CIA, spoke with journalist Bob Woodward about it, and Woodward reported that Saudi Arabia helped organize placement of an explosives-laden vehicle, which went off in front of Fadlallah's home. Several buildings collapsed and 80 people were killed outside an adjacent mosque, but Fadlallah survived.

CHAPTER FIFTEEN

A NEW ENEMY

I srael's intelligence community and the IDF were slow to realize that they faced a very potent enemy in Hezbollah. The wake-up blast came in November 1983: a suicide car bomb that toppled an office building used by Shin Bet as its local headquarters in the port city of Tyre. Twenty-eight Israelis were killed, as well as 32 Lebanese prisoners held inside. Shin Bet's official history calls that the first suicide attack against an Israeli target.

That historical version is challenged, however, because an even taller building nearby—used by Shin Bet and the army—suffered a devastating explosion one year earlier. It caused the deaths of 78 Israelis and around two dozen Arab detainees. A senior military investigatory committee's official conclusion was that the first blast was an accident caused by a gas leak, yet the Lebanese media have always boasted that it was a Hezbollah attack.

Some Israeli investigators agree with the Hezbollah version, and they reveal that part of the car and a leg of the suicide bomber were found in the rubble weeks later. Still, Israel has stuck to the official version of a gas explosion.

The Mossad and Aman intensively probed into the second blast, hoping to trace the bombers to a specific location. Before long, there was a strong focus on Iran's ambassador in Damascus, Ali Akbar Mohtashemi. They concluded that he was the key link between Iran, providing logistical support and training, and Hezbollah men carrying out terrorist operations. They suspected that the ambassador was also involved in plotting the major suicide attacks on the Marines barracks and the U.S. embassy in Beirut.

In the tradition of sending letter bombs in the 1960s to German scientists and in the 1970s to Palestinian terrorists, a parcel was mailed to Mohtashemi in February 1984 at the Iranian embassy in Damascus. It contained a booby-trapped Muslim holy book, a Quran. It exploded but failed to achieve the entire goal: Mohtashemi lost his right hand and part of his left hand, but he survived.

Ironically, in the decades that followed, the militant ambassador would become a reformist publisher and politician in Tehran, supporting pro-democracy causes in his country.

In any event, the exploding book was a waste of time and blood. Hezbollah's growth seemed unstoppable, and it became a more sophisticated force than the PLO. The Shi'ites were better trained, with the backing of their masters in Tehran. Together they innovated a new line of booby traps and mines that were cleverly camouflaged, causing casualties and damage to Israeli forces.

Similar improvised explosive devices would be aimed against U.S. troops in Iraq after 2003, as bombs were planted along roadsides by Iranian-supported militias. Hezbollah experts, honed by their experiences in Lebanon, would infiltrate into Iraq to train their Shi'ite brethren in the anti-American resistance.

The long war in Lebanon became asymmetrical: a regular army facing a guerrilla force. The Israelis eventually realized that the best way to fight guerrillas would be to emulate their tactics. The IDF put soldiers in special small units that staged ambushes, hid explosives, and behaved in unpredictably offensive ways.

Many Israelis, not only in the intelligence community, saw the unexpected and uncomfortable truth of what was unfolding in Lebanon. Israel went into that country to get rid of one enemy—the PLO. But it stayed there, and over the years it faced a more dangerous enemy, Hezbollah.

Israelis had to fight even more fiercely, and the mutual bleeding was not confined to Lebanese soil. It spilled over into Israel.

Hezbollah introduced a new threat, courtesy of its Iranian sponsors: short-range rockets, and then longer-range missiles that could reach many Israeli towns and cities. For the first time since 1948, the civilian population in Israel might be thrust onto the front line, because the military front came to them.

Israel and the radical Lebanese Shi'ites kept hammering each other, and a new crisis would focus on one Israeli airman.

In October 1986 one of Israel's American-made F-4 Phantom warplanes, during a bombing mission over Lebanon, was damaged when one of its own bombs exploded. The pilot and the navigator ejected and safely parachuted to the ground. The pilot was quickly picked up by an Israeli helicopter-borne rescue squad, but the rescuers could not reach the navigator, Ron Arad. Ground fire from gunmen in Lebanon did not let up, and Arad was captured by Shi'ite Muslims.

His captors were not Hezbollah militants, but members of the more traditional Shi'ite movement called Amal. Israeli leaders, pressured by heavy criticism of a lopsided prisoner exchange with a small Palestinian terrorist group two years earlier, were in no rush to offer a deal. The politicians in Jerusalem were reading intelligence analyses from Aman that suggested Arad was not in imminent danger. Meetings were held with Amal representatives in London, aimed at arranging his release. For about 18 months, Israel was certain that Arad was alive, and his family even received letters from him.

But Aman's reading of the situation was wrong. In fact, Amal was sinking quickly in the constellation of Lebanese factions and could not hold on long to its prize captive. Hezbollah paid Amal and took possession of the prisoner. Ron Arad vanished into a black hole.

His mysterious disappearance would haunt Israeli intelligence, the military, politicians, the press, and the public for decades. It is assumed that he died. It is also assumed that his captors, whether Hezbollah or Iran's Revolutionary Guards, did not want him to die, as he could be a precious trading asset. For the operatives and chiefs of Aman and the Mossad, it was truly a low point that an Israeli imprisoned behind enemy lines could not be traced.

Realizing that there was no consistent framework for dealing with such cases, the two agencies created permanent units called Shon, a Hebrew acronym for *Shvu'yim v'Ne'edarim* (Prisoners and Missing). The units would be directed by senior officers, to emphasize the importance of locating anyone who was lost—rooted in the Israeli ethos of leaving no soldier behind.

Among the steps recommended for the Arad case was to kidnap senior members of Hezbollah, so as to have bargaining chips. This was modeled on a success in 1972, when Sayeret Matkal commandos kidnapped five Syrian military officers along the Syria-Lebanon border and exchanged them for Israeli pilots held by Syria.

In July 1989, armed with excellent intelligence, Sayeret Matkal soldiers went into action again inside Lebanon. In the middle of the night, they kidnapped Sheik Abdul Karim Obeid from his home. He was ostensibly a spiritual leader in Hezbollah, but according to the Israelis he directed many acts of violence.

Once again, in the complex Lebanese kaleidoscope, Israeli intelligence was confused by all the facets. Hezbollah stubbornly offered nothing in exchange for Obeid. Either he was not sufficiently important in their organization, or the group had no idea where Arad was—and did not wish to reveal that it did not know. Israel was stuck with Obeid for 15 years and faced international criticism for holding a hostage without trial.

With no progress made on the Arad front, Israeli intelligence and the political echelon decided to escalate. If Obeid turned out to be merely a tail, now Israel would aim at the snake's head. A decision was made to kidnap Abbas Musawi, who only recently had become secretary-general of Hezbollah. Teams of Sayeret Matkal and naval commandos—known as Flotilla 13—practiced various scenarios: grabbing Musawi from an office, from a home, or from a car.

The commander of Aman, General Uri Saguy, spotted an opportunity in February 1992: a newspaper item that said Musawi would visit a Shi'ite village in southern Lebanon. The Israelis would not be far away.

When Musawi was driven southward out of Beirut in a convoy on February 16, the line of vehicles was watched constantly by an Israeli air force drone flying undetectably high above. The pilotless plane transmitted real-time pictures to a command center in the Kirya in Tel Aviv. General Saguy and his analysts realized, to their disappointment, that there were too many cars and people around Musawi, so a snatch operation would be too dangerous.

Without much deliberation, the chief of staff, General Ehud Barak—with General Saguy reluctantly agreeing but some other officers opposed—decided, on the spot, to eliminate the Hezbollah leader. American-made Apache helicopters, on standby at a base in northern Israel, were summoned. Not knowing which car contained Musawi, the pilots were ordered to destroy the entire convoy.

One of the Israeli pilots later spoke of making his own decision, while airborne, to hit the procession of "good-looking black Mercedes cars" and one Land Rover far from any buildings to reduce civilian casualties.

He was not told beforehand who the main target would be, and he said "professional behavior" meant not asking questions. "We knew they weren't sending us out for nothing," he said. The five-minute attack was like a shooting gallery. Four helicopters fired missile after missile to liquidate all the Hezbollah targets. The gruesome results, shattered and smoking remnants of expensive German- and British-made vehicles, formed a killing field.

The death toll included Musawi, his wife, their son, and at least five security guards. This was the first assassination by Israeli attack helicopters, several years before the practice—officially aimed at blocking future terrorism—became legalized by an attorney general as "targeted prevention." America would come to call the method "targeted killing," when aimed against al-Qaeda years later.

Barak did manage to get an okay by telephone from Prime Minister Yitzhak Shamir and Defense Minister Moshe Arens, around a minute before the rockets struck. The political level did adhere to tradition by taking responsibility for an assassination.

This particular killing would lead to terrible blowback for Israel, a mere 30 days later.

First, it rapidly became clear that Hezbollah would not be caving in. Musawi was replaced by a new leader, Hassan Nasrallah, who turned out to be much more charismatic, vigorous, wily, and dangerous. Nasrallah would become one of Israel's bitterest enemies, causing a lot of trouble for the Jewish state—including starting a war in 2006 that disrupted normal life for Israelis.

According to Israeli intelligence, the new leader consulted with his Iranian masters—the supreme leader Ayatollah Ali Khamenei and President Hashemi Rafsanjani—and together they decided to avenge Musawi in a big way. And they had the capability to do that, far from the expected field of battle.

Israeli security agencies were prepared for some level of retaliation. There was the fairly standard shower of Katyusha rockets fired into northern Israel by Hezbollah gunners. Then, when the security officer at the Israeli embassy in Ankara was killed by a car bomb on March 7, Israelis naturally considered that to be Hezbollah's response to the death of Musawi.

There were, however, conflicting claims of responsibility for that blast in Turkey. Hezbollah never made a habit of publicly announcing its operations outside Lebanon, and Iranian intelligence certainly never declared anything.

Yet, without doubt, it was the two of them—Hezbollah and Iran—that committed a much more astounding act aimed against Israel. Their agents blew up the Israeli embassy in Buenos Aires. They chose Argentina because Iran's Ministry of Intelligence and Security (MOIS) already had assets in South America, including sleeper cells that had melted into friendly Shi'ite communities in several countries.

A truck laden with explosives was detonated by a suicide bomber in front of Israel's embassy, in an elegant neighborhood, on March 17. Twenty-nine people, including four Israeli diplomats, were killed.

Yaakov Perry, the head of Shin Bet, had just been in Buenos Aires—as part of a tour of Israeli and Jewish facilities in South America with the head of the agency's security department. They met with Argentine counterparts to discuss the dangers of Middle Eastern terrorism, but they thought they had no reason to think that Argentina would be targeted within a few days.

Separate and joint investigations by the Mossad, the CIA, and Argentina's state intelligence agency SIDE found that the attack was a joint project of Hezbollah with Iranian government agents. MOIS officers, under diplomatic cover at Iran's embassy, had activated local sleeper cells and arranged the logistics: procuring the truck and delivering the explosives in diplomatic pouches from Tehran.

A few more Iranian intelligence officers had flown into neighboring countries, Brazil and Paraguay, and the operation was planned and executed with impressive speed.

People in Israel were truly shocked. This was the first time that one of its embassies had been destroyed. Israeli intelligence began to reconsider whether killing Musawi had been such a good idea.

An even bigger blow—again in Buenos Aires—two years later drove home the message that Israel was involved in a war that it barely understood. No one can mess blithely with the Iranians, who are proud to be leading what they see as a historic rise of Shi'ite Islam. They have very long memories. They plot in complex ways. They get even, and sometimes doubly so.

In 1994, yet again, it was a truck bomb. This time the target was in a working-class neighborhood of small markets: the seven-story headquarters of AMIA, Argentina's national Jewish organization. On July 15, an explosion brought down the entire building. Eighty-five people were killed and over 300 injured.

The driver was vaporized, and no pieces remained of him to put together. There were no documents, no clothing, and no fingerprints. But the Mossad managed to piece together a logical conclusion that he was from a Shi'ite village in Lebanon's Bekaa Valley, because a plaque was quickly erected to honor a Hezbollah fighter killed on that particular date. And a pro-Hezbollah television station in Lebanon announced that Musawi's killing by Israel in 1992 had now been avenged.

Having destroyed an Israeli embassy, Hezbollah fell in love with the tactic as a stunning blow to the Jews and their sovereign state. Hezbollah would plot similar bombings, time and again.

In 1996, Aman received a piece of intelligence that seemed to be a secret message between a terrorist in the Middle East and a partner overseas. A junior intelligence officer in the military's counter-terrorism unit—who happened to be good with hunches—tried to identify the person who was far away. Sticking with it beyond where others would have quit, he located a suspect in a Southeast Asian country.

The man's name was not familiar to the Mossad, but the fact that he was in touch with Hezbollah was enough to set off a sense of alarm. Knowing that the Lebanese Shi'ite militants were making major efforts to extend their global reach, the Israelis chose to be safe, rather than sorry. Bitter experience, notably the Buenos Aires bombs, had taught them not to ignore clues in unexpected countries.

The identity of the suspect was passed to Mossad officers in charge of foreign liaison, who arranged for the man—native of another Asian nation—to be arrested and interrogated. The questioning, accompanied by strong local police pressure, was highly effective. The man said that he was a Muslim student who recently had been to Qom, the spiritual center in Iran. He spent time there with a Lebanese colleague who turned out to be a recruiter for Hezbollah. He was offered a training program in Lebanon's Bekaa Valley and agreed.

He also told interrogators that his mission, in the country where he had been caught, had been to purchase forged passports.

Pressed further, the man revealed that he had been in Thailand, just a few days before, with a senior Hezbollah operative on a highly murderous mission. They stole a fuel tanker truck, killed the driver, stuffed his corpse inside the fuel tank, and then took the truck to a workshop in Bangkok that they had leased earlier.

They installed two tons of explosives in the truck—enough to destroy whole city blocks. The plan was to fly in a suicide bomber from Lebanon and destroy Israel's embassy in Bangkok. But, judging by the lack of any headlines about it in the news, the truck obviously never exploded. The detainee who was questioned did not know why.

It turned out—luckily for the Israelis and thousands of Thai innocents— that the vehicle had gotten stuck in an awful traffic jam in Bangkok on the appointed morning, caused by a car accident that attracted a lot of police. The Lebanese bomber saw the officers, panicked, parked the tanker truck on the side of the road, and ran away.

Thai police towed away the truck—unaware that it had explosives and a dead driver in the huge tank—and left it at a police station. They discovered that the truck had been stolen, and the driver was listed as a missing person, but they believed it was merely a local crime.

After a few days, a senior police officer asked his subordinates why the truck was still there. He insisted that they check the truck more carefully. They opened the fuel tank and found the corpse and the explosives.

After the capture of the terrorist who was compelled to be talkative, it was clear that Israel's embassy in Bangkok was the intended target. Hezbollah was truly showing that it had worldwide ambitions, and defensive measures would increasingly require better international cooperation. Israel intelligence would have plenty to do.

Sometime later, Israel was informed that Jordan had captured a Hezbollah man—apparently plotting to fire rockets into Israel. Israeli liaison operatives quickly realized that the suspect was the same Hezbollah commander who had run the fuel tanker truck plot in Bangkok.

One of the heads of Jordan's main security agency promised that the Lebanese suspect would never be released. But within three weeks, he was set free. Israeli officials naturally complained; but the Jordanians said they felt they had no choice, because Hezbollah had threatened to attack Jordan.

The takeaway lesson for the Mossad was that liaison relationships are a fine thing, but ultimately every country acts on its own self-interests. No one, even longtime colleagues for decades, can fully be relied upon. Israelis had to do many things on their own.

The Mossad continued—almost by rote—to play the game according to the rules it understood. Ron Arad was still missing, and the Mossad intended to squeeze someone in Lebanon for information.

True, the kidnapping plan aimed at Musawi had produced a killing field and then twin Buenos Aires massacres. The Israelis would still, however, make an effort to obtain a new bargaining chip: this time, a man they also hoped could provide new information.

A case officer in Aman's Unit 504 managed to recruit a young Lebanese woman, a university graduate from Beirut who worked as a housekeeper for a prominent family in southern Lebanon. It was Mustafa Dirani's household.

He was the security chief for Amal and was the last official of that Shi'ite organization to hold Arad. Israeli intelligence believed that Dirani sold Arad for $300,000 to Iran's Revolutionary Guards.

It was decided to kidnap Dirani and bring him to Israel. The young woman who was spying for Aman provided information about his daily routine and habits—even a sketch of the Dirani home—so that the kidnap squad could make specific plans. Based on the details she provided, the technological unit of Aman built a mock-up of the house; and Sayeret Matkal commandos practiced snatching their target.

In May 1994, the soldiers grabbed him in his house in the middle of the night, and they spirited him away to Israel. Dirani joined Sheik Obeid as the second bargaining chip for the Israelis.

The Lebanese woman, by then, was dead. Israeli intelligence learned later that she had been sleeping with both Dirani and his brother, whether for information-gathering purposes or just because such things happen. When the brothers discovered that they were sharing her affections, instead of being angry at each other, they killed her.

Israeli interrogators found that Dirani was a very tough nut to crack. He claimed that he did not sell Arad—that Lebanese guards had lost Arad during an Israeli air raid on a nearby village. Unit 504's interrogators were not convinced by Dirani's version, and Israeli newspapers would eventually publish details of how the questioners tortured him.

In a court affidavit filed by his Israeli lawyer, Dirani would claim that one of the torturers—a 504 officer codenamed "George"—put a stick up his rectum. He also would claim that an Israeli soldier pulled down his own trousers and threatened to rape Dirani. Israel's Supreme Court refused to believe the allegations, but they proved to be correct.

It turned out that the rough methods of Unit 504's interrogators had been used for a long time in questioning terrorism suspects and enemy soldiers. Shin Bet's interrogation experts were aware of what the 504 men were doing and rejected those tactics out of hand. "Those guys think they are a law unto themselves," said a senior Shin Bet official. "When the public finds out, they will disgrace all of us."

It might seem strange that a security operative from an enemy state, kidnapped by Israel's army and held in an Israeli prison, would be permitted to file legal complaints with Israel's highest court and to demand millions of dollars in compensation. Yet that is the eternal paradox facing Israeli intelligence. It operates as though on a constant war footing, yet it often has to dance to the tune of democratic law and human rights.

Dirani proved to be almost worthless. He and Sheik Obeid were not valuable, light bargaining chips. They both became heavy millstones for Israel. The two Lebanese men were released in 2004, part of a prisoner swap. The deal was mediated by the German intelligence service BND, which proved again to be friendly, useful, and ready to assist Israel.

Frustrated by Hezbollah and not yet fully grasping its wide and dangerous scope, the Mossad stepped up efforts aimed at cracking the militant Shi'ite enemy. In an increasingly dirty war, particularly after the embassy and the Jewish center in Argentina were bombed, no tactics seemed out of bounds.

By the early 1990s, Israeli intelligence identified the mastermind of the two bombings in South America as Imad Mughniyeh. He had become much more than the TWA hijacker who thrust himself in 1985 into the infamy of the FBI's most-wanted list—with a bounty of $5 million offered on his head at age 22. In his 30s, he was the major figure in the construction of Hezbollah as a military force—and the point man with Iran's MOIS and al-Quds Force.

Aman and the Mossad—having learned bitter lessons after assassinating Musawi—were not going to repeat the mistake by targeting Nasrallah. The two agencies realized that killing the top figure of this particular organization would not achieve the desired goal of disrupting its operational capabilities.

However, "targeted prevention" was still considered a powerful option if aimed at the right person: the one in charge of planning and executing the terrorist actions against Israel. That person was Mughniyeh—and he understood very well that he would be a prime target.

After the killing of Musawi, Mughniyeh fled to Iran and found shelter with the Revolutionary Guards. He underwent plastic surgery to change his facial appearance, hoping to fool his pursuers, who had only the one famous photograph of him –taken when he was waving his pistol in the TWA cockpit window.

Losing sight of Mughniyeh, the Mossad deliberated how to lure him back to terra cognita, a known land such as Lebanon. The Mossad needed a lead.

The Israelis spotted his brother Fuad, who was also a Hezbollah activist. He owned a car-repair facility in a Shi'ite neighborhood of southern Beirut. The Mossad reportedly tried to recruit Fuad, but then concocted another plan. If he would not cooperate, he would become bait at the end of a fishing line— dead bait.

In December 1994, the Mossad activated a team of Lebanese agents led by a man named Ahmed Halek. A powerful car bomb was planted in front of Fuad's garage, and the notorious Mughniyeh's lesser known brother was killed. It was not revenge for his refusing to work for Israel. In his death, he became a tool in a dirty war becoming ever dirtier.

It was hoped that Imad could not resist the Shi'ite fraternal duty of attending Fuad's funeral. Israeli intelligence hoped that Imad would be there. But the elusive and super-cautious Hezbollah military chief did not show up, at least not in a way they could recognize.

He did, however, launch a vengeance plan. Mughniyeh ordered an investigation to find his brother's murderers, and a number of Lebanese agents working for the Mossad were arrested by Hezbollah.

Halek and his wife, Hanan, managed to escape to Israeli-controlled southern Lebanon. Their security was provided by Israel's Christian ally, the South Lebanon Army (SLA). After a while, the couple was persuaded that they would be much more secure if they were resettled abroad.

They agreed, and they moved to a foreign country. But after a few months, they returned to southern Lebanon and complained that they had been unable to adjust to a new nation. Once again they were provided with around-the-clock security guards and were warned to keep a low profile.

Mughniyeh and his security teams kept searching and they spotted the weak link in Ahmed Halek's chain: his love for women and alcohol. They sent a southern Lebanese agent—Ramzi Nahara, the drug dealer who for many years had been an informer for Israeli intelligence but then was imprisoned.

Nahara was grateful to Hezbollah leaders for his freedom. They believed that he had changed to their side, so they put his name on a list of prisoners to be released in a swap with Israel. So now it was time to pay his debt to Hezbollah.

Nahara and a few helpers invited Halek to a drinking party where he was promised a chance to meet beautiful women. Halek left his security guards behind and went to the party. Nahara put a drug in his drink. Halek fell asleep, was thrown into the trunk of a car, and driven northward to Beirut. There, he was interrogated by Hezbollah and Syrian intelligence. Mughniyeh personally took part in torturing Halek by cutting off a few of his fingers.

Halek admitted that he had spied for Israel for many years. His wife was also arrested.

Halek provided detailed descriptions of his spycraft training in Cyprus and in Israel itself. He was put on trial by Lebanon in 1996, sentenced to death, and executed by a firing squad. His last request was that his wife—who was also convicted and sentenced to 15 years—be allowed to travel to Israel to collect $100,000, which he had been promised by the Mossad. Obviously, the Lebanese refused to let her go.

As for Nahara's role as a double agent now working for Hezbollah, Israeli intelligence was not about to forgive and forget. It took a few years, but a cleverly disguised roadside bomb in southern Lebanon destroyed Nahara's Mercedes and killed him.

The tit-for-tat war between Israel and Hezbollah continued at a high intensity until the Israelis decided to leave Lebanon in May 2000. The Shi'ite fighters kept spilling the blood of Israelis and the SLA. The sacrifice, in exchange for little or no gain, had become intolerable.

Similar to the American public when considering Vietnam in the 1970s, the Israeli public was asking, "What are we doing there?"

Ehud Barak—the former Sayeret Matkal commando who now held the posts of prime minister and defense minister—made up his mind. Israeli troops would be withdrawn from Lebanon, and 18 years of occupation would come to an end.

To avoid casualties, the Israelis pulled out in the middle of the night: a hasty departure that left behind some of their Lebanese agents. Many were resettled in Israel, including people on the Mossad payroll and SLA soldiers with their families.

Hezbollah portrayed the evacuation as its historic victory: It had pushed the Zionists out of Lebanon. Some of the Shi'ite factions vowed to keep battling to eject the Jews from Palestine, as well.

There was, at last, a ceasefire agreement. The tranquility promised in 1982 by Prime Minister Menachem Begin returned, at least for a while, to both sides of the Israel-Lebanon border. Yet Hezbollah remained a sworn enemy of Israel. Nasrallah promised that the battle against Israel would resume—sooner or later.

Israel's intelligence and the military, while licking their wounds, knew that they had scores of scores still to settle. Imad Mughniyeh remained at the top of the Mossad's most-wanted list.

The Israelis did not have to wait long for an opportunity. In June 2000, top commanders of Hezbollah—dubbed the Fabulous Five by Israeli analysts—visited Shi'ite border installations at the frontier with Israel. Among the five was Mughniyeh.

An IDF observer spotted the visiting group, and on-line cameras transmitted their images back to Aman's center in the Kirya. An intelligence officer there identified all of them—most importantly, Mughniyeh, despite his new facial features.

Preparations immediately began on the Israeli side, to muster either a sniper to the scene quickly or an aircraft that could fire a missile. As with almost all assassinations, a go-ahead would be needed from the prime minister.

In this instance, Barak did not give the okay. To the chagrin of some intelligence officers, Barak decided that shooting at Mughniyeh would be considered a violation of the withdrawal agreement. This showed that, while prime ministers sometimes made cold-blooded decisions, they frequently felt constrained by considerations of international implications. Many governments would have been angry at Israel for breaking a deal that had been so hard to arrange.

Yet America's FBI and the European Union had Mughniyeh on their "most wanted" lists, offering millions of dollars of bounty on his head. U.S. counter-terrorism agencies found him to be extremely slippery, but they came close to capturing him once. The National Security Agency intercepted his travel plans, learning that he would be flying—with a close Hezbollah colleague—from Tehran to Damascus, by way of Kuwait. The CIA asked Kuwaiti authorities to come up with a pretext to hold that airliner on the runway, until U.S. Navy SEAL commandos could get to the scene. The SEALs would arrest Mughniyeh.

The Kuwaitis delayed the plane for about an hour, but then—as Americans involved recalled later—lost their nerve. Fearing that Hezbollah would take revenge against them, the Kuwaitis let Mughniyeh leave. Considering that this was only a few years after America saved Kuwait's rulers and restored them to their throne, by ejecting Iraq's invaders in 1991, some U.S. officials complained bitterly about ingratitude.

As for the Israelis, they would wait until 2008 for another shot at Mughniyeh, while continuing to be on the receiving end of his bloody plots.

When the mighty Israeli army rolled into Lebanon in 1982, one might have predicted that it could soon declare victory and leave. The official cause was irritation stemming from a PLO mini-state, and the effect was its dissolution. A huge sense of triumph might have been expected.

However, the normal relationship between cause and effect was broken in Lebanon by the bloody and unusual nature of a conflict that took many lives—with no progress to show for it, for anyone.

CHAPTER SIXTEEN

BIOLOGICAL PENETRATION

An old man, leaning on his cane, shuffled slowly along Rue Mouffe-tard—a famous pedestrians-only thoroughfare frequented by tourists on the vivacious Left Bank of Paris. Drifting out of one of the many restaurants, as if on cinematic cue, came the voice of Yves Montand singing the immortal "Autumn Leaves."

It was a classic scene in the 5th arrondissement of the City of Light, and Professor Marcus Klingberg was slowly heading to his favorite café to read his favorite newspaper, the Communist Party daily *L'Humanité*.

It was April 2005. Klingberg was in his late 80s and appeared fragile. Yet, his daily strolls could be seen as a real-life incarnation of what the prophet Ezekiel envisioned in the Bible: the resurrection of the dead from the Valley of Dry Bones. For decades one of Israel's leading scientists—with a job about which he was supposed to say nothing—Dr. Klingberg had been in the valley of the vanished, and now he was back from the dead.

His family and its lawyers had persuaded Israeli judges that Klingberg's days were numbered and death would come soon, and thus he should be released from prison. Yet to anyone watching him walk, and hearing him talk, on Rue Mouffetard and in his nearby apartment, it was clear that predictions of his imminent passing were premature. But the deed was done. Klingberg was now a free man in Paris.

In scientific circles, he had been known as a brilliant epidemiologist. Within Israel's intelligence community, he was considered the most effective spy the Soviet Union ever planted in the Jewish state. His name became synonymous with treason. But, speaking soon after his release, he did not consider himself a traitor.

Later in the day, Klingberg planned to meet his daughter, Sylvia. He hoped that she would arrive with his grandson, a rising star in the French Communist Party. With pride, the aged scientist and spy declared: "We are three generations. Me, my daughter, and my grandson. Ideologues. Believers in Communism."

Then he would return to his small apartment and would surf the internet, hoping that Israeli news websites might carry something negative about the man he hated above all: Yehiel Horev. For two decades, Horev had pursued and even persecuted leakers and alleged threats to the airtight secrecy of sensitive projects in Israel.

Admirers of Victor Hugo novels and Broadway musicals might think that if Dr. Klingberg or any other Israeli under suspicion was Jean Valjean, then Yehiel Horev was the unyielding, obsessive Inspector Javert.

Horev was the much-feared head of Malmab: an acronym for *Memuneh al-haBitachon b'Ma'arechet haBitachon* (the One in Charge of Security in the Defense Ministry). Malmab was the field security unit of the ministry, and it developed in parallel with the nuclear smuggling and security "Science Liaison Bureau" founded by Binyamin Blumberg—and led later by the longtime Shin Bet kidnapping expert Rafi Eitan.

Dr. Klingberg vanished into the Israeli prison system in 1983. He was gone for 20 years, including very strict house arrest for the last five years of that time. Israel's military censor prevented any news media from mentioning his name, his disappearance, or his conviction on charges of aggravated espionage.

The truth, which Klingberg did not deny, was that he provided secret Israeli defense and scientific information to Soviet intelligence officers over a very long period. Israeli security officials identify Klingberg as the spy who caused the worst damage to the nation's most sensitive defense systems. As well as transferring hidden data on everything he knew—including, according to reports, non-conventional weapons produced and held by Israel—he demonstrated how negligent his nation's counter-intelligence efforts could be.

Klingberg should have been caught back in the early 1960s. He worked, after all, in one of the most secretive and guarded places in the country: the Israel Institute for Biological Research (IIBR), where he served as deputy director.

The high-walled Institute contains laboratories where Israel has manufactured an arsenal of chemical and biological weapons. Many commentators would say that using them would almost as unthinkable as using nuclear bombs.

Reports about the existence of non-conventional weapons was never acknowledged by Israel's government. The sophisticated work at Nes Tziona included the development of countermeasures to protect Israelis, in case Arabs or Iranians might attack with chemical or biological arms.

Klingberg's life is an intriguing story: an extreme exemplar of Jewish destiny enveloped in Holocaust survival, Communist ideology, scientific achievements, access to top secrets, and above all living in denial.

Avraham Mordecai-Marcus Klingberg was born in Warsaw, Poland, in 1918. World War I was just ending, but momentous events continued to swirl all around Europe. Russia was caught in civil war after its Bolshevik Revolution, and Poland had strangely redrawn borders and a vigorous campaign for self-determination.

Klingberg's parents were rich and religious, and one of his grandfathers was a renowned rabbi. Despite his Orthodox roots, the young man had a secular, liberal education. When he matriculated at the medical school at Warsaw University in 1935, he rubbed shoulders with students more radical than he.

Klingberg was captivated by Marxist ideas and the need for the working class to rise up in a "proletarian revolution."

His grandfather did not like the young Klingberg's inclinations, but the old man displayed a sense of humor about it: "Well, Mordecai, you won't be a rabbi in *Eretz Yisrael* (the Land of Israel), but it is consolation, perhaps, that you'll be a rabbi in the Communist Party."

When the Second World War broke out in September 1939, Klingberg was about half-way through medical school. Poland was conquered within the month and was divided between Nazi Germany and Soviet Russia as part of a pre-war conspiracy. The 21-year-old student saved himself by finding shelter in the Soviet Union. He left behind his entire family, and they were all murdered by the Nazis in the Holocaust.

In his own old age, Klingberg sounded regretful and even guilt-ridden as he insisted that he had acted on the orders of his sick father: "I left Poland because of the Germans, at Father's request. Mother was against it. But Father said, 'You have to leave. At least one member of the family has to stay alive, and you should go.'"

The emotional parting from his parents was a scar that never healed, though he covered that pain as just one of the many masks he wore. His parents' deaths would haunt Klingberg all his life.

He continued his medical studies in the Soviet system at the University of Minsk, only to suffer another interruption. In June 1941, Germany invaded the Soviet Union—as Adolf Hitler double-crossed Josef Stalin—and Klingberg boasted, more than 60 years later: "At 10 a.m. on the morning after the invasion, I volunteered for the Red Army, and I am proud of that to this day."

He served at the front for four months and suffered light leg wounds from shrapnel. After recovery, he was transferred to another unit, where he was allowed to practice the profession for which he had been studying: epidemiology, the study of how diseases spread. "The Russians called me Mark," he said. "In Poland, I was Marek."

In 1943, he took an advanced course in Moscow and was part of a team that dealt with an epidemic that left thousands of people dead in the Ural Mountains. "When the disease broke out, no one knew the cause," he related. "But we were able to stop it and prevent its spread." The cause of the epidemic was a fungus, which developed in wheat that rotted under the snow and emitted a toxin. Another contribution he made was in researching typhoid fever.

The war years further strengthened Klingberg's belief in Communism and in the unique, positive, global role of the Soviet Union.

Klingberg was discharged at the end of the war with the rank of captain. Like many Jews who had found shelter in Soviet territory, he returned to his homeland. Of the Jews who came back to Poland, quite a few quickly emigrated to Palestine. Klingberg was a staunch believer in Communism, so he decided to stay in Poland and contribute to the creation of a socialist society there under Stalin's tutelage.

He married Wanda Yashinskaya, who was a microbiologist and a Warsaw Ghetto survivor. Wanda was made of tough stuff. She was determined, confident, and opinionated. When Wanda decided that they should not live in a Poland where the soil was tainted with the blood of millions of Jews, her husband caved in.

The couple left in 1946, first for Sweden but with the hope of continuing on to what generations of Yiddish-speakers called the *goldene medina* (golden country): the United States of America.

Paperwork and finances left them stuck in Sweden, where Wanda gave birth to their only child, Sylvia, in 1948. The winter was rough, and the Klingbergs were split on whether to remain in Scandinavia.

According to him, "Wanda wanted to stay in Sweden. But I was offered a chance to volunteer and help Israel in its War of Independence. I wasn't a Zionist, but since I didn't like Sweden, I decided to take the offer. She loathed the idea of going to Israel, but she and the baby joined me."

For young Dr. Klingberg, the decision was justified by one more fact: "I did it also because, at that time, the Soviet Union supported Israel."

Four days after Klingberg arrived in Israel, he was drafted into the medical corps of the nascent Israeli army. He joined a department that was dealing with the prevention of diseases, and between the battle zones and the arrival of Jewish immigrants in various states of health, there was plenty to do.

In light of his military experience and his medical degree, Klingberg was quickly promoted to the rank of lieutenant colonel. He and his family were given an apartment in Jaffa, a previously Arab port city that pre-dated its new Jewish neighbor, Tel Aviv.

The Israel Defense Forces did not ask any questions about his background or his motivations. No security scanning was required. The IDF needed professionals, and it was taken for granted—or accepted merely on his say-so—that Dr. Klingberg truly was a qualified doctor and skillful epidemiologist. Before long, his wife also found a job as a microbiologist with the medical corps.

Klingberg monitored the IDF's hygiene and vaccinated servicemen against malaria and other sicknesses. The Israeli army, as a mirror image of the society at large, was a tight-knit, intimate community. It was rather easy for this prestigious Polish immigrant to meet, rub shoulders with, and befriend the top echelon: from the chief of staff, General Dayan, to Prime Minister Ben-Gurion.

In 1953, after clashes with his immediate superior in the medical corps, Klingberg resigned as head of the disease prevention department but remained in uniform with another medical unit.

That was the year when, "for the first time since my childhood, I cried like a baby," he reminisced. "I didn't cry when I said farewell to my parents and my brother during the war, and not even when I was informed that they were murdered in a concentration camp." What prompted him and Wanda to weep was the news they heard over the radio on March 5, 1953: that Stalin had just died. "The tears shed by my strong-willed wife further emphasized for me the depth of the tragedy."

In 1957, a budget crunch forced the closure of the medical unit in which Klingberg had been serving. He was officially discharged from the IDF, but he was not unemployed for even a single day. He gladly accepted a senior post at the IIBR. His wife already worked there, and she eventually completed her Ph.D.

The Institute's locale, Nes Tziona, had a noteworthy role in Israel's creation. It was one of the first Jewish agricultural villages, established in Turkish-ruled Palestine in 1883 with the help of the French Jewish philanthropist Baron Edmond de Rothschild. Young Jewish immigrants from Europe settled there, a quarter-century before Tel Aviv was built on sand dunes 15 miles to the northwest. The settlers—in what would become the heartland of the State of Israel—battled malaria, Arab gangs, and other crises to establish a Zionist foothold in the Promised Land of the Bible where Jews had a kingdom long ago.

All around the Institute and its imposing walls, set atop a hill, are orchards: grapefruits and oranges dotting the trees with color, the beauty of citrus blossoms in the spring, as well as the sight and scent of strawberry fields.

The Institute's original buildings were much older than the secretive laboratories. Decorated by glorious arches and other features of classic Arabesque architecture, these houses had been home to a wealthy Palestinian Arab landowner. As part of the fog of the 1948-1949 war, the Arabs either left or were forced out, and the Israeli government became the landowner.

Over the years, modern buildings were built, some as tall as five stories with glass, steel, some traditional Middle Eastern motifs, and modern anti-intrusion systems. Expensive world-class labs were added for "applied research" in biology, microbiology, chemistry, and pharmacology.

Administratively, the Institute belongs to the Prime Minister's Office, but responsibility for its security and for guarding its secrets lies with Malmab—the tough-as-nails security agency within the Defense Ministry.

The biological institute, after all, does not exist for the purpose of publishing treatises or winning Nobel Prizes. Its very existence stems from Israel's perceived need for self-protection of the highest order. Ben-Gurion was obsessed with having a significant technological advantage over his country's Arab neighbors. Many parts of his vision became classified programs, although it was no secret that the IDF had the *Heyl Mada*—the Science Corps, known by the Hebrew acronym Hemed, led by Munia Mardor and Professor David Ernst Bergman.

Mardor would become the head of Rafael, the state-owned Armaments Development Authority. In 2002, it would morph into Rafael Advanced Defense Systems Ltd., owned by shareholders but doing vast quantities of secret work, including the weaponization of many scientific innovations. Professor Bergman, of course, had become the one-man Israeli Atomic Energy Commission in the 1950s.

Mardor and Bergman, who proved for decades that they were adept at keeping secrets, intended to grow the Institute at Nes Tziona into a complex of "national laboratories" in the mold of America's most prestigious defense research centers and laboratories. The Israelis were well aware that the United States set an impressive example of what could be accomplished when people with fine minds, a strong sense of dedication, and assurance of full support from their government are brought together in a brainy hothouse.

The Institute became one of the most clandestine compounds in Israel. Until the mid-1990s, its location was not even marked on maps of the country. That ruse was deemed moot after Arab websites published the coordinates of its precise location, along with pictures of Nes Tziona taken by commercial satellites. Yet electronic spies, high overhead, cannot read minds or see inside buildings. No foreigners and very few Israelis could know or guess, with any precision, what was taking place inside the facility.

Sources claimed, without giving details, that biological and chemical weapons were developed there—as well as protective measures against an enemy attack using those kinds of non-conventional arms. International treaties ban the use of such weapons, but Israelis from Ben-Gurion's time until the present day believe that the Middle East is a region of fervent hatred, deception, and rule-breaking. The Israelis were not going to gamble their own existence on the likelihood that treaties would be honored.

Israeli scientists and engineers are among the world's best, so creating a range of offensive measures, antidotes, and defensive mechanisms was well within their capabilities. Quantities and exact locations of stockpiles remain strictly classified.

Examples abound of how sensitive Israel has been about the work done at Nes Tziona, but some specifics about how the authorities preserved secrecy were themselves blocked from publication.

The Institute's researchers partnered, at times, with the Ministry of Defense, the armed forces, and other parts of the Israeli government.

One of the most innovative attacks on a terrorist was death by chocolate. In 1977, boxes of poisoned chocolates were sent to Dr. Wadia Haddad, the lethally ambitious military chief of the Popular Front for the Liberation of Palestine. The Israelis knew that Haddad operated Ilich Ramirez Sanchez—the Venezuelan terrorism subcontractor best known as Carlos. Haddad was also the mastermind behind the hijacking of Israeli and Western airliners.

It was fairly easy to discover that the evil doctor loved chocolates, and poisonous sweets were prepared. Haddad, thinking they were from a trusted colleague, ate them; and that was apparently the cause of his death a few months later in East Germany, where doctors were baffled by the 50-year-old's disease.

Poisons meant to work in untraceable ways became an Israeli specialty, and Russia's espionage chiefs must have been happy to learn all about many kinds of innovations and inventions by having a spy for almost three decades inside the Nes Tziona institute.

Klingberg was not just any spy. He had a phenomenal memory: retaining names, dates, and places—able to describe in great detail the appearance of people he met and what they wore.

Klingberg kept the genesis of his treason cloaked in double and triple stories. In 1983, after he broke down during interrogation by Shin Bet investigators, he said that he had been recruited in 1957 during a cocktail party at the Soviet embassy in Tel Aviv. The confession was legally sufficient for Shin Bet, and it did not matter precisely how his espionage had begun.

In 2007, when his memoirs were published in Hebrew, he admitted that the prior version was a lie. "I was in the embassy only once, in 1959, with the authorization of Binyamin Blumberg," he wrote of the founder of Malmab and the chief security officer in the Defense Ministry.

The convicted spy wrote that Blumberg "sent me to meet a Russian scientist couple who had come especially for the first international conference of microbiologists held in Israel. Even Ben-Gurion came to the opening of the conference in Jerusalem. But I did not meet with my handler at that meeting."

Shin Bet investigators did not believe either version from Klingberg. They suspected that he had been recruited by Soviet espionage during World War II, and already was a trained, committed agent when he arrived in Israel in 1948.

Klingberg's book added another twist to the mystery, though readers had to keep in mind that the author's track record for authenticity was poor. His memoirs claimed that he was recruited during his Israeli military service, in 1950.

He wrote that he had been recuperating from a road accident, and while staying in a rehabilitation center he was approached by a young Israeli couple who showed high interest in his World War II reminiscences. Klingberg confided to them that he was a senior army officer in the health service, and that further piqued their interest. The couple suggested that they all get together with some Russians friends, and Klingberg said yes.

Again putting a fog around the start of his espionage, he wrote: "After two years in Israel, I was thirsty for such a contact." He never met the couple again, but it seems that the man and woman were "helpers"—sympathizers, but not paid agents—of Soviet intelligence. Their job was to spot and develop potential targets for recruitment.

The next stage could have been torn from the pages of a cheap novel, but this—if Klingberg the memoirist was finally telling the truth—was how cliché-ridden an approach by the KGB could be. He said he received a telephone call, a few weeks after parting from the shadowy recruiters. The accented male voice identified himself thus: "I am *tovarisch* Sokolov," using the Russian word for "comrade."

Israel and the Soviet Union were still friends. Two years earlier, in 1948, Moscow had supported the establishment of a Jewish state and agreed to arms shipments from Czechoslovakia, one of the Communist satellite states. Czech weapons, including aircraft, played a decisive role in Israel's War of Independence victory.

The man on the phone, according to Klingberg, "spoke Russian and told me that he had gotten my number from the couple I met at the rehabilitation center, and he asked to meet me."

It was arranged that Sokolov would come by car and pick up Klingberg in a narrow alley in Jaffa. The Russian, an accredited diplomat at the Soviet embassy in adjacent Tel Aviv, was certainly an experienced case officer. He was full of praise and bonhomie, according to Klingberg—the start of a very long string of compliments, lasting for many years, designed to build up an agent's self-confidence and courage—but he also seemed worried that Israeli agents might be watching.

Sokolov drove Klingberg in wide circles for almost an hour—to shake any "tail"—before the Russian started asking the Israeli about his life. The chit-chat ended with an enigmatic sentence. "You helped us a great deal in the past during our difficult times in the war," said the Soviet diplomat. "I can assure you that we remember, with appreciation, people like you."

Klingberg, a man obsessed with his own honor and value, swallowed fully the bait built of flattery.

According to Klingberg, Sokolov had a second meeting and then a third with him. They agreed to address each other by first names—"Mark" and "Viktor." Only at the third meeting did Viktor make a pass designed to consummate the relationship: "Look, we want to be in touch with you and might need your help."

Klingberg recalled: "I certainly didn't say no. I gave him the impression that I feel committed and that the Soviet Union is close to my heart. Nothing seemed to me dramatic."

That allegiance to Moscow was certainly genuine, whenever or wherever Klingberg really was recruited to be a spy. He wrote that he would meet Sokolov, his handler, three or four times a year for the next decade or so. They set their meeting places by using classic espionage tradecraft: one man leaving a chalk mark on a certain building, then the other man chalking another building. That was the signal that the meeting would take place, at nightfall, at a location between the marks.

Klingberg was not posted immediately to the secretive biological institute, but his varied assignments for the Israeli army made him seem highly interesting and valuable for Soviet intelligence.

When he entered Nes Tziona in 1957, embarking on 25 years of seemingly solid service there, Klingberg rapidly rose to become the deputy director. The

Israeli government paid for study sabbaticals abroad, and he proudly published research papers about epidemics.

Klingberg attended many conferences outside Israel, and these were perfect opportunities to rendezvous with Soviet handlers. There were also numerous meetings inside the Jewish state: almost always at the "Red" Church in southern Tel Aviv—a Russian Orthodox compound, rather obviously under Moscow's strong influence. Some of the priests and nuns were actually trained officers of the KGB or the military intelligence agency GRU. Because of the military nature of the Institute, Klingberg was run by the GRU.

He and his Soviet handlers must have been highly professional and cautious, because Shin Bet counter-intelligence teams did not detect Klingberg's secret meetings. One security officer at the Institute claimed that he felt somewhat suspicious as early as 1960, and in the mid-1960s a woman at the World Health Organization in Geneva told Israeli security that Klingberg had been meeting with scientists from Poland.

Upon his return to Israel, he was summoned by Shin Bet for a polygraph test. This was no small matter. He was a senior official and a member of Mapai, the ruling political party. He was personally in touch with Prime Minister Eshkol, Dayan, and other VIPs.

Klingberg pretended to be offended and reacted very angrily to the lie detector invitation. He arrived at Shin Bet headquarters under protest, yet he was hooked up to the very same polygraph that the Israelis had gotten a decade earlier from the FBI. He was asked a series of questions, but he got through the ordeal without a hitch. The graphing pen stayed fairly steady, with no signs of dissembling.

Victor Cohen, Shin Bet's senior investigator, admitted that the test was a failure. "We asked him the wrong questions," Cohen explained. Klingberg was asked about reported contacts with agents of Poland's security service, when he should have been asked about a relationship with Russian handlers.

A few years later, a lie detector was wired onto Klingberg's palms and fingertips again. Reports of unauthorized contacts had been received, and they had to be checked out, but this time Shin Bet interrogators treated him much more respectfully. Instead of individual, often challenging, and skeptical questions, Klingberg was engaged in a conversation. He emerged as pure and clean as driven snow.

Suspicions were cast again in 1982, when Shin Bet received information that Klingberg was expected to meet his handler at a scientific conference in Switzerland. The Mossad was put in charge of surveillance, and a team did its best to watch the scientist at all times. The watchful eyes turned up nothing.

There was no meeting in Geneva with any Soviets that time, according to Klingberg, because he sincerely had broken his ties with the Russians. He said, many years later, that he leaked no secrets after 1976.

Counterintelligence teams continued to lay traps, and one trap took the form of a Soviet Jew who had recently gotten to the Promised Land. Shin Bet questioned the man upon his arrival, having noticed something suspicious, and he readily admitted that the KGB had recruited him to spy in Israel. Shin Bet then "doubled" the man, by persuading him to pretend that he was still serving the KGB—while occasionally meeting secretly with his true employers at Shin Bet to keep them fully briefed.

This spook game paid off. One day, the new arrival received a coded message from KGB headquarters in Moscow to create a signal for someone by making a chalk mark on a specific wall in Tel Aviv. He did not know what the signal meant, or for whom it was intended.

The Russian Jew did as instructed and informed his contact at Shin Bet. An Israeli counter-intelligence team laid ambush, and a few hours later an unknown person showed up, saw the message, and continued walking. Shin Bet shadowed him all the way to his home and discovered it was Klingberg.

One investigator said: "This time, the fourth time, we decided that Klingberg would not escape our net." Shin Bet carefully studied Klingberg's personality, concluding that he had a strong desire for recognition and official honors. This was January 1983.

Shin Bet agents posed as a Mossad team looking for someone brilliant and reliable to go overseas on a secret mission. They told Klingberg that Malaysia, a Muslim country that did not have diplomatic relations with Israel, wanted the help of an Israeli expert on diseases. Flattered by the request, Klingberg said immediately that he would be glad to help. He was told to inform his wife only that he would be out of the country.

On the day set for his flight to the Far East, two Shin Bet operatives picked up Klingberg, but instead of driving him to the airport they headed to a safe house in Tel Aviv. There, two interrogators were waiting for Klingberg. The fiction about a foreign trip would give them time to do their work, with no intervention from his wife or others.

"They had nothing against me to nail me down, not a shred of information that could be admitted as evidence in court," Klingberg recalled later. "Not a phone call, not a slip of paper. There was nothing. If I had not opened my mouth, they would have let me go."

Yet, he did talk. "I don't understand it myself," Klingberg said while shaking his head. "After all, I knew the Shin Bet people. They promised me that if I told them everything they would release me. What stupidity on my part! How could I have believed them?"

The Shin Bet account of Klingberg's interrogation portrayed him as stubborn for 34 days, refusing to admit any crimes. The sessions were long, and without a confession the security agency had insufficient evidence to support an indictment in court.

The Shin Bet interrogators were on the verge of despair. But on the likely last day—when it was clear that a court would not extend Klingberg's period of arrest any longer—one of the questioners had a creative, out-of-the-box idea. Chaim Ben-Ami was a veteran of many investigations, and he decided to use his strong *basso profundo* voice to shout at Klingberg that he was a traitor. The taunting was not about a betrayal of Israel by espionage, but for betraying his parents' memories by letting them stay in Poland to face death while he escaped to the Soviet Union.

Ben-Ami recalled: "He looked at me, said nothing, and then started crying." Klingberg, choking back tears, asked Ben-Ami to call in the other interrogator—who played the role of "the good cop"—because the spy was finally willing to provide a confession.

During his trial, Klingberg argued that Shin Bet extracted his confession by illegitimate means, in return for a promise of leniency or outright release. "But it was my word against theirs," the spy had to acknowledge. "The judges believed them, of course—not me."

Klingberg wrote in his memoirs that he had confessed only because he was shown photographs of his daughter in Paris: a hint, as he took it, that Israeli intelligence knew everything about her and could easily harm her at any moment.

At the time, Klingberg said, he felt suicidal. There was intense pressure from his wife Wanda—who was permitted to visit—not to reveal anything. "It is true that my wife did not like the fact that I had talked in the interrogation, but she is not the reason that I tried to kill myself," Klingberg said in Paris. "I tried to commit suicide twice. The first time was even before I made a confession. That was after four days of interrogation. I tried to stick something metallic into the power outlet in the room and electrocute myself. But it didn't work."

The second time was after he confessed. "I swallowed medicine. I asked my wife to bring me my blood thinner pills. But to say that she tried to get me to commit suicide? Absolutely not. The decision was mine. I saw that it was all over, and I didn't want my family to suffer because of me." His attempt at an overdose failed.

Wanda Yashinskaya did, in fact, have strong reasons to be worried when her husband started talking to the Shin Bet. After she died in 1990 and her cremated remains were placed in a cemetery in Paris, Klingberg revealed that his wife had been his partner in espionage.

While she held her own job at the top-secret Biological Institute, Wanda provided the GRU with bacteria and virus samples and some other formulas and secrets. Confirmation of the deceptive duo's partnership raised the suspicion that the Soviet Union planted both of them in Israel at the very start.

Klingberg was found guilty of treason and espionage, and he was sentenced to 20 years in prison. The entire process—arrest, interrogation, indictment, court hearings, and the verdict—took place in total secrecy. Not a word about him or the charges appeared in the mostly hyperactive and free Israel press.

Even in prison, he was given a cover identity: a prisoner ostensibly named Avraham Greenberg, in order to prevent leakage of the case to the public at home and abroad.

The censorship was heavy and strict. Journalists who took an interest in the case were immediately visited by Shin Bet agents and warned to publish nothing about it.

As for Klingberg's agreement never to use his real name, even inside the prison walls, he explained after his release: "I was threatened with worse prison conditions and the loss of rights, especially visiting rights. It was made clear to my wife and daughter that if they revealed the fact of my arrest, they would not be allowed to visit me. Thus, they were forced to tell anyone who asked—friends, mainly—that I was hospitalized in a Swiss sanatorium."

The *Rashomon* of varied stories about Klingberg from various angles included not only when and where he had started working for the Soviets. The vexatious narrative extended to why: the scientific spy's primary motive.

Shin Bet and Malmab interrogators reached the surprising conclusion that the main reason was blackmail. According to their narrative, Klingberg was not actually a fully qualified medical doctor. He did not finish his studies in Poland because of the war. In the 1950s, to get a pay raise at the Institute, he was asked to provide a certificate or diploma to show that he had completed his medical training and exams.

He approached the Soviet embassy in Tel Aviv for help in obtaining a diploma from the University of Minsk as evidence of his studies there. Intelligence officers at the embassy apparently discovered the truth, but they did arrange to forge a diploma for Klingberg—and, in return, they compelled him to work for them. As with most efforts to seduce and induce people to sell out their country, once they begin they are trapped.

Klingberg, however, rejected this explanation. To him, honor was more important than gold, and the thought of being unqualified angered him. "I am a certified medical doctor," he insisted with a force that belied his almost nine decades. "I completed my studies. I wasn't pressured. I agreed to work for the Soviet Union because they saved my life. And out of belief in the cause of Communism. I wanted to help them to balance their inferior knowledge against the Americans and the West during the Cold War."

One truth is shared by both sides. Shin Bet agreed that Klingberg was not spying out of greed and was not paid for his services. The professional assessment of the damage done, however, is grave. Shin Bet and defense officials believe that Klingberg helped the enemies of the state by handing over biological and chemical secrets: an important, though never discussed, factor in Israel's ultimate lines of defense. Israeli intelligence assumes that the Russians relayed all the information to their Arab partners, in various deals and intelligence exchanges.

Klingberg, for his part, showed no remorse. "I do not regret anything I did, even though I am not proud of what I did," he said. "If I were approached today, I would certainly not agree to work for the Russians. But I did it because I felt it was the right thing to do. Why? Because of the Cold War. I wanted the two blocs in the Cold War to be at the same level, out of a desire for a more balanced world."

It is the same kind of argument that American and, especially British, traitors recited to their interrogators and prosecutors over the years after being caught spying for Russia.

The Klingberg case, partially and unintentionally, helped to lift the cloud of secrecy that shrouded the biological institute for half a century. After his release was made public, it was suddenly no longer a taboo in the Israeli media to talk about the place. This was regrettable, in the eyes of the Nes Tziona directors and the security officials at the Ministry of Defense.

In the new spirit of uncovering some truths, it was revealed in 2009 that the head of the Institute—Dr. Avigdor Shafferman, who ruled the facility with an iron fist—had used Israeli soldiers as guinea pigs to develop a possible anthrax vaccine of doubtful value.

A French newsletter reported that, in return for sharing test results from the vaccine, the Pentagon and the United States Army financed a $200 million project enabling the Institute to build a pharmaceutical production line that apparently was not needed.

It would take Shin Bet a few years to recover from the Klingberg case— clearly a major defeat at the hands of the Soviets. Israel's intelligence community also had to repair the damage done to its reputation in the eyes of American espionage counterparts.

The Israelis found solace in "Golf Ball," the code name they gave to one of the most imaginative counter-intelligence operations in the history of Shin Bet.

It began by pure chance, and noticing an unmatched pair of socks on Alexander Lomov's feet was a key part of the unexpected opportunity.

Lomov was a non-Jewish Russian who arrived in Israel with his wife Alexi in the spring of 1986 to assume the title of administrator at the "Red" Russian Church. He would manage a collection of properties, as well as a few dozen priests and nuns, practically owned by the Soviet government—as opposed to the "White" Russian Church that remained loyal to the czar deposed in 1917 and would never cooperate with the Reds.

Lomov's religious managerial role was merely a cover, for he was in fact a professional intelligence officer employed by the overseas directorate of the KGB. Alexi was his radio operator, fully trained in encryption and code books. After the Six-Day War of June 1967, when the Soviets broke diplomatic relations with Israel, the Russian Church became the headquarters for KGB spying in the Jewish state.

Shin Bet, as a matter of routine, mounted around-the-clock surveillance of the administrators. It did not take long to discover that the Lomovs—who lived in the Red Church's famous Russian Compound in Jerusalem—were not in love with each other.

Marital strife signaled opportunity for Shin Bet officers, who prided themselves on noticing even the most minute detail. Lomov's socks often did not match, and this suggested stress or a drinking problem. The Israelis started imagining various techniques of taking advantage of the undercover Russian: situations that might involve blackmail or other psychological pressure.

Continued surveillance confirmed that Lomov was often drunk and occasionally beat his wife. Shin Bet more intensively worked on ways of inserting some leverage between them, hoping that Alexi would betray him and become a mole for the Israelis.

It was noticed that she often shopped in a certain Jerusalem supermarket. One day, at that store, Alexi met and chatted with another Russian-speaking woman, who was a very good listener. Alexi started dishing all of her ugly family secrets. One thing led to another, and the new "friend" introduced Alexi to a circle of friends. One of them was a young, handsome fellow who started to romance the loveless and desperate Alexi.

He happened to be a subcontractor for Shin Bet. He was not a full-time employee, but someone who could be hired for the purpose of political seduction.

This was an almost classical "honey trap," as the technique is known in the spy trade. It usually, however, involved the use of females to trap males. In recent years, the gender gap has narrowed rapidly—and all sorts of combinations of males and females have been effective.

Before long, the Israeli lover boy offered Alexi a deal. He said he had a friend who could help her start a new life in America. All she would have to do was meet them, and tell them everything she knew about espionage and politics. Alexi agreed.

She met Shin Bet operatives, who struck an explicit deal with her. She would provide all the code books for KGB communications at the Jerusalem "station," and in return she would be given a new identity and settled in the United States.

Shin Bet had indeed been in touch already with the CIA, which agreed to accept the female radio operator into a "rehabilitation" program in America. Alexi proved to be a gold mine. The code books she supplied helped the Israeli and Western intelligence communities intercept Russian intelligence messages in many countries: to expose a few more spy networks, and to reconstruct some of the past activities of the Soviet Union.

This defection had a happy ending. Alexi left her husband a note in their home: "I am in the company of good friends. If you want to repair our relations and to have a new beginning with me, please call this number in the next 24 hours."

Shin Bet officers did not believe that Alexander Lomov would do it. But he did. He dialed the number, and he joined his wife. The couple was debriefed by Shin Bet for a week and then flown to the United States for further questioning by the CIA and the start of a new life. When last seen by the Israelis, the Lomovs were getting along better.

For Shin Bet, there was a measure of revenge against the Soviets for decades of high-level espionage by Marcus Klingberg. In addition, the Lomov affair brought relations between the CIA and Israeli intelligence to a new zenith of cooperation and trust.

CHAPTER SEVENTEEN

AMBIGUITY AND MONOPOLY

The director of the Mossad, Yitzhak Hofi, arrived in Paris in early April 1979, traveling under a bogus name and wearing a disguise. The espionage agency often consulted and used Israelis who worked in theaters as experts on changing a person's appearance. An addition as simple as a glued-on beard, a wig, or eyeglasses could make someone look completely different.

Unlike routine visits, in which the head of a foreign security service has a formal liaison session or a courtesy call on a host country to share information, Hofi's unheralded stay in Paris was hidden from France's security services.

Hofi was there on official but unacknowledged business. He was following the Mossad and military traditions that put the top commander in the field: at the front, overseeing a dangerous operation. His proximity can help when there is a need for uninterrupted communication and an instant decision.

A psychological factor is even more important. The message the Mossad chief conveys to his people is: I am with you, and the entire organization is behind you 100 percent.

Hofi was described by a longtime senior operative in the Mossad as a man "of steel and infinite patience" and "a born commander," yet in the early hours of April 6 he was nervously waiting inside the Israeli embassy for some news.

Then, the coded message arrived: "Mission accomplished." Hofi flashed a big smile and headed back to Israel immediately.

Five-hundred miles to the south, his Kidon boys had just successfully completed their latest act of stealth. In the pre-dawn hours, an explosion in a warehouse at La Seyne sur Mer, an industrial part of the port of Toulon, severely damaged two cores of a nuclear reactor.

These cores had been nearly ready to be loaded onto a ship headed for Iraq. They were to be installed in a nuclear facility that Saddam Hussein was constructing just south of his capital, Baghdad. The reactor, which he called Tammuz—the name of a Babylonian deity in ancient Iraq—was known to the French as Osirak.

Iraq's nuclear program was of great concern to Israel. Prime Minister Yitzhak Rabin and Defense Minister Shimon Peres, in 1974 to 1977, kept warning about it. They used secret and open diplomacy, trying to persuade France, Italy, Brazil, and other countries to stop helping Saddam fulfill his megalomaniacal dreams of having weapons of mass destruction.

Israel asked the United States to exercise any influence it might have, and in consultations Israeli intelligence found that its basic assessment of the Iraqi program matched the CIA's view. They differed only about the date by which Saddam would be capable of building nuclear bombs.

The situation foreshadowed what Israel and the United States would face 35 years later, when debating how to confront the nuclear program of Iraq's neighbor, Iran.

When Menachem Begin and his Likud party won the 1977 election and formed Israel's first right-wing government, Israeli politics had a sensational change of orientation. Yet the country's efforts on the Iraq issue continued as before. Begin and his foreign minister, Moshe Dayan, repeatedly tried to persuade France's leaders that it was irresponsible and immoral to allow a menace such as Saddam to have a nuclear reactor.

Israel's new leaders stepped up their diplomatic campaign—but they also had something else in mind.

Officially, the 40-megawatt reactor was supposed to be for scientific research purposes. But it was clear, certainly to Israeli leaders, that Saddam wanted his new toy for a variety of reasons: to establish hegemony over the region; to threaten his arch-enemy, Iran; and to dominate the other oil-exporting nations of the Middle East. Posing a nuclear threat to Israel would be part of that formula.

This was an especially emotive topic for Prime Minister Begin, who—more than any other Israeli leader—was obsessed by the Holocaust. He often spoke about Jewish history, anti-Semitism, and the murder of six million Jews in Europe. For Begin, it was always as though it had just happened yesterday—and must never happen again.

He ordered Hofi to increase the Mossad's collection efforts aimed at Iraq's progressing nuclear program, but at the same time to prepare plans of action. Aman used its research and technological departments to assess Iraq's intentions and capabilities, while the Mossad worked at learning everything it could about the construction of the reactor.

The Mossad recruited agents among the foreign, mainly French, workers who were involved in the project in Baghdad. Operatives made efforts to learn all they could from scientists involved with the Iraqis. Occasionally, Caesarea operatives would terrorize them—and European companies involved—to pressure them into quitting the program.

In 1979, when Begin realized that the intimidation campaign and diplomacy were failing and the French government would not back out from its long-term, lucrative deal with Iraq, he ordered Hofi to shift gears and step up sabotage planning.

Begin's conviction was that Israel had to do everything in its power to stop the Iraqi program. He approved the Mossad's plan to bomb the reactor cores in the French harbor, an attack meant to cause substantial delay in Iraq's plans—and, hopefully, to make the French think again.

Caesarea operatives collected everything they could learn about the planned delivery of the cores from La Seyne sur Mer: when they would leave the factory, how they would be trucked to the port, at what time the transfers would take place, and where they would be held before the ship sailed. The point of maximum vulnerability seemed to be the warehouse near the piers, and the best time to strike appeared to be over the weekend—when very few people would be around to notice interlopers or to be injured by a blast. There also would be fewer guards than on a weekday.

Caesarea smuggled a large quantity of explosives into France, and then Kidon teams planted five bombs all around the two reactor cores. The blasts that followed caused severe damage to the cores.

A few hours later, another Mossad unit went into action. This was the psychological warfare department, which composed a press release on behalf of the nonexistent French Ecological Group, claiming credit for the bombing at the harbor to express its opposition to nuclear power. News agencies and TV stations duly reported the claim.

Diverting attention from Israel did not last long. It seemed obvious to the international media that the notorious Mossad was behind the blasts. It was barely believable that unknown amateurs could penetrate the perimeter, evade the guards, use the exact amount of explosives needed to crack the cores without collateral damage, and not leave any fingerprints or other evidence. And Israel, after all its public and private complaints about Iraq, certainly had a motive.

Successful as it was, the sabotage in the south of France did not change the reality much. France still refused to cancel the contracts and offered Iraq replacement cores. Saddam Hussein was not deterred, either, and his engineers and scientists continued building Osirak.

Menachem Begin and his cabinet also realized, to their disappointment, that little or nothing had been accomplished. Back at Square One, Begin was as determined as ever to stop Saddam's push for nuclear might.

In mid-1980, he ordered the intelligence community and the Israel Defense Forces to come up with a military option: a strike that would be more likely to derail Iraq's plans.

Several scenarios were produced and discussed. These included using agents—or Israeli special operations soldiers—to plant bombs at the reactor site. But in the middle of Iraq? That was dismissed as too risky, especially when operatives would have to carry a large amount of explosives with them.

Sayeret Matkal commandos had managed many deep incursions into Arab countries, but had never done something as big as this would entail—perhaps hundreds of soldiers, hundreds of miles away, near an enemy capital.

Israeli leaders were left with only one option: an air option. That was not bad at all, as Israel's air force was always considered the long arm of Israeli defense.

A bureaucratic process was put into motion. First, Begin had to persuade his cabinet colleagues that sending the air force to attack Tammuz/Osirak—its longest bombing mission ever—would be doable and its ramifications limited. After long deliberations, he got the majority he needed.

Simultaneously, instructions were passed from Begin, via the defense minister, to the IDF chief of staff and the air force: Start preparing for a secret mission, which was not revealed or fully defined to them. The pilots selected did not know where, when, and how they would be flying. As they practiced bombing runs from various angles, they did not know what the target was.

Aman analysts had begun in 1979 to accumulate all possible information about the Iraqi reactor: how it was built, and what spot on the structure would be most vulnerable. Intelligence exchanges with counterparts in a few other countries produced a lot of data about the building and also about anti-aircraft guns, missiles, and radar around the reactor.

The Mossad was still needed to provide updated information on developments at the Osirak complex, and the Israelis managed to recruit some of the Iraqi technicians being trained in France for reactor operations. That was a Mossad technique, which could be called a "travel-trap." It might be hard to reach and recruit an Arab in his own country, but he is more vulnerable when he is enjoying the promiscuous environment of a Western country, something he lacks at home. He might be open to offers of entertainment, cash, and favors, or to threats of blackmail or violence.

The air force's own intelligence unit focused on the best route to fly, how many planes were needed, what load of munitions would be required for maximum effective destruction, how best to avoid detection by friendly or enemy radars along the way, and what resistance the pilots might meet from Iraqi air defenses. Some knowledge came from Israeli advance reconnaissance flights, some of them intentionally skirting the borders of Jordan and Saudi Arabia to get those nations' militaries accustomed to Israeli warplanes.

Planning to have the attack planes flying very low for most of the 90-minute journey to Baghdad, Israeli intelligence located and charted electricity and communication cables in several enemy countries—and that mission alone involved putting spies at risk, in every sense behind the lines.

The key element to prepare for the attack by combining the vast array of quantitative and qualitative data was the use of "operational research" by the air force. This is a field of applied mathematics that originated in Great Britain before World War II. It uses mathematical methods to compute the optimal use of limited resources. Israel's operational research team, mostly young mathematicians, calculated that the best way to cause the maximum damage to the reactor would be by dropping heavy bombs—old-style and "stupid," in defense parlance—rather than laser-guided "smart bombs."

Planners in the air force examined the humiliating failure suffered by United States special forces in Iran in April 1980, when a mission to rescue diplomats held hostage ended in a collision on a desert airstrip, one airplane and seven helicopters lost, and eight American servicemen dead. The entire plan had been too complicated, as the Israelis saw it, and that strengthened their determination to make the air strike on Iraq's reactor "a KISS operation," as they dubbed it in English: "Keep it simple, stupid."

There was also the issue of what day and time would be best for hitting the Iraqi reactor in terms of weather, natural light and glare, and work patterns at the facility. Again, Israel preferred to strike when a minimal number of employees would be present.

Still, a debate continued within Israeli intelligence and the military about the wisdom of such an attack. International reaction might be highly negative, and there was great concern that hitting Iraq would ruin the implementation of the Camp David peace accords with Egypt. Iraq might strike back at Israel. And even if the raid were successful, for how long would the Iraqi nuclear program be stopped?

These were the same questions Israel's security establishment—decades later—would face when similar nuclear threats were detected in other Middle East countries.

The discussion about Osirak crossed the usual lines, as the positions held did not take the form of agency versus agency. Although the entire subject was cloaked in secrecy, the internal debate was relatively open: Mossad and Aman analysts were encouraged to express their views.

Some of the most senior intelligence officials opposed attacking Iraq at that time—including the Mossad director, Hofi, who preferred sabotage and diplomatic pressure. His deputy and future successor, Nahum Admoni, favored an attack. The same divisions were found in Aman, where the director—General Yehoshua Saguy—was against launching a strike, at least at that stage, while his deputies were generally in favor.

The only voice that really mattered was Menachem Begin's. And he was intent on demolishing Iraq's nuclear potential.

Preparing for the attack meant that more people were brought into the circle of knowledge, but not a word was leaked to the public.

Dates for an attack in 1981 were chosen at least three times, only to be postponed. Time was running out. The attack would have to be done, in the Israeli view, before the reactor would go "hot" by installing uranium rods. Showing concern for radioactive fallout, Begin said, "The children of Baghdad should not suffer."

The cancellations were usually because of weather conditions, but once because there was a leak within political circles. The opposition leader, Shimon Peres, who considers himself one of the founding fathers of Israel's nuclear arsenal and thus an expert on these topics, expressed his concern.

Peres had received information about the attack plan from Uzi Even, a member of the Israel Atomic Energy Commission who had worked at Dimona. Professor Even was also a member of a special task force, created by Aman's technical department, to assess Iraq's nuclear progress. His study concluded that the Osirak reactor would not be able to produce fissile material, suitable for bombs, for a very long time. Uzi Even breached his secrecy pledge and, without authorization, told what he knew to Peres.

The opposition leader went to Begin and warned him not to launch an attack, because Israel would be so strongly condemned internationally that it would be a pariah state. "We will be like a thistle standing alone in the desert," Peres intoned.

Begin, angry about the leak, was unstoppable. He decided to postpone the operation, but he insisted that a new date be set right away.

Finally, eight attack planes would fly on Sunday morning, June 7. American-made F-16A fighter-bombers were to carry out the attack, escorted by F-15 fighter planes to defend the bombers, if necessary.

They flew over Jordan, and King Hussein looked up from his yacht in the Gulf of Aqaba and noticed Israeli airplanes heading east on some mission unknown. Aman overheard a report from the king to a military control post in his capital, but it seemed that neighboring Iraq was not informed. The jets continued at a very low altitude—as low as 150 feet—over Saudi Arabia, heading into Iraqi airspace.

The pilots had, in their gear, Iraqi money provided by the Mossad—just in case they had to bail out and somehow buy their way to freedom.

While they were flying, around a dozen military and intelligence chiefs gathered in the situation room—known in Hebrew as *ha-Bor* (the "Pit")—inside the defense ministry headquarters compound in Tel Aviv.

One senior officer was missing. Yehoshua Saguy was not invited—by order of the IDF chief of staff, Rafael Eitan. This was a pre-emptive strike by the top general who suspected that his intelligence chief, because he opposed the operation, would leak it and force another cancellation.

The 90-minute flight to Baghdad was smooth. The reactor dome came into sight, "shining in the sun," said Relik Shafir, one of the eight pilots in the formation who later would be a brigadier general in the air force. "We faced no problems. I was much more emotional about the historical significance of the mission, rather than any operational difficulties. Everything went according to plan. The training was actually much more difficult than the real thing."

As the Israeli pilots flew away, heading almost straight up to 42,000 feet, they felt the massive gravity of seven times their weight. The Iraqis did fire at them from the ground, including at least one missile, but they missed. And one Iraqi air force MiG scrambled but never caught up with the Israelis.

They left behind a completely destroyed burning ruin of a nuclear facility. The iconic dome of the reactor collapsed inward and was erased from the face of the Earth.

The successful mission was meant to be kept secret, with Israel preserving deniability. There was even a deception option. For two days, the Iraqis thought the attack was the work of the Iranians—as they were near the beginning of a bitter eight-year war with them.

Prime Minister Begin, however, decided to change the strategy. He ordered his press secretary to issue a statement taking responsibility for the attack on Osirak. Begin was proud, not ashamed, and he wanted to send a double message: not only "never again" in a Holocaust context, but also that Israel would not tolerate any effort by any country in the Middle East to have nuclear weapons.

He did not say it in so many words, but this strategy could be interpreted as the Begin Doctrine. A lot of it was based on fear and the feeling that Jews were always in peril. The State of Israel, in his perception, was besieged and in danger of annihilation. But also hidden between the lines was a fortress mentality: an Israeli determination to maintain its nuclear monopoly in the region.

While the attack was admired by many in the world, it was formally denounced by many governments—including Israel's friends in the West. They were concerned about the implications. For the first time, one country holding nuclear weapons had taken violent action against another nation on the nuclear threshold.

The Reagan Administration joined in the condemnation and even punished Israel—postponing the delivery of the next set of American-made planes, but for only two months. Privately, Ronald Reagan was delighted, as he told a top aide: "It shows that the Israelis have claws, a sense of strategy, and are able to take care of problems before they develop."

The same sentiment was expressed, though in secret, by some Arab and European officials. Even France seemed quite happy that its customer had been knocked out of the nuclear market. The French could not say it in public, but they admitted—years later—that the Israeli decision had been bold and correct.

Israel did not take much time, however, to rest on its laurels. Israeli intelligence noted that Saddam Hussein drew some lessons from the Osirak attack and re-started his program, but this time diversifying it: building facilities in various locations and not putting all his nuclear eggs in one basket. Instead of a plutonium-based program at a reactor, Saddam opted for a uranium-based track using centrifuges.

Of even more concern was the development of nuclear weapons in Pakistan. True, that nation was far away from Israel and—despite its Islamic and often radical sentiments—it never joined with Arab countries in their wars against the Jewish state. Yet, there were reasons for the Mossad to pay close attention.

Pakistan had developed its own nuclear arsenal, based on drawings that showed how to enrich weapons-grade uranium by using centrifuges—without the need for a nuclear reactor. A Pakistani scientist who was considered the father of his country's nuclear bomb, A. Q. Khan, stole the drawings from a European consortium in the Netherlands called Urenco.

When Israel's Lakam obtained similar drawings, with future Hollywood mogul Arnon Milchan facilitating, that was from another part of the same Dutch-based consortium.

Israeli intelligence feared that the Pakistani bomb would eventually become an Islamic bomb. It was a reasonable fear. In the late 1970s, when Khan was helping his nation build its first bomb, Pakistani leaders were approached by Libya's Colonel Qaddafi, who offered them money in return for one nuclear device. Fortunately for most of the world, the offer was rejected.

There was a possibility that Saudi Arabia, a close religious and strategic ally of Pakistan, would also share in a widened nuclear arsenal. It was quite natural that the Mossad would try to find out as much as possible about Pakistan's nuclear capabilities and intentions.

In that era, when Israel did not yet have spy satellites and Pakistan was too far away for reconnaissance aircraft flights, the Mossad had to be inventive to keep an eye on Pakistan. Teaming up with India—always highly vigilant toward its hostile neighbor—was one route. Most Indians were not friendly toward Israel, however, as they enjoyed status as leaders of the Non-Aligned Movement that had close links with the Arab world.

An excellent opportunity arose in 1985, when Pakistan was hoping to hire experts who could renovate and upgrade Soviet military equipment. Israeli defense contractors had a lot of experience at that, so some of them teamed up with a Belgian company to make a pitch to the Pakistanis.

Negotiations advanced to the point that the Pakistani military invited a delegation from Israel. Several Israeli corporations that did military work sent representatives, and so did the Defense Ministry's Lakam unit, in its capacity as the guardian of technological secrets. Lakam wanted to ensure that these companies would not sell or reveal more than they were permitted to share.

When the Mossad heard about the group getting ready to leave for Pakistan, it decided to jump on the wagon. But it had very different intentions, not rooted in Israeli-Pakistani commerce. A senior Mossad operative joined the delegation, and all the Israelis had false foreign passports provided by the spy agency.

Everything went smoothly, and the business meetings in the capital, Islamabad, with defense officials seemed promising. But then, one afternoon, when the delegation had a half-day off, the man from the Mossad suggested—actually, he ordered—his fellow Israelis to board their bus, and they traveled to a location outside the capital. It was Kahuta, where Pakistan assembled its nuclear weapons.

Posing as innocent tourists, the Mossad guy and the group—somehow imagining that they were not under surveillance—went about taking photographs and soil samples. Upon returning to their hotel, they were confronted by a senior officer from Pakistani intelligence. He demanded that the rolls of film be handed over, though the Mossad man probably managed to keep one of the rolls.

That was the end of the trip. The angry Pakistanis could have detained the Israelis as spies, but instead decided to expel them on the first flight the next day. The business delegates were also unhappy because the Mossad had ruined their chance of getting a nice contract. The whole trip now seemed devised as a cover for an intelligence operation, and they felt like extras in a scenario staged by the Mossad from the outset.

Some of the participants claimed later that if they had been able to make their deal, they might have influenced the Pakistanis to break off their dangerous liaisons with Iran and Libya.

Yet, the overall Israeli intelligence assessment was that A.Q. Khan would never have agreed to be restrained. He was determined to spread nuclear know-how and profit from it. In the 1990s he traveled through the Middle East, offering his services to various countries. Most governments declined to hire him, but Libya and Iran signed lucrative contracts with him. That was enough for Khan to gain the reputation of being the world's greatest nuclear proliferator.

The Mossad made sure to track Khan's travels. "We knew about his movements, but the larger picture escaped us. We didn't realize how bold, daring, and greedy he would be. He's one of the rare examples of a single person determining the course of history," Shabtai Shavit, who was then the director of the agency, admitted years later.

"So we didn't attach too much importance to his meetings and offerings. I regret that we didn't assassinate him. That could have saved Israel a lot of worries."

While doing all it could to preserve its nuclear monopoly, Israeli intelligence also continued its policy of nuclear ambiguity.

The notion of ambiguity was first conjured up by Peres's delicate dance of words in 1963, when he was chatting with President John Kennedy at the White House. Israel would "not be the first to introduce" nuclear weapons into the Middle East, Peres had told the president. That almost immediately became Israel's policy.

It was a unique choice for a nation with nuclear weapons. Israel would always refuse stubbornly to confirm that it had—or did not have—a nuclear arsenal, though the whole world believed that it did. Officials and the military censor enforced an almost ridiculous policy: turning Dimona and everything about it into a taboo. The Israeli media and the public were not allowed, for years, even to discuss the ramifications of having a nuclear option.

One nuclear technician threatened to jeopardize the decades-old policy, and he made a mockery of the enormous security around it.

Mordecai Vanunu, a Moroccan-born Jew who immigrated with his parents to Israel in the 1950s thanks to secret efforts by Israeli intelligence, developed strong but mercurial opinions and behavior.

First, as was traditional in his community, he studied at a religious school. Later, he stopped wearing a yarmulke (*kippa* is the Hebrew term) on his head, and he was open to the temptations of the secular world. Throughout, he felt that as a Sephardic (Eastern) Jew he was rejected by what he saw as the dominant Ashkenazic (European) culture in Israel.

In 1977, at age 22, while studying at the local university of the desert town Beersheba, he applied for a job at the Dimona nuclear reactor, administered by the Israel Atomic Energy Commission. After passing the exam, he underwent a short course in nuclear physics and chemistry, including lessons on plutonium and uranium with which the new recruits would be working.

Vanunu started working as a technician on the night shift. The routine was boring, and he compensated for that by plunging into the bustling life of the university by day. He volunteered to pose as a nude model for art classes, and he also shifted his political views from right-wing Likud politics to left-wing radicalism.

His newly adopted ideology was deepened by the Israeli invasion of Lebanon in 1982. His extracurricular behavior was noticed by the university's chief security officer. Israel being a small society with a shared sense of mission, security officers around the country tend to work closely together. Even at an academic institution, they feel obliged to cooperate with the government's security apparatus.

The university security officer told his counterpart at Dimona about Vanunu's activities. The man at Dimona reported to Malmab—the Defense Ministry's security office in charge of enforcing the ambiguity policy and protecting all defense-based scientific institutions. Those included the Dimona reactor and the biological institute at Nes Tziona.

The counter-espionage department of Shin Bet was also brought into the picture, and the authorities together decided that it would be best to put pressure on Vanunu to leave. They warned him about his political and personal behavior.

Vanunu only became more defiant. For reasons he never explained, he started wandering around the Dimona facility's secret corridors, taking photographs with a camera that he smuggled in.

That was a clear security breach, and he should have been spotted in the heavily guarded facility. But officials never knew that Vanunu had snapped photos.

The security chiefs did find an excuse to fire him in November 1985, when there were some budget cuts at the atomic energy commission. Vanunu complained that he was a victim of both political and ethnic discrimination, but he left Dimona.

He still had his rolls of film, however, and when he left the country soon after losing his job, he felt fed up with Judaism and the Jewish state.

Allowing him to leave Israel so easily was yet another in a string of failures by Malmab and Shin Bet. Israelis with classified jobs frequently are visited and reminded of security requirements before they go on foreign trips. Vanunu was overlooked and his actions neglected.

Vanunu was in a soul-searching mood. His first destination was in the Far East, where he explored alternative religions. He went on to Sydney, Australia, in May 1986, and found a job at an Anglican church. And he found the light.

The wayward Israeli became friends with the priest and converted to Christianity. He also met Oscar Guerrero, a Colombian vagabond with no fixed address and no fixed profession. Vanunu confided in him that he had worked at Israel's top-secret reactor and had two interesting rolls of color film with him.

The Colombian, a highly entrepreneurial traveler, marveled at Vanunu as a chicken about to lay golden eggs. He persuaded the Israeli that the story could be sold, and for enough money to last a lifetime. The idea appealed to Vanunu.

Guerrero appointed himself Vanunu's literary agent, in effect. They developed the snapshots, and Guerrero contacted several international publications to offer a "sensational scoop." Strangely, no one was interested except for the British *Sunday Times*. The free-spending newspaper, owned by the Australian-born press magnate Rupert Murdoch, sent an investigative reporter to Sydney to meet the Israeli and assess his fantastic tale.

The reporter was impressed, and a deal was struck. Vanunu provided the photos and was flown to London in September 1986 for further debriefings. The *Sunday Times* cut out the middleman, refusing to deal with Guerrero.

In London, Vanunu was taken care of by Insight, the investigative team of the *Sunday Times*, which placed him in a nice hotel and promised him a book deal, with an advance of roughly $300,000 if his story could be verified. Assisted by nuclear scientists, the journalists started to grill Vanunu. He told them everything he knew, which included a lot that he never should have known if security at Dimona had been conducted properly.

He provided a detailed sketch of six hitherto unknown, below-ground-level sections of the Dimona complex. That could explain why the American inspectors in the 1960s inside Dimona never saw the truly important parts. Above ground, the building appeared to be a two-story, little-used unimportant warehouse.

Scientists corroborated Vanunu's story, and the *Sunday Times* was preparing to publish one of the world's great exclusives: an accurate and detailed look inside Israel's secret nuclear bomb factory.

Near the end of September, the British newspaper sought a comment from the Israeli embassy in London by giving it an outline of the Vanunu story. The embassy issued a denial and portrayed Vanunu as a minor technician who would not know anything, anyway.

What later tipped the balance in favor of publishing the story was the somewhat panicked reaction by Peres, now the prime minister. He summoned a group of Israeli newspaper editors and briefed them, off the record, about the coming big story from London. Peres begged them to play it down.

As is perversely customary with off-the-record briefings in Israel, the information was quickly leaked.

The *Sunday Times* realized that despite the embassy's denial, Israel's most senior authorities were taking the Vanunu story very seriously.

In the meantime, angry at both Vanunu and the *Sunday Times* for abandoning him, Guerrero went to a rival newspaper—the *Sunday Mirror*—with his own, slightly garbled version of the nuclear revelations. The *Mirror* did not believe in the Colombian at all, but paid him some money and used a couple of Vanunu's photos to publish a two-page barb that poked fun at the *Sunday Times* for falling for patent nonsense.

Israel's nuclear potential was being used as a weapon in a newspaper circulation war that raged between Murdoch and his arch-rival, *Mirror* owner Robert Maxwell. Maxwell, a Czech-born Jew who converted to Christianity, had become a born-again pro-Israel activist. After he mysteriously fell off his yacht and drowned in the Mediterranean in 1991, published rumors would claim that he was a Mossad agent who in 1986 provided a tip-off about Vanunu. Some books suggested that the Mossad sent frogmen to murder their sayan, or helper, to shut him up. Those tales made little sense.

Moreover, the Mossad did not need Maxwell to know about Vanunu and his escapades. The agency learned about it from the *Sunday Times* reporters. At least twice, they contacted Israel for comment and verification: once, calling the embassy, and even earlier calling a journalist in Israel to ask about Vanunu's credibility. The journalist thought he should inform his brother, who happened to be a senior Aman officer. Now the intelligence community knew.

Prime Minister Peres ordered the Mossad to find the former nuclear worker and bring him back to Israel. At Mossad headquarters, some senior members suggested that the best solution would be to assassinate Vanunu. But that was ruled out. Since the death of the kidnapped Alexander Ibor in 1954, no Israeli citizen was killed by his own government.

The Mossad had to come up with a snatch mission to bring Vanunu home to face trial for spilling secrets.

One more string was attached: Peres ordered that the kidnapping not take place on British soil. He feared that whether it was a success or a failure, Britain's Iron Lady—Prime Minister Margaret Thatcher—would be very angry at Israel if her nation's sovereignty were violated.

Caesarea operatives—closely supervised by the department head, Shabtai Shavit—stepped up efforts to find Vanunu in Britain. They flew in, using false passports and armed with cover stories. Shavit's deputy was the on-the-spot project manager in London.

It would not be easy, with Vanunu changing hotels regularly. The Mossad manhunt benefited from the pure luck of a labor strike against the *Times*. There were picket lines outside the newspaper's offices, which provided a perfect cover for a Mossad team to pose as a television news crew, hoping to spot Vanunu and his minders from the Insight team as they came and went.

That worked. And from then on, it was relatively easy to keep an eye on Vanunu. Still, they faced two problems: how to establish contact with him, and how to compel him to leave Britain so that Peres's orders could be obeyed.

Good luck stroked their mission again. Vanunu was angry, by now, about the delays in publishing his story. He told his handlers from the *Sunday Times* that he would love some female companionship. The newspaper team would say later that it did not arrange for a prostitute, out of fear that eventually that would make them look like pimps.

Frustrated and lonely, Vanunu became careless about his security, and the *Sunday Times* handlers could not hold him back. He started wandering the streets of London alone, and one evening eye contact was made.

Vanunu saw a woman who seemed interested in him. She was plump and bleached-blonde, wearing high heels and playing hard to get. She introduced herself as "Cindy," but years later her true identity would be revealed by the *Sunday Times*: Cheryl Bar-Hanin, an American Jew who moved to Israel, married an intelligence officer, and was recruited to work for Caesarea.

Mordecai and "Cindy" went out on a few dates over the next week. The Mossad was exploiting his sexual hunger and his frustration with the British press. Cindy then suggested a way to get away from it all. She said that her sister had an apartment in Rome, and that they should fly there for a memorable weekend.

Against the advice of his *Sunday Times* babysitters, Vanunu took the bait. After hearing about the girlfriend, the British reporters cautioned him not to leave the country. But he did leave.

After landing in Rome, he drove with Cindy to what he assumed would be their love nest. It was a Mossad honey trap. Kidon team members were waiting for him in the apartment. They pounced on Vanunu, injected him with a sedative, put him in a rental car, drove to a marina 200 miles from Rome, and boarded a yacht. It pulled out and rendezvoused with an Israeli Navy ship, the *Noga*, which had cadets on board on a training mission.

The cadets and the crew were told to go below deck—and not look—when the strangers arrived. The Kidon team members, carrying their sedated prisoner, locked themselves inside a cabin, and the ship sailed to Israel.

While Vanunu was a captive in chains in the eastern Mediterranean, the *Sunday Times* finally published its major spread—with a front-page headline screaming, "REVEALED: THE SECRETS OF ISRAEL'S NUCLEAR ARSENAL." It included Vanunu's inside story of the work conducted at Dimona, and a physicist's assessment that Israel must have around 200 nuclear and thermonuclear bombs.

The world was not really surprised. It always assumed that Israel had a substantial atomic arsenal. Yet, it was fascinating to see Vanunu's photographs.

Several governments deplored his having been kidnapped in Italy's capital, but officials also admired Israel's decisive action: bringing a citizen home to face trial for violating the law by revealing sensitive secrets. Vanunu had revealed them only to a newspaper, not directly to an enemy. Still, he was indicted for espionage and treason.

Israel's supreme court rejected a claim by Vanunu's lawyer that the former Dimona worker had been brought illegally to the country. Vanunu was sentenced to 18 years in prison, and he served the entire term. Israeli officials were not even tempted to grant leniency to the nuclear spy, even though prison officials reported that he was almost losing his sanity in a long period of solitary confinement.

That harsh attitude was the product of Yehiel Horev's pressure. The Malmab chief would not forgive or forget the Israeli who betrayed one of Israel's sacred secrets.

There certainly was an element of revenge, but also a measure of face-saving. Security chiefs were ashamed of their initial failures to stop Vanunu, and they compensated for their own shortcomings by taking it out on him.

The vendetta against him continued, even after he served his term. He was released in 2004, yet Shin Bet and Malmab claimed that he continued to be a security risk because of the knowledge in his head. Thus, they insisted that he be banned from leaving Israel, and his movements were restricted.

Even in 2012, Vanunu could occasionally be spotted strolling the streets of Tel Aviv or sipping coffee at an outdoor table –almost always alone. He certainly had friends worldwide, and even a couple in America that formally adopted him, but his quest had been a lonely one: trying to force his country to tell the truth about its own strength.

Israel's leaders still preferred ambiguity and showed they would take action to preserve it.

CHAPTER EIGHTEEN

SPYING ON FRIENDS

Inside CIA headquarters in Langley, Virginia—in a corridor leading to the toilets, in a segregated section where foreign visitors come on official business—hung a large poster showing a notorious spy.

It was a photo of Jonathan Jay Pollard, an American who in 1985 was caught spying for Israel. The poster's implicit message to employees of the United States intelligence community was: Don't do what he did, and you won't end up like him. Pollard is serving a life sentence in prison.

When Mossad liaisons were the visitors, the poster conveyed an extra meaning. It was a bitter reminder of the difficulties the organization has had in dealing with the CIA, and more widely with the entire U.S. military and security establishment.

"Those were harsh times for us," said a former Mossad head of station in Washington, referring to the Pollard fall-out. "There was a decade in which we were punished for a crime we did not commit."

He said he was reminded of the Biblical phrase about the sins of the father being visited upon the children. The Mossad visitors felt they should not be punished by the Americans for something that other Israelis had done; indeed, the CIA acknowledged that it was not the Mossad, but another unit, that ran Pollard. Still, it added up to Israel betraying the United States.

The secret operation unraveled on November 21, 1985, when Pollard sat nervously in his Ford Mustang just outside the front gate of the Israeli embassy in Washington. With him were his wife, Anne Henderson-Pollard, their birth certificates, family photographs, their cat, and the cat's vaccination records. The Pollards were hoping to flee the country right then and there, if possible simply by vanishing into the world of diplomatic immunity.

When the heavy steel doors opened for a few moments, Pollard gunned the engine and pulled into the Israeli compound. Security guards looked puzzled and drew their guns, even as the driver told them that he needed help—refuge from the FBI agents following him.

Indeed, several carloads of FBI agents lurked outside the gate, and they used an intercom placed there for visitors to tell the Israeli guards that the people who had just driven inside were wanted for questioning. The embassy's administrator and chief security officer turned away the Pollards. They were forced to leave, and the FBI arrested them outside the grounds.

Pollard was a civilian who had worked for the U.S. Navy for six years, most of that time in intelligence and counterterrorism units. Lest that sound too swashbuckling, he was only a desk man. But he was a man whose desk included a computer with access to almost every secret collected and stored by America's huge intelligence network.

While Pollard considered himself a loyal American, he was also a fervent supporter of Israel. He was born in Texas in 1954 to a Jewish family that moved to South Bend, Indiana.

Pollard went to Stanford University, one of the nation's finest, where his international relations professors found him to have an overactive imagination. He claimed to be a colonel in the Israeli army, and he even told acquaintances that the Mossad was grooming him to be a spy in America.

Pollard's stories always involved Israel, and he left some people with the impression that the Mossad was paying his tuition fees. While the tales did not all seem credible, they were told with such conviction that it was hard to believe they were totally false—but they were.

He was hired by the United States Navy as a civilian intelligence analyst in 1979, and he was later assigned to an anti-terrorism center that was created in 1984 in response to the upsurge of Hezbollah attacks in Lebanon. His job gave him access to facts, clues, and rumors collected by U.S. agencies and agents across a wide range of countries.

Pollard also held Washington's most valuable library card—a "courier card" that permitted him to visit high-security archives and carry documents back to his office for analysis.

The nightmare of why his American employers failed to detect his erratic personality traits in school, his exaggerated boasts and his outright lies, would go on to haunt security officers in Washington for years.

Before joining the Navy, Pollard had applied for a more prestigious job at the CIA but was rejected. The Agency never told the Navy about its assessment of Pollard as "a fanciful liar, a closet spy, a Zionist zealot, and a drug abuser."

Pollard set out to live his fantasies. Through a New York businessman he knew, Pollard was introduced in May 1984 to an Israeli air force colonel, Aviem Sella, who was on leave in New York, studying for a post-graduate degree.

It was conspiracy at first sight. Pollard told the colonel that he had absolute proof that the United States was not sharing all the intelligence data it should with Israel, and Pollard said that made him livid. For instance, he said, Iraq had a highly active chemical weapons program, and America was not giving that information to Israel. Pollard hastened to add that his goal was to help the Jewish state, which he truly loved, and not ever to hurt America.

Sella, one of Israel's finest pilots—one of the élite who who had bombed Iraq's nuclear reactor—listened with interest.

Colonel Sella dutifully sent a message to the air force in Tel Aviv about the angry American intelligence analyst who offered to keep Israel fully informed.

His report made its way to Aman and to the Mossad. Yet the Mossad director, Nahum Admoni—who succeeded Yitzhak Hofi in late 1982—immediately decided that he did not want to risk angering the United States by running a spy there.

The report also went to Rafi Eitan, the veteran "Mr. Kidnap" who now had the very limited role of directing Lakam—the small defense ministry agency for technological and nuclear espionage. Eitan had grand ambitions to expand his agency, and the offer made by Pollard as a "walk-in" seemed to be great timing.

In weighing whether to use him, Eitan had to consider what most Israeli intelligence chiefs had decided many years earlier: not to use local Jews as spies for Israel inside their own countries. Egyptian and Iraqi Jews who served Israel had been tortured and hanged after being caught, and their families and communities had suffered.

Yet, Israeli officials might be forgiven for assuming that they could get away with almost anything inside the United States. Ronald Reagan, who became president in 1981, got off to a somewhat bumpy start with Israel—as he sold sophisticated weapons to Saudi Arabia, steamrollering opposition by pro-Israel lobbyists, and then condemned Israel for its invasion of Lebanon in 1982.

After attacks by Syria and Hezbollah on Americans in Lebanon, though, Reagan turned strongly pro-Israel. He gave enthusiastic backing to a formal memorandum on strategic cooperation with Israel, which included more port visits to Haifa by America's Sixth Fleet, the pre-positioning of U.S. military equipment in Israel, joint training exercises, and heightened cooperation between the intelligence communities.

CIA veterans with long years of service in the Middle East concluded that Israel could do almost anything and be forgiven by official Washington. One American intelligence officer told a Mossad contact, only half jokingly, that Israel was lucky it never became the 51st state.

"Why are we so lucky?" the Israeli wondered.

"Because then," said the CIA agent, "you would only have two U.S. senators, and this way you have at least 60."

Still, the intelligence communities of both countries knew enough to be suspicious of each other. The FBI was especially wary of Israel's aggressive acquisition of technology.

No one was better qualified than Rafi Eitan to know about the sensitivities of spying in America. He himself was involved in the suspected disappearance of uranium from Numec in Pennsylvania. As a seasoned professional, he also knew enough to be suspicious of an over-eager walk-in like Pollard. It could be a "sting" operation by the U.S. authorities or a trap of another sort.

Eitan also knew, however, that the young American's input could be priceless. Despite formal exchange agreements, Israel's intelligence community always assumed that the United States was not sharing everything. Pollard could fill the gaps.

Knowing that Lakam had enjoyed unquestioned backing from the top political echelon in decades past, Eitan felt he had an implicit green light to proceed.

He used "Avi" Sella, on his study break in New York, as a local case officer. The colonel was instructed to continue his contacts with Pollard, and he had several guarded conversations with him from telephone booths. In the summer of 1984, Sella met with Pollard in Washington and purposefully forged a friendship. They spoke for hours about Israeli history and strategy.

Pollard also handed over classified documents. The Lakam agency's science attachés in New York and Washington assisted Sella by photocopying papers and rushing the copies to Eitan in Tel Aviv.

The results were astounding. Now the Israelis could see what the Americans had: a lot of information on issues of major importance to Israel's defense.

There was information on some of the newest weapons systems obtained by Israel's Arab neighbors: lists and descriptions of arms recently purchased by Egypt, Jordan, and Saudi Arabia. Because those three countries were seen as pro-America moderates, the United States had always refused to share its intelligence about them with Israel. Now, Eitan realized, Israel had a new window into those countries. And this was just a sample of what Pollard could deliver.

The American agent's enthusiasm was overwhelming. After he was promoted within the Navy's anti-terrorism center in October 1984, he told the Israelis that his higher security clearance could get them almost any document in the American intelligence networks—including photographs taken by spy satellites. Israel, at that time, did not have its own roving eyes in orbit.

Eitan was so pleased that he decided to launch a new phase. Pollard and Anne Henderson, then his fiancée, were flown to Paris at Lakam's expense in November 1984. There, a little surprise awaited them. Sella was on the scene, taking them out to fancy dinners—and then introducing Pollard to his new case officer, Yossi Yagur.

Yagur, an employee of Israel Aircraft Industries, was now Lakam's science attaché at the Israeli consulate in New York. In case the worst should happen, Yagur was protected by diplomatic immunity.

As a further surprise, Pollard got to meet the legendary Eitan, whose exploits (such as kidnapping Eichmann) were outlined to the young American to impress him. Eitan was introduced as director of the entire operation involving Pollard. Eitan and Yagur sat down with their volunteer agent to discuss their next moves, including specific documents they hoped he could acquire.

In more relaxed moments, Sella encouraged Jonathan and Anne to admire the windows of some of the French capital's most elegant jewelry stores. When Henderson saw a large sapphire and diamond ring she liked, Sella urged, "Go ahead and buy it." The Israeli paid, on condition that they make it their engagement ring.

It cost around $10,000, and in many ways it was the tangible mark of the Pollards' engagement by Israel. The couple would marry the following August in Venice and spend a three-week honeymoon in Italy—which was not only paid for by Israel, but included a detour to Tel Aviv to meet Eitan again.

In compensation for expenses and as a token of their appreciation, the Israelis told Pollard, he would be paid $1,500 a month. In addition to Anne's ring, Pollard was immediately given $10,000 in cash, and Eitan told him that a Swiss bank account had been opened for him. His fees would be deposited directly, for Pollard's use in 10 years.

By then, the American replied, he would hope to live in Israel. Yagur responded to that by showing him an Israeli passport already prepared for Pollard with his photograph and the false name "Danny Cohen." Pollard was pleased.

The diamond ring and the cash were part of a classic technique to ensnare a secret agent and keep him. The spy who tells his controllers he is acting voluntarily, out of ideological affection for the country he is helping—or disgruntled hatred of the nation he is betraying—can easily be overcome by fear or change his mind. Being a volunteer, he feels he can withdraw at any time.

A paid agent cannot. He feels obliged to deliver, and in the background lies the threat of blackmail.

Pollard's motivation was a combination of Zionism and excitement. He felt certain that he was helping Israel defend itself, and he had the thrill of being a spy, with exotic trips and secret payments.

As soon as he returned from Europe, Pollard got right to work. He brought an entire suitcase full of documents—and the fabled satellite photographs of the Middle East—to a house in Maryland, where he met Yagur. The Lakam officer taught Pollard some code words to be used in case communication or cancellation of an expected meeting was necessary.

Yagur told Pollard to come, every other Friday, to a special photocopying facility in a Washington apartment building where Irit Erb resided. She worked as a secretary for the Lakam office in the Israeli embassy.

The apartment she used belonged to an American Jew, working as a lawyer in Israel, who apparently did not know what the defense ministry was doing in his Washington residence. There was so much high-speed and high-quality copying hardware there that a special electronic shielding system was installed, to block electromagnetic waves from causing interference to the neighbors' television sets.

The Israeli handlers knew how to keep Pollard interested in his work: They stroked his ego. Yagur frequently told Pollard that he was extremely valuable, and that various parts of Israel's intelligence and defense communities were using the information he had provided. Because Pollard was in the business of analyzing such matters, he was not satisfied by generous but general platitudes. He insisted that Yagur find out, line by line, agency by agency, who in Israel was using the secret documents and how.

The various agency chiefs in Tel Aviv—and officials as senior as the prime minister himself—had to have known that Eitan's scoops were coming from

Washington. After all, only an American source could have provided satellite photographs. Yet no one asked Eitan who his agent was. Revealing details would violate compartmentalization.

Thanks to their eccentric but effective spy, the Israelis received CIA analyses, copies of messages exchanged among American facilities in the region, details of Syrian chemical weapons, reports on Iraqi efforts to revive its nuclear program, and lists of Soviet arms deliveries as seen by U.S. secret agents and satellites.

The photographs and analyses provided by Pollard allowed the Israelis, for nearly a year until he was caught, to monitor in detail the movement of various navies' vessels in the Mediterranean. There was also a CIA file on Pakistan's efforts to build a nuclear weapon, which could be the "Islamic bomb" that Israelis long had feared.

The most valuable pieces of purloined intelligence, in terms of enabling the Israelis to carry out a specific mission, were the aerial photographs of PLO headquarters in Tunis. There were also reports on the air defense systems of the North African states on the way to Tunisia, including Colonel Qaddafi's Libya. Israel's air force bombed the PLO complex on October 1, 1985, in the most distant Israeli bombing raid ever at that time. It flattened much of Yasser Arafat's post-Lebanon base, and Pollard took pleasure in knowing that he had helped make it happen.

The spy was, however, driving himself too hard. His enthusiasm gave way to fatigue, and the Navy's Anti-Terrorism Alert Center (ATAC) noted that his job performance markedly declined. He was doing a full-time job analyzing data and reports for the Navy, and then a full-time moonlighting job as a spy.

His boss at ATAC, Commander Jerry Agee, began to have doubts about Pollard after catching him telling lies about some trivial matters. Agee started paying attention and noticed stacks of secret documents on Pollard's desk, many of them unrelated to his assigned projects.

The boss noticed that every Friday, Pollard was accessing Middle East message traffic and more computerized files than usual. Naval counterintelligence planted surveillance cameras over Pollard's desk, and it looked like he was amassing his own intelligence library.

He was detained for questioning on November 18, 1985. He told naval intelligence agents that he could help them uncover a multinational spy ring of which he was aware. They let him call his wife, and while pretending to explain that he would be coming home late that night, he also told Anne to "take the cactus to friends." It was a code they had developed earlier, indicating that he was in trouble and any secret documents at home should be removed at once.

Ironically, the Pollards were scheduled to have dinner that evening with Avi Sella, who was no longer their primary contact but was on a visit to the United States. Sella had told the Pollards that the air force had promoted him to brigadier general, and they ought to go out to celebrate. Instead, as Anne left for the dinner date, she was in a state of panic.

"Jay is in trouble," she told Sella at a Chinese restaurant on K Street. The new Israeli general sensed severe danger and nervously told Anne not to admit that they had ever met. They never saw each other again.

Pollard was allowed to go home that night, after the first round of questioning. He and Anne decided to call their case officer and got through to Yagur in New York. Pollard demanded asylum and transport to Israel. Yagur said: "You're probably being followed. If you shake your surveillance, come in and we'll try to help." The remark was unusually sloppy for an espionage handler: If Yagur believed that his agent was being followed, he should have known that Pollard's telephone was being wiretapped, too.

Israel and the Pollards would all pay for their lack of professionalism in this most delicate and dangerous operation. The Israelis were in an unseemly race to see who could flee fastest. Yagur and Sella flew home from New York; Erb and her boss, deputy Lakam attaché at the Washington embassy Ilan Ravid, left for Israel from the capital.

Israel's intelligence operatives were making a clean getaway, but they were abandoning their paid agent in America.

Three days after the Pollards' arrest, Israel first admitted the possibility of having been involved with the couple. There was worldwide amazement that Israeli intelligence would have been so stupid as to have allowed an agent to be arrested at Israel's embassy. And the assumption, which surprised the international press, was that the Mossad had acted stupidly.

Within a few days, however, it was revealed that "a scientific agency named Lakam"—whose existence never had been mentioned before—was responsible. Officials tried to dismiss the humiliating affair as a mere "rogue operation." The Israeli government announced that Lakam would be dismantled.

On the American side, there was puzzled anger and a sense of betrayal. President Reagan, thinking of the juicy aid with which he nourished Israel, said: "I don't understand why they are doing it."

His astonishment also stemmed from the fact that at that very time, agents of the two countries were in the middle of a secret project—so sensitive that U.S. government agents lied to Congress about it, and Israeli agents hid it from the Mossad. This was Irangate, or the Iran-Contra affair, and it proved that the road to Hell is paved with good intentions.

The idea was to win the release of Western hostages by Hezbollah in Lebanon. As one step in a sequence of secret moves in 1985, American arms would be supplied to Iran. The incredible irony was that Iran was an enemy of the United States and Israel, labeling them "the Great Satan" and "the Little Satan."

Here was the scheme: Israel delivered weapons to Iran, which was then struggling in a brutal war against Iraq. The United States would replenish Israel's arsenals. The Saudis would pay for the deal, and part of the money would be illegally funneled—behind the backs of Congress and the CIA—to the Contra rebels fighting a leftwing government in Nicaragua.

Iran did issue instructions to Hezbollah, and a few hostages were released. But the affair came to a halt when a Beirut newspaper leaked its essence. The Reagan Administration was greatly embarrassed, in part because the president's policy of "never dealing with terrorists" was plainly violated by his own employees.

When Jonathan Pollard's espionage activities were revealed, most American authorities were not very surprised. The CIA, for one, always assumed that Israeli spies were active in the United States. A secret study by the agency declared that after gathering intelligence on its Arab neighbors, the second and third priorities of Israeli intelligence were the "collection of information on secret U.S. policy or decisions, if any, concerning Israel," and the "collection of scientific intelligence in the United States and other developed countries."

Believing that there was now an opportunity to send Israeli intelligence a very stern message—that it should stop all espionage in the United States— federal prosecutors came down very hard on Pollard. The government attorneys declared: "This defendant has admitted that he sold to Israel a volume of classified documents, ten feet by six feet by six feet" if all gathered into one huge pile.

Defense Secretary Caspar Weinberger wrote his own letter to Judge Aubrey Robinson: "It is difficult for me to conceive of a greater harm to national security than that caused by the defendant." Weinberger said privately that Pollard deserved to be hanged or shot, adding that repairing the damage he caused could cost the United States a billion dollars.

Pollard, meantime, made the mistake of boasting that he had been "quite literally, Israel's eyes and ears over an immense geographic area stretching from the Atlantic to the Indian Ocean." His own memo to the judge also offered the opinion that the information he gave to Israel "was so unique" that the country's political leaders must "have known about the existence of an agent working in the American intelligence establishment."

The way the Israeli handlers had "tasked" him, he said, indicated "a highly coordinated effort between the naval, army, and air force intelligence services."

True as the assessment may have been, inflating the importance of his undercover work certainly did not get him a lighter sentence.

On March 4, 1987, nine months after pleading guilty in a bargain that was supposed to mean he would not have to spend the rest of his days in prison, Pollard was given a life sentence anyway. Weinberger's letter had swayed the judge. Pollard's wife Anne was sentenced to five years, and she served three.

The Israeli government, though caught red-handed in November 1985, evaded questions for a few days but then had no choice but to admit that Pollard's actions were an Israeli operation. Prime Minister Shimon Peres told President Reagan by telephone that it had not been authorized and would not happen again.

Eitan—feeling under pressure to resign—testified later to an Israeli inquiry committee, apparently referring to special operations going back even earlier than kidnapping Eichmann in 1960: "All my actions, including Pollard, were done with the knowledge of those in charge. I do not intend to be used as a scapegoat to cover up the knowledge and responsibility of others."

The others to whom Eitan referred were the leaders of two government administrations in Jerusalem: Prime Minister Yitzhak Shamir, who had been a senior Mossad man; Prime Minister Shimon Peres, who had created Lakam; Defense Minister Moshe Arens, whose background was in military aeronautics; and Defense Minister Yitzhak Rabin, a former army chief of staff.

They might not have been aware of Jonathan Pollard's name, but they must have had high appreciation of where the intelligence "product" was coming from.

U.S. investigators rushed to Tel Aviv to test the Israelis' assertion that the American probe would get all possible assistance. The Israeli liaison assigned to "help" them was Avraham Shalom, the Shin Bet chief who later would stumble and fall in a scandal over the killing of bus hijackers. Shalom would protect the intelligence community's interests, but definitely not Pollard's.

Documents provided by Pollard were returned to the Americans. True, Israel was assumed to be keeping extra copies, but now prosecutors could see the full scope of what Israel had been given.

At the same time, Israeli intelligence maintained its standard, strong instinct for deception. That was why Shalom, the cover-up king, got the liaison job. The Americans were introduced to "everyone" involved with Pollard, but somehow Avi Sella was not mentioned.

Later, when the Americans discovered Sella's role, they demanded that his promotion to be commander of one of Israel's most important air bases be cancelled. The United States threatened to halt all cooperation with the air force. Sella was forced to retire from the military.

The Americans were also annoyed to see that Eitan—after the abolition of his agency, Lakam—was given a plum job as head of Israel Chemicals, the largest state-owned industry.

Instead of pleasing U.S. investigators with the provision of documents and some testimony, Israeli intelligence was getting on their nerves even further by treating Eitan and Sella so kindly.

Lakam's duties were now to be spread among various parts of the government and private companies. After all, Israel still had its complex military-industrial requirements. They could not change, simply because America was angry.

When it came to public relations and politics, however, Israel had suffered a setback. The trusting relationship that it had with the United States, though never really perfect, was severely dented by the revelation of what Pollard had been doing.

As for the spy himself, he quite justifiably felt betrayed—similar to the fate of the imprisoned Jews who had worked for Israeli intelligence in Egypt in the

1950s. As in most criminal cases, Israel could have demanded that in exchange for its cooperation, its agent would be given a light sentence. But Israel did not ask for that.

This behavior led Pollard and his supporters—as his cause would come to be associated mainly with right-wing Israelis and American Jews—to think that Israel did not want him to be released. Perhaps it was feared that, as a new immigrant there, he would give so many speeches that he would be a nuisance. He also might be regarded as a living stain on the country's conscience.

He was not totally abandoned, however. The Israeli government paid millions for his legal defense and helped Anne—who divorced Jonathan—to recover and settle in Israel. More importantly, the government eventually started lobbying publicly for his release. Cabinet members, members of parliament, and ambassadors visited him in prison. He was given a document showing that he had been granted Israeli citizenship, under his real name.

Prime ministers asked, at every meeting with American presidents, whether Pollard could be granted clemency.

It almost happened in 1998, during peace talks the Americans were hosting between Israel and the Palestinians in Maryland. President Bill Clinton nearly agreed to a demand by Prime Minister Benjamin Netanyahu that Pollard be freed as part of a deal to evacuate some West Bank land. But the CIA director, George Tenet, threatened to resign if Pollard were released. He and other American intelligence officials contended that it would set a terrible precedent to be lenient in any way with Pollard—who violated his duties of secrecy. They wanted everyone with a security clearance to see that spying, no matter for which foreign country, would be dealt with extremely harshly.

For years to come, the Jewish community in America and Israel would continue to feel the fallout of this ugly affair. The FBI, noted for always being suspicious, never abandoned the belief that Israeli intelligence had penetrated even more deeply into the U.S. government. For many FBI agents, Pollard was just the tip of an Israeli iceberg.

That approach led to misinterpretation of even the tiniest clues. For years, the Mossad and then the Foreign Ministry had a code name for the CIA: "Mega." In 1997, the Israeli ambassador in Washington received a request from Jerusalem to find out what the American thinking was on a development in Israeli-Palestinian negotiations. After conferring with the State Department, which was quite routine, the ambassador, Eliyahu Ben-Elissar—ironically a former Mossad operative—turned to Yoram Hessel, the Mossad station chief based at the embassy, whose prime responsibility was to liaise with the CIA.

Since this was over the weekend, Hessel was at home. Knowing he was on an open phone line, Ben-Elissar asked Hessel to find out what "Mega" thought about the topic.

The phone conversation was monitored by America's NSA and passed to the FBI. The G-Men immediately guessed that Mega was the code name of a very senior Israeli agent who was still totally undercover.

FBI suspicions have also haunted many Jews employed in the U.S. government. The FBI frequently did not trust them, and when a Jew was called in for extra security screening, that person's loyalty to America was being questioned.

AIPAC—the pro-Israel lobby group—was also targeted by investigators. Some of AIPAC's employees were routinely involved in collecting information from open sources which had relevance to U.S.-Israel relations. They met regularly with State Department and Pentagon officials and with Israeli diplomats, visiting officials, and cabinet ministers.

To federal investigators, these meetings looked like a guilty fabric of improper links. In 2005, trying to confirm the suspicions, the FBI concocted some information about a supposed terrorist threat to Israelis in Kurdistan, in northern Iraq, and sent that to Larry Franklin, a non-Jewish Pentagon official with pro-Israel leanings. Franklin, in one of his encounters with AIPAC officials Steve Rosen and Keith Weissman, passed on the information. A short while later, Rosen and Weissman gave the warning to an Israeli diplomat. To them, it was a matter of life and death. For the FBI, it was *prima facie* proof of espionage.

Charges were filed against Franklin, Rosen, and Weissman. The Pentagon analyst pleaded guilty, as part of a plea bargain, and was sentenced to 10 months of house arrest. Rosen and Weissman were harassed by investigators and prosecutors for years, but charges were dropped in 2009.

Pollard remained in jail since 1985, still serving his life sentence. Israelis kept pressing for his release, directly by pleading to U.S. administrations, and indirectly by trying to cook up clandestine deals.

The Committee to Release Jonathan Pollard, backed by the Israeli government, raised the possibility of swapping him for an Israeli army officer who was imprisoned after entertaining a recruitment approach by the CIA.

His name—Yossi Amit—was not well known, in part because of judicial gag orders and military censorship in Israel that made media coverage difficult. Yet the basic notion that the CIA probed into Israeli secrets, while Israel did some spying inside the U.S., was far from shocking to officials who were truly in the know.

It was true that the Mossad and the CIA reached an understanding in the early 1950s that they would not spy on each other, but perhaps the real deal was that they should not get caught doing it.

American intelligence certainly used the National Security Agency to listen in on security-related conversations and data in Israel. U.S. diplomats based in Tel Aviv and Jerusalem gathered all they could from open sources—so as to be well informed about Israeli political intentions, as well as technological and military capabilities.

In rare cases, it can now be stated with confidence, the United States did send spies into Israel. They were on specific missions to learn about military, economic, and scientific projects—including the nuclear program. Defense Minister Rabin remarked immediately after Pollard's arrest, but without details, that Israel had discovered five American spies in the late 1970s and early 1980s in sensitive nuclear and industrial facilities.

Israeli intelligence, for its part, was more aggressive inside the United States. The main goal, however, was not to figure out what the administration in power intended to do. That kind of analysis was openly available from knowledgeable people at the Israeli embassy and the AIPAC lobby.

The only field where the Israelis were anxious to know the very latest was technology. For that purpose, they had few inhibitions against covert operations, paying American agents or tasking Israeli official visitors to steal secrets. Thus, the FBI or U.S. Customs agents would occasionally expose Israelis—or Americans working for Israel—who were breaking the law.

If there were a competition of ignominy, Israeli losses would outnumber America's embarrassments. The only exposed case in which the CIA was close to running an Israeli as an agent was that of Amit. When the Pollard case came to light, a member of the U.S. Senate Intelligence Committee let it slip that American spies had run at least one Israeli soldier as an agent. The senator was almost surely referring to Amit.

While Pollard suffered in prison and campaigned to have his life sentence cut short, Amit was spending seven years in a cell in Israel's most heavily guarded prison at Ramle, 20 miles east of Tel Aviv.

Amit was a former major in Aman's agent-running Unit 504. His crime: unauthorized contacts with the CIA.

He was born in 1945 in Haifa. His father was a police officer, and Yossi studied at a military academy. In 1963, after graduating, he joined the IDF, passed the officer training course with flying colors, and served in a special forces unit.

Amit was wounded in a battle with Palestinian guerrillas in Lebanon. After recovering, he joined Unit 504 and ran Arab agents in Lebanon, Syria, Jordan, and Egypt. Amit did well there, and at the callow age of 32 he was commander of the unit's northern base, which was responsible for operations in Lebanon.

He became privy to the unit's most guarded secrets, including operations that most anyone would call dirty. Amit admitted, years later, that he participated in extrajudicial liquidations of Palestinian agents who betrayed Israel.

He also came across drug dealers whom the Mossad and 504 exploited and turned a blind eye to their activities. Some nights he would return home from his secret meetings with drug smugglers deep inside Lebanon, his clothes reeking of hashish.

Though Amit was a tough, bright, and ambitious intelligence officer, the scenes he witnessed scarred his soul. His promising career came to an unexpected end in 1978, when police detectives arrested him on suspicion of drug dealing. Major Amit denied the charge, but a court martial was convened. Military doctors declared that he was mentally unstable and had suicidal tendencies, so he was ruled unfit to stand trial.

Amit attributed his mental state to the dark side of his work for Unit 504. He was discharged from the army and forced into a mental hospital for three years. Electroshock therapy only seemed to make his condition worse.

In 1981 he returned to his wife Tzila and their children in Haifa. He did odd jobs, and among other things he worked as a private investigator.

Three years later, he happened to meet an officer in the U.S. Navy, whose ship was docked in the port of Haifa. The man called himself "David"—with no last name given. The two of them seemed to get along wonderfully.

Amit told David about his work in Israeli intelligence and complained about always being short of money and having difficulty finding a decently paying job. The American confided to Amit that he would soon retire from the navy and set-up a textile business in Germany. Perhaps there would be a place there for his new friend Yossi?

Amit loved the idea. In 1985, he flew to Frankfurt at his own expense to meet David. They met in a hotel and discussed their future partnership in textiles.

David, it seems, was either a CIA talent scout or a genuine naval officer who was ordered to keep in touch with the Israeli intelligence major he had just happened to meet.

The American did Amit favors, such as paying for a visit to a medical clinic, where his old physical injuries were assessed.

David then introduced Yossi to another friend, "Bob," mysteriously calling him "one of the good guys." Bob, as though making casual conversation, mentioned everything he knew about the Israeli—and that included quite a lot that Amit had never told David. Bob's brown shoes were so distinctive, with dots and other design details, that Amit could not help but notice them.

Bob said, "We need your help," and asked for details about Unit 504 and Israeli military intelligence in general.

Amit said he would love to work for the Americans—and stated, "I'm crazy about intelligence work"—but he stipulated that he would not agree to do anything for them within the borders of Israel. Instead, he suggested that they use his knowledge of Arab countries, notably Syria and Lebanon, which he knew well after running agents there.

Amit asked for a salary, a United States passport, and help in leaving Israel. Bob said, "I think we can work something out," and asked Amit for more details about Israel. Amit declined.

Bob then said, "Okay. You want to work for us? We have to work out some details, and first we have to check your reliability." Amit agreed to take a lie detector test and to an evaluation of his personality.

The polygraph quiz included, again and again, whether anyone in Israel knew about his trip to Germany. The Americans obviously suspected that Amit was a double agent, sent by Israeli intelligence to trap the Americans—just the same suspicions that Israel would have about any walk-in.

Another member of the CIA team—a woman who called herself "Lesley"—praised Amit for his test results and told him he had a very high IQ. The Israeli could not tell, of course, whether she was merely using flattery to win his confidence and cooperation.

At a certain stage during the test, the Americans departed from the room, leaving their documents on the table. Amit did not touch the papers or even peek at them. As a trained intelligence operator, he knew the papers had been left there deliberately to test his honesty.

Later, Bob told Amit that they needed more time to check out the possibility of recruiting him. The American with the memorable footwear took $2,000 in cash from his pocket and offered it to Amit "to cover your expenses." Amit refused to take the money.

David called later and asked if he could be in touch in the future. "Remember that I'll be calling myself 'Herbert' when I call," he said. Amit still wanted this job, whatever it might be, but he got the impression he was not being hired.

On his flight home to Israel, he was certain he saw Bob on the airplane. There was no beard or long hair now, so those had obviously been false. But it was unmistakably Bob: His height and his distinctive brown shoes were those of the man he had met the previous day. Amit still had the eye for details of a good intelligence officer.

He never heard from Bob or David again.

As time went by after the meetings in Germany, Amit's frustration grew. He was still having nightmares about his military intelligence experiences, and he was almost perpetually in a foul mood. He started talking too much—even about his close brush with the CIA.

One of his friends took seriously what most listeners took to be false boasting. This man was an Arab Israeli with a very unusual background. He was part of a large family that had worked for Israeli intelligence in the formerly Syrian Golan Heights and in Lebanon. When the spies were exposed, they were hurriedly relocated to Israel. He ended up in Aman's 504, serving in Yossi Amit's unit as an expert tracker.

Betraying his friend, but feeling he was doing his duty, the Arab Israeli went to the police and told them of Amit's babbling. The police passed the information to Shin Bet.

Now, a counterespionage section responsible for "Westerners" came into the picture. This department was in charge of foiling and exposing espionage acts of any organization or individual that did not fit the definition of Arab or Communist espionage.

Amit was put under surveillance, and authorities said a search of his apartment uncovered classified documents about military intelligence operations, including lists of Arab agents and details of contacts with drug traffickers.

He was arrested in March 1986 at his Haifa home. He cooperated fully with Shin Bet interrogators, and he told them all about his meetings with the CIA team in Germany.

Amit also said he had been motivated by emotional problems and by not liking his commanders in the army. He hoped that his punishment would therefore be light or non-existent, and he imagined that Shin Bet might ask him to re-contact the Americans and serve as a double agent to penetrate the CIA.

He had an excellent memory and described the rendezvous locations, the discussions, the names used by the Americans, and the man with the brown shoes on the flight home from Germany.

Shin Bet found it easy to consult travel and passport-control records, to discover that a CIA man—under diplomatic cover in Tel Aviv—named Tom Waltz had been on that flight.

Waltz had served in the CIA station in the U.S. embassy in Bonn and was transferred in 1982 to Tel Aviv to work on counter-terrorism issues. At his liaison meetings with Shin Bet and the Mossad, they would exchange information on and assessments of radical Arab organizations. It was something of a surprise to Shin Bet that Waltz was also trying to recruit a former Unit 504 officer to spy for America.

Despite all the information provided to Shin Bet and prosecutors by Amit, Haifa's district court was hard on him. In April 1987, he was sentenced to 12 years in prison.

The trial had been conducted entirely behind closed doors. The Israeli public was not told a word about Amit, his alleged involvement with drugs, his shadowy military service, and his contacts with U.S. intelligence.

Whenever Amit—after serving his time behind bars—made some effort to leak his story to journalists, the military censor prevented publication. When a Hebrew-language newspaper in the United States did print a version of the story, saying an Israeli army major had been arrested for spying for Syria, that angered Amit even more. He figured that the article must have been an Israeli government attempt to destroy him with a false charge of treason. He now virulently hated what he called "the Establishment."

Some government officials privy to the truth thought that perhaps—at the very least—Israel should complain to the United States about the CIA attempt to recruit an Israeli officer, as though that were equivalent to the Pollard case in America. The officials thought that might prompt the Americans to admit their dalliance with Amit, and that might prompt U.S. officials to lean toward swapping Pollard.

When word reached Amit, behind bars in Ramle Prison, that a possible prisoner exchange was brewing, his intelligence instincts again went into action. He managed to get his hands on a piece of government stationery—because the envelopes were printed in the prison—and he wrote a letter to the U.S. embassy that said he did not want to be swapped.

Israeli intelligence did mention the case, at least once, to the Americans. Yosef Harmelin, who was head of Shin Bet from 1964 to 1974 and then again from 1986 to 1988, raised the subject with the CIA station chief in Tel Aviv. The CIA officer blanched, at first, but then denied any knowledge of a Yossi Amit. Later, he did come back to say that Amit had been a walk-in, volunteering to spy for America, and that the CIA had rejected him.

Israel did not bring it up again and did not ask that Waltz be withdrawn.

Around that time, an American military attaché was caught taking photographs in Israel's closed military zone near the Lebanese border. Some Israeli intelligence officials suggested kicking him out of the country—as a kind of revenge for America's rough treatment of the Pollard affair. But there were no expulsions by Israel, as it did not wish to cause further damage to a relationship that was already dented.

Some American Jews felt that the most lasting impact caused by Pollard's espionage—aside from his long ordeal in prison—was an uncomfortable rift between them and the State of Israel. They wondered if Israeli intelligence saw them as pawns in a large game devoid of any amusement.

By recruiting Pollard and taking advantage of his divided loyalties, Israelis proved themselves insensitive to the facts of life for the small Jewish minority in the United States. American Jews justly felt well accepted, overwhelmingly comfortable, and successful. They wished Israel well, and many were happy to give when asked to donate to Israeli causes. But they were, first and foremost, loyal to the United States and its interests.

With few exceptions, they certainly would not want their non-Jewish neighbors to think that American Jews loved Israel more than they loved the United States.

When spymasters in the Jewish state undermined the equanimity of life in America for Jews, Israel was taking one step too far.

CHAPTER NINETEEN

COVERUPS AND UPRISING

M any Israelis never thought about it, but the occupation of the West Bank and Gaza that began with victory in 1967 became a chronic conundrum: a millstone that the Jewish state, dedicated to democracy and human rights, could barely support.

By the late 1980s, a prolonged and destructive round of violence would break out. Perhaps it could have been prevented, if Israel's leadership—including the intelligence community—had not viewed the Palestinians almost exclusively through the gun sights of a rifle.

Israeli officials would contend that the PLO and other Palestinian groups committed terrorism to push their demand that the Jewish state be eliminated. The Israelis said the often-icy harshness of the IDF and of Shin Bet in the territories was necessary as a form of self-defense. Israel, however, refused to talk with the PLO and urged the United States to stick with the same ban, as part of Israel's policy of never negotiating with terrorists.

The best that anyone could say, as of early 1984, was that the West Bank and Gaza were relatively calm, with most Palestinians struggling to make a living and stay out of trouble. Israelis, generally far more prosperous, were enjoying a period of tranquility.

But in April 1984, the handling of a bus hijacking underlined how Israel's security services regarded Palestinian militants. The gunmen were captured, and then they were treated like cockroaches. Their crime was horrible, terrorizing innocent passengers, but the justice system of a free country is not supposed to include Shin Bet savagery.

On the night of the incident, Prime Minister Yitzhak Shamir—who was formerly known as a man of violence, before he became a Mossad operative—was attending a meeting of his right-wing Likud party. In 1983, Shamir had succeeded Menachem Begin, whose decline and resignation were hastened by the Lebanon war he started and by the death of his beloved wife.

Facing an election to win his own term in the summer of 1984, Shamir sought to portray himself as totally firm on security issues. His party hinted that Shimon Peres, the Labor leader, was soft on Palestinian terrorism.

Shamir was interrupted by a phone call from Avraham Shalom. He was the Shin Bet director who had been involved in the kidnapping of Adolf Eichmann, the mysterious visit to a uranium facility in Pennsylvania, and running damage control with the Americans after Jonathan Pollard was caught spying.

The prime minister thought he knew the most likely subject of Shalom's call. Shin Bet was on the verge of cracking a case so sensitive that it could have led to a war with the entire Arab world. In this instance, the terrorists being pursued were Jewish settlers who started a murder campaign against Palestinian politicians in the West Bank and plotted to blow up the major mosques in Jerusalem. Muslims worldwide would be outraged if that plot were to be carried out.

This phone call, however, was not about the Jewish terrorists. Because Shamir had authorized Shin Bet to plant informers among the settlers, the plotters would be arrested—but sometime later.

Shalom, on this night, was reporting that an Israeli bus on line number 300, from Tel Aviv heading south, had been hijacked. The fear was that the hijackers would take the Israeli passengers into occupied Gaza and then cross into Sinai, which in 1982 had returned to Egyptian control.

Shamir was also informed that orders were given to the military to stop the bus. Sayeret Matkal's hostage-rescue commandos and a Shin Bet operations team were rushing to the scene. The prime minister felt a certain sense of relief, believing that the security forces could handle this.

Soldiers at a roadblock managed to shoot out the tires of the bus and brought it to a halt in the Gaza Strip, less than six miles from the Egyptian border. Shalom himself arrived on the scene. He was a field and operations man, not a paper-pushing bureaucrat, but he had limited experience in Palestinian issues—unlike Avraham Ahituv, the Shin Bet director he replaced in 1981.

Watching the motionless Bus 300 on the road near Gaza, Shalom knew that the army and police had units specially trained to storm all types of hijacked vehicles and rescue hostages. Shin Bet's job would be to interrogate the four Arab attackers and discover their accomplices, sources of arms, and paymasters.

The Sayeret Matkal soldiers, who had practiced the technique hundreds of times, smashed windows and were inside the bus in seconds. They opened fire immediately, killing two of the terrorists and wounding the other two. The three dozen hostages were free, except for one woman who was killed in her seat.

When Israelis woke up the next morning, they heard good news: that all four bus hijackers were killed.

"But that can't be," said Alex Libak, a newspaper photographer who had witnessed the shootout and vividly remembered the charred bodies of two hijackers—the bus had caught fire in the gunfight—but had also seen soldiers and men in civilian clothes pummeling two wounded terrorists with fists and rifle butts.

His newspaper violated military censorship by publishing his photo of two hijackers being led away. This challenged the official version and would create an avalanche of revelations that would expose decades of misbehavior by Shin

Bet. Until that week, Shin Bet had been almost invisible: an organization that Israelis never discussed.

Puzzled by the photograph, Defense Minister Moshe Arens decided to take two steps: to use old, rarely used emergency laws to shut down that particular newspaper for four days; but also to set up an inquiry commission to look into what happened that night.

Punishing the newspaper added to the credibility of its story, and indeed the commission concluded that two of the terrorists had been alive when the battle was over. Now the question was: Who killed them?

Testimony by Shin Bet men pointed blame at the IDF's General Yitzhak Mordechai, who had been beating the two detainees during a brief "field interrogation."

Shin Bet provided multiple, corroborating witnesses who blamed Mordechai. It eventually emerged that this was a deception campaign directed by the agency director, Shalom. He and his close associates approached the task as thoroughly as they might have planned an assassination, but here it was a character assassination of Mordechai.

This put the decorated general in a Kafkaesque position. He knew that he did not kill the hijackers, but he faced a court martial where no one seemed to believe him—and his entire career could be ruined.

Luckily for the general, a later inquiry commission found that the two terrorists had been very badly wounded during the firefight, and that was why they died. Mordechai was found not guilty.

Around the same time, the deputy director and two other senior Shin Bet men actually turned against their boss, Shalom. At first, they had thought that the agency would get away with yet another in a long string of cover-ups. But now, they were extremely disturbed by a web of lies they felt was damaging Shin Bet.

They knew that since the Six-Day War, under two previous directors, Shin Bet had been torturing Palestinians and systematically lying to courts. The three men were part of the system. Yet now, after years of being accomplices to abuses, they were outraged by the thought of ruining an honorable general's career. And they concluded that lies and cover-ups were poisonous for Shin Bet.

Their goal was not public exposure, as they did not particularly want citizens to know the truth about the agency that was tasked with keeping them safe. The three rebels believed, however, that a professional organization should be telling the truth to itself.

One of them went to see Shalom, who strangely insisted that the meeting not be at Shin Bet headquarters—but at Tel Aviv's main municipal garbage dump. In a scene torn out of an old-fashioned crime novel or movie, the agency director admitted that he had given the order to his operatives to "finish off" the bus hijackers. Shalom added, however, that he was obeying instructions from Prime Minister Shamir.

The three rebels, not satisfied by the private confession, all went to see Shalom and demanded his resignation. They argued that he was ruining Shin Bet with all his cover-ups. The director refused to step down, believing that one of the three was plotting to grab his job. Shalom suspended them, and they were ostracized within the organization.

Before long, staff meetings were convened and—in the style of the Soviet KGB—the order of the day was to denounce the three renegades. According to the officially sponsored smear, they were plotting a *putsch* against Shalom. Rumors then spread that they were involved in drug smuggling from Lebanon.

Undeterred, they decided to go to the new prime minister, Shimon Peres. Because of Israel's Byzantine political system, after a near tie in the July 1984 election, Peres and Shamir had reached a unique agreement: a "rotation" coalition. Shamir was now the foreign minister, and the plan was for them to swap jobs in 1986.

Although Peres met with the three Shin Bet officials—who were practically breaking a blood pledge of absolute silence, not unlike the Costa Nostra's *omerta*—the prime minister did nothing. He refused to be dragged into the Shin Bet's squabble, however serious it was. He felt that the bus hijacking scandal began on Shamir's watch, not his.

This entire dispute was played out in secret, with heavy censorship of the press preventing any morsel from reaching the public. In any event, only a small minority of Israelis would care about the deaths of two Palestinian terrorists.

Despite the realization that Israel, from top to bottom, preferred to bury this entire affair, the trio were practically obsessed with not giving up.

Later dubbed "the three musketeers," these long-time Shin Bet men felt like victims of their own agency. They were wiretapped and under surveillance. For their own protection, they recited everything they knew into tape recorders and hid the recordings for safekeeping, to be found if they met untimely ends.

They used their old tradecraft to avoid detection and went, in the middle of the night, to see Attorney General Yitzhak Zamir and his chief prosecutor, Dorit Beinish. Zamir and Beinish were shocked, hardly believing what they were hearing, and they decided to launch yet another investigation—a full two years after the bus hijacking. Now, Prime Minister Peres had to pay attention, and he joined forces with Shamir.

When Zamir concluded that there was a basis for a criminal investigation and passed the case file to the police, Peres and Shamir responded by firing the attorney general. This was truly a coverup in the style of Nixon during Watergate.

The police kept doing their duty, however, and declared that Shalom and 11 others in Shin Bet should be indicted. It turned out that the head of the operations department, Ehud Yatom—the brother of a future Mossad director—had taken the two wounded hijackers away from the scene on that day in Gaza. Along with subordinates, Yatom headed in a vehicle toward a Shin Bet interrogation center, but on the way he took the two Palestinians out of the van and killed them with stones, sticks, and his own bare hands.

"I smashed their skulls, and I'm proud of everything I've done," Yatom told a reporter years later. "On the way, I received an order from Avraham Shalom to kill the men, so I killed them."

Yatom said his hands were "clean and moral," adding, "I am one of the few who came away from the affair with a healthy soul."

Peres and Shamir arranged one more extra-legal trick. They had installed an attorney general more to their liking, and they arranged for him to visit the president of Israel, Chaim Herzog. Herzog's was primarily a ceremonial job, but, as in many countries, the president had the power of pardon. Herzog agreed to issue pardons to all 12 Shin Bet men who were under investigation— even before they were indicted, tried, or convicted. It was probably relevant that Herzog had been director of Aman: an old hand at black operations.

Most of the dirty dozen left Shin Bet, but not in disgrace. Shalom started a new career as an international security consultant, going back to his old last name, Bendor, for a small measure of anonymity. Yatom tried hard to become the principal of a high school, but the community raised a ruckus that a man who smashed skulls should be an educator. He did go on to be elected a member of Knesset for the Likud Party.

Three million Palestinians, already under occupation for two decades in the West Bank and Gaza, were unimpressed by Israeli niceties such as putting the Shin Bet house back in order. For them, Shin Bet—whether with torture writ large, or minor torturing—was an instrument of oppression.

They exploded.

The detonation of long-simmering rage was not orchestrated, with no central organizers. It was spontaneous: a popular uprising. It was an *intifada*, the Arabic term for "shaking off."

Like other major historical events, a wide array of contributing factors can be seen, even when the precise timing defies explanation. For the Palestinians under occupation, the sad facts of life included economic decline, disappointment in the empty promises of the PLO to win their freedom, and despair from the apathy of the Arab world about their fate. Above all, they were expressing frustration—a message that enough was enough.

The spark was an unintentional tragedy in December 1987. An Israeli truck hit a group of Palestinians in Gaza, killing four and injuring others. To Gazans, it seemed to be murder: the last straw, the breaking point. They took to the streets the next morning. The protest movement spread to the West Bank, and it went on and on.

It was basically a youth movement. Young protesters refused to leave the streets. Day and night, they were out there: throwing stones at Israeli soldiers and military vehicles and at Jewish settlers' cars, burning tires at nearly every intersection, attacking police stations, and tearing down Israeli flags and replacing them with the PLO's national flag of black, white, red, and green. Hardly any guns were used. No terrorist bombs were set. This was a homemade and handmade rebellion.

Institutions on two sides were taken by surprise: the PLO, and Israel's military and Shin Bet.

The PLO—officially embodying the national aspirations of the Palestinian people—was supposed to have its finger on their pulse. But since being forced out of Lebanon by the Israeli invasion of 1982, the PLO was disoriented. It was headquartered in far-off Tunis, and its activists were dispersed all over the Arab world. The organization lost touch with the Palestinian reality under occupation.

Fairly quickly, however, the PLO was able to pull itself together and jump on the protest wagon. It started to lead the intifada, so Yasser Arafat was back in the driver's seat.

Intifada activists and the PLO were helped by a new bit of technology: not the greatest breakthrough, perhaps, but the fax machine was literally a revolutionary instrument. Orders were faxed back and forth, between Tunis and the various Gaza and West Bank committees that were being established to coordinate the violence against the Israeli occupiers.

Once a strategy was developed, Palestinian leaders assigned a high priority to breaking one of the central tools of the occupation: the informers who were working for Israel. They were a central link of a chain that enabled Shin Bet to control the daily lives of the Palestinians and to pacify the territories. There were several thousand informers, ranged across Palestinian society, from factory workers to intellectuals.

Manipulating a host of human weaknesses, Shin Bet recruited them by combining pressure, threats, and favors. Life in the West Bank and Gaza required permits to do almost anything: travel, build a house, open a shop, pursue higher education, and access specialist clinics. Licenses would be withheld or granted, depending on the Palestinian's willingness to cooperate.

Shin Bet operatives could suitably be described as "princes of the territories," moving around like they owned the place. In a modern-day feudal system, they were the lords—each controlling a neighborhood or village where local residents were like serfs who were expected to cooperate. Many of the Palestinians received stipends of up to $200 per month, and they were supposed to keep the Israelis informed about everything.

Now, the informers were at the receiving end of hatred. Protesters targeted them. Their houses were burned. They were abducted, tortured, and sometimes killed. Their families were branded "collaborators" and shunned by Palestinian society.

Israeli security officials, however, were slow to realize what was happening before their eyes. The security apparatus looked at the first protests as unconnected and believed that they could be easily smashed, like Arafat's efforts to stir up a revolution just after the Six-Day War. But this, in fact, was an uncontainable earthquake.

No one typified the odd Israeli mix of confusion and arrogance more than Yitzhak Rabin—serving as defense minister in the uncomfortable coalition of Shamir and Peres. Rabin ordered the IDF to "break the bones" of protesters, and soldiers wielding batons did that quite a lot.

The Israeli government and security chiefs still had trouble absorbing the fact that the intifada was a product of the grassroots. Their outmoded view was that it was all directed from outside, and they had to find an address. They easily found one: PLO headquarters in Tunisia.

They almost had to remind themselves that they already bombed Tunis three years earlier, in 1985. What could they do now? They were determined to find a culprit, someone who was giving the intifada orders.

The Mossad easily alighted upon one of the founders of the PLO, Khalil el-Wazir, known as Abu Jihad. It was no secret that he was Yasser Arafat's deputy and in charge of PLO operations in the West Bank and Gaza. As early as 1965, when Abu Jihad was organizing a Palestine Liberation Army in Damascus, the Mossad operations chief Rafi Eitan proposed assassinating him. Meir Amit and other intelligence bosses decided not to pursue that.

In 1988, however, Abu Jihad—the self-titled "Father of the Holy War"—was deemed a deserving target. One reason was that in March he sent three Palestinians into southern Israel from Egypt. The terrorists hijacked a bus carrying nuclear workers to Dimona, killing three of the Israelis and then themselves dying in an ensuing gunbattle.

The Israeli leadership was alarmed whenever Dimona was approached by enemies in any way. Abu Jihad stood out as a daring and dangerous man. In addition, cabinet ministers were looking for a way to boost the morale of the public in the dark days of the Palestinian intifada.

An assassination plan was immediately requested, and this one would be complex and high-priority. Planners were pleased to find that information needed to penetrate Tunisia was available in abundance. After the PLO moved its headquarters there, the Mossad was hot on its trail and created front companies in the capital city, Tunis—a terrific base for keeping an eye on the Palestinian leadership.

Aman military officers opened a safe that contained "personal target files." The files included everything known about someone Israel might want to get rid of someday: the home address, of course, but also the precise plan of his house; his habits and daily routines; the number of guards, if any; the target's vehicles; and details of his family and friends. All of that and more were in the file about Abu Jihad, truly thick with data.

Caesarea teams visited his neighborhood and subtly photographed his house, while assessing how many guards were on duty and where. The Mossad operatives also pinpointed a landing area on the beach and rented several cars. The operation was ready to be launched.

Israeli navy missile boats ferried special operations commandos to waters just north of Tunisia. Israel's air force flew a Boeing 707 over the Mediterranean, with senior military and Mossad personnel acting as a forward command post and communications center.

This was one of the most coordinated and long-distance missions in Israeli military history. It involved the air force, the navy, the sigint experts of Aman's Unit 8200, and the secretive commandos of Flotilla 13 and Sayeret Matkal.

Before the final go-ahead was given, the Israelis wanted to try to confirm that Abu Jihad was at home. The innovative method chosen was to make a phone call to him, ostensibly from someone he knew. The call was actually made by a Shin Bet man, calling from the Boeing jet over the sea. Shin Bet always had someone with perfect Palestinian Arabic on duty for such purposes—known as a *maz'ik*, or alarm-giver, because his function was usually to get an urgent message to an Arab agent.

Just after midnight on April 16, Abu Jihad answered the phone.

Flotilla 13 frogmen landed first, in motorized rubber craft, to prepare the beachhead. Next came Sayeret Matkal soldiers in civilian clothes, who had practiced how to be assassins. They got into the cars with Mossad operatives, heading for Abu Jihad's villa.

Storming the house at around 2 a.m. at high speed, the soldiers shot at least one guard and a gardener at the front and burst inside. Abu Jihad was at the top of the stairs, and the Israelis shot him dozens of times—but they spared his wife and daughter, who were watching.

The Mossad team, the special operations soldiers, and lastly the Flotilla 13 boat crews all rushed out of Tunisia with no trouble. Everyone returned home safely.

From the intelligence and operational points of view, this was a high-class success. Abu Jihad was dead. Yet, the intifada in the West Bank and Gaza was very much alive.

Seen in a broader perspective, the Palestinian uprising was precisely what Shin Bet was meant to prevent. After all, its name meant "Security Services," and it had battled in 1967 to get the right to be in charge in the territories—instead of Aman getting that responsibility.

Shin Bet had a very narrow focus on preventing terrorism, and it did not recognize that a society was developing in the occupied territories. Shin Bet's top officers did not see the Palestinians as people. They were considered only to be a human reservoir for terrorists.

At its unlabeled headquarters in a northern suburb of Tel Aviv, Shin Bet concentrated on gathering information rather than producing informed analysis. Once again, Israeli intelligence was binding itself to a preconceived idea—

like The Concept preceding the Yom Kippur War in 1973. Hardly anyone wanted to believe that the Palestinians would rise up in mass rebellion.

The intifada's fires burned hot for four years, with the IDF and Shin Bet finding some countermeasures in a mini-war of attrition. No one felt victorious—certainly not the Israelis. Both they and the Palestinian protestors were exhausted: truly burned out.

The immediate results were 185 Israelis killed and around 2,500 Palestinians—almost half of them suspected collaborators killed by other Palestinians.

The bureaucratic lessons included Shin Bet's realization that it needed a research and analysis division, which would provide it with a more complete picture of Palestinian life.

Shin Bet did rearrange its resources and thus was able to recognize the importance of Hamas: the beginning of a Muslim extremist movement within the Palestinian population. Hamas was inspired and, at the start, somewhat directed by Egypt's well-established Muslim Brotherhood.

Israeli analysts could see that, especially in Gaza, many Palestinians had lost faith in the PLO and instead renewed their vows to radical clerics who linked Allah with liberating the land held by "the Jews." Hamas issued its founding charter in August 1988, eight months after the truck accident that sparked the initifada.

They would always be remembered like twins who were born together, the intifada and Hamas. The group's charter was totally uncompromising and declared all of Palestine as a holy land that belonged only to Muslims, with no room for a Jewish state. Before long, Israel would find that Hamas, with its daring methods and glorification of suicide bombers, was a much more dangerous foe than the PLO.

Yet, at the same time, the intifada created the strong feeling—among reasonable majorities on both sides—that something big had to change. Mutual suffering offered no hope and no way forward.

CHAPTER TWENTY

HOPE AND DESPAIR

The strangest thing about the first Gulf War—which followed Iraq's invasion of Kuwait in August 1990—was that the missiles fired by Saddam Hussein at Israel ignited hopes for peace.

The Iraqi dictator's intention had been to draw Israel into the war, because that would shatter the anti-Saddam coalition cobbled together by the United States. The Arab countries that were fighting alongside the Americans and the British surely would quit if the Jewish state were to jump in on "their" side.

So, Saddam did what he could to aggravate the Israelis. His army fired 39 long-range Scud missiles in January and February 1991, trying with limited accuracy to hit Tel Aviv. He also aimed for the nuclear reactor at Dimona. That was partly a measure of revenge for his Osirak reactor having been destroyed in 1981, but, above all, he hoped to provoke the Israelis to enter the war.

It was the first time since the 1948 War of Independence that Tel Aviv was hit by enemy fire. The 1991 Scud missile strikes exposed a soft underbelly: Israel's highly populated core was vulnerable.

Because Aman and the Mossad had warned that there was a significant chance that Iraq would use chemical or biological warheads on the Scuds, millions of Israelis walked around with gas masks and hurried to plastic-sheeted safe rooms whenever an air raid siren was heard.

Saddam was indeed managing to anger the Israelis, and it seemed as natural as sunrise every morning that Iraq would be struck by retaliation. That was basic Israeli military doctrine: not to let any damage to Israel go unanswered. But President George H.W. Bush insisted that Israel not exercise its right of self-defense. He did not want his Arab coalition partners to bolt.

The war and its aftermath triggered a major geostrategic change. Saddam was defeated and, to a degree, humiliated. Positive outcomes for Israel included the dismantling of Iraq's chemical weapons and the apparent end of Saddam's attempts to restart his nuclear arms program.

There was also an effect on the Israeli-Palestinian conflict. Having scored a military victory in the Middle East—a new experience for the Americans—they felt that they could follow that up with peacemaking. Arrangements were difficult, in part because Israel's Prime Minister Yitzhak Shamir refused to negotiate with Yasser Arafat's PLO.

The Bush administration was able to organize the Madrid peace conference in October 1991, and it was a breakthrough in several ways: Shamir found himself sitting with a Palestinian delegation notionally representing West Bank and Gaza residents, and senior officials from Egypt, Jordan, Syria, and Lebanon were also taking part.

Arafat went along with giving a silent nod to the Palestinian negotiators. There was no chance that the PLO leader would get his own seat at the table, in part because he had enthusiastically supported Saddam Hussein during the war. Arafat had gambled and lost, so he was isolated.

Follow-up talks never realized the optimistic promise of the grand get-together in Spain's capital. Shamir was enmeshed in discord with the Bush administration, which had insisted that loan guarantees to help Jewish immigrants would be cut unless Israel stopped building settlements in occupied territories.

Israeli voters usually hate indications of bad relations with Washington, and that was one reason that Shamir lost his bid for reelection in 1991. The Labor Party, led by its same old faces, was back in power, but this time Yitzhak Rabin returned as prime minister; while his intra-party rival, Shimon Peres, became foreign minister.

Peres, who never took *no* for an answer, fervently felt that the time was ripe to have serious peace negotiations with the Palestinians. A few Israeli officials and peace activists who were close to Peres initiated their own clandestine channel with the Tunis-based PLO.

Despite its declared policy and a Knesset-passed law banning contacts with terrorist groups, Israel occasionally had some communications with the PLO—mainly for prisoner swaps. In those cases, it was the Mossad that conducted secret talks. Yet now, the espionage agencies were left in the dark as the clandestine channel proceeded.

It should not have been so, because the Mossad and Aman's high-tech Unit 8200 had wiretaps all over PLO headquarters in Tunis. They were even able to plant microphones in furniture delivered to leaders of the organization.

Much of this was accomplished by a senior PLO security official who had been recruited by the Mossad. He turned out to be a gift from Heaven. Adnan Yasin had been targeted for recruitment by a technique the Mossad had been perfecting for many years: the medi-trap.

The Mossad had learned that one of the best times to take advantage of the vulnerability of a potential agent was when he or she or a close relative needed top-quality medical therapies in Western countries—not readily available in the Middle East. Most people in such a position would do almost anything, including treachery.

Yasin's wife needed expensive cancer treatment, and they were looking for the best doctor they could afford in Paris. Mossad operatives—posing as non-Israelis in another of their traditional techniques, false-flagging—offered their help in finding a great doctor. Yasin agreed. Medical treatment was provided, and the medi-trap was set.

For three years, until Yasin was caught in 1993, he provided vital information on the inner workings of the PLO leadership, including the meetings, travels, and plans of Arafat; his deputy, Mahmoud Abbas (also known as Abu Mazen, a future Palestinian president); and their associates.

By the end of Yasin's brief espionage career, his work was less important to the Mossad. Israel and the PLO were negotiating peace and not plotting to kill each other anymore.

The result of the clandestine channel was a historic and astounding breakthrough: the Oslo Accords. In the Norwegian capital in August 1993, Peres and Abbas signed a deal that would lead to a ceremony on the White House lawn a month later—featuring the indelible sight of a handshake between Prime Minister Rabin and Arafat, with President Bill Clinton as the proud and smiling godfather. Rabin, Peres, and Arafat would share a Nobel Peace Prize that year.

The two sworn enemies, Israel and the PLO, were now promising to be partners for peace. It was a barely believable breakthrough. Until just before that, Israeli intelligence had been plotting assiduously against Arafat. Also, the hunting trails and pools of blood were still fresh from the secret war in which Mossad and PLO operatives tried to kill each other in Europe.

But now, Israel was recognizing the PLO as the legitimate representative of the Palestinian people. The PLO, in turn, recognized the State of Israel.

Arafat would be permitted to return to Gaza and the West Bank—26 years after he fled the clutches of Shin Bet. Yet, even at that celebrated moment, he could not kick his old, deceptive habits. In the car that brought him in from Egypt, Arafat smuggled weapons and a few wanted terrorists.

Shin Bet operatives noticed what he was doing but turned a blind eye to it. The Israelis hoped that, in due course, he would transform from a revolutionary terrorist to a Palestinian nation-builder and peace-seeking statesman.

The intelligence community had to decide how best to monitor Arafat—now that he was practically running a foreign government so close to Israeli borders and citizens.

Aman was traditionally in charge of watching and analyzing Arab nations whose military forces posed potential threats to Israel; but the military analysts had to admit that they were weak in trying to understand the ebbs, flows, deceits, and double-crosses of Palestinian politics.

Shin Bet had been keeping close track of rival factions, usually regarding them as various wings of a Palestinian terrorism threat to Israelis. Shin Bet did not want to lose this significant part of its responsibilities, just because there was a new Palestinian Authority with offices in Gaza and the West Bank.

A division of labor was worked out: a deal that intelligence community leaders called "the Magna Carta." Shin Bet would maintain a close eye on Arafat's movement, his intelligence and security apparatus, and Palestinian organizations opposed to Arafat's peacemaking. Aman's analysts would try to predict changes in the Palestinian Authority's plans, including the constant possibility that the PA would cut off all negotiations and try to rally global support with a unilateral declaration of independence.

Aman contended that it could carry out its routine duty of predicting the likelihood of war, even on this new Palestinian front. Shin Bet insisted that the PA, governing most of the people who had been administered by Israel since 1967, could not simply be labeled "a target country" in the usual Aman way.

Shin Bet developed a strong, mostly cooperative relationship with Arafat's security services. The Israelis pressed them to crack down more emphatically on terrorist factions, and the CIA provided equipment and training to make the Palestinian secret police better at eavesdropping and other skills. Ironically, these Palestinians were the successors to Force 17: Arafat's personal guards whose leader had been the Mossad's assassination target, the Red Prince of the 1970s.

That kind of relationship had to walk delicately on a tightrope. Shin Bet wanted the Palestinian secret service to do the dirty work for Israel: hunting down terrorists. The Palestinians were concerned that they would be hated by their local population as a mercenary force—or as a shield for the Israeli overlords.

Shin Bet, Aman, and the Mossad all gathered information meant to help Israeli negotiators in the peace talks that tried to move forward—mainly with American mediation—in the spirit of the Madrid conference. A senior intelligence officer in Aman was always part of the negotiating team.

There was often a problem of false optimism. Arafat's side would indicate that it was considering some kind of sweeping concession, such as tolerating the presence of large Jewish settlements in parts of the West Bank. Israeli intelligence officers felt that it fell upon them to explain to their negotiators that they should not be excited by Palestinians thinking aloud—as the aim often was to wrest concessions from the Israelis without genuinely giving anything.

The great goals of peace and reconciliation, in fact, never materialized. Both sides would have to share the blame for adhering to most of their traditional suspicions, mistrust, and petty-mindedness.

The final blow to the Oslo process was inflicted by an Israeli on an Israeli: the assassination of Prime Minister Rabin on November 4, 1995, during a peace rally. Moments before, Israel's leader was part of a group singing a peace song on the terrace overlooking a large square in Tel Aviv. While Rabin walked toward his car, with his bodyguards nearby, a young, right-wing Jewish zealot named Yigal Amir fired three bullets into the prime minister's back.

Shin Bet had many failures and questionable episodes in its history, but this was by far its nadir. The agency is, by nature, an intelligence-gathering organization; but, unlike in other Western nations, it also has the responsibility for guarding political VIPs. The personal protection unit is small, but well trained and self-confident in its ability to deal with most eventualities.

Yet, the bodyguards failed. This failure traumatized the Israeli public and shocked the world.

The assassin had been known to Shin Bet. Amir had been at many rallies, hearing rabbis and others declare that Rabin was a danger to the Jewish people—and deserved to die—because he was making concessions to Arabs. Posters at rallies portrayed Rabin as a Nazi SS officer.

Amir's files, fully examined after the murder, named many people in his right-wing circle of friends and acquaintances, including one man who had been recruited by Shin Bet as a mole codenamed "Champagne." Yet the agency failed to understand that the political Right was, literally, dead serious.

Shin Bet already had suffered a huge blow to its prestige more than a decade earlier, when Palestinian bus hijackers were killed and a history of torture was revealed. This was another slap, and Shin Bet was deeply ashamed.

The first Israeli political assassination of such magnitude naturally worsened the friction among various factions in the country. One notable fault line, to paint in broad strokes, was between "pro-peace" left-wing activists and "anti-concession, hard-line" right-wingers. The leftists had just lost their hero, Rabin, and they bitterly blamed rightists for feeding a poisonous atmosphere that led to murder.

Right-wingers rushed forward to spread their own conspiracy theories, mainly to deflect the accusations leveled against them. This was like an Israeli version of the JFK assassination, in which, decades later, people refused to accept the official findings and looked for convoluted explanations—blaming shadowy government elements for the murder.

Israeli rightists tried to create the impression that Shin Bet deliberately neglected to protect Rabin on the fateful night: a kind of "inside job."

As long as stories of that ilk came from fringe elements, they could be dismissed lightly. But the leader of the opposition's trying to spread such tales— that was quite different. Benjamin Netanyahu—who had high hopes of soon becoming prime minister—seemed to be panicking that he would be blamed for inciting the murder. He and other Likud leaders had been the star speakers at rallies with portrayals of Rabin as a Nazi.

Netanyahu personally phoned journalists to call their attention to a possible inside job. He pointed out that Amir, a few years earlier, had been in Russia as an instructor for Jewish students. So Amir had been a paid agent, in a sense, for Nativ—the former intelligence agency tasked with supporting Soviet Jewry.

"Follow the money," Netanyahu solemnly advised, borrowing a phrase from the Watergate scandal in the country where he had spent many years, the United States. He hinted that the intelligence community controlled Amir, a story that Netanyahu seemed to be pushing, apparently to deflect criticism from himself and his appearances at anti-Rabin rallies.

Investigative committees found grievous errors by Shin Bet. They faulted the agency's complacency, its negligence in the area of intelligence-gathering, the poor process of debriefing informants in the months before the murder, and poor on-the-spot security.

A few heads at Shin Bet were chopped. Among those forced out was the agency director, Carmi Gillon, who had taken over only 18 months earlier.

The irony of Gillon's departure was that he was a veteran of the Shin Bet unit in charge of keeping an eye on right-wing extremists. The final words in his master's thesis on that subject for Haifa University had been that "the lone wolf" is the greatest danger: an attacker operating singly and difficult to detect.

Before departing, Gillon asked Rabin's successor, Peres, to let him stay at the job for just a little while—to complete an operation that Shin Bet was planning. Gillon was hoping for a success so that he could leave with some glory and not only shame.

Peres agreed, and that would eventually contribute to his own political downfall in an unexpected chain reaction.

Shin Bet was pursuing the most notorious Palestinian bomb maker, Yehya Ayyash, considered responsible for the bloody deaths of dozens of Israeli civilians at the hands of suicide bombers. Ayyash, with a senior role in the military wing of Hamas, was an expert at designing explosive devices that were difficult to detect. Nicknamed "The Engineer," he fled Shin Bet's pursuit in the West Bank and found shelter in Gaza.

The Israelis were working on a highly innovative way to get him. They identified his principal associates and managed to recruit one of them, providing him with a cellular phone to give to Ayyash as a gift.

The Engineer took the bait, receiving a nice new "mobile." The phone had been remanufactured by Aman's technological toy shop, which installed high-powered explosives.

Ayyash received a cellphone call, answered, and with a loud boom his head was blown off. The Engineer had been out-engineered by an Israeli intelligence designer.

The Israeli public, widely depressed after the murder of Rabin, enjoyed reading and hearing news of the January 1996 assassination of the feared bomb maker in Gaza. But the joy was short-lived, and in the weeks and months to come the Israelis would suffer.

In a massive wave of revenge, Hamas struck back. A series of suicide bombers were sent into Israel, blowing themselves up in buses and other crowded civilian targets. In a single week in late March, 57 Israelis were killed.

The political impact seemed clear. Prime Minister Peres was losing his edge in opinion polls against Netanyahu. Fearing that he would be viewed as too soft on security issues—and thus feeling he had to do something to respond to the suicide bombings—Peres authorized a military incursion into Lebanon against Hezbollah and Palestinian forces in April 1996.

The army's campaign went astray when Israeli artillery mistakenly hit a United Nations refugee camp at Qana, in southern Lebanon, killing more than 100 civilians.

Nothing was going right for Peres. Netanyahu won the May election by a slim margin, and the right wing was back in power.

Netanyahu was far from enthusiastic about the Oslo process and decided to slow it down. The truth was that the negotiations with the PLO already had been doomed to a kind of clinical death by the three bullets fired by Yigal Amir into Yitzhak Rabin's back.

There were sporadic efforts to revive the peace talks, but Arafat was also unhelpful. The Palestinian leader continued to pay lip service to the peace process, but it seemed that he was merely trying to deceive the world about his real intentions.

The always zigzagging Israeli political system took another turn to Labor's zag, after three years of Netanyahu's zig. Ehud Barak was now the Labor party leader—ironically, Netanyahu's former commando commander in Sayeret Matkal. In the 1999 election the left-wing Barak defeated the right-wing Likud leader.

Shin Bet and Aman analysts were divided on whether Arafat was still a peace partner or simply hopeless.

President Clinton clung to his belief that a deal was possible. He was intent on overcoming the tragedy of his friend Rabin's murder and took a last stab at negotiations in the second half of 2000—his final months in office. At his mountain retreat, Camp David, in Maryland, Clinton brought Arafat and Prime Minister Barak together. There were dramatic moments, and Clinton felt that Barak was offering unprecedented concessions, but Arafat refused to reciprocate and sign a deal that might have ended the entire historic conflict.

Arafat instead ignited a second intifada in October 2000, claiming he was provoked by an unnecessary visit by Israeli opposition leader Ariel Sharon to the Temple Mount in east Jerusalem—holy to both Jews and Muslims.

Shin Bet, Aman, and the Israeli army—on one side—and the PLO, now supplemented by Hamas suicide bombers, were once again at the barricades. Palestinians stepped up their atrocities in the heart of Israeli urban centers. Israelis in buses, pizza places, restaurants, and shopping centers became targets for them.

Israel reacted by using fighter planes to bomb Hamas and PLO installations in Gaza and the West Bank. Targets for retaliation included the compound near Ramallah of Arafat's secret service—apparently, the end of Israel's cooperation with those gunmen. That particular air raid angered the CIA, which was doing its best to foster cooperation and still believed that the Palestinian secret service was valuable as a crusher of radicals.

In a slightly more subtle fashion, Shin Bet introduced a new wave of targeted killings, now on an industrial scale. The agency head who took over in 2000, Avi Dichter, was notably more willing to share efforts and information with the other Israeli agencies. He set up a situation room and made a point of hosting representatives of the air force and Aman, so that they together could process the latest intelligence on individuals to be targeted. Helicopters and drone aircraft firing missiles were used to assassinate Palestinians who allegedly organized terrorism.

Israeli attack planners, when considering any act of "targeted prevention," would discuss the likely collateral damage. Definite efforts were made to avoid or minimize harm to uninvolved civilians, and attacks were sometimes cancelled when—even at the last minute—intelligence indicated that children or other innocents were with the target at his house or other attack site. Still, many unintended casualties were caused.

As both sides sank further into a whirlpool of mutual killings, the chances of rescuing the peace process dimmed to near invisibility. Israelis elected Sharon prime minister in February 2001 to restore security, not to pursue negotiations. The intelligence community, meantime, was so busy coping with violence and fighting back that it paid little attention to grievances and social trends among the Palestinians.

Disputes within and between Shin Bet and Aman about Arafat came to an end. The PLO leader was once again, in their eyes, the master terrorist.

The three men in Varash, the acronym for *Va'adat Rashei ha-Sherutim* (the Committee of the Heads of Services), took the fairly unusual step of recommending a new political strategy. Meeting with Sharon and senior cabinet members on March 28, 2002, the night after a Palestinian suicide bomber killed 30 Jews at a Passover Seder meal in a hotel in Netanya, the directors of Shin Bet, Aman, and the Mossad proposed that Arafat be expelled from the Israeli-held territories.

The government decided not to turn the Palestinian leader into a globally admired exile, but Israel would instead keep him confined inside a single building in the West Bank. The presidential compound in Ramallah had been heavily bombed by the air force, and for three years, Arafat never left it.

Living in crowded conditions, with poor hygiene and no running water, his health deteriorated markedly. European peace mediators who visited him were worried about the world icon, in his mid-70s, apparently fading away from day to day. They asked the Israelis to permit Arafat to leave, so he could get medical treatment in Europe.

The intelligence chiefs in Varash convened a special meeting on the subject in late October 2004 and debated whether to grant a favor to the Palestinian leader. On one hand, it would make Israel look kind and just. But there were objections that he was not so terribly ill, and he would probably recover and then go on a worldwide propaganda tour.

The military suggested that it could forcibly evacuate Arafat: grab him, put him on a stretcher, rush him out of the building and take him to a clinic somewhere. Prime Minister Sharon rejected that, saying the hustle and bustle might kill Arafat—and that would look terrible for Israel.

The prime minister actually sided with the softer faction that leaned toward letting Arafat go. Sharon felt that leaving Arafat—certainly a celebrity and to many in the world a hero—to die in his smashed compound, without medical treatment, would do serious diplomatic damage to Israel.

So, France and Jordan were permitted to organize the Palestinian leader's exit: on a stretcher, in a helicopter, on a wheelchair, and then onto a French military airplane. Apparently it was too late to save him. He died in a hospital in Paris within two weeks, in November 2004, but that sparked a new, mysterious controversy. What was the cause of death? The French military doctors treating Arafat refused to specify, at least in any public statement.

Rumors swirled that Israel had poisoned him, perhaps little by little adding lethal substances to the air in his compound in Ramallah or sneaking poison into his food. There also were rumors that Arafat was gay, and it might have been AIDS that killed him.

Israeli intelligence knew of indications that Arafat—who for decades had been "married to the movement"—was not intimately interested in women. This knowledge came into play during a rare encounter between Mossad officials and Israeli journalists, a few years before Arafat's demise.

Intelligence officers invited two journalists to a private chat, mostly about Arafat. The Mossad clearly wanted to spread scandalous stories about Arafat being corrupt, including the notion that he had "stolen money from the revolution" and had millions of dollars hidden in European banks.

A third journalist, who was truly an intelligence junkie, made a point of dropping in to the coffee shop where the conversation was taking place and practically invited himself to join in. Excited by the possibility of taking part in Mossad psychological warfare, he offered to pose as a foreign writer who could approach Arafat's wife Suha and get secrets from her—and he volunteered to sleep with Suha as part of an espionage escapade.

The Mossad said no, thanks.

As for claims that Israeli intelligence poisoned Arafat, there was a resonance of truth based on prior experience. In at least two cases, the Mossad had used poison to try to eliminate enemies. There were, indeed, the Belgian chocolates that killed Palestinian terrorist leader Wadia Haddad in 1978. And in 1997, Mossad men sprayed poison into the ear of a Hamas leader in Jordan. (*See Chapter 22 on assassinations.*)

Closer in time to Arafat's death, there was another case. Shin Bet poisoned a senior Hamas military commander in the West Bank. First, the Israelis tried to kill him by their conventional method of "targeted prevention," but when they failed to get to him they designed an alternative route: adding lethal substances to the man's food.

As for the end of Arafat, Israeli officials denied responsibility and said he had actually died of leukemia. They did concede that he had not gotten timely and proper treatment, because he was trapped in Ramallah by Israeli forces.

Israel said it had not poisoned this longtime foe, but it knew that many around the world would not believe the official story.

Arafat was succeeded by Abu Mazen, who lacked charisma and strong support from the Palestinian people. Prime Minister Sharon practically refused to negotiate with him, believing Abu Mazen lacked the clout to make a deal and referring to him as "a chick without feathers"—a potential leader who never matured.

It was a time of reflection for Israeli politicians who were interested in peace. Some thought more deeply about whether it had been short-sighted to eliminate Abu Jihad, 16 years earlier, in Tunis. He would have been Arafat's successor. Israel had killed a charismatic PLO figure, a man who could have made daring decisions. Perhaps Israel could have patched together a peace process and a lasting deal if a strong Palestinian had still been around.

CHAPTER TWENTY-ONE

AT THE FRONT TOGETHER

Avi Dichter felt no pleasure at all in harboring the biggest "I told you so" in history. What he felt was horror, and not a scintilla of satisfaction, as he watched 9/11 unfold on a TV screen in his office at Shin Bet headquarters in northern Tel Aviv.

As director of the agency, Dichter and his predecessors—as well as former security officials who had become private counter-terrorism consultants—had been trying for nearly 20 years to persuade the Americans to do more about aviation security.

Israel, having learned by trial and error, instituted unique measures that were at once simple and advanced. In 1968, after an airliner belonging to Israel's El Al was hijacked, Israel introduced armed sky marshals and thick metal doors to protect the cockpits.

Israel also was the first to require that passengers be questioned by security personnel before the flight. The method would become more systematic, but also problematic because of privacy infringement. Many foreign tourists—and especially Israeli Arabs and Palestinians—felt they were unfairly targeted by what was clearly a "profiling" system. It was based on experience and intuition about which nationalities, age, gender, and travel history were most likely to be involved with terrorism. Only a tiny minority of Arab travelers would be dangerous in any way, but they all were hassled.

When Israeli security planners spoke of experience, they meant the memory of bloody attacks and an oath to prevent their recurrence. In May 1972, three Japanese Red Army terrorists—acting on their partnership with the Popular Front for the Liberation of Palestine—landed at Lod Airport, grabbed machine guns from their luggage, and opened fire on innocent passengers. Twenty-six were killed, most of them Christian pilgrims from Puerto Rico. Part of the security change at Lod was to search all luggage, pat down almost all passengers, and use X-ray machines on both bags and people.

Israel also became the first country to introduce armed officers dotted throughout the international airport. Areas closely guarded included the luggage hall for arriving passengers and the check-in desks for departures. In almost every other nation, those were practically ignored by police.

All the new security measures, using both humans and machines, were under the jurisdiction of Shin Bet. The agency established a large security department with sub-units for aviation and for shipping.

In late 2000, when Israel was suffering through the second intifada—with terrorists targeting civilians in shopping malls, restaurants, and buses—Shin Bet devised another layer of protection: compelling those places to hire private security guards, trained to Shin Bet standards.

The irony was that the machines and the technology were imported from America. There were plenty available, because manufacturers there found that the U.S. government, airlines, and airports did not want them. Israel saw the need and was the best customer for them.

Makers of such detectors, scanners, and future developments were prepared to satisfy most every Israeli need. Dichter recalled that Shin Bet would not allow El Al to fly to Bangkok, Thailand, until the airport obtained an adequate explosives-detection machine. An American company, InVision Technologies, immediately dispatched a machine to Bangkok—exclusively to meet El Al's need.

Israel was the poster boy for U.S. and Western manufacturers of security gadgets. Nothing sells like success, and Israel exemplified the best aviation security. None of its airliners was hijacked since 1968, and numerous attempts to detonate bombs in mid-air or to attack check-in counters were foiled.

Some of these conspiracies by Arab terrorists were very clever. In April 1986, a Jordanian of Palestinian ancestry—hired by Syrian intelligence—tried to send a human bomb aboard an El Al flight from London. He had met an Irish hotel chambermaid, got her pregnant, and promised to marry her in his hometown in the Holy Land. He told her to fly ahead of him, so she could meet his family, and he gave her a piece of hand luggage for the trip.

The British security at Heathrow Airport did not notice anything odd about the bag. Only the thorough security checks by the Israeli guards at the El Al boarding gate discovered that the bag had a false bottom, concealing a bomb so powerful that it could bring down a jumbo jet.

Had the attack not been foiled at Heathrow, Israel certainly would have launched an all-out war against Syria. The deaths of 400 people on an El Al plane would have felt like a 9/11, in such a small country as Israel.

When Israeli experts tried to sell their knowhow to U.S. air carriers and the Department of Transportation, the Americans refused to invest the kind of financial resources needed to enhance security. They argued that Israel was small, so it was relatively cheap.

The airlines feared that their profit margins, in an already precarious industry, would shrink to nothing. They also pointed out that Israel's national airline was getting a huge government subsidy in the form of a security system. That was not going to happen in the United States.

The Americans also came up with the claim that U.S. aviation would grind to a halt if every passenger and piece of luggage were subjected to security.

Even the deaths in December 1988 of 270 people, when a Pan Am jumbo jet was blown up over Scotland by Muammar Qaddafi's Libyan agents, did not prompt the Americans to do much. Some Israeli privateers benefited from the Lockerbie disaster by being hired by airlines as consultants, but they soon realized that the American corporations were refusing to introduce the necessary measures to make the system safer.

Then came 9/11, and everything changed.

The Twin Towers were destroyed, the Pentagon was hit, and a fourth airliner crashed in Pennsylvania; all told, 3,000 innocent Americans died. The United States immediately launched a war in Afghanistan to chase the al-Qaeda perpetrators.

Shin Bet's Dichter, having watched all that from afar, did not want to cause offense with a loud "I told you so," but after a decade he calculated that a trillion dollars was spent, and many thousands of lives were lost—and it all could have been easily prevented.

It all came down to that day, on the four domestic flights. Nineteen terrorists, unarmed except for box-cutters, passed through the existing system unmolested. They did not seem suspicious, and their hand luggage was not deemed dangerous.

They turned the airplanes themselves into massive weapons. "That's a suicide terrorist's dream," Dichter said, "piloting a missile filled with 50 tons of fuel moving at high speed." They were able to accomplish their goal for one surprisingly simple reason: There were no sky marshals.

Israeli-style armed marshals and metal-reinforced cockpit doors most probably would have stopped the 19 from hijacking the planes and then causing America's worst calamity.

Until that September day, the U.S. aviation security concept was to rely on one circle of defense: intelligence collection to get advance information of plots aimed at American airlines. But that was not enough. The CIA and the FBI, for an entire decade, were aware that al-Qaeda wanted to attack America; and there was some specific information about a few of the hijackers that the agencies did not share with each other.

Not knowing precise attack plans meant that airports and airplanes were defenseless on 9/11 itself.

The Israeli doctrine, designed by Shin Bet, worked very differently. The intelligence circle was very important, but there was also a second one: the security circle, on the spot. That was like having a back-up.

The second circle had various layers. Israel used sophisticated machines for scanning luggage, and computerized tomography (CT) machines which could detect all types of explosives, including the plastic kind. Yet there was—and is—no equipment for detecting intentions. There is no mind-reading machine, and there probably never will be one.

The second circle was meant to compensate for failures of intelligence or inaccurate information. On-the-spot security—the armed guards, the questioning, the machines, and the sky marshals—would further increase the odds of preventing any attempt to hijack planes or down them.

Israeli aviation officials knew that their country's airplanes and facilities would be high-priority targets for terrorists. But Shin Bet was able to engineer a situation in which the least likely airline to be attacked was El Al, because so many attempts had failed. Terrorists would turn to softer targets, which, unfortunately, often meant that havoc was unleashed on the airlines and airports of other countries.

Even in Israel occasionally there were calls, by government financial officials, to save money by cutting out sky marshals. But Dichter's reply was both emphatic and futuristic. The Shin Bet chief declared that even if all passenger planes became pilotless to save money, and everything was self-service so that flight attendants would no longer be employed, there would still have to be armed sky marshals on board.

Finding itself in asymmetrical wars in Afghanistan, in Iraq, and against loosely linked jihadist terrorist networks around the world, America had to build up a set of war doctrines from scratch. Naturally, it turned to any source that had the knowledge and experience at this. Israel clearly fit that bill.

CIA counter-terrorism experts, special operations commanders, and FBI interrogators traveled to Israel to learn from the oracles on unconventional warfare.

In 2003, Dichter hosted Robert Mueller, the FBI director, and some of his assistants. In an unprecedented gesture by Israel, which usually did not like to expose its secretive and unique methods, Mueller was allowed to enter one of the holies of holies: the situation room built by Shin Bet at its high-security headquarters close to Tel Aviv.

He was shown video footage taken by drone aircraft and helicopters, depicting targeted killings by the Israeli air force against terrorists, mainly in Gaza. There were many such Israeli attacks at the time, practically on an industrial scale, and the aerial video often showed Palestinian cars and individuals being identified, chased, and then struck.

What Mueller, visitors from the CIA, and American special operations officers learned is that Israel made a great effort to be accurate, avoiding collateral damage. That could be achieved only by having advance, precise intelligence about the movements and plans of terrorists. The Americans could see that Israeli intelligence often had an agent on the scene to warn of problems that could prompt cancellation of the lethal missions.

The United States adopted and adapted the use of drones for elimination missions, especially along the border between Afghanistan and Pakistan, but would or could not match the Israeli method of having agents in the strike zone. Missions were flown, with controllers—in effect, ground-based pilots doing just what they would do if playing a high-tech video game—sitting comfortably as far away as New Mexico.

Under President Barack Obama, the United States reached its own industrial scale of targeted killings. Drones fired missiles at al-Qaeda and Taliban terrorists in the border zone, but also in other countries beset by Islamist radicals, such as Yemen and Somalia. Sometimes tragic mistakes were made, causing the deaths of children and other non-combatants.

Dichter conceded later that cooperation with the United States was not a one-way street. Shin Bet and Israel's air force actually learned a great deal from the Americans, even about the tactic of targeted killings that was considered to be Israel's innovation.

It became known that one of the first targeted killings was carried out by the United States, in Yemen in November 2002, when Israel was still toying with making that method a regular part of its campaign during the second intifada. In the radically transformed post-9/11 world, countries large and small would have to shatter old conventions.

The first U.S. assassination-by-missile was the achievement of a Predator drone remotely piloted by the CIA. The Agency soon started flying its own fleet of unmanned attack aircraft—independently of the American military.

In this regard, there was a bureaucratic difference. In Israel, drones were flown only by the military. The intelligence community gave up any idea of running its own drones or paramilitary units. There did not seem to be any need for that.

Even as rules of warfare, retaliation, and intelligence-gathering were rapidly re-written in the weeks after 9/11, America seemed unsure of how to fight back most effectively. A mighty nation had been awakened from the complacency of believing that vast oceans protected it from Middle East terrorism. But, President George W. Bush naturally wondered, now what?

Invading Afghanistan was a no-brainer, as that is where Osama Bin Laden resided when he sent the hijackers to America. The British and some other U.S. allies joined in that war—as the world quite justly rose up against a ruthless enemy—but Israel, as usual, was excluded from a Washington-led coalition. Bush and his vice president, Dick Cheney, liked Israel and admired its skills, but consorting with the Jewish state would inevitably prompt Muslim and some other nations to shun the coalition.

The Bush-Cheney team hardly hid its intention to start a second war by attacking Iraq. The Americans declared that Saddam Hussein was refusing to open his nuclear, chemical, and biological weapons programs to international inspectors.

The Mossad was consulted for its analysis of what might occur next in the region. While claims were made later that Israel and its supporters in the United States clamored for a war against Iraq, the truth is that Israeli leaders had no reason to do that. In their view, Saddam's nose had been bloodied in the Gulf War of 1991, and he seemed nicely contained.

On balance, Israeli intelligence said, Iraq probably did have chemical and biological weapons; and the Mossad's suspicion was that some of those might have been smuggled across the border into Syria for safekeeping.

Yet, the Israelis did not share President Bush's absolute certainty that Iraq had weapons of mass destruction, and they expressed concern that Iraq was distracting from the real enemy, Iran.

The Americans, again with the British and a few partners, invaded Iraq in March 2003 and provoked a painful headache that lasted almost a decade. By the classic measure of Middle East trends, Israeli strategists had reasons to be cheerful: In and around Iraq, there were now Arabs battling Arabs and Muslims killing Muslims. And the loudly anti-Israel dictator Saddam was out.

Israeli intelligence could see, however, that a miasma of confusing and rapid events added up to a net gain for the Islamic Republic of Iran. That, in a region of rival hegemons, threatened to be a net loss to Israel.

Iran seemed to be achieving a strong partnership with its fellow Shi'ite Muslims in Iraq—and even a measure of dominion over them. They had been suppressed by Saddam, and while Iraqi Shi'ites had hardly any attention or energy to direct toward Israel, they had many reasons to pledge allegiance to Iran's religious leaders.

By the end of 2003, while battling an insurgency in Iraq that had separate but potent al-Qaeda and Shi'ite elements, American strategic planners were coming around to the notion that neighboring Iran was a major trouble-maker. Senior officers at the Pentagon spoke of Iranian operatives, known to be part of the Revolutionary Guards, crossing into Iraq to deliver and plant bombs that were killing United States soldiers.

Israel had already been fighting its largely secret war against Iran and its clients, notably Hezbollah, for two decades. The Israelis thus were prepared to tell the CIA and the U.S. military a great deal about the al-Quds Force élite of the Revolutionary Guard Corps.

Very much unlike the Israel pattern, however, U.S. forces were constrained by their political masters from crossing into Iran to deal the al-Quds men— their unit using the Arabic name, "the Holy," for Jerusalem—the blow they richly deserved.

The Mossad had its opening now to highlight the dangers posed by Iran both to Israel and to the United States, to its oil suppliers in the Arabian Gulf, and even to American allies in Europe who could soon be within the range of Iranian missiles.

This was around the time that Meir Dagan, whom Ariel Sharon appointed as director of the Mossad in 2002, was completing his dramatic re-direction of priorities: away from Palestinian issues, and focusing instead on Iran.

Dagan and a Mossad department known as Nabak—an acronym for *Neshek Bilti-Conventzionali* (Non-Conventional Weapons)—were building up huge dossiers on the sites within Iran where nuclear enrichment had begun.

International inspectors already suspected, in 2003, that the Iranians were hiding a lot of uranium.

Based in part on their own experience, secretly developing a nuclear arsenal with materials acquired in unorthodox ways, the Israelis were even more suspicious than the International Atomic Energy Agency. Dagan himself became a frequent traveler to Washington, where he presented evidence to the CIA, to the Pentagon, and to members of Congress. The Mossad wanted the United States, as distracted as it was by wars in Afghanistan and now Iraq, to accept that Iran was trying to build nuclear weapons and must be stopped.

The CIA, the military, and the National Security Council in the Bush White House all hesitated, due to varying degrees of concern that the Israelis were "playing" them. Despite the common ideals and interests frequently espoused by American and Israeli politicians, security agencies—including the CIA and the FBI—felt that they were paid to be skeptical. They did not automatically trust any foreigners, with the general exception of the British; Israel's espionage agencies had often shown that they had their own agenda and interests, not always coinciding with America's.

The U.S. intelligence community, many senior officers in the military, and a majority of veteran diplomats in the State Department were still smarting over the espionage conducted by Jonathan Pollard in Washington. Every time Israeli leaders asked the United States to commute his life sentence and set him free, the CIA and other agencies would advise the president not to do so—because Americans who were risking their lives and toiling in secret would never accept that a man who violated his secrecy oath should be released. Still, Israel renewed the request in 2012 when Pollard was reported to be very ill.

Despite the reality of old friction between the American and Israeli intelligence communities, a new focus on Iran as a joint enemy gained ground and a genuine head of steam. The Bush administration—and, after 2008, the Obama White House—showed great interest in applying financial pressure on Iran: freezing the bank accounts, for instance, of al-Quds Force commanders and banning their travel abroad. Over the years, much broader and tougher sanctions against Iranian officials and institutions would be introduced, leading to a significant decision by the European Union to stop purchasing oil from Iran in the summer of 2012.

Dagan's Mossad stepped forward with many more ideas for applying pressure on Iran's economy. Dagan felt that unrest by students, ethnic minorities, and other freedom-seekers in Iran could be stirred up if Iranians were hungry, fuelless, and frustrated at their Islamic government. In 2004 and the years that followed, Israel was a significant partner in United States finance-based efforts to fight terrorists and box in the Iranians.

There was no denying, however, that the entire environment for Israel-U.S. relations had changed from the relatively easygoing days of assuming that both nations were natural friends. Critics, many of them in Washington, but also in academe and in other Western capitals, more frequently cast doubt on the notions of shared democratic values and strategic interests.

Some of the critics focused on the continuing occupation of the West Bank, even after Israel withdrew all its troops and Jewish settlers from the Gaza Strip in 2005. These writers wondered what kind of values were represented by controlling the lives of Palestinians who had no voting rights.

Strategic goals also, at times, seemed out of sync. When Barack Obama came into office at the start of 2009, he immediately tried to distance the United States from Israeli policies. He repeatedly called for a freeze on the construction of Jewish settlements in the West Bank and parts of Jerusalem captured in 1967, as he felt that only then could serious peace negotiations with the Palestinians resume. The talks went nowhere, fizzling out and leaving Obama frustrated at both the Israelis and the Palestinians.

Israel's intelligence community was not unduly alarmed. Mossad and Aman analysts are highly professional and rejected the nonsense promulgated by some right-wing politicians that Obama was a Muslim or, at least, pro-Arab. Because he was determined to be the anti-Bush, he was attempting some new initiatives. His top Middle East advisors said that he had to offer talks with Iran, because only then could he persuade more countries that he was trying everything—and that now they should join in tough sanctions against the Iranians.

Obama's policies in the region were, through little fault of his own, thrown into disarray in 2011 when pro-democracy uprisings occurred in Tunisia, Egypt, Yemen, and then more violently in Bahrain, Libya, and Syria. Egypt's president, the now deposed Hosni Mubarak, had for 29 years been the glue that held together a collection of common interests that helped both the United States and Israel.

Neither the CIA nor the Mossad could save their old friend Mubarak, and officials of his regime who had warm relations with both those agencies were either arrested or disgraced. President Obama and Prime Minister Netanyahu, despite personal and political friction between them, shared a sense of disappointment over losing Egypt as a firm ally.

Netanyahu drove home the point that unrest, and especially gains for Muslim Brotherhood-type parties in various countries, would help expand Iran's influence. The United States government increasingly viewed the Middle East through a prism not too different from Netanyahu's.

Pressure on the Israeli prime minister to make concessions toward Palestinians abated. Obama, especially when he faced re-election in 2012 and wanted Jewish voters to stay in their traditional Democratic camp, stepped up his frequent repetition of his assurance that his administration was "unwavering in our support of Israel's security."

Israelis, including leaders of the intelligence community, took note of his constant insertion of the word "security." Obama desired a secure Israel, but he did not approve of settlements or of the wide borders that a rightwing-dominated cabinet in Jerusalem would want.

The United States and Israeli governments were brought closer by their shared concern over Iran's nuclear program. That had a definite impact, too, on the intelligence communities.

However, there was also a corrosive element: each side feeling that the other was not revealing all of its options and plans. Netanyahu, while visiting Washington, made a point of declaring that Israel's patience with Tehran was wearing thin. He hinted that Israel had military plans for dealing with Iran's nuclear facilities not only on the table, but ready to take to the air.

Senior U.S. officials made it clear, in early 2012, that they did not want the Israelis to attack Iran. Yet, they understood the Israeli attitude—rooted in the core value of being an independent Jewish state—that Jews would never rely on others to fight their battles for them.

Obama, when personally asked by Netanyahu in March to endorse Israel's right to take action of its choosing, declared: "Israel must always have the ability to defend itself, by itself, against any threat."

Netanyahu and his defense minister, Ehud Barak, indicated that they could postpone an attack on Iran's nuclear facilities—and perhaps miss the Israeli military's best window of opportunity to do significant damage—but only if they heard a key assurance from the United States. They wanted Obama to pledge that the U.S. would use its much larger forces to strike Iran if negotiations, sanctions, sabotage, and all other steps should fail.

The President would not give that absolute promise. But he did say that a nuclear-armed Iran would run counter to the interests of both America and Israel, and "I will not hesitate to use force when it is necessary to defend the United States and its interests."

At the huge annual policy conference of the AIPAC lobby, Obama added: "When the chips are down, I have Israel's back!" His motives, facing perhaps his toughest foreign policy challenge, surely included a desire to please pro-Israel voters and campaign contributors.

Obama also wanted to reassure Israel, so that it would not—in the American view—unnecessarily start a new war in the Middle East.

Word leaked out from Israel that the heads of Israel's intelligence agencies opposed the idea of attacking Iran anytime soon. Recently retired agency directors, including Dagan, hinted that they had some doubts about what their air force could accomplish. Current and former espionage chiefs also hinted that there was still a lot more damage on Iran's program to be inflicted through cyberwarfare and other sabotage.

While differences over tactics could not be papered over, the Mossad did take part in a concerted Israeli government campaign to get the world's attention.

Israel's political leaders pointedly combined genuine information and analysis, sometimes exaggerated alarm tied to historical tragedies of the past, and a measure of poker-style bluff. They were emphasizing that if the United States and other large countries did not stop Iran's march toward creating nuclear bombs, Israel would take action. Their campaign clearly succeeded, because the world was listening. The Iran issue was not being ignored.

CHAPTER TWENTY-TWO

ASSASSINS

Kidon is one of the Mossad's most secretive units—if not the most secretive. Whether it is a mini-Mossad within the agency, or even a planet of its own, the fact is that Kidon operatives are obscured by strict secrecy and further protected by military censorship of the Israeli media. Yet, an accurate window into the structure of Kidon, its modes of operation, and the moods and psyches of its members can be found in the pages of a novel.

The author is Mishka Ben-David, and a thorough dossier describing the Kidon unit is nestled in a seemingly innocent book of fiction he wrote, *Duet in Beirut*, published in Hebrew in 2002. Ben-David, though, is not just a novelist. He was an intelligence officer. He was in the Mossad. And if that is not real enough, then consider that he was the chief intelligence officer of Caesarea, the agency's operations department that runs combatants—Jewish and non-Jewish—who penetrate such enemy countries as Syria, Egypt, and Iran.

Caesarea also has, at its service for special occasions, Kidon. This "Bayonet" unit is kept small but sharp, and it recruits men and women who already have proven themselves in their military service or in other intelligence work. They are judged, through a process that includes copious psychological profiling, to have excellent self-discipline. Even more importantly, they have the skills needed for operations that are on the edge. Many of them come from special forces units, such as Sayeret Matkal and Flotilla 13.

They are trained by highly motivated instructors and work in small teams of two or four—each of them known as a *khuliya* (a Hebrew word for "team" or "connected link"). Although Kidon's overall size has never been published, there are several dozen khuliyot, and the entire secretive organization is referred to as "The Team."

They are so compartmentalized that their office is not inside the Mossad headquarters at the Glilot junction. They hardly ever go there, and even with the very few Mossad operatives with whom they interact, they use assumed names—so as to be anonymous even to them.

In the field, they use a third name, and sometimes even fourth and fifth identities.

Their training includes almost anything one might imagine is needed for a thorough intelligence operation: surveillance, shaking off surveillance, and how to study an object—things, buildings, or even people—and memorize everything about it.

They become proficient at remembering codes and securely communicating during missions without raising suspicion. On top of conventional communication gear, this can include an agent touching her nose or pulling her earlobe, or some other form of sanitized signal to colleagues.

One of the skills is to remain cool as a cucumber in all circumstances, and not to be shaken by any unexpected interruption, question, or approach by people—never hinting that you are involved in anything unusual.

In Ben-David's adventure novel, a female Kidon combatant and the senior man who trained her are sent to penetrate a factory in a foreign country that manufactures parts for Iran's nonconventional weapons. They are interrupted when another Kidon team, serving as their perimeter guard, informs them with urgency that unexpected guests are arriving. The guards disperse, according to plan, and the duo know precisely where to go to meet a car that is waiting there for such an eventuality. Everyone keeps their cool. Panic is not in their lexicon.

Kidon personnel excel at the manual skills that are often required in the field: picking or breaking a lock, surreptitiously taking photographs, and planting electronic devices.

They also learn to master a variety of vehicles: not only cars and vans, but also motorcycles, which have become Kidon's vehicle of choice—almost a trademark of a team that leaves few traces.

The Team's members are constantly practicing the use of weapons, and as wide a variety of weapons as has ever been invented. They are very good at firing pistols, often with silencers, whether while standing, running, driving, or riding a motorcycle. They know how to shape, plant, and detonate explosives, including innovatively designed bombs. They are well practiced at stabbing enemies with knives, injecting them with hypodermic needles, or administering poison by way of newly minted delivery methods. In addition, well trained in martial arts, Kidon operatives are adept at using their own hands and feet as weapons.

The description of their skills may seem torn from a James Bond novel or movie, but they are not figments of a writer's imagination. Kidon men and women are authentic intelligence officers who are taught a wide range of crafts. It is a barely concealed fact, within the Mossad, that they are Israel's assassins. Moreover, they are considered to be supreme intelligence officers for all seasons—not simply a death squad.

Because they are the cream of the crop, they are the ones the Mossad director selects for very dangerous missions —including complex intelligence operations of an information-gathering nature—that require the top professionals.

Over the years, although hardly ever intentionally, some stories about Kidon's prowess leaked to the public. With the little that was known about them, The Team's operatives were considered synonymous—in Israel and outside—with assassins, liquidators, and murderers.

The truth about the myth is that since the Mossad's creation in the early 1950s, it has been involved in only a few dozen killing operations—certainly fewer than 50. But the public imagination worldwide has been captured by the notion of constant assassinations, and the Mossad might find it difficult to refute the image with facts. So it does not bother. Indeed, the murderous image is useful.

True, Israel has targeted and killed hundreds, throughout its history, in surgical strikes against individuals who are considered notably dangerous. But the vast majority of those killings were by army units, mainly in uniform, crossing into occupied or enemy territory. Whether in the West Bank and Gaza, or in a raid on the PLO in Beirut, these were generally acknowledged.

The Mossad has never claimed responsibility for any killing or attempted assassination.

Another difference between military-style assassinations and the occasional killings by the Mossad lies in the deniability factor. Soldiers on an official army mission feel that they have back-up—substantial forces ready to help or rescue, if necessary. A small Mossad team is on its own, however, and Israel would rarely recognize and assist them publicly if trouble broke out.

Assuming a foreign army or government is the captor, a soldier in uniform when captured would be protected by the Geneva Conventions. A spy who was captured might well be tortured and executed, as he or she would not have the benefit of "prisoner of war" status under international law.

For Israeli intelligence, killing is a last resort. Before eliminating a target, the Israelis typically try to turn him into an agent, warn him, or terrorize him. If he does not bend or break, then the Mossad might have to remove him from the field of battle.

Analyzing the Mossad's dozens of assassinations in various time periods, three broad categories of targets may be noted: former Nazis, scientists who worked in non-conventional and other weapons programs in enemy countries, and senior operatives and leaders of terrorist organizations. The latter two categories have continued to be threads of Mossad activity woven throughout Israel's clandestine history—and still part of today's tapestry.

The pursuit of Nazi war criminals was never a central tenet of Mossad strategy or priorities, and this assassination category ended in 1965 with the murder of Herbert Cukurs. (*See Chapter 7.*) These were among the rare cases in which revenge and historic justice were the motives.

The first scientists who were targeted—well before the birth of the Kidon unit—were Germans who were not leaders of the Nazi regime but had been employed by it. About half a dozen men, trying to cash in on their technical knowledge, had contracts with the Egyptian missile program in the first half of the 1960s. Egypt hired them to help it develop missiles that could reach Tel Aviv: an ambitious goal and a very dangerous one, in Israel's eyes.

The Mossad conducted a systematic campaign against these Germans. Their families were approached, in the hope that ominous messages would prompt them to persuade their loved ones to quit the Egyptian program. Threatening letters were sent, some bullets were fired at the scientists' cars, and eventually letter bombs arrived in the mail.

Part of the aim was larger than targeting only these scientists. A message was being sent, in effect, to other Germans to think twice and thrice before signing a contract to work for Israel's Arab enemies. The Mossad was making it a dangerous job for any European to accept, so it would not be seen as a safe way of earning some money.

The campaign lasted for only two years and resulted in several injuries, sometimes of innocent people. Egypt's missile program, for various reasons, made little progress and ran out of steam.

Attacks on the Nazis and on the German scientists were not yet the actions of Kidon. The Team did not yet exist. Lacking a specialized assassinations unit, the Mossad relied on its pool of operatives from various units scattered around the agency.

The Egyptians did renew their missile aspirations in the 1980s. Realizing that they could not succeed with a home-grown program, they reached a partnership accord with Argentina. That country was making good progress with its Condor missiles.

Naturally, Israel was alarmed and interested in learning all about this project to build long-range missiles. Experts from Aman managed to obtain invitations to Argentina, and they were even able to examine the Condor prototype.

Luckily for Israeli intelligence, it had a long record of military cooperation with Buenos Aires—a link with dictators that led to much criticism of Israel, but also one of many examples in which relationships with pariah regimes yielded fruit for Israeli intelligence.

The Mossad simultaneously exercised its own talents. It launched a terrorizing campaign, now with Kidon up and running, aimed at European experts who supported the Condor joint venture.

A German engineer who lived in the tiny principality of Monaco and had offices near Salzburg, Austria, was approached gently by Mossad operatives who asked him to cut his ties to the Condor project. They thought that a threat was implicit, but he simply continued his work.

Next, his car was blown up. He was not in it at the time. He stubbornly stayed with his Condor work, so a few weeks later his Salzburg offices were set on fire. That was the German's breaking point, and he quit the program.

Argentina eventually succumbed to pressure by Israel, and, more importantly, by the United States government and ended the project. The Egyptians were left empty-handed and wanted to get something from their investment. They sold their part of the missile work to Saddam Hussein's Iraq.

The Iraqi dictator was a megalomaniac, constantly active on all possible aggressive fronts. Saddam was working on chemical, biological, and nuclear weapons. He was also working on a wide array of delivery systems.

In early 1990, he threatened that he would "scorch half of Israel," wording that was interpreted by Aman analysts as a hint that he seriously intended to launch his missiles westward with chemical warheads atop them.

All of his projects were seen by Israel as major threats, perhaps even to the Jewish state's existence. They naturally became high-priority targets for Israeli intelligence.

The Mossad discovered the key role of an Egyptian nuclear scientist who worked for the Iraqis, Yehia Meshad. Following its traditional pattern, the Mossad first tried to persuade him to cooperate with Israel. When he refused, a Kidon team was sent to locate him. The trail led to a hotel in Paris, a much easier place to strike than Baghdad would be. Meshad was murdered in his room in June 1980. French police found no traces of the killers and concluded that it was a professional job. That was all they ever said about it.

The Iraqi nuclear program continued to make progress, however, and Saddam's regime was investing heavily in ways to launch or drop the bomb he hoped to build. He was attracted by an innovative but doubtful idea: the Super Gun. This was the brainchild of an obsessed Canadian scientist, Gerald Bull, who had made a career of designing weapons for anyone who would finance his pet projects. He did some work for America's Pentagon, for South Africa, and for other clients, and then moved his operations to Europe.

Along the way, Bull offered his services to Israel. His ideas were deemed interesting, but not something that the Israelis needed. They already had technologically advanced delivery systems: warplanes and missiles.

Bull's big gun concept fascinated Saddam: an enormous rifle, to be aimed threateningly at his enemies—very, very far away. Bull was hired to start building, in an Iraqi desert, a mammoth cannon. His calculations indicated that it could even launch a payload into orbit. Pointed at Israel or other countries, the Super Gun would probably not be accurate—but if the warhead were nuclear, it would not have to be.

Bull worked out of his home in Brussels, actually an apartment rented by his Belgian girlfriend. It was on the sixth floor of a modern building in the Uccle district of the capital.

The Mossad, with its former operative, Prime Minister Yitzhak Shamir giving approval, decided to eliminate Bull. After all, he might succeed at perfecting his giant artillery, and thus he was an active danger.

Kidon teams did thorough reconnaissance of Bull's habits, his travels, and his home. Before long, three "Moroccan" men rented an apartment in a different wing of his building. The key they were issued would not open the entrance to Bull's part of the block, but the building's wings were connected through an underground garage. It was an excellent situation: The Team was easily able to get to the target, but it was not living too close to him. No one would remember any connection between them.

One day in March 1990, told by lookouts that Bull was heading back to his apartment—and after checking to be sure that the man's girlfriend was not at home—Kidon men with silencers screwed onto their pistols waited outside his door. As he walked up the hallway, they shot him several times in the head.

Ironically, an Israeli lived in the same wing as Bull. Belgian police were so confused about the crime that, at least for a while, they thought that a Moroccan hit team had killed the Israeli. An assassinated Canadian seemed inexplicable. Bull's son later told investigators that strangers had called his father several times and had warned him to stop working for the Iraqi regime.

The operation in Brussels fit into Kidon's fairly standard procedure, but Gerald Bull was an unusual choice of target. He was neither a Nazi nor an Arab terrorist. He was a Western scientist.

For the Mossad and the political echelon that approves its missions, it is easier to find justification for issuing death warrants on Palestinians, Arabs, and Muslims. This is not precisely a racist attitude, but a pattern based on the realities of the conflict: that Israel's most direct enemies are in those three categories.

True, two decades earlier, the Mossad had pursued German scientists. That decision was a product of its time, when Holocaust memories were still fresh, and all of those Germans helping Nasser's Egypt had previously served Hitler's Third Reich.

It is more complicated when Israel feels compelled occasionally to target citizens of nations that are basically friendly. Indeed, since Bull's slaying, Israeli hit squads never targeted a Westerner.

Ten months later, Saddam Hussein showed that he did not need the Super Gun to strike at Israel. As the Gulf War was raging in early 1991, he showered the Jewish state with 39 Scud missiles. Israeli leaders refrained from retaliating, because of restrictions imposed by the George H.W. Bush administration, and they felt humiliated. They believed that they somehow had to strike back—not simply for the sake of face-saving but to restore deterrence, always a key part of Israeli defense.

IDF Chief of Staff Ehud Barak, a lover of special operations, concocted yet another plan that was truly unprecedented: a plot to assassinate the leader of a foreign country. The target would be Saddam, and the plan would involve Israeli soldiers penetrating deep into Iraq. Barak brought the idea to Defense Minister Moshe Arens. They were both very frustrated by America's handcuffing of Israel. Arens okayed the preparations.

Israel, except for one case, had never before considered killing the leader of a country. The exception was Egypt's Nasser.

As a general rule, Israel's own leaders concluded long ago that if they started down the path of targeting the leaders of states, it would change the rules of the game. The Middle East conflict would be even uglier, and the tactic could backfire.

Therefore, heads of state were out of bounds—even during the heyday of extreme hatred and state-sponsored terrorism.

This deviation, trying to eliminate Iraq's dictator, was justified by the notion that he had violated two taboos: His missile strikes tried to hit Dimona; and he had targeted the largest of civilian targets, Tel Aviv, the icon of modern Israel.

Still, there was a great deal of hesitation on the Israeli side. Prime Minister Yitzhak Rabin, who had replaced Shamir and now also held the defense ministry portfolio, was reluctant.

Rabin found support in his skepticism from the Mossad chief, Shabtai Shavit, who succeeded Nahum Admoni in 1989. Rabin and Shavit concluded that it would be nearly impossible to get close to Saddam for a short-range hit by Kidon teams. They also knew that the Iraqi dictator rarely went out in public and often sent out body doubles instead.

Rabin gave Barak a green light only to practice the plan being developed, but without promising an okay for its final execution.

The plan, codenamed "Bramble Bush," called for finding a day that President Saddam would be making a public appearance outdoors. Mossad and Aman collection units—which had the use of Israel's first reconnaissance satellite—worked hard to keep track of Saddam's schedule and movements.

Iraqi agents working for the Mossad provided the information that he would be attending a ceremony to inaugurate a new bridge over the Tigris River. The agents found a hotel that, while quite distant, would have a clear shot at the ceremony site.

A few Sayeret Matkal commandos were selected to be flown secretly into Iraq by helicopter, and agents would pick them up and drive them to that hotel. On a pre-chosen balcony, they would have a newly developed shoulder-fired missile dubbed "Beyond the Horizon." Plans were made for alternate locations, as well.

On November 5, 1992, a year and a half after the Gulf War ended, the chosen commandos gathered at a large army training base in the Negev Desert for a dress rehearsal. In the audience sat the top brass of the Israeli military, including Barak, Aman chief Uri Saguy, and many intelligence officers.

Almost incredibly, considering their long track record of stunning successes, a fatal mix-up occurred. A missile that was supposed to be a harmless dummy, for what trainers called "a dry run," was mistakenly the "wet run" missile. It exploded within a group of Sayeret Matkal soldiers, killing five of them.

The tragedy for Israel's secretive commandos put an end to the plan titled Bramble Bush. Details started to leak out, as this accident was so major that censorship could not keep a lid on it. Non-Israeli newspapers reported that commandos died while planning to kill Hezbollah's Hassan Nasrallah in Lebanon. Within a few months, it became known that the intended target was Iraq's Saddam.

Prime Minister Rabin had never given the green light for the assassination mission, and the idea was dropped. Israel, since then, has not gone after national leaders—not even Iran's president, Mahmoud Ahmadinejad, who publicly advocated wiping Israel off the map.

Israel's intelligence community returned to its long-term assassinations playbook: pursuing and targeting senior Palestinian planners of violence. That was the strategy after the massacre at the 1972 Munich Olympics, and another catalyst for lethal action came in 1976.

While Sayeret Matkal troops brilliantly ended the hijacking of the Air France plane to Entebbe, Uganda, the Mossad could not rest until it figured out who had formed the team of Arab and German hijackers. The answer turned out to be Wadia Haddad, head of the small Popular Front for the Liberation of Palestine.

Haddad seemed certain to be planning more attacks on Israelis, and they intended to erase him first.

Caesarea, the Mossad's operations department, struggled to find ways to get at Haddad. He had based himself in Baghdad and seemed to travel only between Iraq and Yemen. By late 1977, the Mossad recruited one of Haddad's trusted assistants to spy for Israel. He was the man who delivered the poisonous chocolates to the terrorist chief with the fatal sweet tooth.

The Mossad made a point of watching for whether his faction—which had broken away from Yasser Arafat's mainstream PLO—would continue without Haddad. To the Mossad's delight, it did not. Airplane hijackings became a nuisance of the past.

In the view of Israeli intelligence, it is worthwhile to kill "the snake's head" when an organization is basically a one-man show. Eliminate that one man, and a group that is small and dependent on its mastermind will most likely collapse.

That lesson was almost immediately put into practice again, this time on the French Riviera. In July 1979, Kidon assassins waited with their silenced pistols outside Zuheir Mohsen's apartment near a casino in Cannes and then shot him in the head.

The target was the leader of a Syrian-sponsored Palestinian group that in 1975 sent terrorists onto the beach in Tel Aviv. The Arab attackers holed up in a hotel, and in a furious firefight with Sayeret Matkal soldiers, 11 hostages and seven of the Palestinians were killed.

At least according to the official Israeli view, the Kidon gunmen in Cannes were not meting out revenge for past atrocities. Mohsen had to be eliminated, because he would almost surely organize more such spectaculars.

Now, his chapter in the region's bloody history was over. As in the case of Haddad's splinter group, Mohsen's was buried with its founder. Their two organizations were never heard from again, thanks to assassinations.

The same expectation lay behind an assassination plan hatched by Shabtai Shavit. He had the almost-perfect career of a good Israeli intelligence officer. In his military service, he fought in Sayeret Matkal. Then he joined the Mossad; and that included a spell, undercover, in the Shah's Iran as a case officer who was running agents inside Iraq.

Later, Shavit would head the Caesarea department and became strongly linked with the "special tasks" in the official name of the Mossad.

The special target for October 1995 would be Fathi Shkaki, the leader of a deadly, diminutive terrorist group called Palestinian Islamic Jihad (PIJ). PIJ was established in Gaza in the 1980s, combining a PLO-linked nationalism with a strong emphasis on radical Islam.

Despite its limited size, PIJ proved very effective during the first intifada and, even more so, in the wave of suicide bombings following the 1993 Oslo peace accords. PIJ often seemed in competition with its larger Islamic soul-mate, Hamas, to recruit Palestinians willing to give their lives for the cause—killing more Israelis, with the eventual goal of destabilizing the Jewish state.

Shkaki, despite leading a Sunni Muslim organization, was an enthusiastic supporter of Iran's efforts to spread a Shi'ite Muslim revolution.

In January 1995, two of his followers blew themselves up in the middle of a crowd of off-duty Israeli paratroops—killing 20 of them. This was during the heyday of the Oslo reconciliation with the Palestinians, and the Israeli public was very shocked.

That attack inside Israel, more than anything else, sealed Shkaki's fate. As was his habit, he granted interviews and boasted about his achievement.

Yet, as usual, the Mossad's decision to assassinate him was not a matter of revenge. The goal truly was to decapitate PIJ. Eliminating Shkaki would kill his organization, since there were no deputies to recruit or direct dangerous followers.

The Mossad and Aman, consulting their constantly updated target files, knew almost everything about Shkaki, his personality, his thinking, and his associates. Yet, one important component was missing—his movements. Actually, he hardly ever went anywhere. Shkaki sat in the safe environs of Damascus, sucking at the twin financial teets of Syria's President Hafez al-Assad and of Iran.

Syria was not unknown territory for Mossad and Aman special operatives. They sometimes entered parts of Syria for intelligence-gathering purposes. Yet, careful study by the two agencies concluded that it would be very difficult to reach Shkaki in his Damascus lair.

Caesarea's operational planners would have to wait for an opportunity. That was provided by—of all people—Libya's Colonel Qaddafi.

In the autumn of 1995, Qaddafi invited the leader of one of Shkaki's rival radical Palestinian groups to the Libyan capital, Tripoli. It seemed that the erratic dictator would be offering large amounts of money to his latest favorite.

At Mossad headquarters in Glilot, Caesarea's planners—acting on pure intuition—figured that Shkaki would want his slice of the Libyan pie. Important to the operation was the fact that since 1988, when Libyan agents blew-up a Pan Am airliner over Lockerbie, Scotland, international sanctions blocked all civilian air connections with Libya. One of the very few routes to get there was to take a ferry boat from the island nation of Malta.

If Caesarea's guess was correct, Shkaki would have to leave Damascus and fly to Malta. All the Mossad would have to do would be to watch the airports and passenger lists.

Waiting for a target was an old but innovative method of the joint Mossad-Shin Bet operations department, going back to chasing Soviet-bloc spies in Israel in the 1960s: "the Comb." Lacking a large number of operatives to shadow suspects, the Israelis learned to wait in a particular area after anticipating the target's next move.

Aman intercepted a telephone call between Damascus and Tripoli, discussing details of Shkaki's forthcoming travel. Libya was fairly well covered by Israeli intelligence, and Qaddafi was worth watching. He supported a wide array of radical Palestinian groups. In addition, Libya was believed to be acting on his ambitions of acquiring non-conventional weapons. Israel would have to know about such threats.

When it came to Shkaki, the Mossad's gut feeling was panning out. The Palestinian did, indeed, leave his nest in Damascus. He flew to Valetta, the capital of Malta, heading to Libya in hopes of a handout from Qaddafi for terrorism organizations.

That was the moment that Israeli operatives sprang into action. They knew that he had been in Malta before, on a similar trip, and his personal security habits there were lax. The Mossad figured that he would stay in the same hotel as before—and he did. Shkaki also used the same Libyan passport, under a fake name, as he had previously.

Upon arrival, he felt so unafraid that he went out on a shopping trip. Even terrorists have to buy things for the folks back home. This gave Israeli teams an excellent chance to keep tabs on Shkaki.

The assassins acted as they were taught during their long training. On October 26, 1995, with no apparent hesitation or panic, two of the Israelis got on a motorcycle and headed for Shkaki as he was walking. One of the gunmen shot Shkaki in the head, again showing the much-practiced skill of shooting accurately from a moving motorcycle. The attack took barely 20 seconds.

The Israelis sped off and left hardly any evidence. The motorcycle was untraceable: not bought or stolen locally, but imported onto the island by the Mossad. Its license plate was forged.

The assassins also benefited from the Maltese police announcing only that a Libyan merchant—Shkaki's fake identity—had been mysteriously shot dead.

Perhaps Malta was trying to protect its reputation as a tourist destination, rather than a battleground for Palestinians and Israelis.

The more interesting story that a terrorist chief had been assassinated did not come out for days, and the Israeli combatants were long gone by then. They apparently left the island by boarding a ship that had been pre-positioned nearby by the Mossad.

The death of Shkaki was the last major decision by Prime Minister Rabin, who himself was assassinated the very next week by a Jewish zealot. Had Yigal Amir evaded arrest in Tel Aviv, Israeli intelligence might have thought the shooting was Palestinian retaliation for the Malta hit.

For a while, Shkaki's murder fit into the desirable Mossad scenario: that ending the life of the leader of a small group kills the group. His replacement was a Palestinian professor who taught in Florida, Ramadan Abdullah Shallah. Born in Gaza, and operating out of Damascus, he was designated a "most wanted terrorist" by the FBI in November 1995.

Shallah had no background in operations, so under him the organization was having trouble returning to its full, violent functions. Eventually, he caught on. PIJ suicide bombings resumed, so the killing of Shkaki had provided a respite of only a year or two.

For the Mossad and Israeli political leaders, that was enough to justify the assassination. They could argue that even in a relatively short period, dozens of lives were probably saved.

There was a changing of the guard in Jerusalem in May 1996, as Benjamin Netanyahu was elected prime minister. A year later, Palestinian terrorists showed that they liked his being in power.

Netanyahu, the former Sayeret officer, had pledged to voters that he would be tough on terrorism. He did not believe in the Oslo process, and had it not been for the Clinton administration in Washington he would have stopped negotiations with the PLO. His tough stance encouraged radical Palestinians to feel that they, in turn, should be even harder on the Israelis.

In July 1997, in a brutally sophisticated terrorist attack, Hamas sent two suicide bombers to the busiest market in Jerusalem. One human bomb went off, and the second man waited around as rescue units arrived. He pushed the button on his suicide vest and caused even more casualties. Sixteen Israelis were killed and 170 wounded.

Within hours, Netanyahu summoned the Mossad director, Danny Yatom, to Jerusalem from his headquarters at Glilot. Yatom had been an army general, but he was inexperienced at the Mossad—barely a year in office after replacing Shavit. Yatom had been selected by Shimon Peres for only one reason: the murder of Rabin.

Yatom had been the top military advisor to Prime Minister Rabin, and after the 1995 assassination he claimed that Rabin had promised him the Mossad directorship. There was no supportive evidence of that, neither written nor anyone else's memory, but Peres did not want to be depicted as dishonoring "Rabin's will."

Though he had been a Sayeret Matkal commando, Yatom had developed into a neat and organized headquarters officer who was nicknamed "the Prussian."

In Netanyahu's office just after the slaughter in west Jerusalem, the prime minister demanded a quick response against Hamas. Yatom, trying to impress his boss but perhaps not knowing how complicated intelligence operations could be, said *yes* without expressing any reservations.

Back at his headquarters, he instructed Caesarea and the research department to find him someone to strike. The pool of possibilities, known in the Mossad as the "bank of targets," was limited and poor at the time. There were no suitable and operationally reachable targets available immediately among Hamas leaders.

Netanyahu was impatient and kept pressing Yatom. The Mossad director, in turn, impatiently pressed his underlings. It took a while, but they came up with a few minor targets. These were considered, but dismissed. One man was too unimportant. Another lived in a European country, and that was ruled out. A third, in the United Arab Emirates, would be very difficult to reach.

The process resembled the person who loses a valuable piece of jewelry, then searches only in places around him that are well lit. It is a lazy, but common, approach. In the Mossad's search process, the easy solution they alighted upon was Khaled Meshaal, and the location would be Jordan's capital, Amman.

There were two problems with this choice: Meshaal was not truly important in Hamas and certainly had no role in the group's terrorism campaign. More significantly, Jordan was Israel's strategic asset in the region. King Hussein had met secretly with Israelis—including dozens of times with Mossad chiefs—long before signing a peace treaty in 1994. He provided information and coordinated his political stands with Israel.

Jordanian intelligence was one of the Mossad's best allies, to the point that they acted together against their common enemy: the Palestinians.

The Jordanians were tipping off the Mossad about terrorists, handing them over to Israel on occasion, and letting Israelis observe interrogations of radical Palestinians. Jordanian intelligence even showed a readiness to assassinate Hamas and Hezbollah militants.

Neither Netanyahu nor Yatom gave enough thought to the grave risk of jeopardizing that relationship. An assassination in Jordan, even if successful, could backfire, yet no one in the Mossad's upper ranks seemed to recognize the danger. Everyone seemed to buy into the group-think of being yes men.

The operation was initiated hastily, and that was further hastened by another Hamas attack in early September. This time, the group sent three suicide bombers to the main pedestrian mall in Jerusalem. Five Israelis were killed, and 180 people were wounded.

The prime minister became even more pushy. Kidon did not get to practice for the planned Amman operation as much as it normally liked to do.

A lot of thinking, however, did go into the choice of weapon: not a car bomb that would cause a lot of damage in friendly Jordan's capital; not even a silenced pistol, because, to intelligence operatives, any shooting is considered a "noisy operation." Instead, poison was selected—yet another one prepared by scientists at Israel's super-secret Nes Tziona biological institute. It would be loaded into a hand-held aerosol spray device.

The lethal beauty of this poison was that the victim would not appear to have been murdered. The death would seem to be natural, from a breakdown of body systems.

The Team members practiced how to use the spray. This was done on some crowded Tel Aviv streets. Israeli bystanders would find themselves suddenly approached from behind by someone who opened a Coca Cola can right by their ear. Kidon's team was testing how people would react to the approach and a spraying sound close up.

The head of the Kidon unit would be on the scene in Amman, but most of the others he chose for the mission were not the most experienced operatives. Jordan, after all, was deemed a friendly place where risks would be lower. There were only 10 Israelis on the mission, and that did have the advantage of minimizing the chance of being noticed and caught.

All the while ignoring how Jordan might react, The Team moved into place. The intelligence on Meshaal was almost perfect: where he lived, how he got to and from the Hamas office, who was usually with him, and what the moments of vulnerability might be. Exit routes were mapped out.

An Israeli female doctor from a Tel Aviv hospital—who had done some work for the Mossad from time to time—went to the Intercontinental Hotel in Amman with a top Caesarea officer. He was Mishka Ben-David, the future author of spy novels and the coordinator for the team aiming to eliminate Meshaal.

It was common for Kidon operations to have a doctor standing by. It was unusual, however, that her first aid kit included an antidote, also developed at Nes Tziona, to be used in case the Kidon members came into contact with the poison.

On September 25, 1997, two Kidon assassins were waiting with the aerosol device at the entrance to the Hamas office. Meshaal arrived by car with his driver, but also with his daughter. Her presence was unexpected.

Now things started happening fast, but not as Kidon had envisioned them. The little girl exited the car and rushed toward her father, calling "Baba! Baba!" (Arabic for Daddy). The driver seemed to be chasing her up the walkway. That was the first interruption to the Kidon plan.

A second team, acting as spotters, signaled to the assassins that they should attack immediately—lest the girl and the driver get in the way. The original plan had been to spray the poison into Meshaal's ear only when he reached the office building itself. Now they did it, a few yards in front of the building. The

Palestinian suddenly turned, so he was sprayed on the back of his head, rather than in the ear. Still, the poison would be effective, on any part of the skin.

Meshaal immediately collapsed. Later, he would say, "I felt a loud noise in my ear. It was like a boom, like an electric shock. Then I had a shivering sensation in my body like an electric shock." Soon he began to vomit, and then Meshaal could not breathe on his own.

The driver, the daughter, and some bystanders rushed to him. The two Israelis walked away, with the professional calmness of practiced assassins. They got into a getaway car, driven by none other than the head of Kidon. He was acting as commander of this operation.

Another surprise derailed The Team's plan. A courier for Hamas was walking toward the office, and he saw everything. He was not a bodyguard but showed that he had the instincts of one. He noted the license plate number of the getaway car as it drove off, turned right, and vanished from sight.

The two assassins told their commander, in the car, that someone had just noticed the number. For reasons not fully explained, someone panicked and the two assassins left the car.

A third twist tangled the plot. The Hamas courier ran after the car, took the right turn on foot, and, to his surprise, saw the car parked and the two strangers hurrying off in separate directions. He immediately jumped on one of them. The second returned from his escape route and, using his martial arts skill, hit the courier and knocked him out.

The getaway car, driven by the head of Kidon, managed to leave the scene, but a crowd of Jordanians surrounded the two assassins and the Palestinian they had just rendered unconscious.

The two strangers tried to explain that they had just been mugged, that they were Canadian visitors, and that they just wanted to go back onto the tourist trail. More bad luck was added to this chain of unfortunate events when local police showed up.

While the two Israelis continued to claim that they were mere tourists, a police officer stopped a taxi that was passing and ordered the two foreigners to get inside. The Hamas courier, who was just regaining consciousness, was also loaded into the taxi.

It seemed like a scene from a slapstick movie, but this was real. And it was not funny.

In the crowded taxi, if the two "Canadians" hoped that they would be driven to safety, they were wrong. The courier next to them kept shouting, "Meshaal! Meshaal!" And the Jordanian officer in the taxi had it drive to a nearby police station.

Jordan's police did what they should and called the Canadian embassy to report that two of its citizens were apparently in custody. A diplomat came to the police station and had a brief chat with the two men. He did not think that they were his countrymen.

Meshaal, meantime, was rushed to a hospital. He was unconscious.

Jordanian's domestic security service sent several investigators to the police station, and the two foreigners were harshly questioned. They did not break down and stuck to their story.

The four other Kidon members, including the commander, drove to their respective hotels. They informed the coordinator, Mishka Ben-David, that the operation had not gone as planned and that the two assassins were in trouble.

Ben-David then communicated with the head of Caesarea, at Glilot headquarters. Going up Mossad's chain of command, Yatom and Netanyahu were almost instantly privy to the bad news.

Not losing his nerve, Ben-David drove the remaining four Kidon men to the Israeli embassy in Amman. He next went to the Inter-Continental to inform the doctor and calm her down. His intuition told him not to throw away the antidote, although there was the danger of its being used as evidence.

A few hours after the botched operation, Prime Minister Netanyahu placed a phone call to King Hussein and asked him to meet with the head of the Mossad that very day. That seemed fairly routine, so the king agreed. Not yet informed of the incident, he did not know that Meshaal was in critical condition in a hospital, or that two foreigners had been detained.

Yatom, in Amman that afternoon, informed the astonished king that Israeli intelligence had tried to kill Meshaal there. To say the least, the king was very angry. He felt that Israel had betrayed him and his years of cooperation. He was well aware that Yatom and his family had just spent a relaxed weekend, as a sign of good will, in the Jordanian port city, Aqaba.

In addition, just a few days before the assassination attempt, the king had met with a senior Mossad officer whom he liked: the man in charge of Jordan for the global liaison department, Tevel. Hussein had been pleased to hand over an unusually moderate offer from Hamas: for a 30-year truce with Israel.

Hussein did not know that the Mossad, busy with the offensive strike it was planning and other matters, had not immediately transmitted the truce offer to Prime Minister Netanyahu.

The king demanded that the four Israeli fugitives turn themselves in, right away, to Jordanian authorities. If not, he warned, he would send his commando soldiers to storm the Israeli embassy and seize them by force.

Taking responsibility for dealing with the crisis, Netanyahu ended up spending the whole night at Mossad headquarters. He made the highly unusual offer of providing the antidote that would revive Meshaal. The king accepted the offer.

Ben-David then met with a Jordanian intelligence counterpart. The Mossad man suggested that they go to the hospital with the Israeli doctor to administer the remedy. The Jordanian, not trusting the Israelis and perhaps fearing that they would try to finish off the job, refused the offer and took the antidote away.

The life of a Hamas leader, nearly extinguished by a fairly complex Israeli operation, was now saved by his sworn enemies.

Still, there was the matter of six Mossad team members, trapped in Jordan. A former Mossad deputy director, Efraim Halevy, was summoned from his ambassadorial post in Brussels: first to the agency's headquarters in Tel Aviv, and later to Amman. For many years, as head of Tevel, he had been the key go-between for King Hussein and Israeli prime ministers.

Halevy declared to longtime Mossad colleagues that Israel would have to find a way to make Hussein a hero in the eyes of Palestinians. Halevy suggested that Prime Minister Netanyahu free some of the most senior Hamas men who were held in Israeli prisons. Mossad analysts hated the idea and suggested alternatives, such as providing night vision equipment for Jordan's tank force and upgrading King Hussein's military jets.

Netanyahu said, though after strong reluctance, that he would consider freeing the spiritual leader and founder of Hamas, Sheikh Ahmed Yassin. Halevy flew to Amman, to start bargaining with and mollifying the king.

Hussein explained, in detail, why he was angry at Israel. But he let Halevy leave, by helicopter, with the four Israelis who had felt trapped inside their embassy.

Another ten days of negotiations ensued, launched by Netanyahu himself after a tense 20-minute nighttime helicopter flight from Jerusalem to Amman. Apparently sending a petulant message, the Jordanians did not illuminate the royal helipad, so an Israeli military chopper containing the prime minister and a raft of senior aides flew back and forth over Jordan's capital for a further half an hour. "One mistake," Halevy commented later, "and the whole mission could have ended in national tragedy."

The fate of the two Mossad assassins, jailed by the Jordanians and still claiming to be Canadians, hung in the balance. The deadlock was broken by Ariel Sharon.

Sharon, for many years, was feared by the king. The veteran general and cabinet minister had long thundered that Hussein's family should be forced out of power and replaced with a Palestinian state—as a better solution, in Sharon's eyes, than letting Arabs have sovereignty on the West Bank of the Jordan River.

In almost Mafia style, Sharon made an offer he thought Jordan could not refuse. He hinted to the king that if a solution were not found quickly, Israeli spies would return and strike in Amman again.

The good-guy bad-guy combination worked. A solution was found, but it was a painful one for Israel—and especially for Netanyahu. Yassin, the Hamas founder, was released. And so were the two "Canadians" held by Jordan.

Meshaal recovered fully, the near-death experience serving him well. He had been a small figure in Hamas, but now he would be considered an icon and a leader.

The crisis triggered by the assassination attempt was over, but hard feelings remained. King Hussein—who would die three years later in Amman, after lengthy treatments for cancer at the Mayo Clinic in Minnesota—never forgave or forgot what he considered Israel's treachery.

The Canadian government was also furious over the Mossad's use of genuine Canadian passports. These had been loaned to the Israeli government, or to Jewish Agency representatives, by innocent students from Canada who were visiting Israel. Some of the passports were doctored by changing the photographs.

That was exposed as a standard procedure for Mossad: "borrowing" passports, thus taking advantage of the goodwill of Jews and other visitors in Israel.

Israel promised Canada that it would not happen again, but that promise was not kept. Intelligence operations require their own evaluation system, sometimes weighing truth and honor against necessity.

The release of Hamas founder Sheikh Yassin was patently humiliating to Israeli authorities, as he gave a series of speeches to huge crowds in Gaza and praised suicide bombers heading into the Jewish state. He had a major role in stirring up the second intifada that began in 2000.

Yassin would be killed in March 2004, targeted by the Israeli air force in Gaza. That was eight months before Yasser Arafat's death. Two major leaders passed from the scene in the same year, but no major impact for good or for ill was noticed.

Israeli intelligence has wondered, at various junctures in the long conflict with the Palestinians, whether assassinations were ever very effective. They clearly were not when an operation failed, as with Meshaal in Jordan. They might be temporarily effective, when trying to snuff out small organizations, but certainly not against large groups such as Hezbollah, Hamas, or the PLO, which are solidly rooted in their own societies.

Senior intelligence professionals, regardless of their opinions about assassination as a weapon, realize that there are various sides to the issue. In the Middle East, if you do not smite your enemies, you will be seen as weak. But when you murder an enemy, the gains are often limited: at best delaying terrorist or enemy plots only for a few years.

Several inquiry committees looked into the failure in Jordan, including an internal panel in the Mossad. Yatom first tried to sidestep his responsibility by blaming his deputy, Aliza Magen, the highest-ranking female operative ever in the organization.

The inquiries did lead to the resignation or removal of several other managers in the agency, including the head of Caesarea.

Yatom himself quit in early 1998, after another failure on a smaller scale. In Berne, Switzerland, five Mossad operatives from the Neviot department, tasked with break-ins, were caught by police while bugging the telephones of a Hezbollah operative. Swiss authorities were intent on prosecuting one of the men. After prolonged negotiations, the Israeli government paid a few million dollars in bond and pledged that the Mossad man would return to stand trial.

Yatom had served for less than two years and was replaced by Efraim Halevy, who only a few months before had been smoothing King Hussein's ruffled feathers.

Halevy had very little personal involvement in operations—aside from disguising himself as an ultra-Orthodox Jew back in 1962, when Israel's spies were searching for the kidnapped boy named Yossele. Still, Prime Minister Netanyahu believed that Halevy could provide stability as he navigated the agency through the troubled waters left by the Meshaal affair.

The new Mossad chief started out badly with his Neviot and other operations officers, however. When Swiss prosecutors set a date for the trial of the Mossad man who was out on bond, Halevy felt it was a matter of honor that the operative should fly to Switzerland and take his chances in court.

Many in the Mossad, including two élite officers who wrote to Netanyahu to complain, insisted that their colleague not be forced to go on trial. Halevy insisted, and later he was deeply relieved when the man was given a suspended prison sentence and permitted to return home to Israel.

Years later, he wrote that in intelligence all decisions are "made in circumstances of uncertainty." Halevy continued: "You always have to take risks and be ready to shoulder responsibility for failure, just as you are willing to revel in success."

While some of the broader issues about assassinations were debated in public, there was one deeper impact that never truly surfaced: the psychological and emotional effects on Kidon combatants. Who monitors their stability? What effect might there be on how they feel about their country, when it sends them out to do such things? How damaging is all this to their family relationships and home life? They need counseling sometimes, and Kidon provides it.

The commander of Kidon in the mid-1990s, facing criticism that he felt was totally unfair, became depressed. He left the Mossad a short while after the failure of the Meshaal mission in Jordan.

Kidon combatants are not natural born killers. They are trained. Some who have anonymously made comments truly believe, often with the strong guidance of their instructors, that they murder for good cause. Only a very few members of The Team have expressed doubts and regrets for what they have done. That occurs mostly when an operation has been botched.

There have been numerous occasions in which Kidon teams were recalled home in the middle of a mission—for fear that they were about to be discovered and arrested or publicly exposed. Luckily for them, the poisonous experience in Jordan was the only one that went so badly wrong.

In his novel, Ben-David describes a Kidon operative who suffers a bad conscience for failing on a mission; he then runs his own, unauthorized operation to finish the job and kill the target. It might be assumed that the story is based on the failure in Amman, and the title *Beirut Duet* names a different Arab capital so as to mollify Israel's military censor.

Yet, perhaps the former Mossad man is hinting about something else, or prophesying the possibility of some renegade behavior in the future by a Kidon combatant or commander.

When Meir Dagan was chosen by Prime Minister Sharon to replace Halevy in September 2002, General Dagan prepared himself for the job by studying the Mossad's practices and history. He spoke with many former Mossad officials and read books.

One of the books he read was Ben-David's novel. The genuine new spymaster was impressed by the scenarios, methods, and tricks in the mostly made-up story. Dagan would later comment to his department chiefs: "I want you to be as imaginative as this book is."

CHAPTER TWENTY-THREE

WAR, NEAR AND FAR

I srael's spies would indeed be imaginative and creative—they had to be—in confronting Hezbollah, their dangerous enemy just to the north. The militant Shi'ite movement in Lebanon was high on Meir Dagan's priority list, second only to Iran. They were not truly separate issues, because Hezbollah was considered an embodiment of Iran's regional ambitions.

The big showdown came in July 2006, when Israeli politicians and the army felt they had to respond massively to Hezbollah's kidnapping of two IDF soldiers along the border with Lebanon. The intelligence agencies were very active the entire time: before, during, and after what became known as the Second Lebanon War.

The fighting lasted for 34 days. Israeli troops crossed into Lebanon, parts of that country were pounded by air strikes, and Hezbollah fought back fiercely by firing 4,000 rockets at Israeli civilians.

The results were highly controversial in Israel. Critics charged that Prime Minister Ehud Olmert made a hasty decision to go to war without adequate preparation and thinking. It was a huge commitment, and one that would force more than one-quarter of all Israelis out of their homes—all for the sake of two missing men.

Top IDF commanders were accused of lacking a clear sense of mission and being indecisive about staging a ground invasion. The day-after experts, including retired officers now fitting the mold of armchair generals, said that commando forces could have been flown deep into Lebanon—behind enemy lines—to smother Hezbollah.

Supporters of the war saw a different picture. Israel inflicted significant damage on Hezbollah, and air raids destroyed all of that organization's long-range missiles. Israeli jets also flattened a complex of buildings in southern Beirut that had served as the political and military base for Shi'ite power.

After the United Nations arranged a ceasefire in mid-August, 30,000 U.N. peacekeepers moved into southern Lebanon and created a buffer zone between the Israeli border and Hezbollah forces. The Shi'ite militants were no longer allowed to move around freely, wearing uniforms and bearing weapons like a huge quasi-army.

There also was the helpful fact that leading Sunni Muslim countries—notably Saudi Arabia, Egypt, and the Gulf kingdoms—barely said a word.

They did not support Hezbollah, and they shed no tears when Israel struck hard at Iran's proxy in Lebanon.

Meir Dagan was able personally to feel a fresh wave of understanding. The Mossad chief, traveling without any public announcement and usually with a false name on his documents, held talks in several Arab capitals and exchanged surprisingly similar views about Iran and its hegemonic goals.

Upon his return to headquarters at Glilot, he told his analysts that the Middle East had two worlds: the open, visible one mainly for public consumption; and the covert, underground world in which rivals rally together against common enemies.

Israeli intelligence happily found itself unstained by the war's aftermath, even in the findings of an official investigatory panel. The committee did level some criticism, but that was mainly about field intelligence not being well disseminated from headquarters to soldiers at the front.

There is no doubt, however, that strategic intelligence was excellent. That was the product of combining the humint assets of the Mossad and Aman, together with Aman's Unit 8200 and its unrivaled sigint. Analysts in both agencies also used new names for some traditional ways of collecting data: "osint," meaning intelligence based on open sources, such as websites, newspapers, and radio shows; and "visint," which referred to visual intelligence from observation posts near borders, low-flying planes (including drones), and increasingly satellites orbiting Earth.

Israel's unique strength continued to lie in human intelligence. In the years leading up to the 2006 Lebanese war, the Mossad and Aman managed to recruit important assets inside Lebanon. Communications networks there were easily penetrated, and tapping into all manner of conversations helped the Israelis identify Hezbollah targets that ought to be hit, whenever a war might break out.

The most impressive intelligence was identifying—with great specificity— private houses where Hezbollah hid the long-range missiles that could perhaps reach Tel Aviv. At least a hundred of what were basically domestic launching pads were constructed with the secret help of Iran's al-Quds Force. Iranian engineers designed extensions to the houses with an innovative feature: sliding roofs like missile silos. The convertible tops could be opened to launch a surprise weapon toward Israel.

As a reward, the homeowners and neighbors would get money from Hezbollah, financed by Iran.

That entire network of houses and missiles was destroyed by precise air strikes in the first 34 minutes of the war—reminiscent of the pivotal first three hours of the Six-Day War in 1967. The exact locations in Lebanon were provided by the Mossad and Aman. A retired chief of analysis at Aman called that "the result of years of determined, individual, gray, exhausting intelligence work, and one of Israel's greatest successes in target intelligence."

The loss of Hassan Nasrallah's most potent missiles turned his words into hollow threats. The maverick secretary-general of Hezbollah boasted, in the first days of the war, that he would hit "beyond Haifa," meaning Tel Aviv. He no longer had the capacity to do that.

All he had left were short-range rockets. They certainly were disruptive to normal life, and even fatal, for residents of northern Israel—about a million forced to sleep in shelters or move to safer parts of the country to the south—but the damage and casualties were far less than Hezbollah had hoped to inflict.

Nasrallah, after the war, admitted that he regretted having provoked Israel. He told Hezbollah's TV station that had he known "the Zionists" would react so massively, he would not have ordered the operation to kidnap the two soldiers.

His interview was an echo of secret meetings he had with his master, the commander of the al-Quds Force, Iran's Major-General Qassem Suleimani. Al-Quds was the special unit of the Revolutionary Guards in charge of covert action outside Iran's borders and maintaining ties with pro-Iran militias and terrorists. The United States publicly blamed the al-Quds Force for a campaign of roadside bombs that caused many American casualties inside Iraq.

Israeli intelligence quickly learned that Suleimani strongly scolded Nasrallah over the results of the war. He accused the Lebanese Shi'ite of not being cautious and of failing to coordinate the kidnapping of the two Israelis with him. The Iranian's biggest complaint was that the missile launchers with the sliding roofs were no longer a secret—and no longer in existence. Iran had meant to save them for a much bigger showdown, when Iran and Israel might go to war.

Feeling humiliated and penetrated after the war, Hezbollah launched a witch-hunt for Lebanese who had spied for Israel and claimed to have caught a handful. TV stations in Lebanon showed evidence, including camouflaged communications equipment. Some suspects confessed to having been recruited by Israel 20 years earlier. As usual on such matters, Israel maintained its silence.

Yet, for Israel, the sum total of the Second Lebanon War was a strategic win.

There was no greater indication of Israeli victory than Nasrallah's disappearance. For more than five years after the war, he never dared to show his face in public. His televised rallies were all staged, trying to create the impression that he was addressing masses of supporters. He was actually exposing himself to very few people.

His fear, of course, was that Israel might assassinate him. Indeed, Israelis questioned themselves: Why didn't we kill Nasrallah during the war?

It could be that it was impossible to get him, as he went into hiding as soon as the war began. But it also could be that Israeli intelligence drew upon the lesson of 1992, when Nasrallah's predecessor in Hezbollah—Abbas Musawi—was assassinated. That led to massive retaliation in the form of a flattened Israeli embassy in Argentina.

For Israeli intelligence, the most important target in Hezbollah was not Nasrallah. It was his "defense minister," Imad Mughniyeh. He had been the Mossad's most wanted man—and also on the FBI's official list—for many years. Israel tried to kill Mughniyeh numerous times, not only at the funeral of his brother in 1994, where he did not show up.

He was very elusive. Knowing he was a target, he changed his face, he changed his safe houses often, he changed his vehicles, and he barely traveled: only to Damascus, Syria, and to his masters in Iran. Until Dagan became the Mossad chief, those locales were out of bounds for Israeli assassination operations.

In the end, the Mossad showed that it could be patient as a hawk waiting for its prey. Waiting and watching, for one mistake. One opportunity.

That came in February 2008 in Damascus.

Syria was a dangerous place for Mossad operatives. The government had a large security apparatus, unusually adept at spying on its own people. Foreigners, too, were under constant watch. When the Mossad wanted to operate in Damascus, it would be highly unlikely that Israelis would pose as citizens of a Western country—the usual technique in most places. It would be wiser to melt into Syrian crowds on the streets. And a Kidon team managed to do that.

The Mossad had done it, in fact, four years earlier in Damascus. Izzedin el-Khalil, a senior operative in the military wing of Hamas—the Palestinian Islamic movement—was killed by a bomb planted under his car in September 2004. That was an important operational landmark. For the first time, the Mossad proved that it could execute a lethal mission in a front-line enemy capital other than Beirut, even in such a tightly controlled police state as Syria.

That mission gave the Kidon unit a great deal of confidence that it could carry out such strikes under the most challenging conditions imaginable. That was fully in accord with the undeclared motto of the Mossad, that everything is do-able.

Piecing together humint and telephone intercepts, Israeli intelligence managed to learn a great deal about Mughniyeh's private life and tracked his movements, finally aware of his post-plastic surgery appearance. They took advantage of two human weaknesses, quite uncharacteristic for a master terrorist on the run.

First, hosted by Syrian intelligence in one of its guest apartments, and in constant contact with Iranian "diplomats," Mughniyeh felt totally comfortable in Damascus. Living for decades with the assumption that he was an assassination target, he must have craved a place to feel safe. He let down his guard when in Syria, moving around with full self-confidence and no fear.

He also permitted himself to do, in Damascus, what he did not do at home in Lebanon: fool around with women. That, too, meant that he was literally a man about town, in moving cars more than a cautious man would be. Spies for the Mossad took note of routes that he repeatedly took.

A Kidon team, acting with great care in an enemy capital, managed to plant a bomb in or on Mughniyeh's Japanese four-wheel-drive vehicle on February 12, 2008. The terrorist's career ended with a blast. His body parts were scattered, but no one else was killed.

This was a triumph for the men and women of Israeli intelligence. They had accomplished the nearly impossible. Their feeling was similar to the satisfaction Americans would enjoy, three years later, when Navy Seals found and killed Osama bin Laden.

In Beirut, Nasrallah was paralyzed with shock. He and Mughniyeh had practically grown up together, running Hezbollah hand in hand for 16 years. Mughniyeh had been in charge of the organization's clandestine dealings with Syria and Iran. He coordinated the acquisition of missiles and other weapons from those two countries, and he plotted all of Hezbollah's terrorist attacks.

Mughniyeh had also been responsible for the personal security of the secretary-general. One can only imagine what went through Nasrallah's head when he heard of the violent death of his closest confidant.

The message of this flawless hit, which left no traces, was clear: If the Israelis could get Mughniyeh in Syria, they could get Nasrallah in Lebanon.

Eliminating Mughniyeh did have a strong impact on the military capabilities of Hezbollah. When debating the plusses and minuses of assassinations, Israeli intelligence typically felt frustrated when the head of a large, well-established terrorist group could be replaced quickly by a deputy.

Yet, in this case, the removal of Mughniyeh truly made a difference. The fear factor—the impact on Nasrallah—was strong. He would now waste a lot more time and energy on protecting himself, and on searching for Israeli spies in Hezbollah.

Furthermore, no one man was able to manage all of Mughniyeh's roles. His duties were divided among four men, who formed a kind of collective that directed Hezbollah's "military" operations. The strongest of them was Mustafa Bader al-Din, a brother-in-law of Mughniyeh, who was clearly a man of violence. He had been indicted for the murder of a former Lebanese prime minister, Rafik Hariri, a pro-Western billionaire killed by a huge car bomb on the orders of the Syrian government in 2005.

The next known assassination by the Mossad was, compared with eliminating Mughniyeh and Khalil in Damascus, like a stroll in the park. At least, that was the expectation.

The arena chosen was Dubai, the bustling and always growing port city in the United Arab Emirates. Its openness made it a major attraction for Western businesspeople, front companies for Iran's Revolutionary Guards, and Palestinian terrorists. Thus, it offered a wealth of possibilities for spies to melt into the foreign community, and also a wealth of targets for espionage operations.

Situated just across the Persian Gulf from Iran, Dubai was clearly a hub for Iranian subterfuges to circumvent sanctions. The UAE had an excellent financial system, used by Iran's front companies and by individuals who wanted banking with no questions asked. It was no wonder that A.Q. Khan's nuclear network operated out of Dubai. And it was similarly predictable that Western intelligence agencies considered the city a window into Iran. The CIA had a large presence in Dubai, under diplomatic cover or using deeper legends.

The Mossad did not have a permanent station in Dubai, but its operatives used borrowed identities to pass through very often. They felt almost at home there.

The assassination target chosen was a shadowy Hamas operative named Mahmoud al-Mabhouh. He was well known to the Israeli intelligence community.

Mabhouh had personally led Hamas's first lethal attack in 1989, just a few years after the organization's establishment: the kidnappings and killings of two Israeli soldiers. In separate incidents, three months apart, Mabhouh and his men drove from Gaza into Israel. They disguised themselves as Orthodox Jews in a car with Israeli license plates. Taking advantage of the transportation habits of off-duty IDF soldiers, the Hamas attackers picked up their hitchhiking victims, then assaulted and killed them.

Though he was wanted in Israel by Shin Bet for the murders, that was not the reason the Mossad set out to get Mabhouh. The motive was not revenge. The Israelis were focused on the greater danger he had become.

After the second killing in Israel, Mabhouh had escaped to Egypt and from there to Syria. In Damascus, he rose through the Hamas ranks and became the chief of logistics and of the supply of weapons to Hamas's military wing operating in Gaza.

Despite the religious differences between the Sunni Muslims of Hamas and Shi'ite Iran, the al-Quds Force of the Revolutionary Guards became the biggest supplier of arms to Hamas. Weapons were shipped to ports along the Red Sea in Sudan, then smuggled into Egypt and on to the underground tunnels from Sinai to Gaza. Mabhouh was in charge of these supply lines, which enabled Hamas to rain home-made and Iranian rockets onto southern towns in Israel.

While Mabhouh was not in the top leadership of the political or military wings of Hamas, the Mossad and Aman considered him a key figure and an important target. The Israelis believed that getting him out of the way would disrupt the arms-smuggling conveyor belt from Iran to Gaza—at least for a while.

With relative ease, Kidon teams located Mabhouh in Damascus and put him under surveillance. The Palestinian knew that Israelis were shadowing him and tried to evade them. Granting a rare interview, he made sure to keep his face covered and claimed that Israeli intelligence had tried to kill him three times. Once, he said, he spotted assassins trying to attach a bomb to his car.

Proud of his skill, Mabhouh said, "As far as the Israelis, my hands are stained with their blood. Thank God that I am very cautious."

In fact, he was not. The Mossad, in 2010, would help him achieve an aspiration he had declared on TV: "I hope to become a martyr."

Israeli intelligence established that he regularly visited Dubai, where he would conduct meetings with Hamas's Iranian suppliers in office buildings and hotels. Aman's Unit 8200 monitored his phone calls and other communications.

Once the decision was made to eliminate Mabhouh, the Caesarea unit's planners considered where would be best to execute the operation. Despite the few previous successes in Damascus, Dubai was judged to be a much safer place.

In early January, Dagan presented the assassination plan to Benjamin Netanyahu. Fourteen years earlier, Netanyahu—the first time he was prime minister—approved the operation to kill Khaled Meshaal of Hamas in Amman; that turned out to be a fiasco. Yet this time, he showed no hesitation in sanctioning the Mabhouh killing.

There were key differences. Israel had no official relations with Dubai, and it was not an important strategic ally like Jordan was. The plan also looked reasonable to Netanyahu, with a high chance of success.

On January 19, Mabhouh flew from Damascus to Dubai. He was using a false name and passport. Arriving in the afternoon, he checked into the Al Bustan Rotana, a five-star hotel. His bodyguards would not be arriving from Syria until the next day, so Mabhouh went out alone for a few hours. He returned with a shopping bag.

Back in his hotel room in the evening, he called his wife and went to bed. Late that night, she was unable to reach him on his cellphone or at the hotel. She alerted the Hamas office in Damascus, which then sent people to the hotel in Dubai. At their insistence, hotel managers opened the door to Room 230 and found Mabhouh. He was on the bed, dead.

A local doctor examined him and declared that the visitor had died of heart failure. Hamas seemed willing to accept that explanation. His family, however, insisted that that could not be true. He had seemed to be a healthy man.

The body was taken to the Dubai morgue, where an official autopsy con-firmed the verdict of heart failure. By now it was known that the dead man was a Hamas official, and Dubai authorities—thriving on tourism and business without scandal—did not really want to know the truth.

The family remained dubious of Dubai and insisted on a fuller investiga-tion. Tissue and blood samples from Mabhouh's corpse were sent to a more trusted laboratory in France for intensive testing. More than a week later, the results showed traces of a muscle-relaxant drug, succinylcholine, in his body. In large doses, it could totally paralyze a man for a while, rendering him unable to struggle against anything.

Hamas's version was that Mabhouh must have been sedated with that drug and then strangled or suffocated with a pillow. Because of minor burns on his chest, Hamas claimed he had first been tortured. Those red marks also could have meant that a defibrillator was used, on a maximum-voltage setting, to stop the man's heart.

Either way, an important goal of the killers must have been to make the murder look like a natural death. That could explain not deploying the one-shot poison spray used on Hamas's Meshaal. Pathologists might identify that as a link to Israel, now that the secret formula had been blown during the operation in Jordan.

It took the Dubai police six weeks to show some interest in running a serious investigation. Once the probe did begin, a new media star was born: General Dahi Khalfan, the Dubai police chief. He took the central role and seemed to enjoy becoming the famous face of the unfolding mystery. He would introduce even more faces.

All in all, in a series of press conference in which he starred, he showed the visages of 27 people who, he claimed, were Mossad operatives involved in murdering Mabhouh. Their faces were taken from their passports and from video cameras peppered around Dubai.

General Khalfan contacted the international police agency Interpol, asking for assistance in the investigation. Interpol asked the respective countries and concluded that all the passports were doctored or fabricated. Some of them belonged to real people, and only the photos were changed. Others were manufactured by expert forgers.

Israel's government said nothing, but international media quickly found that there were Israelis with dual nationalities whose names and passports were used in the operation. When they were reluctantly interviewed, they explained that they had no idea how their passports found their way to Dubai.

In fact, Israeli intelligence never stole the identity of its own nation's citizens. The Mossad, at least within Israel, was a law-abiding agency. Therefore, as in several precedents, it usually would borrow the passports of Jews who were new immigrants or Jewish students in Israel on a long stay.

Those newcomers willingly loaned their documents, though all they had been told was that the passport was needed "for the state" or "for the Jewish Agency." They did not ask many questions, and the borrowers did not mention the Mossad. In most cases, permission was obtained.

When operating outside Israel's borders and often in hostile nations, the Mossad could not send out its operatives only with a cover story. Israelis were not welcome. The Mossad needed to procure convincing foreign identities. It was much better to have genuine identities and not fabricate them out of thin air.

The agency preferred to rely on those borrowings, but occasionally it would run out of options and the Mossad would go to fairly extreme efforts—investing time, money, and energy—to obtain even one genuine foreign passport.

A passport scheme was uncovered in 2004 by the government of New Zealand. The Mossad had gone through a series of convoluted steps to apply for one genuine passport, using the name and personal details of a New Zealand citizen.

A mid-level operative from the Caesarea department had arrived, a few years earlier, in Australia—supposedly, to open a travel agency catering to the many Israeli young people who, just after their military service, typically traveled to the Far East and the Pacific.

His real business, serving as Mossad project manager for the procurement of passports, was supported by two other Caesarea operatives and the help of a Jewish sayan in New Zealand. The sayan helped them identify a man with cerebral palsy who was confined to his house and hardly ever went out.

The Israelis were able to get a copy of the man's birth certificate and used it to file a passport application, using his name and a post office box address. It seemed to be a clever idea, because the passport would be mailed and there would be no contact between him and the authorities.

Everything went according to plan, until a government official became suspicious and phoned the applicant. One of the Israelis answered, but to the official the accent sounded Canadian. He asked about that, and the ridiculous answer was that the applicant had never left the country (having no passport) but used to spend a lot of time with Canadians in New Zealand.

The police and security service put the applicant under surveillance, and they were able to establish that he, the local sayan, and colleagues who had arrived from Australia were all connected. Sensing trouble, the Israeli who had filed the application fled. The two others were arrested and sentenced to short prison terms for passport fraud.

The Israeli government apologized very publicly and pledged that it would not happen again.

That promise was reminiscent of another pledge made in 1996, after the botched attempt to assassinate Meshaal in Jordan. At that time, the Mossad used Canadian passports; when that was revealed, Canada's government was very angry. Israel promised that its spies would never again hide under a Maple Leaf identity.

Indeed, in the Dubai police chief's list of fake passports, there were no Canadians. It was quite a motley crew, however: 12 British, six Irish, four French, four Australian, and one German.

In the international media, in foreign intelligence agencies, and among the Israeli public, this appeared improbably sloppy. Twenty-seven operatives, endangering themselves by being seen on security cameras in the airport, opening and closing sliding doors, riding up and down elevators, posing as pudgy tennis players, changing eyeglasses and wigs, and pretending to be talking on the cellphone to somebody? Acting like bulls in a china shop seemed amateurish, and in contradiction with the image of the Mossad.

From Dagan's point of view, however, the scene looked quite different. There had been a lot of impressive successes. First, Israeli intelligence had collected precise information on Mabhouh and his movements. A Kidon operative had managed to follow Mabhouh on his flight from Damascus to Dubai.

The fact that Dubai was a modern "smart city," covered to its teeth with cameras, was well known to the Mossad from earlier reconnaissance trips. Visual security systems were a modern fact of life, and the Israeli operatives were all changing their glasses, facial hair, wigs, and clothing so that none would ever be readily identified.

Some Israelis, seeing the photos and video clips released by Dubai police in newspapers and on TV, claimed that they recognized some of the Mossad men and women. But, overall, there was an impressive sense of patriotism that kept everyone's mouth shut. Perhaps they gossiped about it at Friday night dinners, but no one spilled any names to the foreign press or foreign governments.

As assessed by the Mossad, the mission was a success. Mabhouh was dead. All the combatants returned home safely. Their real names were totally unknown.

General Khalfan, with all the limelight he enjoyed, ended up frustrated. Early in the probe, he had vowed to find and arrest the Israelis involved. But now, perhaps inspired by a B-movie he had seen, he publicly called out to Mossad director Dagan by name: "Be a man, and admit what you did."

Dagan, in his third-floor office at headquarters in Glilot, was amused by Khalfan's melodramatic act. Around that time, he happened to be speaking with an official of another country, who mentioned that he would be traveling to Dubai and would see the police chief.

When Dagan was asked if he would like some message to be passed to Khalfan, the Israeli said: "No, just give him a kiss on the forehead on my behalf." Dagan certainly did not seem worried at all by Khalfan's bluster.

The police chief had been exaggerating, anyway. His very public line-up of the 27 mugshots was fattened by Mossad operatives who had visited Dubai at other times. They may have been involved peripherally in the Mabhouh operation, but there were not so many in Dubai on the day of the killing.

The size of The Team sent to the Arab emirate was not much different from other Mossad assassinations. Between eight and 16 Kidon and Caesarea members were typically needed for tasks that included warning of anything unexpected about to occur, and perimeter security to ensure that escape routes were available.

The only troubling fallout for the Mossad, it seemed, could be the ire of foreign governments over the use—and forgery—of their passports. Ireland, Britain, and Australia protested. A security guard from Israel's embassy in Dublin was expelled.

London was a far more significant capital, so the reaction of the British was taken more seriously. After all, the Mossad had felt the wrath of Britain in the past, after blunders that included an Israeli official courier stupidly losing a sack full of United Kingdom passports.

After the Dubai caper, the British government expelled the Mossad station chief, and indeed seemed very angry, with members of parliament lined up to protest publicly the violation of Her Majesty's sovereignty.

But very soon, clandestine intelligence ties returned to normal. A new station chief was accepted, and—around the time that Dagan retired in December 2010—Dagan paid a friendly visit to London to introduce his successor, Tamir Pardo, to MI6 and MI5. Both Israelis were hosted by the heads of the two British secret services.

In Canberra, also, the Israeli embassy's Mossad station chief was expelled. But there was an interesting twist. Dagan had previously decided to close the station anyway, because it was not a very productive location and thus not cost-effective. Australia's intelligence service had seemed offended by that, as though it was a matter of pride, and had asked the Mossad to stay.

But now, after the abuse of Australian passports in Dubai, there was a public outcry. The Australian government felt it had to act, and a tacit deal was reached. The Mossad station for Southeast Asia would indeed be moved to another country.

In Dagan's view, there was very little damage done by the limited revelations from Dubai. A wider message was emerging: Anyone who bought arms and supplies to be used against Israel might—in a manner of speaking—wake up dead one day.

Once again, the Mossad had gotten away with murder.

CHAPTER TWENTY-FOUR

ENFORCING MONOPOLY

T he Mossad director, Meir Dagan, was on his way to a routine chat with the prime minister on Ehud Olmert's once-a-week Tel Aviv day.

When Israel's leader had a secret talk scheduled, his office calendar showed two Hebrew letters—*pey* and *aleph*—the initials for *p'gisha ishit*, words meaning "a personal meeting." This referred usually to chats with leaders of the Mossad, Shin Bet, Aman, and the Israel Atomic Energy Commission.

Until 1984, the meetings were truly personal—usually just two people, or as Israelis put it, "four eyes." However, since the killings of the bus hijackers by Shin Bet—after which Prime Minister Yitzhak Shamir and the agency's chief, Avraham Shalom, accused each other of giving the order—the routine was changed. A note-taker of the prime minister's office would always be present.

On this summer day in 2007, Dagan was going to brief Olmert on various intelligence matters, with nothing unusual on the agenda. Half-way from the Mossad's Glilot headquarters to the prime minister's modest, two-story office in the Kirya compound, Dagan got a phone call.

His chief intelligence officer had news, but worded it cautiously. "That thing we are working on? It's certain."

Dagan immediately understood and told the chief analyst to rush to the Kirya to join the meeting. The two senior Mossad men laid out for the prime minister what Israeli spy satellites—and now spies on the ground—had been able to verify in an obscure part of eastern Syria, about 300 miles northeast of Damascus. The Syrians were close to completing the construction of a nuclear reactor.

The Mossad's "non-conventional weapons" researchers assessed that the reactor was closely modeled on a North Korean design, built with the help of advisors from that country, and that the goal was to produce plutonium as the fissile material for bombs. The site was called Al-Kibar, according to Syrian officials in phone calls intercepted by Aman's Unit 8200. The Mossad had gotten its hands on photos, apparently taken by Syrians, showing the inside of the building and a visit by a senior North Korean nuclear official.

Olmert was suddenly reminded why his job was one of the most difficult on the planet. New challenges arose with little or no warning, and they demanded decisiveness. This was far beyond his previous jobs as a lawyer, politician, and mayor of Jerusalem.

He had become prime minister only in January of the previous year, when Ariel Sharon suddenly had to be replaced as prime minister. A severe stroke in January 2006 silenced and paralyzed one of the strongest and most loquacious of Israeli leaders, and Sharon would apparently live out his days in a vegetative state.

Hearing about Syria's secret project, Olmert turned grimly serious.

"What are we going to do about it?" he reflexively asked.

Within minutes, it was clear that the question was rhetorical. The two Mossad men and the prime minister all knew that Israel would have to demolish the Syrian reactor.

Dagan was installed as Mossad chief for just such a day. Prime Minister Sharon—who appointed him in September 2002—instructed the retired general to enhance the spy agency's work to make it more relevant to burning national-security issues.

Sharon believed the Mossad had just gone through five years, under Efraim Halevy, with very little of relevance being accomplished. Perhaps that was too harsh a judgment, since under Halevy's directorship the Mossad continued to recruit agents, run them, and collect information. The ground was well prepared for what Dagan would do later. Yet, Halevy's image was cemented as a cautious and cerebral intelligence officer who—unlike Dagan—avoided risks.

Dagan was born Meir Huberman in 1945 in Novosibirsk, in the Soviet Union, to Polish Holocaust survivors who had fled eastward and found shelter there. They later migrated to Israel and settled in Bat Yam, a poor town south of Tel Aviv. His grandparents had been murdered by the Nazis, and he would indeed keep a photo of one of his grandfathers, kneeling before arrogant German soldiers just before his death, on display all through his career.

The Hubermans were part of a large community of newcomers, denigrated by long-time Bat Yam residents as "the refugees." Young Meir recalled how one of his teachers told the class that Jews who survived the Holocaust must have done something wrong and probably were collaborators with Nazis.

This made a strong impression on the boy. It would help shape his determination to show that he deserved to be respected—not tainted by prejudice about survivors from the Diaspora. He wanted full acceptance as an Israeli. In the 1960s, there was nothing more Israeli for a young man than to become a fighter in an élite unit.

He got his wish, and as a special forces soldier he was wounded twice in combat and received medals. By 1970 he was a captain and found himself in the Gaza Strip, occupied by Israel three years earlier in the Six-Day War. He served there under General Ariel Sharon, a connection that would turn into a long-lasting friendship built on mutual admiration.

Dagan led an innovative and violent team, called Sayeret Rimon, that hunted for Palestinian terrorists. He and his troops staged ambushes and made a habit of popping out of the ground without warning to kill militants. Arab news media, before long, were spreading rumors about an Israeli named Dagan who cut off Palestinians' heads—sometimes while they were still alive.

Years later, Sharon would launch a different version of that rumor, by saying that Dagan's specialty was "separating Arabs' heads from their bodies." Other Israeli politicians wondered why Sharon thought that was an amusing or acceptable thing to say.

Dagan's image as a tough guy helped him rise through the ranks of the military. In the 1980s he served in Lebanon and again focused on chasing Palestinian and Hezbollah terrorists. He was occasionally involved with Aman's Unit 504, which had a record of dirty operations, including extrajudicial killings.

However limited those operations might have been, they were magnified in the retelling. Within the IDF, Dagan also gained a more positive reputation as a cunning planner of daring operations. He reached the rank of general and served as the commander of operations for the general staff, and in 1995 he retired from the military. He was 50 years old.

While serving in uniform, he had not bothered to quash the rumors of being a man of violence. Fear could be a useful weapon against the enemy— and a way to build his self-image. Yet, after retiring from the Mossad, Dagan would reject all such descriptions, saying, "I have never been a killer, and I don't like to kill."

But he confirmed that his unit had killed dozens of terrorists, specifically when "anyone armed refused to surrender." Dagan did add proudly that for every one who was killed, "dozens were taken prisoner."

He retired to his house in a quiet, beautiful part of northern Israel to have more time for his hobbies, including painting. His canvasses often portrayed rural Middle Easterners, both Jews and Arabs, in bucolic scenes. Dagan also traveled the world, including an adventure across Central Asia with two long-time friends, who both were also retired generals.

Dagan was called back into government service in 1996 to lead a small counter-terrorism bureau in the prime minister's office, first under Shimon Peres. Later, under Benjamin Netanyahu, Dagan decided he did not like the self-promoting politician nicknamed "Bibi."

Heading a small unit with limited resources, kind of a fifth wheel outside the main intelligence agencies, Dagan did not have much to do in that job. But he did learn the importance of economic factors: Follow the money, when examining terrorist groups. He and his unit initiated a more systematic approach for tracing terrorists through financial sites and not just gun sights.

Under his leadership, the Central Bank of Israel, the tax authorities, and other financial institutions joined forces to accomplish that goal. He would take that tool with him to the Mossad, making it an important part of the counter-terrorism unit there.

His time at the prime minister's office also taught him the importance of international coordination in tracking financial transfers, and cooperation with the United States was especially important. That sowed the seeds of an overall improvement in security cooperation with the American government, particularly with the CIA. Dagan was thus developing from being a tough soldier with dirt under his fingernails, into a refined man of the world.

When Sharon became prime minister in 2001, he naturally thought of Dagan as the perfect man to head the Mossad. Four of the previous nine directors had been army generals, like Dagan, and his was the kind of no-nonsense leadership that seemed necessary at a time of multi-faceted dangers.

Israel was challenged by the second Palestinian intifada, which had swept Sharon into office. He also saw a need to re-order the country's priorities so it could act against non-Palestinian threats, such as Iran and Hezbollah.

When Halevy—who had restored calm within the Mossad, after the Meshaal murder snafu in Jordan—retired from his extended interim role, Dagan got the job.

His arrival at the *Ramsad* or agency director's office, on the third floor of the headquarters at Glilot, was a hard landing. As an outsider, Dagan was not welcomed by the old-timers. Hardly anyone within the Mossad liked his image as someone tough, even cruel, as though he ruled by fear.

The old guard spread jokes about Dagan, like his supposedly beginning their weekly meeting by asking: "So, who are we going to assassinate today?"

Dagan hoped to re-shape the organization in his own image. He felt the resistance within the Mossad and decided to move fiercely to quash it—reminiscent of Sharon's nickname, "the Bulldozer." He replaced his deputy, then brought in a new one again and again.

When he found that one of these deputies was leaking information to a journalist, Dagan went to the prime minister, and asked Olmert to order Shin Bet—in charge of domestic investigations—to probe the Mossad deputy. Dagan was certain who the leaker was, but he wanted to go through the motions.

Shin Bet's findings arrived quickly and did not surprise Dagan. His deputy had been wiretapped and photographed while meeting with a journalist. Dagan gave him a choice: either write a letter of resignation immediately, or be subject to a criminal investigation that could lead to his indictment for breaching state secrets. Of course, the man quit.

The Mossad does not have a press officer, and Mossad people are not authorized to talk to the media. Yet, in many instances, current agency employees find a way to circumvent that restriction. They relay information to former Mossad staffers, who in turn pass it on to reporters. Most of the information that changes hands in this way is office gossip. The Israeli media have very little knowledge of the missions and serious work of the Mossad, so TV, radio, newspapers, and websites settle for the crumbs of information that are available.

Several in the agency's top management resigned, in what was becoming a bitter atmosphere under Dagan. He proved, however, the validity of Charles de Gaulle's aphorism that graveyards are filled with people who thought they were indispensable.

Dagan replaced the old guard with younger men and women, who proved more enthusiastic, more flexible, and more prepared to follow his direction. Yet, after his retirement years later, he would admit that he could have handled the situation better: perhaps by dealing with each person in a direct, one-on-one manner, and not as a collective.

Two years into his term, Dagan had firmly established his authority and could re-define Mossad priorities and missions.

Trying to shift the direction of the agency, with its approximately 3,000 staff members, was like turning a big ship. Dagan realized that it was going in the wrong direction.

At first, under the spell of the 9/11 tragedy in the United States, he made the Mossad's top mission the monitoring of—and battle against—what Israeli intelligence called "global jihad," meaning al-Qaeda and other loosely affiliated Islamist cells all around the world.

There was, indeed, some basis for setting that as the priority. Aman's 8200 electronic surveillance teams, Mossad's humint capabilities, and liaisons with international counterparts uncovered several plots by Muslim zealots to bomb Israeli embassies in Singapore and the Philippines, to target Israeli and Jewish facilities in Tunisia and Turkey, and to shoot down an Israeli airliner leaving Mombasa, Kenya.

In addition, exchanging information about al-Qaeda—and about Islamist networks inspired by Osama bin Laden in dozens of countries—gave the Mossad and its friends in the CIA a lot to talk about.

Quite soon, however, Dagan and analysts in the Mossad's research department realized that networks inspired by al-Qaeda were not seriously interested in battling Israel and the Jews. Their main priority was and has been causing bloody trouble to America and pro-Western Arab regimes.

Dagan had to consider re-ordering priorities again. In light of Iran's nuclear and missile programs, plus the rhetoric of its leaders who declared Israel an illegitimate state to be wiped off the map—it seemed wise to place the Islamic Republic at the very top of the priority list. Intelligence collection and analysis aimed at Iran would be more than doubled.

A second priority, just behind on the list, would be Iran's terrorist proxies, who carried out the Islamic Republic's dirty work by periodically pricking Israel: Hezbollah and Hamas.

To establish these priorities, however, Dagan had to overcome one major obstacle: the military analysts at Aman. That agency was, by law, in charge of Israel's NIE—the National Intelligence Estimate—and did not like the Mossad to encroach onto its turf by trying to set new national priorities.

Aman still believed in the classic approach: that prime importance went to monitoring the military capabilities of Israel's nearest neighbors.

Dagan dismissed Aman's contention, by offering his own checklist of the neighbors. In an acrimonious debate, he argued that Egypt could not pose a threat to Israel. Certainly Syria, with its outmoded and rusty military, could not. And Saddam Hussein's Iraq, after America's spring 2003 invasion, had been removed from the military equation. Israelis, in government and out, were justifiably relieved when Saddam was captured, tried by an Iraqi court, and hanged.

This debate unexpectedly settled itself, with a slap in the face to the two quarrelling sides. On Christmas Eve 2003, the world woke up to a public announcement: Colonel Muammar Qaddafi's Libya was giving up its weapons of mass destruction, which included a nascent nuclear program and a large arsenal of chemical weapons.

The announcement took Israeli intelligence completely by surprise, and its directors did not like surprises. The Mossad claimed that it was Aman's fault, for dropping Libya from the list of "objectives" for information-gathering because of tight budgets. The result was that in recent years, very few Israeli intelligence operations were mounted inside or against Libya.

The Mossad felt embarrassed by the fact that the CIA and British MI6—two of its closest counterparts—had been negotiating with Qaddafi for weeks to clinch the deal. Those intelligence communities did not share the information with the Mossad.

What really grabbed the Israeli agencies in the Libya story was the revelation that Colonel Qaddafi's nuclear program had been born out of the efforts and expertise of the Pakistani merchant of atomic knowhow, A.Q. Khan. He had signed an agreement with Qaddafi to deliver a turn-key project. Drawings, the centrifuges, scientists experienced at enriching uranium, and engineers who could assemble the bomb could all be provided by Khan.

Dagan and his chief intelligence officer wondered to themselves: Since they missed the whole Libyan deal, what else had they missed? The research department was ordered in 2004 to go back into its archives and examine every piece of humint and sigint information it had accumulated, in the past decade, about Khan's activities as a nuclear traveling salesman. Intelligence agencies often gather more data than they can read and analyze, and individual intercepts and data points are not always immediately pieced together into a coherent mosaic.

The Mossad realized that—in addition to Libya—Khan had traveled to Saudi Arabia, Egypt, and Syria. Further evaluation concluded that the Saudis and Egyptians, being in the American camp, would be less likely to have the gall to launch a nuclear program.

Syria could be a different case. It was anti-America, making overtures to Iran, and supporting Hezbollah in Lebanon more than ever. The then-new Syrian dictator, Bashar al-Assad, was inexperienced and might miscalculate in his ambitions to outdo his late father Hafez.

The more Mossad researchers dug, the more they found. For the first time, Israeli analysts were seeing hints of nuclear work in Syria. They noticed that the Assad regime, at the start of the 21st century, had clandestine contacts with North Korea that were difficult to explain. The subject was, almost surely, not the already-known cooperation in the field of Scud missiles. There was something else going on: secret, high-level, and troubling.

Dagan had his agency zoom in on Syria, by all measures available. The Mossad first turned to the CIA and other friendly liaison links to ask whether they were aware of Syria's having nuclear contacts with North Korea. Western intelligence agencies all knew about missile sales and cooperation between Damascus and Pyongyang. Yet, neither the Americans nor the French (the latter having relatively good coverage of Syria due to their colonial past) knew a thing about nuclear links.

Israeli intelligence realized that it would have to rely upon itself. That was a commonly held view in Israel on many topics, even when international cooperation seemed to be available. "It's part of their ethos," commented Dennis Ross, a longtime Middle East advisor to American presidents, "not to contract out their security."

Within the Israeli intelligence community, through most of 2007, there was an urgent sense of being faced with a new mystery in Syria. This was, therefore, no time to re-open old Mossad-Aman wounds about who missed Libya's weapons program. The divisions were healed.

Military intelligence had Unit 8200 improve its eavesdropping on Syrian communications and signals. Israeli satellites, first launched in 1988, were reoriented so that their orbits would put them over Syria more often. The Mossad's agent-running Tsomet department was instructed to do all it could to penetrate Syria's leadership and to uncover the mysterious, unresolved contacts with North Korea.

This substantial extra work for Israeli intelligence required additional budgetary resources. Dagan turned to Prime Minister Olmert to ask for more money and found, in Olmert, an ally. "Whatever you need," was the message, "you'll get it."

Israel's air force now was able to afford a lot more high-altitude reconnaissance flights. Intelligence analysts were working much longer hours, poring over photos taken by Israeli satellites.

Some of the information was from sigint sources—intercepted communications. But that was far from easy. It seemed that only a very few Syrians knew what was going on. Israeli intelligence tried to listen in on all their conversations, including those of President Assad and his close advisor and coordinator of covert projects, Brigadier General Muhammad Suleiman.

The combined espionage effort was narrowing onto several places and projects deemed highly suspicious. The first breakthrough came in the form of a building, seen in reconnaissance photos: 130 feet by 130 feet, and about 70 feet tall, within a military complex in an obscure desert in northeastern Syria, not far from the Euphrates River.

The Syrians tried to block aerial views of whatever was being built by putting a large roof over the scene. That meant that something was being constructed, something worth concealing, but Israeli agencies could not tell what was inside.

The next, crucial step would involve risking the lives of Israelis: sending operatives into Syria to get close, to see what the Syrians were building. For a variety of operational reasons, a decision was made to send combatants of the Mossad's Kidon unit—who excelled at sensitive, dangerous surveillance and not only assassinations—in addition to an army special forces unit.

They sampled the soil, water, and vegetation around the site, but did not find any traces of radioactive materials. Yet, other evidence they carried back to Israel did lead to the pieces of the puzzle falling into place.

The mystery began to be solved. It truly was a nuclear project.

The teams returned there on several reconnaissance missions and obtained, every time, additional information. It became clear that North Korean experts were helping Syria build a nuclear facility. Unknown was whether it was a collection of centrifuges, which would take a long time to enrich uranium for bombs. Or was it a nuclear reactor, which could, alarmingly, provide plutonium for bombs more quickly?

Whatever it was, how close to completion was the project? The answer would be significant. Israeli leaders might feel they had to bomb the building urgently, or they might decide they had time to wait and see.

In March 2007, irrefutably incriminating evidence arrived. These were photos taken inside the mysterious building. Who took the photos is the most closely guarded secret of the operation. It could have been Mossad combatants who managed to penetrate the facility. The Israelis also might have recruited a Syrian, or even a North Korean, to take snapshots inside and provide them to the Mossad. The most likely scenario: Israelis extracted the photographs from a laptop computer or a memory drive carelessly carried abroad by a Syrian official.

There was now strong pictorial evidence that Syria was building a graphite reactor of the Yongbyon type, used by North Korea to make its own nuclear bombs. Israel understood that the Communist pariah state, always desperate for hard currency, did it for the money.

Even more important and troubling was the assessment by the Mossad's non-conventional weapons department that the reactor could be ready to "go hot" within a few months, and then it would take a little over a year to produce enough plutonium for a nuclear bomb.

One more piece of evidence was troubling. Large pipes and a pumping station, for cooling the reactor with Euphrates River water, seemed to be complete—ready for use.

An additional item of data contributed to Israel's decision-making process. The Mossad concluded that Iran had no role whatsoever in the construction of the reactor. Despite a growing friendship between Syria and Iran, the Iranians were not privy to the secret. An alliance between nations, however close, still can be constrained by a large degree of compartmentalization.

That was the information that Dagan and his chief intelligence officer were bringing to their briefing for Olmert in Tel Aviv—the meeting that concluded with a consensus that the building would have to be flattened.

That was, of course, much easier said than done.

The burden of decision-making was now slowly shifting from the intelligence community to the IDF and, above all, to a political process led by Olmert and his cabinet.

Faced with a huge decision, any Israeli prime minister, early on, tests the waters of the Potomac to hear what the American administration has to say on the subject. Almost all major choices were made by Israel after consulting with or telling the United States—although the Israelis rarely stood still for a long period to field questions and get bogged down in soul-searching and indecision.

They saw George W. Bush's administration as the most friendly to Israel since the Reagan era. But being entangled in two wars, in Iraq and Afghanistan, the Americans might react in unexpected ways.

It was traditional to send the director of the Mossad to Washington to test those waters. Olmert dispatched Dagan, who showed the CIA and the Pentagon a dossier and asked: Do you Americans know about this?

They did not.

Olmert, paying his own visit to Washington in June 2007, addressed President Bush face to face: "George, I am asking you to bomb the compound."

Bush decided, however, that bombing Syria without obvious provocation would cause "severe blowback." He suggested that Western countries should instead expose the Syrian reactor project, by providing photographic evidence to the world's media, to force the Damascus government to dismantle it.

Olmert's reply to the president, in July, was: "Your strategy is very disturbing to me."

The prime minister concluded that, if action were needed, Israel would have to do it alone. Olmert found himself suddenly in the same position as was the late Menachem Begin in 1981. Olmert had to decide whether he would follow in the footsteps of his predecessor and enforce the Begin Doctrine—that no enemy of Israel would be allowed to have nuclear weapons.

Consulting with very few advisors, Olmert reached his own decision that he would follow the Begin line. It was almost instinctive, based on strategic analysis and a sense of Jewish history, that Israel needed to maintain a nuclear monopoly in the Middle East. Still, many questions needed to be resolved.

The preferred option would be sabotage: to send a very limited number of Israelis to destroy the facility. That was removed from the table, when IDF special forces and the Mossad said they could not reliably get there with all the explosives and other materials they would need.

The discussion itself recalled 1981, when the option of sending a large contingent of soldiers was ruled out: too visible, too risky, and the probability of success unknown.

Attention turned, as it did then, to an aerial attack. Analysts in Israel's air force started applying their specialty—using the mathematics of operational research—and calculated how many planes would be needed, what load to carry, what routes to fly, and what air-defense hazards they might encounter.

The political decision-making process, in the meantime, got into full gear. The first question was one of timing. The Mossad's non-conventional weapons department determined the window of opportunity to be a matter of just a few months, running only to the end of autumn of 2007. At that point, the reactor would become operational.

The very few Israelis privy to the secret were shaken by that. They feared that if the reactor were bombed after going hot, radiation would spread. That would cause the worst possible pollution in the Euphrates River, which flows from Turkey, via Syria, to Iraq, and provides the livelihood for millions of people.

If such contamination were to happen, Israel would be blamed for a colossal ecological disaster. International reactions might be reminiscent of old anti-Semitic accusations that Jews poisoned wells. The Muslim world would be up in arms.

Olmert slightly expanded the number of people who were involved in these discussions. Over a matter of weeks, he hosted five serious meetings of his inner cabinet—14 people in all—with every minister encouraged to express his or her genuine views.

The ministers were helped to come to a conclusive decision by the knowledge that the Israeli intelligence community and the military, this time, spoke with one voice. That was a huge difference from the deliberations leading to the Osirak attack 26 years earlier. All the intelligence agency chiefs, their deputies, and their top analysts now favored demolishing Syria's reactor project—including Dagan, the Aman chief General Amos Yadlin, who was one of the pilots who struck Iraq in 1981, and the IDF chief of staff, Lt.-General Gabi Ashkenazi.

A strong consensus seemed to be emerging. Ministers supported Olmert's position that—in the spirit of Begin—Syria would have to be stopped from getting nuclear weapons. But there was one very prominent exception.

To the astonishment of his colleagues, Defense Minister Ehud Barak kept voicing strong objections. He did not say that he was, in principle, opposed to bombing Syria; but he suggested that Israel still had time, that there was no need to rush.

Barak even tried to prevent other generals from expressing their views in cabinet meetings, saying that he would be the sole defense or military voice. Olmert overruled him on that claim.

A rift between the two Ehuds was growing. Olmert tried to figure out Barak's true motives. He reached the conclusion that these were selfish political interests, and that Barak was prepared to sacrifice national interests for his own good.

Looming over the debate were tensions left by the Lebanon war in the summer of 2006, when Israel battled Hezbollah and many Israelis criticized the political and military decisionmakers' deficiencies. An investigatory committee was due to release its report in January 2008. Olmert, Dagan, and Ashkenazi could not avoid the conclusion that Barak was waiting for that release—probably hoping that Olmert would be forced to resign and Barak could be prime minister again, or he could be defense minister in a cabinet that would give him more influence.

Barak argued against those suspicions, saying his true concern was that Olmert made hasty and unreliable military decisions.

Dagan, however, lost all faith in Barak. And that would make a difference in future crises.

The decisive factor regarding whether to bomb the reactor was the question of Syrian retaliation.

Israeli intelligence knew that Syria's powerful missiles were always on standby, and if an order were given, they could hit any target they chose in Israel. Destinations, it was believed, were pre-set: from the Dimona reactor, to the Kirya military headquarters in Tel Aviv, to the Knesset in Jerusalem, as well as air bases, power stations, and other key facilities.

If Israel believed there was a likelihood of Syrian retaliation, then preparation of the home front would normally be necessary. That would require mobilization of reservists and civil defense workers, which would be detected by the Syrians. That could lead to a miscalculation. Syria might even pre-emptively strike Israel, and an all-out war could result.

That lethal scenario almost happened in 1996, and the man responsible was a faker within the Mossad.

Yehuda Gil was considered a living legend within the spy agency. Born in Libya and fluent in Italian, Arabic, and other languages, he became a role-model case officer who recruited Palestinian agents to fight terrorism and Arab military officers to spy on their own countries. In addition, as an instructor in the Mossad academy, he shared his lifetime of experience and escapades, training new generations of up and coming case officers.

Gil was considered a star katsa: embodying all the skills of that job in locating, contacting, persuading, then running a foreign agent. In 1974, he was tasked with recruiting a Syrian general who was on a trip to Europe. That was shortly after the Yom Kippur War, and Israel desperately needed a new crop of agents in Arab countries. The general proved to be irresistibly corruptible.

Gil, operating with the Mossad tradecraft of false-flagging, introduced himself as an Italian working for a corporation with close ties to the NATO alliance. He started showering the general with gifts, including a refrigerator that was imported for him from the United States.

The general was requested to provide some information, as a test of his willingness to go along. Very quickly, it was clear that while he was greedy he was not treacherous. He agreed to give some data that might be helpful to a corporation, but he refused to betray his country's big secrets.

Gil was faced with a dilemma. Being proud of his track record, he did not want to return to headquarters in Israel as a failure. He started writing reports based on his own speculation, imagination, and knowledge he gained from reading newspapers. Gil certainly knew what his bosses would expect to hear from a senior Syrian general.

As for the money he was supposed to pay to the agent, Gil kept that at home under his mattress.

Luckily for him, the general was not able to leave Damascus too often: maybe once a year, to visit his daughter in Europe. Gil did not have to invent too many reports. Since the general was considered a high-quality agent, Mossad headquarters expected great stuff—but not too often.

There were authentic meetings, and they continued even after the general retired. The Syrian still refused, however, to reveal significant secrets. He also rejected Gil's offers of money and did not seem to feel that he was a spy in any sense. The meetings petered out.

Gil also retired, but the Mossad employed him part-time to run the senior Syrian source. Gil kept stuffing his reports with made-up details, even as he kept stuffing money into his mattress.

Whenever it was suggested that he be accompanied by another case officer or by a military specialist from Aman who could ask more precise questions, Gil refused to permit that. He argued that the Syrian general would not meet anyone but him.

In 1996, 22 years into the bogus operation, Gil fabricated his most dangerous report. Advised by Aman that he should ask about certain movements of Syrian military units, he answered with one of his imaginative, intelligent guesses.

That report set the Israeli military on fire. Aman analysts concluded—based on Gil's false information—that Syrian forces planned a quick invasion to grab part of the Golan Heights. In response to that chimera, Israel's army was mobilized in the north, preparing for war.

Luckily, the Syrians did not miscalculate, and their reaction was mild. There was no war by mistake.

Red flags about Yehuda Gil went up in both the Mossad and Aman. After several internal investigations, the organizations concluded that he was probably inventing things. At one point, he was followed on a supposed mission by a Kidon tracker—using the best, since Gil knew how to detect and avoid surveillance. It was apparent that Gil was not meeting with anyone.

Back in Israel, he was arrested and put on trial. Gil was sentenced to five years in prison.

Now, in the summer of 2007, with a looming nuclear threat in Syria, the fear of miscalculation was even greater. Israel, after all, was about to do something quite provocative—and likely to be considered an act of war prompting a Syrian response.

The decision required on the part of Olmert and his cabinet seemed momentous. Ministers spoke of the possibility of the Israeli people facing thousands of retaliatory missiles flying in from Syria and from Hezbollah in Lebanon. Some might even carry chemical weapons.

Despite those dark thoughts, the inner cabinet voted, 13 to 1, in favor of an attack. Even Barak voted yes. The only no was cast by the former Shin Bet director, Avi Dichter, now a cabinet minister, who feared the bloody toll that might be inflicted on Israeli civilians by Syrian retaliation.

Despite all the deliberations, meetings, and up to 2,500 Israelis involved in planning, the secret was not leaked or even hinted—quite astounding for a talkative society.

Everyone trusted with knowledge about the plan was required to sign a special secrecy pledge, even those who already had the highest security clearances, such as cabinet ministers and heads of intelligence agencies. The only one exempted was Prime Minister Olmert.

On the night of the attack, September 6, Olmert was in the "Bor" (the Pit), the IDF's situation room, flanked by a few assistants and military generals. Eight F-16s took off from a base in northern Israel, flying westward, northward, and then eastward into Syria.

Unlike the "stupid" heavy bombs dropped in the Osirak attack in 1981, this time Israel used "smart" weapons. Shortly after midnight, the pilots fired precision missiles from a safe distance. Within two minutes, the attack was over.

To keep the Israelis safe, their advanced electronics jammed and blinded Syria's air-defense system. This time, on top of what Israel had accomplished before, the electronic warfare was raised to a new level. The Syrian radars seemed to be working, just fine, even when they were not. Syria's defense personnel had no idea that their system, which detected absolutely nothing, was down.

The Israeli pilots adhered to radio silence and communicated with headquarters only after about 30 minutes. Olmert, other top politicians, and generals were relieved and delighted to hear that the target was destroyed.

Despite their analysis that Syria would not retaliate, they could not rule out the possibility. To minimize the chance, a firm decision was made to keep the entire affair secret. If President Assad were not publicly humiliated, he would probably decide to do and say nothing. Indeed, Israel still has never publicly confirmed that it hit Syria that night.

A war of misinformation would follow. The Syrians apparently did not know what to make of Israel's silence. Fearing that Israel might announce it first and embarrass them, the Syrians declared they had repelled an Israeli air incursion. Later, they said that Israel had bombed a deserted military structure. They also pointed to the one mistake the Israeli air force made as evidence of the incident: One of the pilots released an auxiliary fuel tank from his F-16, on the way home. The tank was found in a field in Turkey; it had Hebrew markings on it. Deniability would now be more difficult.

After Syria's government started talking about an Israeli attack, word leaked from Israel that the target had been a nuclear facility. Syrian officials adamantly denied that. They refused, for months, to let the International Atomic Energy Agency visit the site; in the meantime, the Syrians cleared away all the rubble and replaced the soil. Finally, when international inspectors were allowed there, they detected a few traces of uranium. Syria claimed these were from uranium-tipped Israeli missiles, but the IAEA did not believe that fiction.

The inspectors concluded that the structure, now gone, had contained a North Korea-type nuclear reactor. This finding was bolstered by a fairly complete report made public by the CIA. Intelligence agencies discovered that dozens of people were killed when Israel bombed the building, both Syrians and North Koreans. North Korea never said a word about it.

Israeli intelligence prepared files to be sent to foreign government leaders and friendly intelligence agencies. The cooperative relationship that meant the most was with the United States. Olmert spoke by phone with President Bush, and Dagan flew to Washington to give briefings—even meeting the president at the White House. Both sides seemed comfortable with the fact that Israel had not informed the Americans, in any detailed way, before the bombing raid. Deniability was preserved.

Intelligence professionals at the CIA and in the Pentagon praised Israel for having precise information and for being decisive and leak-proof.

While Israel proved to the Middle East that the Begin Doctrine worked for a second time, the mission was incomplete for Dagan and his Mossad.

On August 1, 2008, President Assad's close aide, General Suleiman, was felled by one bullet. He was sitting on the terrace of his villa on the Syrian coastline, enjoying the Mediterranean breeze while entertaining guests for dinner. They apparently did not notice that an Israeli naval vessel was anchored offshore, with an expert sniper on deck. The ship was bobbing on the sea, of course. Yet one shot, at a great distance, did the job.

The general was killed, but his guests were unharmed.

No less impressive was the precision of the information gathered about Suleiman's party: what time it would start, and where he would be sitting.

The mission, thus accomplished, was to send a message to his master, the president: Don't mess with us. Another objective was getting rid of a powerful official who worked on Syria's very special relations with both Hezbollah and Iran.

CHAPTER TWENTY-FIVE

INTO THE FUTURE

There always seemed to be an immediate challenge or crisis for Israel's intelligence agencies, and none seemed more important than the multi-pronged covert offensive aimed at sabotaging—or at least retarding—Iran's nuclear program.

Israeli leaders monitored the issue extremely closely, knowing that they might feel compelled to unleash their country's military muscle to combat the Islamic Republic's nuclear capability. Thanks to significant delays, for which former Mossad director Meir Dagan claimed credit, the fateful year for a decision was changed from 2010 to 2011 and then to 2012, and likely beyond that.

Yet, even as Dagan was replaced at the end of 2010, after eight highly active years, by his deputy Tamir Pardo, there was a need to look ahead to the next, seemingly inevitable crises.

Reviewing the past, it becomes clear that Israeli intelligence always has had its eye on the future. It consistently has tried to be on the cutting edge in utilizing human and technological resources. The Mossad, Aman, and Shin Bet pride themselves on being innovative; and they hope and believe that they are ahead of their peers—the other espionage and security agencies, large and small, worldwide.

Israel's was one of the first intelligence communities to introduce computers, as early as the 1950s, long before other governments used them for any function at all.

Israel was the first nation to take advantage of drones, for pilotless intelligence gathering and for striking enemies.

Israel was the sixth country to join the nuclear club, although doggedly refusing to confirm that fact, and one of only a handful of nations to launch satellites.

Israel is a leading country in the new virtual battlefield of cyberwarfare. Increasingly and by necessity, spy agencies are expanding from the physical world to the digital world.

Cyberspace has largely been a blessing for Israel and its intelligence agencies. It is becoming less relevant that the Jewish state is so physically tiny, because in technology it is the giant of the Middle East.

Vastly increased reliance on computers elevated Aman's role within the community, since the conduct of cyber-activities is in that military agency's hands. Aman has immersed itself in a new dimension where bloodless wars are waged. Many objectives can now be fought over, without soldiers or machinery ever clashing face to face.

Three forms of cyber-activity are useful, relevant, and exploited by the military: intelligence gathering, offensive steps, and defensive moves.

For collecting information and for operations, cyber-based methods are not eliminating human intelligence, an area at which the Israelis have excelled. Technology, however, is now invaluable in helping humint—offering a wealth of useful shortcuts. Almost every human activity today is linked with computers, is recorded by them, and leaves tracks on a network that can be found and penetrated by cyber-espionage.

It would be foolish for anyone using a computer in any manner to think that privacy and secrecy exist anymore. If Israeli intelligence agencies believe that some needed data resides in the computer networks of almost any foreign government, military, company, or individual, Israel's ability to ferret out the data and to undetectably procure it is far above average.

Smart use of cyberspace obviates the need for old-fashioned shots in the dark, including fishing expeditions for information in the real world that burn up travel budgets and put operatives at risk. Like other intelligence communities, Israel's became expert at break-ins; yet those, in a physical sense, are less important in our era of networked computers and the internet.

Information is much more available, and data more obtainable than ever. Israeli software and hardware developers, including many who learned their skills in the military's Unit 8200, invented much of the networking equipment used around the world. They know all the "back door" entrances, and they are adept at cracking all types of computer code.

Intelligence agencies can also use chat rooms, social networks, e-mail exchanges, and other websites to identify important information very far from home, and to dig deeper to learn more—all from a safe distance.

A katsa, or case officer, may well find it necessary to establish personal contact a few times with agents employed abroad. Psychological factors are still strong, and the reasons that a foreigner is supplying secrets about his or her own country need to be understood. Yet, for routine and follow-up meetings, there is less need for an Israeli to enter enemy lands—the "target" countries—or to bring their agents to the neutral "base" countries.

Compared with ages past, there is far less need to arrange a clandestine rendezvous with an agent, with laborious coding and decoding of messages by hand. Elaborate signals, such as "dead letter drops" for leaving packages and messages under false rocks in the woods, have become relics of the past displayed in spy museums.

Because the internet leaves a lot of room to the imagination, there are new opportunities for "false-flag" recruitment. You can introduce yourself as something entirely different than you are. It used to be that if an Israeli operative were pretending to be Belgian, for example, he would have to be someone selected to credibly pass himself off as a Belgian. On the internet, such disguises are relatively simple.

United States intelligence agencies have also learned that technology in the hands of terrorists can be turned against them. Anytime an enemy of America or Israel uses a telephone—and especially a smartphone, with its mobile connection to the internet—an intelligence agency has a very good chance of detecting where he is and intercepting his messages. Not surprisingly, al-Qaeda and other terrorist groups gave up using telephones and depend only on couriers who carry messages in medieval style.

Israel has developed offensive capabilities that could be unleashed against enemy nations that have modern infrastructure. The United States is very advanced in this category of warfare, but the fact is that large and small countries—America and Israel, for instance—can be nearly equal in their power to stage cyber-attacks that could cripple a foe.

It is possible for most any nation with terrific technology experts to shut down electricity, water supplies, and the aviation system of the enemy without endangering a single one of its own soldiers. Specialists can take destructive action, while sitting comfortably at control panels and in situation rooms thousands of miles away.

A modern nation could theoretically be brought to a halt, if one country decides to bring chaos to another's society.

Intelligence agencies have also developed the ability to feed false information into the enemy's computer-based systems. Planting the Stuxnet worm in Iran's nuclear computers was just one example of the limitless possibilities in offensive cyberwar. Israel was also able to blind the Syrian anti-aircraft defense system, when the nuclear reactor in Syria was destroyed in 2007.

However, these weapons are double-edged swords. The more a country is technologically advanced—certainly including Israel—the more it is vulnerable, because it inevitably has much of its own vital information in computer networks that might be pierced.

Israel and its intelligence agencies devote increasing resources to defending themselves from cyber-assaults. They invent and activate virus detectors and firewalls, and—of course—they make sure not to connect the public websites of the Mossad and many other sensitive institutions to the important intranets used by agency employees.

The problem is that a country must defend not only its *real* military and strategic installations, but also its entire *virtual* home front. Traffic lights are controlled by computers, as are sewers, hospitals, and myriad other civilian systems. Cyberwar turns every individual in the country into someone who could be hit by the enemy and could suffer.

There is also the somewhat troubling fact that the enemy need not be a state. Terrorist groups can hack into databases with various levels of skill—from the rudimentary to the surprisingly complex. Some hackers often change their locations and their modes of entry into computer networks. Israel, to defend its infrastructure and hit back, may have to go through the frustration of punching at a moving target.

The future for Israel and its intelligence community may be full of double-edged swords. Almost anything that Israel has acquired or developed, its enemies are also aiming to get.

The one thing that the opponents cannot match—at least, not so far—are Israel's humint assets. Analysts at Aman and the Mossad know the neighboring countries very well; and many Israelis speak a wide variety of languages, often thanks to the origins of their own parents and grandparents.

Meantime, the espionage and security agencies of Israel's enemies seem to focus nervously on pleasing their masters; and that often means telling an authoritarian ruler precisely what he wants to hear. Be they Iranians, Lebanese radicals, Egyptians, or other Arabs, the rival security services consistently have failed to understand Israeli society. In simple terms, hardly any of them ever met a Jew.

They mainly come from dictatorships and cannot imagine the workings of a society that is open and democratic. They tend to judge Israel's every move according to their own core values and experiences.

That has given Israel a genuine qualitative edge over the years. But Israeli society is changing. It is becoming less educated on average, less productive, more introverted, less attuned to the world's opinions, and increasingly torn by tensions between rich and poor.

The secret agencies, it is true, are peopled by exceptional individuals. Yet, Israel's intelligence community has always been a reflection of the entire nation. It cannot be better than the society in which it resides.

In fact, coming from a free and open country, Israelis find it quite challenging to assess the intentions of the surrounding dictatorships. The ideal piece of intelligence would be knowledge of exactly what is going on between the ears of only one man—the leader. Despite all of Israel's technological advances, no machine can read minds and intentions.

When longtime Arab rulers were toppled in the pro-freedom uprisings of 2011, Israel was taken by surprise. Intelligence analysts contended—when looking at their largest neighbor, Egypt—that they predicted the possibility of an anti-Israel, Islamic regime in Cairo; but only after the eventual death of President Hosni Mubarak. He had been, practically, an ally for Israel and certainly for the United States. Israeli strategists wished that he could still be around, but changing the course of history is beyond the capabilities of even the best espionage agencies.

Israel's analysts did all they could to keep up with a rapidly changing set of Arab governments, and intelligence professionals shunned simplistic questions, such as, "Is it good for us?" Yet top politicians wanted to know how their country would be impacted by popular movements, hope mixed with violence, and a demand for freedom in Arab lands that could lead to an honest desire for peace. Events could also lead to hatred of Israel being stirred up by new leaders.

Israelis genuinely felt threatened by Iran's radicalism and its growing power. When leaders in Jerusalem warned that they would not tolerate a nuclear-armed Iran, they emphasized that they could not take the risk that the mullahs might one day use the world's most potent weapons. The Mossad and Aman could not claim to know what today's Supreme Leader, or tomorrow's, might do.

Iran's nuclear program, combined with its support of terrorism, is currently at the heart of Israel's most urgent concerns; but crisis management has become part of life for Israelis. This is certainly not their first crisis, and it will not be their last.

As usual, there are many options for attempting to resolve it. Elected officials, military chiefs, and, indeed, the people of Israel naturally want to have the best possible information—and they have enjoyed the fruits of a very impressive intelligence community. Now, the leaders must decide. Israel should not expect the secret agencies to be more than they have proved to be: an excellent example of what a small nation with meager resources can do by using them to the utmost. The community's history has demonstrated both the maximal achievements and the inescapable limitations of intelligence.

ENDNOTES

Chapter 1

Meir Dagan, just before leaving the Mossad in December 2010, invited 30 journalists to the agency's guest house at Glilot and briefed them on his views. It was intended to be off-the-record, but within hours lengthy reports were in the media. After that, he appeared in several public forums in Israel and made statements that were controversial and disliked by Prime Minister Benjamin Netanyahu and Defense Minister Ehud Barak. Details of his views also emerged at the Saban Forum of the Brookings Institution in December 2011 in Washington, DC.

On the Shah of Iran's nuclear ambitions, see Yossi Melman and Meir Javedanfar, *The Nuclear Sphinx of Tehran* (Carroll & Graf, 2007), Chapter 5, "The Grandfather of Iran's Bomb."

Mohammed ElBaradei, former head of the International Atomic Energy Agency, offers his perspectives in his memoir, *The Age of Deception: Nuclear Diplomacy in Treacherous Times* (Metropolitan Books, 2011).

On various plans hatched by the CIA and Israeli intelligence to stop Iran's nuclear program, including a plot to supply flawed bomb-design blueprints to Iran, see James Risen, *State of War: The Secret History of the CIA and the Bush Administration* (Free Press, 2006).

An article reporting cooperation by Israel and U.S. intelligence in producing and testing the Stuxnet virus appeared in *The New York Times* on January 15, 2011. A virus analyst at the California-based networking security firm Symantec spoke to one of the authors in April 2012 about Stuxnet and its computer-code cousin Duqu.

Commenting on the huge explosion at an Iranian missile base in December 2011, Israel's deputy prime minister in charge of strategic affairs, a former IDF chief of staff, Moshe (Boogie) Yaalon, claimed that the base was developing a 10,000-kilometer-range missile meant to threaten the United States. He spoke at briefings for journalists and experts in New York in January 2012.

Dagan's meeting with Nicholas Burns, a U.S. undersecretary of state, in August 2007 was summarized in a State Department cable that was apparently authentic, released by Wikileaks in November 2010. Dagan is quoted as outlining his five-part plan for destabilizing Iran and persuading that country to stop its nuclear weapons program.

Dagan gave his first interview to American television when he spoke to the CBS News program *60 Minutes*, aired on March 11, 2012. He publicly predicted that an Israeli air assault on Iran would prompt Iranians to support their Islamic regime, while on a panel at a Jerusalem Post conference in New York on April 29, 2012.

President Barack Obama and Netanyahu declared their views on Iran's nuclear program in speeches to the American Israel Public Affairs Committee's annual policy conference in Washington on March 4 and 5, 2012, respectively.

Obama said that he was "not bluffing" when interviewed by Jeffrey Goldberg, national correspondent of *The Atlantic*, as reported at TheAtlantic.com on March 2, 2012.

Chapter 2

Moshe Tziper, the son of the allegedly disloyal Avner Israel, spoke with one of the authors in June 2011.

Rafael Eitan, "Mr. Kidnap," was interviewed in 2011 by one of the authors about the operation to find "a Bulgarian needle in an Italian haystack."

Amos Manor, former Shin Bet director, spoke of being "ashamed" of Avner Israel's death, interviewed by one of the authors; see *Ha'aretz* of March 9, 2006, by Yossi Melman.

The final days of the pre-state Shai were described by Hagai Eshed, *One-Man Mossad: Reuven Shiloah, Father of Israeli Intelligence* (in Hebrew by Edanim/Yediot Aharonot, 1988), p. 120.

Isser Harel's agents did police-type work and opened "thousands of letters," according to Tom Segev, *1949: The First Israelis* (Domino Press, 1984), pp. 292, 294.

Some of Avri El-Ad's activities were written about by El-Ad himself in *Decline of Honor* (Regency Books, 1976), pp. 60-2; see also Aviezer Golan, *Operation Susannah* (Harper and Row, 1978).

While El-Ad was secretly sentenced to 10 years' imprisonment, no Israeli official accepted responsibility for ordering the sabotage campaign in Egypt. Israelis called it The Rotten Business, or the Lavon Affair, and all the potential decisionmakers—IDF chief of staff Moshe Dayan, Aman chief Benyamin Gibli, and Defense Minister Pinhas Lavon—denied any knowledge.

The story of Ze'ev Avni was recounted in Moshe Zak, *Israel and the Soviet Union: A Forty-Year Dialogue* (Maariv Book Guild, 1988), pp. 301-2; and by El-Ad, *Decline of Honor*, pp. 282-4.

Chapter 3

The most complete account of ex-Chicago White Sox player Moe Berg's secret second career is in Nicholas Dawidoff, *The Catcher Was a Spy: The Mysterious Life of Moe Berg* (Vintage, 1995).

Reuven Shiloah's June 1951 visit to Washington is described by Eshed in *One-Man Mossad*, pp. 164-5.

James J. Angleton's background, including his suspicious nature, is in David C. Martin, *Wilderness of Mirrors* (Harper and Row, 1980), pp. 10-12.

"Jim saw in Israel a true ally ..." Teddy Kollek, who procured arms and then many friendships for Israel in the United States, and later was the long-time mayor of Jerusalem, is quoted in Martin, *Wilderness*, p. 20.

The story of Elyashiv Ben-Horin and his recruitment efforts in Washington is in Dan Raviv and Yossi Melman, *Friends In Deed: Inside the U.S.-Israel Alliance* (Hyperion, 1994), pp. 63-4.

"Russians were infiltrating Israel's army": Stephen Green, *Taking Sides: America's Secret Relations with a Militant Israel* (William Morrow, 1984), p. 19, quoting a memorandum from acting Secretary of State Robert Lovett to Secretary of Defense James Forrestal; also Martin, *Wilderness*, p. 20.

Israel started feeding data about Soviet life, and allowed the CIA to use Israeli intelligence assets: in Martin, p. 21; and Eshed, p. 163.

"Shiloah persuaded the prime minister" to cooperate with the United States on intelligence: in Harel, *Security and Democracy*, pp. 381-2.

Amos Manor's quotations are from his interview in March 2006 with one of the authors.

Chapter 4

Victor Grayevsky, who had become an Israeli radio journalist and executive, spoke with one of the authors a year before his death at age 82 in 2007. See Yossi Melman, "Trade Secrets," in *Ha'aretz*, March 10, 2006.

Manor, former head of Shin Bet who forged the intelligence alliance with the United States, spoke with one of the authors in March 2006. Manor died in August 2007 at age 88.

"Israel's great friend in Washington helped to maintain the smoke screen ..." Angleton's apparent role in 1956 was reported by the British newspaper, *The Guardian*, on May 13, 1987.

Nir Baruch, the Israeli spy in Cuba who helped the CIA, told his story to one of the authors on condition that it not be published until he died. See Yossi Melman in *Ha'aretz* on March 3, 2011, after Baruch passed away at age 88.

"Angleton had one major responsibility," running the CIA's connection with Israel in a "compartmented fashion": ex-CIA director William Colby, quoted in John Ranelagh, *The Agency: The Rise and Decline of the CIA* (Weidenfeld and Nicolson, 1986), pp. 560-3.

On King Abdullah and continued clandestine relations between Jordan and Israel, see Yossi Melman and Dan Raviv, *Behind the Uprising* (Greenwood Press, 1989).

On Hosni Zaim of Syria being on Western intelligence payrolls: Avi Shlaim, *Collusion Across the Jordan* (Oxford University Press, 1988), p. 423; Copeland, *Game Player*, pp. 93-101. The Israeli connection was revealed at a Tel Aviv University seminar in April 1989.

"Israeli military advisers trained Kurdish guerrillas": Future Mossad directors Zvi Zamir and Nahum Admoni both made undercover trips to the Kurds, and Aryeh (Lova) Eliav revealed his activities in his Hebrew book, *Rings of Testimony* (Am Oved, 1984), pp. 156-164.

Ben-Gurion's secret trip to Turkey and "engine problems that forced an emergency landing": Samuel Segev, *The Iranian Triangle: The Secret Relations Between Israel-Iran-USA* (Maariv Books, 1981), p. 88.

"...the Mossad trained Turkish secret agents in counterintelligence techniques and the use of technical devices": Yossi Melman, *The CIA Report on the Intelligence Services of Israel* (Erez, 1982), pp. 59-60, quoting a classified report dated 1976 and found by Iranian militants in the U.S. Embassy in Tehran in 1979.

On Israeli operatives persuading Iran to let the CIA build a listening post, see Meir Doron and Joseph Gelman, *Confidential: The Life of Secret Agent Turned Hollywood Tycoon Arnon Milchan*, (Gefen Books, 2011), pp. 68-70.

Chapter 5

The gathering of French, British, and Israeli leaders around a table in a French mansion in 1956 is based on an interview by one of the authors with Asher Ben-Natan in December 1988; also, on an article by Mordecai Bar-On, then an aide to Moshe Dayan, in *Yediot Aharonot*, October 24, 1986.

Isser Harel "had to take a back seat" on war plans: article in *Ma'ariv*, October 24, 1986, as the 30th anniversary of the Sinai/Suez war approached.

On the nuclear research reactor delivered by the United States at Nahal Sorek, see Green, *Taking Sides*, pp. 149-150.

"Bourgès-Maunoury... signed top secret documents": Many details from Shimon Peres's point of view are in Matti Golan, *Peres* (Schocken Books, 1982), p. 54.

After resignations from the atomic energy commission, "... they were pleased that fewer people would now have the privilege of knowing what Israel was doing": Peter Pringle and James Spiegelman, *The Nuclear Barons: The Inside Story of How They Created our Nuclear Nightmare* (Michael Joseph, 1982), pp. 295-6; and Golan, *Road to Peace*, p. 51.

"He knew how to keep a secret ...": Shimon Peres, who in 2007 would become Israel's president, gave his assessment of Binyamin Blumberg to one of the authors in April 2005. See Yossi Melman, *Ha'aretz*, April 22, 2005.

"The spy-priest sent a highly critical cable" to Paris after visiting the Negev: Golan, *Road to Peace*, pp. 57-58.

On Blumberg and "what did he have to keep an eye on at the Defense Ministry?": Baruch Nir was interviewed by one of the authors in June 2005.

"Lakam was established behind my back and without my knowledge": Harel was quoted in the newspaper *Yediot Aharonot*, May 29, 1987.

Dimona was "not a textile factory, a distillation facility, or a metallurgical laboratory": See Avner Cohen, *Israel and the Bomb* (Columbia University Press, 1998), p. 85.

America's defense secretary saying "the plant is not for peaceful purposes" is in Cohen, *ibid.*, p. 89. A chapter in Cohen's book, "The Dimona Visits (1964-1967)," is the most thorough account of U.S. government inspection attempts, pp. 175-194.

On David Ben-Gurion's revelation of an atomic reactor in December 1960, see Amos Perlmutter, Michael Handel, and Uri Bar-Joseph, *Two Minutes Over Baghdad* (Vallentine Mitchell and Co., 1982), p. 26. Also, *The New York Times*, "Ben-Gurion Explains Project" and "Israel Assured U.S. on Reactors," December 22, 1960.

Avner Cohen wrote about the delicate verbal dance between Ben-Gurion and John F. Kennedy in *Israel and the Bomb* and again in *The Worst-Kept Secret: Israel's Bargain with the Bomb* (Columbia University Press, 2010); and also in his article in 1995, "Stumbling Into Opacity: The Untold Ben Gurion-Kennedy Dimona Exchange (1961-1963)."

Ben-Gurion spoke of the need to "build up a deterrent force" several times—for instance, in a meeting with newspaper editors in the summer of 1963, according to Zaki Shalom, *Ben-Gurion's Political Struggles, 1963-1967: A Lion in Winter*, p. 41.

On Peres's promise to Kennedy not to "be the first" to introduce nuclear weapons into the region, see "Let the World Worry," by Yossi Melman in *Ha'aretz*, December 13, 2006.

Details of Israel's deception efforts aimed at American nuclear inspectors were revealed to the authors in September 1992 by Abba Eban, the former foreign minister who died in 2002.

John Hadden, former CIA station chief in Tel Aviv, reminisced about nuclear secrets, alcohol, and Mrs. Ben-Gurion when interviewed in 1991 by Dan Raviv and Yossi Melman for *Friends In Deed: Inside the U.S.-Israel Alliance*, pp. 121-131.

Retired U.S. government officials revealed to one of the authors, in Washington in 2011, that Yitzhak Rabin—as Israel's ambassador to the United States—produced a new formula in late 1968 that until there is a nuclear test, Israel will not be considered to possess nuclear weapons. See Avner Cohen, *Israel and the Bomb*, pp. 317-8, who reveals that Rabin's notion came up in talks with Paul Warnke, a Defense Department official in the outgoing Lyndon Johnson administration. Warnke was trying to persuade Israel to sign the Nuclear Non-Proliferation Treaty. Israel always refused to do so.

Richard Nixon's administration, which took office in late January 1969, accepted Israel as an undeclared nuclear power, "if Israel kept its nuclear profile low." U.S. inspectors' visits to Dimona stopped. See Cohen, *ibid.*, pp. 323 and 334-7.

Chapter 6

Levi Levi's confirmation that in Kazakhstan he had contacts with the Soviet NKVD, a predecessor of the KGB, and more information about Levi were in Polish documents—declassified after the fall of the former Communist government—shared with the authors in October 2010 by Leszek Gluchowski, a Polish-Canadian historian.

On the role of sayanim (helpers), one book claims they must all be Jewish. See Victor Ostrovsky and Claire Hoy, *By Way of Deception: The Making and Unmaking of a Mossad Officer* (St. Martin's Press, 1990), pp. 86-7. Ostrovsky, who asserts he was an officer compelled to leave the Mossad after being unfairly blamed for an error, was—according to Israeli officials—only a cadet at the agency's academy. While they denied many highly critical statements in his book, Israel's government did see it as potentially damaging and unwisely tried to prevent its publication in the United States. The controversy helped make it a best seller. As for a "list" of 7,000 sayanim worldwide, Ostrovsky and Hoy wrote: "One thing you know for sure is that even if a Jewish person knows it is the Mossad, he might not agree to work with you—but he won't turn you in."

Ex-Israeli operative Avri El-Ad in his book, *Decline of Honor*, pp. 267-8, told of the message tapped out by Motke Kedar: "Don't let them drag you down."

The refusal to grant Kedar a new hearing was reported by *Hadashot*, November 14, 1986; and by *Yediot Aharonot*, February, 4, 1990. Those newspapers also quoted Yehoshafat Harkabi, the former Aman chief, who said recruits for spy missions are "not uncomplicated."

Isser Harel's boast that judges and courts decided the fate of aberrant agents, and "no traitor was ever executed," is in his book, *Security and Democracy*, pp. 270-3; and in the *Jerusalem Post* magazine, January 20, 1989.

Harel's feeling that creation of an operations unit was like a "birth" was related during a rare interview with Harel, conducted by author Yossi Melman in Harel's house in Tzahala on December 12, 2002, two months before Harel's death at age 91.

Aharon Cohen's espionage against Israel, and his trial, are reported by Michael Bar-Zohar, *Isser Harel and Israel's Security Service*, pp. 106-8, 148.

For more on Yair Racheli's account of "the Comb" method of surveillance for counter-espionage, see "Parallel Underworlds" by Yossi Melman in *Ha'aretz*, May 16, 2003.

On Harel blaming the FBI for failing to share all information about Kurt Sitta, see Harel, *Soviet Espionage*, pp. 169-175; also *Ma'ariv*, November 14, 1986.

For Israel Be'er's claim, until his dying day, that he was innocent of espionage: Harel, *Soviet Espionage*, pp. 131-6.

A recent and thorough book on the Israeli mission to kidnap the notorious Nazi war criminal in Argentina was *Hunting Eichmann* by Neal Bascomb (Houghton Mifflin Harcourt, 2010).

Indications that hunting for Nazis was not a high priority for Harel before Eichmann was located include two memos between Shin Bet and the Mossad in 1952, each suggesting that the other organization should deal with hunting for Eichmann. One said, "We have found that we do not have the means to devote suitable attention to dealing with the matter." They were revealed when the Mossad took the rare step, in early 2012, of putting relics from the capture of Eichmann—including the false passport in the name Ze'ev Zichroni—on display at Beit HaTfutsot (The Diaspora Museum) in Ramat-Aviv. A Mossad archivist said the exhibit had been inside the agency's headquarters. See *Ha'aretz*, in Hebrew on April 12, and in English on April 15, 2012, at Haaretz.com.

Simon Wiesenthal's employment by the Mossad was revealed by historian Tom Segev in *Simon Wiesenthal: The Life and Legends* (Knopf Doubleday, 2010), pp. 9 and 182.

Moshe Tavor, one of the Israelis who kidnapped Eichmann, was interviewed by Saguy Green in *Yediot Aharonot*, "The Safecracker of the Mossad," April 18, 2006, only three weeks before Tavor's death at age 89.

Harel published his version of the Eichmann kidnapping in 1975, *The House on Garibaldi Street* (re-released by Frank Cass Publishers, 1997).

On the surprise and joy in Israel's parliament when the capture of Eichmann was announced: Ze'ev Schiff and Eitan Haber, *Israel, Army, and Defense: A Dictionary* (Zmora Bitan Modan, 1976), pp. 36-7; Dennis Eisenberg, Uri Dan, and Eli Landau, *The Mossad: Inside Stories* (New American Library, 1978), pp. 177-198 and 212-227; and Stewart Steven, *The Spymasters of Israel* (Ballantine Books, 1980), pp. 130-9.

Although Eichmann is the only person put to death by Israel's judicial system, there was the somewhat legal execution of Captain Meir Toubianski, shot on the orders of military intelligence chief Isser Beeri in 1948.

"I believe that he has no idea where Mengele is," Zvi Malchin said to Harel, according to Malchin himself—writing in Hebrew in 1987 as Peter Mann with co-author Uri Dan; and then in English with Harry Stein, *Eichmann in My Hands* (Warner Books, 1990).

Harel said that Mengele moved to Paraguay, then Brazil: Reuters, "Israeli Who Captured Eichmann," April 6, 1989.

"Don't touch Mossinson," the request from Ben-Gurion to Francisco Franco of Spain: according to Yigal Mossinson, interviewed by the authors, December 6, 1988.

Among those telling of the successful boyhunt for Yossele Schumacher: Stewart Steven, *Spymasters*, pp. 141-151; and Eisenberg, Dan, and Landau, *The Mossad*, pp. 36-53.

One of the Israeli journalists recruited by Harel to write about the dangers of German scientists in Egypt was Samuel (Shmuel) Segev, interviewed about this mission by one of the authors on October 21, 1988. The mission was also chronicled in Bar-Zohar, *Isser Harel*, p. 240.

Amos Manor, nominal chief of Shin Bet, spoke to one of the authors in March 2006 about the advice he gave to a stubborn Harel when Harel had his final falling-out with Ben-Gurion.

Chapter 7

"It was a command." David Ben-Gurion giving the Mossad directorship to Meir Amit is told by Eitan Haber, *War Will Break Out Today: Memoirs of Brigadier General Israel Lior, Aide-de-Camp to Prime Ministers Levi Eshkol and Golda Meir* (published in Hebrew by Edanim/Yediot Aharonot, 1988), p. 62.

Isser Harel being forced to testify to an inquiry about the campaign against German scientists was written in Hebrew by Yair Kotler, *Joe Returns to the Limelight* (Modan, 1988), pp. 40, 61, 66-8; also Eitan Haber, *ibid.*, p. 62; and *Yediot Aharonot*, October 16, 1987, which quotes Harel himself.

Yitzhak Shamir resigned: Kotler, *Joe Returns*, p. 61; Steven, *Spymasters of Israel*, pp. 186-187.

"A woman could not gather information in the Arab world," an attitude that changed in the next 20 years, was said to one of the authors in 1988 by a long-time Mossad male operative, who wished to remain anonymous.

On using prostitutes for sexual blackmail missions, the late Hesi Carmel, a Mossad operative who became a French journalist and author, spoke with one of the authors in June 2001.

On the Mossad's virtual monopoly over foreign intelligence collection, with some military exceptions for Aman: Melman, *The CIA Report*, pp. 41-56; and Walter Laqueur, *A World of Secrets: The Use and Limits of Intelligence* (Basic Books, 1985), p. 220.

"It was more effective and less complicated to kill" a Nazi war criminal such as Herbert Cukurs, Meir Amit told one of the authors in an interview in August 2007. Amit died in July 2009 at age 88.

In telling of some of the successes by the Keshet operations department, later renamed Neviot, Mossad veterans did not wish to reveal precisely where the legendary Yaacov Barda and others were active against Arab targets.

On planting misleading stories in the press as Mossad "psychological warfare," senior Mossad veteran David Kimche was interviewed by one of the authors in June 2007. He died in March 2010 at age 82.

A more complete account of the secret meetings between Israeli officials and King Hussein of Jordan can be found in Yossi Melman and Dan Raviv, *Behind the Uprising* (Greenwood Press, 1989).

On the unsolved disappearance and murder of a Moroccan dissident, with Mossad operatives involved: "The Murder of Mehdi Ben Barka," *Time* magazine, December 29, 1975. Also: Steven, *Spymasters*, pp. 240-252. In the Israeli press, *Monitin* magazine in June 1987 and *Yediot Aharonot* on October 16 and 19, 1987, had some details.

Chapter 8

Former Aman and Mossad director Meir Amit spoke with one of the authors in January 2009, six months before his death.

Otto Skorzeny's role as an organizer of Odessa, an organization of former SS officers, and its "rat lines" that smuggled Nazis to South America, is recounted in many books and is neatly summarized in Michael Benson, *Inside Secret Societies* (Kensington Publishing, 2005), p. 132.

The negative view of Israeli intelligence by the late CIA Arabist, Archie Roosevelt Jr., is cited by Stephen Dorril, *MI6: Inside the Covert World of Her Majesty's Secret Intelligence Service* (Touchstone, 2002), p. 654.

Ex-Mossad chief Meir Amit told how the Israelis found and recruited Skorzeny in a public lecture in April 1997 in Tel Aviv, and in an interview with one of the authors in May 1997. Rafi Eitan and Avraham Ahituv also shared their versions with one of the authors in May 2006. See also Michael Bar-Zohar and Nissim Mishal, *The Mossad* (in Hebrew, Miskal/Yediot Aharonot, 2010), pp. 108-9.

Amit spoke about his 1966 meeting in Paris with Egypt's Colonel Khalil, in the interview with one of the authors in May 1997.

The motto of Sayeret Matkal is *"Ha-me'iz M'natze'ach"* (The Darer Wins). Two books in Hebrew detail some of the history of the élite military unit: Avner Shur, *Border Crosser* (Kinneret/Zmora-Bitan/Dvir, 2008), and Moshe Zonder, *The Elite Unit of Israel* (Keter, 2000).

The risky proposals to steal a MiG-21 warplane from Egypt or from Poland—what became Operation Diamond—were related to one of the authors by Amit in 1997. Also: Gad Shimron, *The Mossad and the Myth* (Keter Publishing, 2011), pp. 144-6.

Books in the past said there was a female Israeli, sent to Iraq as part of Operation Diamond, to help persuade the pilot Munir Redfa to defect; however, well-informed sources recently told the authors that no Mossad woman was involved.

The story of Abbas Hilmi, the Egyptian pilot who defected to Israel, and his untimely end in Argentina was related to one of the authors by an Israeli intelligence veteran of Aman's Unit 154, which handled Hilmi's interrogation.

The Israeli spy Eli Cohen was transmitting too much intelligence from Damascus for his own safety: Samuel Segev, *Alone in Damascus: The Life and Death of Eli Cohen* (Keter, 1986), pp. 23 and 60; and Steven, *Spymasters of Israel*, pp. 202-4.

The public campaign by Cohen's family to have his body handed over to Israel by Syria's government can be seen at www.EliCohen.org.

Masoud Buton, an operative for Aman and the Mossad in several Arab countries, wrote his autobiography with Israeli journalist Ronni Shaked, *From Jerusalem to Damascus and Back: An Intelligence Agent Behind Enemy Lines* (in Hebrew, Lavi Publishing, 2012). Buton died in 2011 in France, where he worked as a dishwasher in a restaurant before finding success as a trader of various goods. Ex-Mossad chief Amit called Buton a liar, quoted by YnetNews.com, "Spy: Eli Cohen Died because of Failure," November 5, 2006.

Yaakov (Jacob) Nahmias recalled the agent he ran in Egypt, Wolfgang Lotz, in the documentary film *The Champagne Spy*, directed by Nadav Schirman (2007).

"It was a cardinal error," permitting Lotz to have two marriages: Avraham Shalom, a former head of Shin Bet, said that in Schirman's film.

Interviews with Lotz's son, Oded Gur-Arie, living in the United States, and with others who knew Lotz/Gur-Arie, are in Yossi Melman, "Double Dad," *Ha'aretz* weekend magazine, March 9, 2007.

Amit remarked on the art of running double agents, in his interview with one of the authors in 1997.

"I never got drunk. I outdrank them": Victor Grayevsky told one of the authors in an interview in 2006. See Yossi Melman, "Our Man in the KGB," in *Ha'aretz*, October 5, 2006.

Amit spoke of disinformation "tailored" by three Israeli agencies, in his interview with one of the authors in 1997.

A longtime Shin Bet commander who ran the Yated double-agent operation, David Ronen, was interviewed by one of the authors in March 2011. See Yossi Melman, "How Israel Won the Six-Day War," in *Ha'aretz*, March 31, 2011.

"Let them believe their tall tale," Isser Harel said to one of the authors, quoted in "How Israel Won the Six-Day War," *Ha'aretz*, March 31, 2011.

Chapter 9

Yasser Arafat's escape from the West Bank in 1967: See Ehud Yaari, *Fatah* (in Hebrew from Levin-Epstein, 1970), pp. 101-2.

On Yosef Harmelin's rise to be director of Shin Bet, see *Hadashot* newspaper of June 19, 1987. Also, *Ma'ariv* of April 7, 1988.

On the "masqueraders" unit in Arab communities, Shmuel Moriah was interviewed by one of the authors in June 1996 when he revealed for the first time the existence of the unit. See Yossi Melman quoted in "Israeli Agents Licensed to Wed," *The Reading Eagle* (Pennsylvania), September 30, 1998, p. A2, as well as many other newspapers citing his *Ha'aretz* article. Also, "Sixty Years Later, Spies' Lives Revealed," in *Yediot Aharonot*'s English-language YnetNews.com, February 20, 2011.

"The double life they were living cost them emotionally," said Amos Manor, retired head of Shin Bet, in an interview with one of the authors in March 2006.

"The Palestinians were in a state of shock," David Kimche said when interviewed by one of the authors in September 2007. He also told of his Khartoum trip in the summer of 1967. Kimche died in 2010.

Harmelin (Shin Bet) and Yariv (Aman) spreading rumors of how tough the Israeli hard line would be: recounted by longtime Israeli officer Shlomo Gazit, *The Stick and the Carrot: The Israeli Administration in Judea and Samaria* (in Hebrew from Zmora Bitan, 1985), pp. 133, 223, 284.

Shin Bet agents spread across the West Bank and Gaza often gave advance information of attacks, according to a CIA report on the Israeli intelligence community discovered in the United States embassy in Tehran and published by the Iranian militants who took the diplomats hostages there in 1979. See Melman, *The CIA Report on the Intelligence Services of Israel*, p. 93.

Most Palestinians preferred peace, quiet, and prosperity, and not armed uprisings, according to Yaari, *Fatah*, pp. 91-103.

Harmelin did not believe in physically abusive interrogations, according to the Israeli newspaper *Hadashot*, November 6, 1987.

Chapter 10

Zvi Zamir was a colorless general who became Mossad director in 1968. He is profiled by Eitan Haber and Ze'ev Schiff in *Israel, Army and Defense*, p. 195.

The revelation that Yosef Harmelin only reluctantly fired a Shin Bet department chief because of the Munich Olympics massacre was in the Hebrew newspaper *Hadashot*, November 6, 1987.

Zadok Ofir, the Israeli intelligence case officer who was shot in Brussels by a PLO man he was trying to recruit, told his story to one of the authors, in Tel Aviv, in December 2007.

Former Mossad director Zamir himself informed the authors that there was no formal Committee X to decide on life or death for individual terrorists. He also lambasted Steven Spielberg's movie, *Munich*, which was based on a best selling book by Canadian journalist George Jonas, *Vengeance* (British edition published by Collins, 1984; American re-release by Simon and Schuster, 2005). Jonas based his book on conversations and travels with an Israeli, "Avner," who claimed to have led a Mossad assassination squad. Several published reports say that man is a New York-based security consultant, Juval Aviv. Zamir was among those who said that the story's details were entirely invented and that Aviv was not part of a Mossad hit team.

Another book on the killings of Palestinian terrorists in Europe by the Mossad, after the Munich Olympics massacre, is by David B. Tinnin with Dag Christensen, *The Hit Team* (British edition by Futura Books, 1977).

"What can I say, that it consoled me?" Shin Bet man Baruch Cohen's widow Nurit was quoted in the Hebrew magazine, *Monitin*, in February 1988.

Ali Hassan Salameh is described as "Arafat's young protégé" in Simon Reeve, *One Day in September: The Full Story of the Munich Olympics Massacre* (Skyhorse Publishing, 2011), which is one of several books reporting that the CIA paid for Salameh's trip to Hawaii and Florida in 1977. Salameh is also said to have briefed officers at CIA headquarters in Langley, Virginia. See also Michael Bar-Zohar and Eitan Haber, *The Quest for the Red Prince: Israel's Relentless Manhunt for One of the World's Deadliest and Most Wanted Arab Terrorists* (Lyons Press, 2002).

David Ignatius, then with *The Wall Street Journal*, in February 1983 broke the news that Salameh had been the liaison between the PLO and the CIA. Ignatius reported that Salameh kept rejecting offers of payments from the Agency. In his regular column in *The Washington Post* on November 12, 2004, Ignatius wrote: "I'm told that it was blessed, from the beginning, by Arafat, who wanted to open a channel to the Americans." Ignatius added: "Arafat remained a believer in the secret power of the CIA; that was one of his many mistakes." A thinly veiled account of the CIA-PLO connection is in the first novel by Ignatius, *Agents of Innocence* (W.W. Norton, 1987).

Uri Dan, the late Israeli journalist, profiled Sylvia Raphael when writing in *The New York Post*, February 19, 2005, about her death from cancer in South Africa at age 67.

Her story is also recounted in Hebrew by former Mossad operative Gad Shimron in *The Mossad and Its Myth* (Keter Publishing, 2011), pp. 175-7.

Eliezer Palmor, then Israel's ambassador to Norway, told of his daughter's discovery of Raphael's romance with her defense lawyer, in a conversation with one of the authors in December 2011.

A BBC Panorama documentary in January 2006 stated that when Black September leader Ali Hassan Salameh was assassinated in Beirut, Erika Chambers herself pressed the transmitter button that detonated the car bomb.

A German journalist who wrote about Chambers is Wilhelm Dietl, who himself was a covert case officer for his country's BND for 11 years. Dietl wrote a memoir and was interviewed by one of the authors: see Yossi Melman, "Cover Story," in *Ha'aretz*, June 14, 2007.

Erika Chambers's father, a well known race car driver for MG in Britain, wrote two memoirs: Marcus Chambers, *Works Wonders: Competition Manager Recalls an Historic Era of Motorsport* (Motor Racing Publications Ltd, 1995); and *With a Little Bit of Luck!* (Mercian Manuals Ltd, 2008). They make no mention of his daughter who vanished. He died at age 98 in 2009.

In discussing "Avner," the main source for the book *Vengeance* and Steven Spielberg's movie *Munich*, Zamir called him an imposter in an interview by one of the authors on February 17, 2005.

There was a further absurdity after the incident in Rome in 1973 in which the Egyptian, Ashraf Marwan—secretly working for the Mossad—set up the arrest of Palestinian terrorists with missiles. Twenty years later, an Italian investigative magistrate issued an official charge that Zamir and the Mossad were responsible for the destruction of an Italian military plane—a kind of revenge, as the judge saw it, for Italy's release of the Palestinians with their rockets. Zamir and the Israeli government strongly denied the charge, arguing that Israel does not down the airplanes of friendly countries.

Chapter 11

Meir Amit, former Mossad director, spoke with one of the authors in August 2007.

"The two Israelis were lucky that the host country suspected nothing." The scientist who in 1988 told one of the authors about supplying photocopies to Lakam asked for anonymity.

More information on arms smuggling to newborn Israel, with cooperation from Jewish and Gentile criminals in America, is in Raviv and Melman, *Friends In Deed: Inside the U.S.-Israel Alliance*, pp. 36-46.

Eliyahu Sakharov, the furniture manufacturer who smuggled nuclear materials for Israel, described his experiences in letters to old friends and government officials. He published some of the details in a book in Hebrew, *Ma'as Ba-Tzel* (meaning *Deed in the Shadow*; Ministry of Defense Publishing, 2000), translated into English as *Memoirs*. The book had many deletions ordered by Israel's military censor, and the ministry's security officers vetted the manuscript attentively.

Avraham Hermoni of Lakam was in diplomatic lists as scientific counselor in the Israeli embassy in Washington from 1968 to 1972, according to Charles Babcock, "U.S. an Intelligence Target of the Israelis, Officials Say," *The Washington Post*, June 5, 1986.

The issue of what Carl Duckett of the CIA told members of the U.S. Nuclear Regulatory Commission—and what Edward Teller told Duckett—is discussed by Avner Cohen in *Israel and the Bomb*, pp. 297-8, and footnotes on pp. 421-2.

Victor Gilinsky, former NRC member, gave his understanding of Duckett's message in 1976—including the references to Numec—in a letter to *The New York Review of Books*, May 13, 2004.

Ken Follett's *Triple* (Signet, 1980) is a novel clearly inspired by Israel's clever acquisition of 200 tons of yellowcake uranium by means of a ship-to-ship transfer. Investigative journalists with Britain's *Sunday Times* wrote an excellent non-fiction account: Elaine Davenport, Paul Eddy, and Peter Gillman, *The Plumbat Affair* (A. Deutsch, 1978). But the role played by Blumberg, Sakharov, and Lakam was unknown until now.

On Alfred Frauenknecht visiting Israel, viewing the Kfir's inaugural flight, but feeling abandoned, see Steven, *Spymasters*, pp. 210-220; and Eisenberg, Dan, and Landau, *The Mossad*, pp. 177-198, 212-227.

For more about Hollywood producer Arnon Milchan and his secret work with Lakam's Binyamin Blumberg, see Yossi Melman, "Discreet", in *Ha'aretz*, April 23, 2005.

An almost complete account of Milchan's parallel, clandestine career is in Meir Doron and Joseph Gelman, *Confidential: The Life of Secret Agent Turned Hollywood Tycoon Arnon Milchan* (Gefen Books, 2011). On p. 268, the book reveals the role played by Milchan in obtaining blueprints for centrifuges from Urenco. After their initial manuscript was complete, Milchan partially cooperated with Doron and Gelman.

The use of older centrifuges inside the Dimona complex to test the effectiveness of a computer worm to be injected into Iran's nuclear centrifuge system was revealed by "Israeli Test on Worm Called Crucial in Iran Nuclear Delay," *The New York Times*, January 15, 2011.

The statement that just before the war of June 1967, Israel would only have to "connect a few wires" to have an operational atomic bomb, is in oral testimony by retired General Tzvi Tzur, a former IDF chief of staff, who in 1967 was a special assistant to the defense minister in charge of Lakam and the nuclear project. Before his death in 2004, Tzur recorded his memories for the Rabin Center in Tel Aviv. Parts were published in *Ha'aretz* on September 16, 2011.

Lt. Colonel Dov Tamari's recollection of being ordered to prepare to place Israel's first atomic bomb atop a mountain in Egypt's Sinai was in *Ha'aretz* of September 16, 2011.

The assertion that Israel conducted its first nuclear test in September 1979, apparently with South Africa's cooperation, is based on American officials, as is the description of the

Jericho missile—a secret Israeli project based on a French missile—as being capable or designed to carry a nuclear warhead.

Binyamin Blumberg's post-retirement life in Tel Aviv, under the name Vered, was described by several former intelligence operatives after 2002. His one and only interview was in the Hebrew-language newspaper *Ma'ariv*, April 6, 2012.

A Man Without Qualities was an unfinished but widely read three-volume novel from the 1930s by Austrian writer Robert Musil.

Chapter 12

Aman is generally overshadowed by the Mossad, and this position is somewhat reminiscent of America's National Security Agency. With electronic and communications monitoring capabilities far larger than Aman's, the NSA lives in the shadow of the CIA. But it is the NSA's eavesdropping and data analysis that lay the groundwork for American intelligence successes. See James Bamford, *The Puzzle Palace: A Report on America's Most Secret Agency* (Houghton Mifflin, 1982).

A longer account of the Egyptian brigadier general, codenamed Koret by the Mossad, who spied for Israel, can be found in David Arbel and Uri Neeman, *Unforgivable Delusion* (in Hebrew, Miskal-Yediot-Chemed Books, 2005), pp. 204-214. Theirs is one of the best books on the intelligence failure in the 1973 Yom Kippur War. The authors are former senior Mossad intelligence analysts.

On the Egyptian who worked for the Mossad at the port of Alexandria, and how his "war indicator" was ignored in Tel Aviv, see Yossi Melman, "Regards from Alexandria," *Ha'aretz*, October 8, 2008.

King Hussein of Jordan's secret meetings with Israeli leaders are chronicled in Yossi Melman and Dan Raviv, *Behind the Uprising* (Greenwood Press, 1989).

Ashraf Marwan, the high-ranking Egyptian who was close to Presidents Nasser and Sadat, was the Mossad's best foreign agent. Some in Israeli intelligence still suspect that he ultimately was serving Egypt. See Yossi Melman, "The Truth about Israel's Egyptian Spy," *Ha'aretz*, December 17, 2010.

Valuable information about the Egyptian spy can be found in a Hebrew book by Uri Bar-Joseph, *The Angel: Ashraf Marwan, the Mossad, and the Yom Kippur War* (Kinneret-Zmora Bitan-Dvir, 2010).

Questions about what Israeli and U.S. intelligence knew, in the months before the October 1973 war, were discussed in 1998 by a unique panel of Israeli, American, and Arab officials, published as Richard B. Parker (editor), *The October War: A Retrospective* (University of Florida Press, 2001), pp. 130-143.

Golda Meir's despair during the 1973 war, including thoughts of suicide, were related by her personal secretary and confidante, Lou Kaddar, in the *Davar* newspaper weekly supplement, December 7, 1987.

The creation of the "Devil's Advocate Department" inside Aman is discussed by its former head, retired Colonel Shmuel Even, in "The Revision Process in Intelligence," an essay in Amos Gilboa and Ephraim Lapid (eds.), *Israel's Silent Defender: An Inside Look at Sixty Years of Israeli Intelligence* (Gefen Publishing and the Israel Intelligence Heritage and Commemoration Center, 2012), p. 309.

The rescue of hijacked Air France passengers at Entebbe airport in Uganda by Israeli commandos is recounted in many books, including William Stevenson, *90 Minutes at Entebbe* (Bantam Books, 1976).

Chapter 13

On the frequent declarations by Mossad directors that the peak moments of their careers came when they helped Jews move to Israel: The authors heard these phrases or similar ones from Isser Harel, Meir Amit, Zvi Zamir, Shabtai Shavit, and Efraim Halevy in the various interviews conducted with them since the 1970s.

Shlomo Hillel told the story of his secret work in Iraq in his book in Hebrew, *East Wind: On a Secret Mission to the Arab Lands* (Edanim/Yediot Aharonot and Ministry of Defense, 1985). Also see Howard M. Sachar, *A History of Israel* (Alfred A. Knopf, 1985), pp. 398-403.

On Nativ and Bitzur and their role in Jewish intelligence, see *Ha'aretz* articles by Yossi Melman: "Return of the Nativ" on July 2, 2009; and "Why the Mossad Must Remain an Intelligence Service for All Jews" on November 4, 2010.

On Yeshayahu (Shaike) Dan and his deals with Romania's dictator Nicolae Ceausescu, one of the authors interviewed Dan in 1990, four years before his death. Also, a former cabinet minister in charge of immigration, Yaakov Tzur, was interviewed by one of the authors in May 2002.

Yaakov Kedmi, the head of Nativ in the late 1990s whose activism began as a daring student in Moscow, was interviewed by one of the authors in July 2007. He told his own life story and related the anecdote about Mossad chief Nahum Admoni telling the KGB, "We never spied against you."

The rescue of Tunisian Jews, arranged by Mossad men in Morocco thanks to the French navy, was revealed in *Ha'aretz* on May 29, 1987; also *Yediot Aharonot*, January 22, 1988, and Reuters news agency, December 28, 1988.

Leo Gleser told his story exclusively to one of the authors. See Yossi Melman, "Jewish Cowboy," *Ha'aretz*, March 30, 2006.

Milt Bearden, formerly with the CIA, was interviewed by one of the authors in summer 2007.

Chapter 14

Nahik Navot, the Mossad veteran tied intimately to the war in Lebanon, spoke with the authors. See Yossi Melman, "Waltz Without Bashir," *Ha'aretz*, September 22, 2010.

Despite Israeli press restrictions and official censorship, stories of involvement with drug smugglers popped up, time and again, starting with *Foreign Report* (Economist Intelligence Unit, London) in early July 1993. Also, London's *Sunday Times* had an article on December 25, 1996; it is interesting that it was written by Israeli journalist Uzi Mahanaimi, who had been an officer in Unit 504 and was the son of a brigadier general in Aman.

Regarding the creation of Hezbollah, see Shimon Shapira, *Hizbullah: Between Iran and Lebanon* (in Hebrew, HaKibbutz HaMeuchad, 2000), pp. 96-134.

The CIA's car bomb in 1985 aimed at Hezbollah's Muhammad Fadlallah was revealed by Bob Woodward in *Veil: The Secret Wars of the CIA, 1981-1987* (Simon & Schuster, 1987), p. 506. See Woodward, in *The Washington Post* on May 12, 1985.

Chapter 15

An attempt to kill Iran's ambassador to Syria, Ali Akbar Mohtashemi, in February 1984 by sending him an exploding Quran, is related by Yossef Bodansky in *Terror: The Inside Story of the Terrorist Conspiracy in America* (SPI Books, 1994), pp. 34-6.

The pilot of one of the Israeli helicopters that attacked Hezbollah's leader Abbas Musawi spoke to Felix Frish, with the Israeli website NRG.com (affiliated with the newspaper *Ma'ariv*), February 16, 2008.

Security questions surrounding the two bombings in Argentina, the Israeli embassy in 1992 and the Jewish center in 1994, were reported by Yossi Melman, in *Ha'aretz*, December 25, 1997. In the article, Shin Bet director Yaakov Perry denied that he did not take seriously the dangers in South America. On the contrary, he said, "I always emphasized that South America had the potential for terrorist attacks against us, because of the proximity of

Muslim immigrant communities from the Middle East." He also said there was a thorough internal investigation, and Shin Bet was not found to have failed.

American intelligence sources shared the story of the Southeast Asian extremist, caught on a far-off Asian island and involved in the Hezbollah plot to bomb the Israeli embassy in Thailand. They revealed that an Asian security service turned over the man to the CIA, which tried to turn him into a double agent. They felt that telling the tale after 15 years would pose no harm.

The kidnapping, including the use of a female Lebanese agent, and interrogation of Mustafa Dirani was reported by Yossi Melman in *Ha'aretz* on April 20, 2010.

Shin Bet interrogators rejected rough methods used by Aman's Unit 504, according to a Shin Bet man who spoke with one of the authors in June 2007.

Chapter 16

Descriptions of Marcus Klingberg, after he served prison time in Israel for espionage, are based on a visit to Klingberg in Paris by one of the authors in April 2006. See Yossi Melman, "I Spy," in *Ha'aretz*, June 1, 2006.

Additional information comes from Klingberg's memoir, written with his lawyer Michael Sfard, *Ha-Meragel ha-Acharon (The Last Spy)*, published by Ma'ariv Books (Tel Aviv, 2007).

Various sources revealed that a Mossad agent delivered poisoned chocolates to a Palestinian terrorist leader, Wadi Haddad, and—with the motive given as his group's hijacking of an airliner to Entebbe, Uganda, as "the last straw"—see Aaron J. Klein, *Striking Back: The 1972 Munich Olympics Massacre and Israel's Deadly Response* (Random House, 2005), pp. 207-8.

In failing to detect Klinberg's disloyalty, "We asked the wrong questions." So said Victor Cohen, a Shin Bet investigator, when interviewed by one of the authors in March 2003.

Chaim Ben-Ami, the Shin Bet interrogator who made Klingberg break, spoke to one of the authors in June 2005. See Yossi Melman, "The Best Keeper of Secrets in the World," in *Ha'aretz*, September 21, 2007. A play written by Melman, "The Good Son," based on the interrogation of Klingberg, was performed by Tel Aviv's Cameri Theater in the summer of 2006.

"I agreed to work for the Soviet Union because they saved my life. And out of belief in the cause of Communism." So said Klingberg during his extensive interview by one of the authors in Paris in April 2006.

On an anthrax vaccine that was tested on Israeli soldiers, see Yossi Melman, "Defense Attempting to Block Report About Anthrax Trial," *Ha'aretz*, January 27, 2009.

The French newsletter that revealed a $200 million American investment, thanks to Israeli data on the anthrax tests, is www.IntelligenceOnline.com, number 591, April 2, 2009. It said that Israeli courts had banned publication of some details, but added that the United States wanted and received the results of tests on humans.

Chapter 17

Yitzhak Hofi was described as a man "of steel and infinite patience" and "a born commander" by another former Mossad director, Efraim Halevy, in his essay in Gilboa and Lapid (eds.), *Israel's Silent Defender*, p. 289.

Details of the Mossad's sabotage at the French port of La Seyne sur Mer in 1979 are based on interviews with Western intelligence veterans who were familiar with the incident.

The task of choosing an air route, and mapping electricity wires in enemy lands on the way to Baghdad were written about by the air intelligence officer of the attack operation in June 1981, Lt. Colonel Shamai Golan, "Aerial Intelligence for the Attack on Iraq's Nuclear Reactor," in *Israel's Silent Defender*, pp. 101-5. Golan also writes that King Hussein reported on the Israeli jets overhead, but there was no sign of a Saudi or Iraqi response to that.

The role played by Professor Uzi Even, in telling Shimon Peres about a plan to attack Iraq's nuclear reactor, was relayed by Even to one of the authors in November 2011.

Details of the attack on Osirak, first called Operation Ammunition Hill but later known as Operation Opera, are in Shlomo Nakdimon, *Tammuz in Flames* (in Hebrew, Yediot Aharonot Books, 1986); and Nakdimon, *First Strike: The Exclusive Story of How Israel Foiled Iraq's Attempt to Get the Bomb* (Summit Books, 1987). Nakdimon was a close advisor to Prime Minister Begin.

Relik Shafir, one of the eight Israeli pilots who bombed the Iraqi nuclear reactor, spoke with one of the authors in March 2005. See Yossi Melman, "War Games," at TabletMag. com, April 15, 2010.

Details of the raid on Osirak are also in an article marking the 30th anniversary of the attack, in *Israel Defense*, a Hebrew magazine, December 23, 2011.

On the Reagan Administration's official condemnation of the Israeli raid on Iraq, the national security advisor in the White House at the time, Richard Allen, wrote an op-ed in the *New York Times*, June 6, 2010.

On Ronald Reagan saying the Israelis have "claws" and "a sense of strategy," Richard Allen is quoted by Seymour Hersh, *The Samson Option* (Random House, 1991), p. 9.

Former Mossad director Shabtai Shavit told one of the authors that he regretted not assassinating Pakistan's A.Q. Khan. See Melman and Javedanfar, *The Nuclear Sphinx of Tehran*, pp. 151-6.

The story of the nuclear spy Mordecai Vanunu is based on the authors' previous book, *Every Spy a Prince*, pp. 360-379; and on additional research, including interviews with Yehiel Horev, head of the defense security agency Malmab; and Chaim Carmon, who held a similar post overseeing Dimona security. See Yossi Melman, "Who's Afraid of Mordecai Vanunu?" in *Ha'aretz*, March 19, 2004.

The authors also interviewed Mordecai Vanunu's brother, Meir, who ran a one-man campaign for his brother's freedom.

The claim that British newspaper tycoon Robert Maxwell was a Mossad agent or sayan features prominently in Gordon Thomas, *Gideon's Spies* (St. Martin's Griffin, 2009); and in Hersh, *Samson Option*, pp. 312-5. Thomas's book goes on to highlight a somewhat absurd claim that the Mossad murdered Maxwell after he tried to blackmail the agency.

Chapter 18

Jonathan Jay Pollard's boasts at Stanford University about being in the Israeli military or the Mossad were reported by *The Washington Post*, November 24, 1985.

In a letter to the authors in November 1990, Pollard said that federal authorities invented charges of quirky behavior to create "a legend of instability, to discredit and isolate me." Prosecutors insisted he had a long record of weaving incredible tales.

The CIA's assessment of Pollard as "a fanciful liar" was reported by *U.S. News and World Report*, June 1, 1987.

Pollard, when interviewed in the federal prison at Butner, North Carolina, in 1997 by Ben Caspit of the newspaper *Ma'ariv*, said he was especially concerned that Israel did not have U.S. information about Iraq's chemical weapons program. See New Jersey's *Metro West Jewish News*, May 22, 1997.

An official Israeli inquiry commission criticized senior political leaders for deciding not to ask what Lakam was doing. Pollard told Caspit: "[Defense Minister] Moshe Arens was deeply involved with my activities. He knew everything. He okayed everything. Arens's fingerprints were on all of the tasking orders I received." In the article, Arens replied that Pollard's claim was incorrect.

Pollard's time spent in Paris with Rafi Eitan and other Israeli handlers is related in Wolf Blitzer, *Territory of Lies* (Harper and Row, 1989), pp. 90-1. The use of a Washington apartment for massive photocopying is on pp. 96, 130-1.

Anne Pollard's final dinner with Avi Sella is on pp. 142-4.

On Ronald Reagan saying "I don't know why they are doing it," *Los Angeles Times*, November 27, 1985.

A longer account of the Iran-Contra affair is in Chapter 15, "The Chaos of Irangate," in *Every Spy a Prince*, pp. 324-342.

The CIA's assessment of the priorities of Israeli intelligence, including spying on the United States, is in Melman, *CIA Report*, p. 9.

Pollard's own memo to the judge, about his intelligence tasking, was reported by *Time* magazine, March 16, 1987.

"I do not intend to be used as a scapegoat," said Rafi Eitan, quoted in the Hebrew newspaper *Hadashot*, March 15, 1987.

President Clinton nearly released Pollard, according to George Tenet, *At the Center of the Storm: My Years at the CIA* (Harper Collins, 2007), pp. 66-72. Memoirs by President Bill Clinton and Middle East mediator Dennis Ross confirmed Tenet's threat to resign; although leaders of the American Jewish community say Tenet, for some reason, vehemently denied to them that he had blocked Pollard's freedom by threatening to quit. See Marc Perelman, "Former CIA Chief Changes Tune on Pollard Story," *Forward*, May 18, 2007.

The story of Yossi Amit, who was nearly recruited by the CIA, is recounted in Chapter 15, "Drug Deals," in Yossi Melman and Eitan Haber, *The Spies: Israel's Counter-Espionage Wars* (in Hebrew, Yediot Aharonot Books, 2002), pp. 245-256. The senator who apparently referred to Amit, although not by name, was David Durenberger, Republican of Minnesota.

Chapter 19

The Shin Bet scandal stemming from the Bus 300 hijack in Gaza in 1984 has been the subject of many Israeli newspaper articles, TV reports, and documentaries since Raviv and Melman, *Every Spy a Prince*, wrote of the case in 1990, pp. 278-300. The most recent and complete was, "The Breaking Line" by Gidi Weitz, in Hebrew in the *Ha'aretz* supplement of September 28, 2011, pp. 14-26, based on a documentary aired four days later, on October 2, on Israel's Channel 10.

Ehud Yatom, the Shin Bet man who admitted killing the two bus hijackers and said he was proud of it, spoke to *Yediot Aharonot*, quoted by, among others, British newspapers *The Independent* ("Shin Bet Man Proud of Murdering Two Arabs") on July 24, 1996, and *The Daily Telegraph* ("Justice Minister's Resignation Adds to Netanyahu's Troubles"), on August 9, 1996.

The Israeli human rights group B'Tselem provides casualty tolls from the intifada that began in 1988. These figures are available on its website, btselem.org/statistics/first_intifada_tables.

The story of Ahmed Yasin, the PLO security official in Tunis who spied for the Mossad, was told by several Arabic-language newspapers, including *A-Sharq al-Awsat* of December 19, 2003.

The proposal by Rafi Eitan, in the mid-1960s, to assassinate the PLO's Abu Jihad was related to one of the authors by Eitan in an interview in March 2012. See also *Yediot Aharonot*, March 23, 2012.

The assassination of Abu Jihad was recounted in Raviv and Melman, *Every Spy a Prince*, pp. 395-8. Also see Daniel Byman, *A High Price: The Triumphs and Failures of Israeli Counterterrorism* (Oxford University Press, 2011), p. 54; and, in Hebrew, Moshe Zonder, *Sayeret Matkal: The Elite Unit of Israel* (Keter, 2000), pp. 238-240.

Chapter 20

As revealed after the assassination of Prime Minister Yitzhak Rabin, the mole planted by Shin Bet in extreme right-wing circles and codenamed "Champagne" was Avishai Raviv, a young right-wing activist. It is mere coincidence that his last name is the same as one of the authors', for they are not related.

Benjamin Netanyahu telephoned one of the authors, barely three days after the murder of Yitzhak Rabin in 1995, and suggested to him to write an article that would raise the question of assassin Amir's connection to Israeli intelligence and Netanyahu's idea of "following the money."

The division of labor between Aman and Shin Bet when it came to monitoring the Palestinian Authority, dubbed "the Magna Carta," is in Ephraim Lavie, "Intelligence Challenges in the Palestinian Arena," in Gilboa and Lapid (eds.), *Israel's Silent Defender,* pp. 135-9. Dr. Lavie, a retired Aman colonel, writes: "I am of the opinion that in real-time situations between Israel and the Palestinians, IDI [Israel Defense Intelligence, meaning Aman] did not provide the decision makers with early warnings and suitable assessments."

Dov Weisglass, a close advisor to former prime minister Ariel Sharon, spoke with one of the authors and denied that Israel had poisoned Yasser Arafat. See Yossi Melman, "What Killed Yasser Arafat?" in his column, "The Arms Race," at *Haaretz.com,* July 14, 2011.

Chapter 21

The views and reminiscences of Avi Dichter, director of Shin Bet from 2000 to 2005, were shared with the authors several times in the years that followed.

American officials and former officials in Washington, who preferred not to be named, told the authors of suspicions that the Israelis were "playing" America, on subjects including Iran, in the years just after 9/11.

The notion of shared democratic values and strategic interests that bound the United States and Israel is fully discussed, with both examples and counterexamples, in Melman and Raviv, *Friends in Deed: Inside the U.S.-Israel Alliance.*

Critics of the America-Israel relationship who garnered significant attention included two professors, John J. Mearsheimer and Stephen M. Walt, *The Israel Lobby and U.S. Foreign Policy* (Farrar, Straus and Giroux, 2007).

Vigorous responses to the Mearsheimer-Walt contention that American political leaders were manipulated by Israel and not acting in the best interests of the U.S. included articles by another professor, Alan Dershowitz, who called *The Israel Lobby* "illogical and conspiratorial." Also, see a book by the head of the Anti-Defamation League, Abraham Foxman, *The Deadliest Lies: The Israel Lobby and the Myth of Jewish Control* (Palgrave Macmillan, 2007).

Chapter 22

Most of the material in this chapter is based on interviews with senior Mossad and Aman people associated with—or with knowledge of—the principal episodes discussed in this chapter. They refused to be named.

The attacks on German scientists working for Egypt in the 1960s are not known for certain to have killed anyone, but one scientist, Heinz Krug, vanished from his office in Germany in 1962—apparently after receiving threats.

The Israeli raid on Entebbe airport, that rescued around a hundred hostages, is told in Chapter 12 of this book.

The story of Palestinian terrorist Wadia Haddad, poisoned by chocolates, is told by Aharon Klein, *Striking Back: The 1972 Munich Olympics Massacre And Israel's Deadly Response* (Random House, 2005). The authors have received a slightly different version from sources.

On the assassination of Fathi Shkaki in Valetta, Malta, see (in Hebrew) Yossi Melman, *Ha'aretz*, October 30, 1995.

On the attempt to assassinate Khaled Meshaal in Jordan, numerous articles and books have been written. The quote of Meshaal is in Alan Cowell, "The Daring Attack That Blew Up in Israel's Face," *New York Times*, October 15, 1997.

King Hussein's anger at Israel, and the Hamas truce proposal he handed to a Mossad officer days before the attack on Meshaal, are told by former Mossad director Efraim Halevy, who heard it from Hussein himself. See Halevy's memoir, *Man in the Shadows* (St. Martin's Press, 2006), pp. 164-175.

On Halevy's insistence that a Mossad operative fly to Switzerland to stand trial: *Man in the Shadows*, pp. 185-9.

Chapter 23

On "one of Israel's greatest successes in target intelligence," in the Lebanon war of 2006, see General Amos Gilboa, "Intelligence and the Lebanese Arena," in Gilboa and Lapid (eds.), *Israel's Silent Defender*, pp. 118-9.

Mahmoud al-Mabhouh, assassinated by the Mossad in Dubai in January 2010, earlier had granted an interview to Al-Jazeera Television, in which he claimed he was "cautious" but hoped to become a martyr. It was broadcast only after his death. See "To Israel, I am Stained With Blood," at AlJazeera.net, posted February 7, 2010.

Details of what occurred in Dubai, and the Mossad's reaction to what the local police and others were saying, were gleaned from Israelis who were close to the decision-making, and from American officials who spoke later with the Israelis.

On official British anger, see London's *The Daily Telegraph*, March 24, 2010. On Australia's anger, see the same newspaper on February 26, 2010.

Chapter 24

Israel has continued to be secretive about the decisions that led to bombing Syria's nuclear reactor project in September 2007, but interviews conducted by one of the authors in the United States in 2010 and 2011 revealed details of the planning and the operation. Israeli and American officials asked for anonymity.

Meir Dagan's reminiscences about his command of the Sayeret Rimon commandos in the Gaza Strip were partly in his testimony in a court case, when a former soldier was accused of murder and claimed that killing had been commonplace under Dagan; as reported by Ynet.co.il on November 8, 2011.

Dennis Ross, former advisor to five American presidents, spoke of Israel's "ethos" in an interview with one of the authors in March 2012.

Remembering Ehud Olmert's request that the United States bomb the Syrian reactor project: George W. Bush, *Decision Points* (Crown, 2010), p. 421.

Bush's vice president also wrote about his own recommendation that the United States strike the Syrian building: Dick Cheney, *In My Time: A Personal and Political Memoir* (Threshold, 2011), pp. 470-2.

Yehuda Gil, long considered a star within the Mossad but then imprisoned for faking reports about Syria, told his story to one of the authors at Gil's home in October 2009 and unconvincingly claimed Mossad director Danny Yatom had framed him. See Yossi Melman's "Inside Intel" column at Haaretz.com on October 26, 2010. Further details are in Yatom's memoir in Hebrew, *Shutaf Sod* (*Privy to Secrets: From Sayeret Matkal until the Mossad*) (Yediot Aharonot, 2009), pp. 42-52.

Although U.S. intelligence officials praised Israel for being leak-proof on the destruction of Syria's reactor, the CIA released a dossier and video presentation—including the photos Israel had procured of the inside of the building and of a North Korean official visiting there—to Congress on April 24, 2008. It was immediately given to news reporters. Israel still preferred not to humiliate or provoke Syria with any confirmation. For a CIA statement on the matter, see: https://www.cia.gov/news-information/press-releases-statements/press-release-archive-2008/cia-director-hayden-announces-findings-on-covert-syrian-reactor.html.

The International Atomic Energy Agency, from its headquarters in Vienna, issued a report on May 24, 2011, that accused Syria of telling untruths about the structure at "the Dair Alzour site," reporting that samples taken after it was bulldozed established a connection with nuclear work, but also regretting that Israel took military action instead of informing the IAEA. See: http://www.iaea.org/Publications/Documents/Board/2011/gov2011-30.pdf.

Among those who wrote that Israel assassinated General Suleiman in Syria was Uzi Mahanaimi in the British *Sunday Times*, August 10, 2008; though the details, also in his writing about the air raid that flattened Syria's reactor the previous September, may not be precise. See also Hugh McLeod and Ian Black, "Top Assad Aide Assassinated at Syrian Resort," *The Guardian*, August, 4, 2008.

ACKNOWLEDGMENTS

In producing this, our fifth, book written jointly, we truly learned that it takes a village to reach an important goal. In Washington, in Tel Aviv, as well as in other locales where research and interviews were conducted, we relied on the assistance of people who wanted Israel and its unique challenges and solutions to be better understood.

The vast majority of well informed and experienced individuals in the field of intelligence, who helped us so much by explaining what happened and why, prefer to remain anonymous. You know who you are. We won't forget you, but we'll do you the favor of not naming you.

Yet we would be remiss not to thank the team that helped turn years of conversations and notes into a book. Our wives, Dori Phaff and Billie Melman, contributed not only support but many hours of work in getting many of the tasks done. Paul Skolnick, a master of all things digital, extended himself far beyond expectations as our manager of production. Hillel Kuttler was our strong editor.

The publicity team is ably headed by Sandy Trupp, and our on-line strategies are provided by Michael Conniff at Post Time Media Inc.

Valuable encouragement came also from our families and from Robert Zimmerman, Larry Miller (including a key part of the title), Howard Arenstein, Steve Rabinowitz, Barry Schochet, Kate Brown, and others at and around our respective workplaces.

All errors, of course, are our own.

Please see our website, www.IsraelSpy.com. And follow us on Twitter at @SpiesArmageddon.

A brief note about methodology: Portions of the book in Chapters 2 through 10, 13 through 16, 18, 21 and 25 originated from reporting by Yossi Melman in Israel and those chapters were submitted to that country's military censor. Very minor deletions were made as a result.

INDEX

Z

CPSIA information can be obtained at www.ICGtesting.com
Printed in the USA
LVOW05s0320130813

347599LV00001B/119/P